# The
# Cook's
# Handbook

# The
# Cook's
# Handbook

The ultimate cooking course to perfecting
your culinary skills and techniques

Contributing Editor: Carole Clements

HERMES HOUSE

This edition published in 2001 by Hermes House

© Anness Publishing Limited 1998, 2001

Hermes House is an imprint of Anness Publishing Limited
Hermes House, 88-89 Blackfriars Road, London SE1 8HA

Published in the USA by Hermes House, Anness Publishing Inc.
27 West 20th Street, New York, NY 10011

A CIP catalogue record for this book is available from the British Library

*Publisher* Joanna Lorenz
*Authors* Norma MacMillan and Frances Cleary
*Project Editor* Carole Clements
*Designer* Sheila Volpe
*Cover Design* Mark Latter
*Photography* Amanda Heywood
*Food Styling* Frances Cleary, Carole Handslip, Elizabeth Wolf-Cohen
*Steps* Marilyn Forbes, Cara Hobday and Nicola Fowler

Previously published as *The Ultimate Cooking Course and Kitchen Encyclopedia*

The author would like to thank Jill Eggleton
for her help in testing recipes

The publishers wish to thank Cuisinarts Corporation,
1 Cummings Point Road, Stamford, Connecticut 06904

Printed and bound in China

3 5 7 9 10 8 6 4

# ~ CONTENTS ~

~

# ~ INTRODUCTION ~

Whether you are a complete novice, an experienced cook or an occasional dabbler, there are times when everyone longs for basic techniques and methods to be laid out clearly and simply. This book does just that.

In addition, there are lots of recipes and recipe ideas too, so you can try out the skills you are learning or brushing up. The recipes are designed to illustrate a particular technique. When you read these recipes, take a moment to assess any additional techniques required. Look them up in the index, if you want to review.

## USEFUL EQUIPMENT

To be able to cook efficiently and with pleasure, you need good equipment. That is not to say that you should invest in an extensive and expensive collection of pots, pans, tools and gadgets, but a basic range is essential.

In addition, buy the best equipment you can afford, adding more as your budget allows. Well made equipment lasts and is a sound investment; inexpensive pans and tins are likely to dent, break or develop 'hot spots' where food will stick and burn, so will need replacing. Flimsy tools will make food preparation more time consuming and frustrating.

### For the top of the stove

When choosing pots and pans, look for those with heavy bottoms, sturdy insulated handles and knobs and tight-fitting lids. Bear in mind, too, how much the pan will weigh when full – a large pot for pasta or stock must not be too heavy for you to lift.

Copper conducts heat best, but is hard to care for. Aluminium is good, as is cast iron, although the latter needs scrupulous care to prevent rust. A vitreous enamel coating on cast iron is a good compromise. Stainless steel is lightweight and durable, but it conducts heat unevenly. A composite or clad bottom containing another metal can improve heat conduction.

- **Stove top essentials**: At least 3 saucepans with lids (2, 3 and 5 pint/1, 2 and 3 litre); small and large frying pans with lids; large flameproof casserole with lid; stockpot or pasta pan with lid.
- **Helpful equipment**: Omelette pan, double saucepan, wok, pancake pan, sauté pan, ridged grill pan, steamer.

### For the oven

Cake and bun tins and baking sheets should be made of shiny metal (aluminium, tin or stainless steel) for even heat distribution. Pie and flan tins should be dull metal, glass or ceramic. Roasting tins can be made of any material, but they must be sturdy.

- **Baking and roasting essentials**: 2 round sandwich tins; 8 in (20 cm) or 9 in (23 cm) round and square cake tins; large baking tin (13 × 9 in/33 × 23 cm); large and small loaf tins; deep bun tin; 9 in (23 cm) pie tin; oval or round pie dish; 9 in (23 cm) flan tin with removable bottom, or flan ring; 9 in (23 cm) springform cake tin; Swiss roll tin; 2 baking sheets; roasting tin with rack; large soufflé dish; shallow and deep baking dishes; grill pan with rack; wire rack; oven gloves; oven and meat thermometers.

- **Helpful equipment**: Sandwich tins, round and square cake tins, pie tins, flan tins, springform tins and tartlet tins in alternative sizes; individual soufflé dishes, gratin dishes, ramekins, metal skewers.

### Cutting tools

A good set of knives is the most important tool in food preparation. Yet so many cooks make do with flimsy, dull or nicked knives, which can turn even the chopping of onions into an arduous task.

Knives made of carbon steel can be given the sharpest edge, but they rust and discolour easily so must be washed and dried immediately after use. High-carbon stainless steel knives will take a sharp edge and they resist discoloration, but are more expensive. Ordinary stainless steel knives are very difficult to sharpen efficiently.

Whatever knives you choose, keep them sharp. More accidents occur with blunt knives than sharp ones.

- **Cutting essentials**: Chef's knife with 10 in (25 cm) blade, paring knife with 3 in (7.5 cm) blade, flexible vegetable knife with serrated edge and pointed tip, rigid serrated knife with 10–12 in (25–30 cm) blade, sturdy kitchen scissors, knife block or magnetized bar, several cutting boards in different sizes for different uses.
- **Helpful cutting tools**: Filleting knife with thin flexible 7 in (18 cm) blade and sharp point, boning knife with thin 6 in (15 cm) blade, utility knife with 6 in (15 cm) blade, grapefruit knife with curved serrated blade, poultry shears, carving knife and fork.

**Preparation tools**
You can do a lot with just a big bowl
and a sturdy spoon, but there are
many tools that make cooking easier.
• **Preparation essentials**: 4 mixing
bowls in varying sizes, wooden spoons,
long-handled slotted spoon, ladle,
wooden spatula, rubber spatulas in
varying sizes, palette knife with
flexible 10 in (25 cm) blade, fish slice,
tongs, large balloon whisk, hand-held
electric mixer, potato masher, lemon
squeezer, colander, kitchen scales, jug
and measuring spoons, vegetable
peeler, grater, 2 sieves (1 metal, 1
nylon), long 2-pronged fork, rolling
pin, pastry brush, can and bottle
openers, corkscrew, kitchen timer,
paper towels, wraps, string.
• **Helpful equipment**: Salad spinner,
food processor and/or blender, potato
ricer, meat mallet, rotary grater,
nutmeg grater, citrus zester, canelle
knife, apple corer, melon baller,
pastry blender, pastry scraper, trussing
needle, cherry stoner, pasta machine,
table-top electric mixer, baking
parchment.

## BUYING AND STORING FOOD

A well-stocked kitchen makes meal
preparation easy. The key is planning
– planning menus for the next few
days or the week ahead, then making
a shopping list that includes fresh
foods as well as those frequently used
foods whose stocks are running low or
that are near or past their use-by date.
Allow yourself to be a little flexible,
though. When shopping, take
advantage of fresh seasonal foods and
special offers.

Knowing how and where to store
food – both fresh and preserved – and
how long to keep it will be a great help
in shopping to stock the kitchen.

**In the refrigerator**
All foods in the refrigerator or freezer
should be well wrapped or stored in
sealed containers. This preserves
flavour and moisture, and prevents
the flavours and odours of other,
stronger foods being transferred. It is
essential to keep raw meat and poultry
well wrapped as their drippings can
transfer bacteria to other foods.
  Perishable fresh foods, such as
meats, poultry, fish and seafood, eggs,
cheese and other dairy products, and
many fruits and vegetables must be
kept refrigerated at a temperature of
35–40°F (1–5°C). For longer storage,
many can also be frozen at 0°F (−18°C)
or lower. Cooked leftovers must also
be refrigerated or frozen. Check fridge
and freezer temperatures with a special
thermometer. If temperatures are too
high, food will spoil rapidly.

**Storing fresh fruits**
Those fruits that can be kept at room
temperature while still unripe include
apricots, kiwi fruits, mangoes,

nectarines, papayas, peaches, pears,
pineapples and plums. Once ripe, all
these should be refrigerated and eaten
within 2–3 days.
  Fruits that can be stored at cool
room temperature include apples
(although they will be crisper if
refrigerated), bananas, dates,
grapefruit and oranges. Apples can be
kept at room temperature for a few
days, dates for several weeks, and
grapefruit and oranges for up to a
week; beyond that, refrigerate them.
  Unless you intend to eat them on
the day of purchase, refrigerate fully
ripe and perishable fresh fruits. These
include berries, cherries, figs, grapes,
lemons, limes, melons, pomegranates
and tangerines. They can be kept
refrigerated for 2–3 days.

**Storing fresh vegetables**
Like fruits, there are some vegetables
that can stored at room temperature.
A dark, cool place (about 50°F/10°C)
with good ventilation is ideal.
Suitable vegetables are garlic, onions,
potatoes and sweet potatoes, swede
and pumpkin. All can be kept for
about 2 months. Store tomatoes at
room temperature until they are ripe.
After that, refrigerate.
  Perishable vegetables should be
refrigerated. Some, such as peas or
sweetcorn, should be used quickly,
while others, like carrots or cabbage,
can be kept for a longer period. In
most cases, do not wash the vegetable
until just before using. Celery, frisée,
escarole, spring greens, herbs, lettuce,
spinach and watercress should be
washed before storage.

### Storing canned and dry foods

Full cupboard shelves are a boon for a busy cook, but canned and dry foods can deteriorate if not stored properly or if left too long on the shelf. Kitchen cupboards should be cool (no more than 65°F/18°C) and dry. Staples such as flour, salt, sugar, pasta and grains are best stored in moisture-proof containers. If necessary, remove them from their wrappings and decant them into canisters or jars. Whole-grain products (wholemeal flour and pasta, brown rice, etc) cannot be kept as long as refined ones.

Dried herbs and spices will keep their flavour and scent best if stored in the dark. Light is their enemy, so store them in a cupboard or drawer, rather than on an open spice rack. Oil, too, should be stored in a cool dark place, in an airtight container. Refrigerate nut oils to preserve them longer.

### Herbs and spices

The judicious use of a herb or spice, or both, can transform a dish. It's fun to experiment, once you know what you like and which seasonings go well with what foods.

Whenever possible, use fresh herbs, for their wonderful flavour, scent and colour. They're widely available in supermarkets and are also easy to grow, even in pots on a windowsill. Fresh herbs impart their flavour very quickly, so chop just before using and add to hot dishes towards the end of cooking. If fresh herbs are not available, you can, of course, substitute dried. Use them in a ratio of 1 teaspoon dried to 1 tablespoon fresh.

Most spices, both whole and ground, need time to impart their aroma and flavour to a dish. Some are pungent and spicy-hot, others are sweet and fragrant. If you can, grind spices freshly, using a spice mill, nutmeg grater or mortar and pestle. The difference in flavour and aroma between pre-ground and freshly ground is amazing.

## GETTING THE TIMING RIGHT

Successful meal preparation is as much dependent on organization as on culinary skills. The initial planning of a menu – whether for the family supper or a dinner party – must give consideration to many things: a good range of flavours, colours and textures, as well as a balance in protein, fat, fibre and other healthy considerations.

That done, it then becomes a question of what you can prepare ahead, and what remains to be done at the last minute so that all is ready at the same time. For the beginner, this can be daunting.

The first step is to read all the recipes before making a final choice. The main dish, with simple accompaniments such as vegetables or a salad and bread, is a good starting point. Surround that with a cold starter (if there is to be one) and a cold dessert that can be made ahead of time. This way you can concentrate your efforts at each stage.

If you do choose two or more hot dishes, consider their cooking times and oven temperatures. If you have only one oven, and the temperatures required for the two dishes are different, this will present difficulties.

Next, make a shopping list. Check that you have all the equipment you require. Once you have everything to hand, you can start the preparation.

Read each recipe through again so you know what lies ahead, and try to estimate how long each preparation stage will take. Review techniques in the preparation that are unfamiliar, using the index to locate them, if necessary. Set the time you want to serve the meal, and work back from there so you know when to start the preparation. It's not a bad idea to write down all these times, as if you were planning military strategy.

If you are serving a starter, you'll need to plan what can be cooked unattended while you are at the table. If your chosen dessert is frozen, it may need some time out of the freezer before serving, so decide when to transfer it from freezer to refrigerator.

Remember to allow time for the final draining of vegetables, or carving of meat, or seasoning of a sauce. It is usually the case that all of these need to be done at the same time – but you only have one pair of hands. So decide what can wait and what will keep hot. Also allow time for plates to be cleared from the table if you are serving more than one course.

If any recipe requires the oven to be preheated or tins to be prepared, do this first. Pots of boiling salted water for cooking vegetables or pasta can be brought to the boil while you are doing the chopping and slicing.

Set out all the ingredients required and prepare them as specified in the recipe. If more than one dish calls for the same ingredients, say chopped onion or parsley, you can prepare the total amount at the same time.

Now start cooking, following your timetable. Check the recipe as you work, and don't be distracted. Keep tasting and sniffing the food as you go – that's much of the fun!

## MEASURING TECHNIQUES

Cooks with years of experience may not need to measure ingredients, but if you are a beginner or are trying a new recipe for the first time, it is best to follow instructions carefully. Also, measuring ingredients precisely will ensure consistent results.

Both imperial and metric measures are given in this book. When preparing a recipe, use all imperial or all metric measures. Eggs are size 3 unless specified otherwise and recipes have been tested using a conventional not fan-assisted oven.

### USEFUL CONVERSIONS

| Imperial | Metric |
|---|---|
| 1 teaspoon | a 5 ml spoon |
| 3 teaspoons = | |
| 1 tablespoon | a 15 ml spoon |
| ¼ pint (5 fl oz) | 150 ml |
| ½ pint (10 fl oz) | 300 ml |
| ¾ pint (15 fl oz) | 450 ml |
| 1 pint (20 fl oz) | 600 ml |
| 1½ pints | 900 ml |
| 2 pints | 1.2 litres |
| 1 oz | 30 g |
| 2 oz | 55 g |
| 3 oz | 85 g |
| 4 oz (¼ lb) | 115 g |
| 8 oz (½ lb) | 225 g |
| 12 oz (¾ lb) | 340 g |
| 1 lb (16 oz) | 450 g |
| 1 lb 2 oz | 500 g |
| 2¼ lb | 1 kg |
| 225°F/Gas ¼ | 110°C |
| 250°F/Gas ½ | 130°C |
| 275°F/Gas 1 | 140°C |
| 300°F/Gas 2 | 150°C |
| 325°F/Gas 3 | 170°C |
| 350°F/Gas 4 | 180°C |
| 375°F/Gas 5 | 190°C |
| 400°F/Gas 6 | 200°C |
| 425°F/Gas 7 | 220°C |
| 450°F/Gas 8 | 230°C |
| 475°F/Gas 9 | 240°C |

**1 ▲ For liquids measured in fl oz or pints (ml or litres)**: Use a glass or clear plastic measuring jug. Put it on a flat surface and pour in the liquid. Bend down and check that the liquid is level with the marking on the jug, as specified in the recipe.

**3 ▲ For measuring dry ingredients in a spoon**: Fill the spoon, scooping up the ingredient. Level the surface even with the rim of the spoon, using the straight edge of a knife.

**5 ▲ For measuring brown sugar in a cup or spoon**: If the recipe specifies firmly packed brown sugar, scoop the sugar and press it firmly into the cup or spoon. Level the surface.

**2 ▲ For liquids measured in spoons**: Pour the liquid into the measuring spoon, to the brim, and then pour it into the mixing bowl. Do not hold the spoon over the bowl when measuring because liquid may overflow.

**4 ▲ For measuring dry ingredients by weight**: Scoop or pour on to the scales, watching the dial or reading carefully. Balance scales give more accurate readings than spring scales.

**6 ▲ For measuring butter**: Cut with a sharp knife and weigh, or cut off the specified amount following the markings on the wrapping paper.

# POULTRY

~

*With chicken and other birds a mainstay of weekday meals and holiday gatherings, knowing how to handle poultry helps you make the most of it. It is simple to make your own stock for great gravy and economical to joint or bone poultry yourself.*

# TRUSSING POULTRY

Trussing holds a bird together during cooking so that it keeps a neat, attractive shape. If the bird is stuffed, trussing prevents the stuffing falling out. You can truss with strong string or with poultry skewers.

An alternative to the method shown here is to use a long trussing needle and fine cotton string: make 2 passes, in alternate directions, through the body at the open end, from wing to wing, and tie. Then pass the needle through the parson's nose and tie the string around the ends of the drumsticks.

Remove all trussing before serving.

**1 ▲ For an unstuffed bird:** Set it breast down and pull the flap of neck skin over the neck opening. Turn the bird breast up and fold each wing tip back, over the neck skin, to secure firmly behind the shoulder.

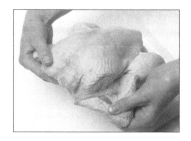

**2 ▲** Press the legs firmly down and into the breast. If there is a band of skin across the parson's nose, fold back the ends of the drumsticks and tuck them under the skin.

**3 ▲** Otherwise, cross the knuckle ends of the drumsticks or bring them tightly together. Loop a length of string several times around the drumstick ends, then tie a knot and trim off excess string.

**4 ▲ For a stuffed bird:** Fold the wing tips back as above. After stuffing the neck end, fold the flap of skin over the opening and secure it with a skewer, then fold over the wing tips.

**5 ▲** Put any stuffing or flavourings (herbs, lemon halves, apple quarters and so on) in the body cavity, then secure the ends of the drumsticks as above, tying in the parson's nose, too.

**6 ▲** Alternatively, the cavity opening can be closed with skewers: insert 2 or more skewers across the opening, threading them through the skin several times.

**7 ▲** Lace the skewers together with string. Tie the drumsticks together over the skewers.

**Stuffing tips**
When stuffing poultry, the stuffing should be cool, not hot or chilled. Pack it loosely into the bird because it will expand during cooking. Cook any left-over stuffing separately in a baking dish. Do not stuff poultry until just before putting it into the oven or pot. It is not a good idea to stuff the body cavity of a large bird because the stuffing could inhibit heat penetration, and thus not kill all harmful bacteria.

# Pot-roast Chicken with Sausage Stuffing

**SERVES 6**

| |
|---|
| 2 × 2½lb (1.12 kg) chickens |
| 2 tablespoons vegetable oil |
| 12 fl oz (360 ml) chicken stock or half wine and half stock |
| 1 bay leaf |

FOR THE STUFFING

| |
|---|
| 1 lb (450 g) pork sausagemeat |
| 1 small onion, chopped |
| 1–2 garlic cloves, finely chopped |
| 1 teaspoon hot paprika |
| ½ teaspoon hot pepper flakes (optional) |
| ½ teaspoon dried thyme |
| ¼ teaspoon ground allspice |
| 1½ oz (45 g) coarse fresh breadcrumbs |
| 1 egg, beaten to mix |
| salt and pepper |

**1** Preheat a 350°F/180°C/Gas 4 oven.

**2** ▲ For the stuffing, put the sausagemeat, onion and garlic in a frying pan and fry over moderate heat until the sausagemeat is lightly browned and crumbly, stirring and turning so it cooks evenly. Remove from the heat and mix in the remaining stuffing ingredients with salt and pepper to taste.

**3** Divide the stuffing between the chickens, packing it into the body cavities (or, if preferred, stuff the neck end and bake left-over stuffing separately). Truss the birds.

**4** ▼ Heat the oil in a flameproof casserole just big enough to hold the chickens. Brown the birds all over.

### ~ VARIATION ~

For Pot-roast Guinea Fowl, use 2 guinea fowl instead of chickens.

**5** ▲ Add the stock and bay leaf and season. Cover and bring to the boil, then transfer to the oven. Pot-roast for 1¼ hours or until the birds are cooked (the juices will run clear).

**6** Untruss the chickens and spoon the stuffing on to a serving platter. Arrange the birds and serve with the strained cooking liquid.

# ROASTING POULTRY

Where would family gatherings be without the time-honoured roast bird? But beyond the favourite chicken, all types of poultry can be roasted – from small poussins to large turkeys. However, older tougher birds are better pot-roasted.

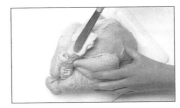

**1 ▲** Wipe the bird inside and out with damp paper towels. Stuff the bird if the recipe directs and truss it. Spread the breast of chicken with softened or melted butter or oil; bard the breast of a lean game bird; prick the skin of duck and goose.

**2 ▲** Set the bird breast up on a rack in a small roasting tin or shallow baking dish. If you are roasting a lean game bird, set the bird in the tin breast down.

---

**Protect and flavour**
Before roasting, loosen the skin on the breast by gently easing it away from the flesh with your fingers. Press in softened butter – mixed with herbs or garlic for extra flavour – and smooth back the skin.

---

**3 ▲** Roast the bird, basting it every 10 minutes after the first ½ hour with the accumulated juices and fat in the tin. Turn if directed. If browning too quickly, cover loosely with foil.

**4 ▲** Transfer the bird to a carving board and leave to rest for at least 15 minutes before serving. During that time, make a simple sauce or gravy with the juices in the tin (page 38).

**Simple Roast Chicken**
Squeeze the juice from a halved lemon over a 3–3½ lb (1.35–1.5 kg) chicken, then push the lemon halves into the body cavity. Smear ½ oz (15 g) softened butter over the breast. Roast in a 375°F/190°C/Gas 5 oven for about 1¼ hours. Skim all fat from the roasting juices, then add 4 fl oz (120 ml) water and bring to the boil, stirring well to mix in the browned bits. Season with salt and pepper, and serve this sauce with the chicken. *Serves 4.*

## ROASTING TIMES FOR POULTRY

*Note: Cooking times given here are for unstuffed birds. For stuffed birds, add 20 minutes to the total roasting time.*

| | | |
|---|---|---|
| Poussin | 1–1½ lb (450–700 g) | 1–1¼ hours at 350°F/180°C/Gas 4 |
| Chicken | 2½–3 lb (1.12–1.35 kg) | 1–1¼ hours at 375°F/190°C/Gas 5 |
| | 3½–4 lb (1.5–1.8 kg) | 1¼–1¾ hours at 375°F/190°C/Gas 5 |
| | 4½–5 lb (2–2.25 kg) | 1½–2 hours at 375°F/190°C/Gas 5 |
| | 5–6 lb (2.25–2.7 kg) | 1¾–2½ hours at 375°F/190°C/Gas 5 |
| Capon | 5–7 lb (2.25–3 kg) | 1¾–2 hours at 325°F/170°C/Gas 3 |
| Duck | 3–5 lb (1.35–2.25 kg) | 1¾–2¼ hours at 400°F/200°C/Gas 6 |
| Goose | 8–10 lb (3.6–4.5 kg) | 2½–3 hours at 350°F/180°C/Gas 4 |
| | 10–12 lb (4.5–5.4 kg) | 3–3½ hours at 350°F/180°C/Gas 4 |
| Turkey (whole bird) | 6–8 lb (2.7–3.6 kg) | 3–3½ hours at 325°F/170°C/Gas 3 |
| | 8–12 lb (3.6–5.4 kg) | 3–4 hours at 325°F/170°C/Gas 3 |
| | 12–16 lb (5.4–7.2 kg) | 4–5 hours at 325°F/170°C/Gas 3 |
| Turkey (whole breast) | 4–6 lb (1.8–2.7 kg) | 1½–2¼ hours at 325°F/170°C/Gas 3 |
| | 6–8 lb (2.7–3.6 kg) | 2¼–3¼ hours at 325°F/170°C/Gas 3 |

# Poussins Waldorf

**SERVES 6**

6 poussins, each weighing about 1¼ lb (575 g)

salt and pepper

1½–2 oz (45–55 g) butter, melted

**FOR THE STUFFING**

1 oz (30 g) butter

1 onion, finely chopped

10 oz (300 g) cooked rice

2 celery stalks, finely chopped

2 red apples, cored and finely diced

2 oz (55 g) walnuts, chopped

5 tablespoons cream sherry or apple juice

2 tablespoons lemon juice

**1** Preheat a 350°F/180°C/Gas 4 oven.

**2** For the stuffing, melt the butter in a small frying pan and fry the onion, stirring occasionally, until soft. Tip the onion and butter into a bowl and add the remaining stuffing ingredients. Season with salt and pepper and mix well.

**3** ◄ Divide the stuffing among the poussins, stuffing the body cavities. Truss. Arrange in a roasting tin. Sprinkle with salt and pepper and drizzle over the melted butter.

**4** Roast for about 1¼–1½ hours. Untruss before serving.

---

# CARVING POULTRY

Carving a bird neatly for serving makes the presentation attractive. You will need a sharp long-bladed knife, or an electric knife, plus a long 2-pronged fork and a carving board with a well to catch the juices.

Cut away any trussing string. For a stuffed bird, spoon the stuffing from the cavity into a serving dish. For easier carving, remove the wishbone.

Insert the fork into one breast to hold the bird steady. Cut through the skin to the ball and socket joint on that side of the body, then slice through it to sever the leg from the body. Repeat on the other side.

**1** ▲ Slice through the ball and socket joint in each leg to sever the thigh and drumstick. If carving turkey, slice the meat off the thigh and drumstick, parallel to the bone, turning to get even slices; leave chicken thighs and drumsticks whole.

**2** ▲ To carve the breast of a turkey or chicken, cut ⅛–¼ in (3–5 mm) thick slices at an angle, slicing down on both sides of the breastbone. For smaller birds, remove the meat on each side of the breastbone in a single piece, then slice across.

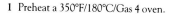

# PREPARING DUCK AND GOOSE FOR ROASTING

Duck and goose are bony birds, with most of their rich meat in the breast. There is a thick layer of fat under the skin which could make the birds greasy if it is not removed before cooking or melted out during cooking.

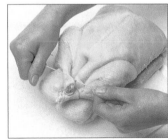

**Lean by nature**
Wild duck and geese are not as fatty as many farm-raised birds, and should be prepared as you would a game bird so the meat doesn't dry out: bard the breast with rashers of bacon or slices of pork fat.

**1** ▲ Pull out any fat from the body and neck cavities. With a skewer or cocktail stick, prick the skin all over the breast of the bird. This will allow the melted fat to run out while the bird is cooking.

**2** ▲ Tie the ends of the drumsticks together with string as for a chicken.

---

# Duck with Peach Sauce

**SERVES 4**

1 × 5–6 lb (2.25–2.7 kg) duck, prepared for roasting

salt and pepper

5 ripe but firm peaches

8 fl oz (240 ml) orange juice

4 tablespoons peach brandy or Southern Comfort, or peach nectar

1 teaspoon cornflour

2 teaspoons water

2 teaspoons Dijon mustard

fresh parsley or watercress, to garnish

**1** Preheat a 400°F/200°C/Gas 6 oven.

**2** Rub the duck all over with salt and pepper. Put it breast up on a rack in a roasting tin and roast for 1¼ hours.

**3** Meanwhile, peel the peaches: dip in boiling water for 30 seconds, then in iced water to remove the skin. Cut them in half and remove the stones. Purée 2 peach halves with the orange juice in a blender or food processor.

**4** Put the remaining peach halves in a saucepan. Sprinkle with the alcohol or peach nectar. Set aside.

**5** ▲ Pour off the duck fat from the roasting tin. Place the duck in the tin, without the rack, and pour the orange and peach mixture over it. Roast, basting occasionally with the sauce in the tin, for about 15 minutes more or until the duck is cooked (lift it with a long 2-pronged fork: the juices that run out of the cavity should be clear).

**6** ▲ Transfer the duck to a carving board and keep warm. Skim all the fat from the sauce, then set the tin over moderate heat and bring to the boil. Blend the cornflour with the water and stir into the sauce. Simmer, stirring, until thickened.

**7** Quarter the duck. Warm the peach halves, then remove with a slotted spoon. Add the mustard to the pan and mix well. Stir this mixture into the sauce and taste. Serve the duck with the peaches, garnished with parsley or watercress. Serve the sauce separately.

# SPATCHCOCKING POULTRY

Whole chickens, poussins, guinea fowl and game birds can be split open in half and opened up flat like a book, to resemble the wings of a butterfly. They will then cook evenly under the grill or on a barbecue. A heavy chef's knife can be used to split the bird, but sturdy kitchen scissors or poultry shears are easier to handle.

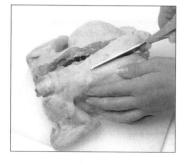

**1** ▲ Set the bird breast down. Cut through the skin and rib cage along one side of the backbone, working from the tail end to the neck. Repeat on the other side of the backbone to cut it free. Keep the backbone for stock, if wished.

**2** ▲ Turn the bird breast up. With the heel of your hand, press firmly on the breastbone to break it and flatten the breast.

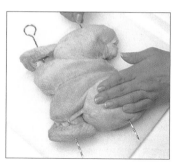

**3** ▲ Fold the wing tips back behind the shoulders. Thread a long metal skewer through one wing and the top of the breast and out through the other wing.

**4** ▲ Thread a second skewer through the thighs and bottom of the breast. These skewers will keep the bird flat while it is being cooked, and will make it easy to turn over.

**Testing poultry**
Overcooked poultry is dry, tough and tasteless, so knowing when a bird is done is crucial. The most reliable test for a whole bird is to insert an instant-read thermometer deep into the thigh meat (the internal temperature should be 175°F/79°C). Without a thermometer, you can test by piercing the thigh with a skewer or the tip of a knife: the juices that run out should be clear, not pink. Or lift the bird with a long 2-pronged fork and tilt it so that you can check the colour of the juices that run out of the cavity into the roasting tin. Pieces of poultry, particularly breasts, can be tested by pressing them with a finger: the meat should be firm but still slightly springy.

### GRILLING TIMES FOR POULTRY

*Note: Cook 4–6 in (10–15 cm) from the heat; thinner pieces, less than 1 in (2.5 cm), nearer the heat. If the poultry seems to be browning too quickly, turn down the heat slightly.*

| | |
|---|---|
| Poussin, spatchcocked | 20–25 minutes |
| Spring chicken, split in half or spatchcocked | 25–30 minutes |
| Roasting chicken, split in half or spatchcocked | 30–40 minutes |
| Chicken breast, drumstick, thigh | 30–35 minutes |
| Skinless boneless chicken breast | 10–12 minutes |
| Boneless duck breast | 10–12 minutes |

# Grilled Spatchcocked Poussins

**SERVES 4**

salt and pepper

4 poussins, each weighing about 1 lb (450 g), spatchcocked

olive oil

FOR THE ONION AND HERB SAUCE

2 tablespoons dry sherry

2 tablespoons lemon juice

2 tablespoons olive oil

2 oz (55 g) spring onions, chopped

1 garlic clove, finely chopped

4 tablespoons chopped mixed fresh herbs such as tarragon, parsley, thyme, marjoram, lemon balm

4 ▲ Meanwhile, for the sauce, whisk together the wine, lemon juice, olive oil, spring onions and garlic. Season with salt and pepper.

5 ▼ When the poussins are done, transfer them to a deep serving platter. Whisk the herbs into the sauce, then spoon it over the poussins. Cover tightly with another platter or with foil and leave to rest for 15 minutes before serving.

1 Preheat the grill to high, or prepare a charcoal fire.

2 ▲ Season the birds, then brush them with a little olive oil. Set them on the rack in the grill pan, about 4 in (10 cm) from the heat, or on the barbecue 6 in (15 cm) above the coals.

3 ▲ Cook for 20–25 minutes or until tender. Turn and brush with more oil halfway through the cooking.

# JOINTING POULTRY

Although chickens and other poultry are sold already jointed into halves, quarters, breasts, thighs and drumsticks, sometimes it makes sense to buy a whole bird and to do the job yourself. That way you can prepare 4 larger pieces or 8 smaller ones, depending on the recipe, and you can cut the pieces so the backbone and other bony bits (which can be saved for stock) are not included. In addition, a whole bird is cheaper to buy than pieces.

A sharp knife and sturdy kitchen scissors or poultry shears make the job of jointing poultry very easy.

**1 ▲** With the sharp knife, cut through the skin on one side of the body down to where the thigh joins the body. Bend the leg out away from the body and twist it to break the ball and socket joint.

**2 ▲** Hold the leg out away from the body and cut through the ball and socket joint, taking the 'oyster meat' from the backbone with the leg. Repeat on the other side.

**Safe handling of raw poultry**
Raw poultry may harbour potentially harmful organisms, such as salmonella bacteria, so it is vital to take care in its preparation. Always wash your hands, the chopping board, knife and poultry shears in hot soapy water before and after handling the poultry. It is a good idea to use a chopping board that can be washed at high temperature in a dishwasher and, if possible, to keep the chopping board just for the preparation of raw poultry. Thaw frozen poultry completely before cooking.

**3 ▲** To separate the breast from the back, cut through the flap of skin just below the rib cage, cutting towards the neck. Pull the breast and back apart and cut through the joints that connect them on each side. Reserve the back for stock.

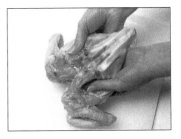

**4 ▲** Turn the whole breast over, skin side down. Take one side of the breast in each hand and bend back firmly so the breastbone pops free. Loosen the bone on both sides with your fingers and, with the help of the knife, remove it.

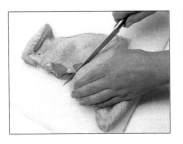

**5 ▲** Cut the breast lengthways in half, cutting through the wishbone. You now have 2 breasts with wings attached and 2 leg portions.

**6 ▲** For 8 pieces, cut each breast in half at an angle so that some breast meat is included with a wing portion. Trim off any protruding bones.

**7 ▲** With the knife, cut each leg portion through the ball and socket joint to separate the thigh and drumstick.

# Simple Chicken Curry

**SERVES 4**

2 tablespoons vegetable oil

1 onion, chopped

1 green or red pepper, seeded and diced

1 garlic clove, finely chopped

1½ tablespoons curry powder

½ teaspoon dried thyme

1 lb (450 g) tomatoes, skinned, seeded and chopped, or canned chopped tomatoes

2 tablespoons lemon juice

4 fl oz (120 ml) water

2 oz (55 g) currants or raisins

salt and pepper

1 × 3½ lb (1.5 kg) chicken, cut into 8 pieces and the pieces skinned

cooked rice, to serve

1  Preheat a 350°F/180°C/Gas 4 oven.

2  Heat the oil in a wide, deep frying pan that has an ovenproof handle or in a flameproof casserole. Add the onion, diced pepper and garlic. Cook, stirring occasionally, until the vegetables are soft.

3  ▲  Stir in the curry powder and thyme, then add the tomatoes, lemon juice and water. Bring the sauce to the boil, stirring frequently. Stir in the currants or raisins. Season to taste with salt and pepper.

4  ▲  Put the chicken pieces in the frying pan or casserole, arranging them in one layer. Turn to coat them with the sauce. Cover the pan and transfer to the oven. Cook it for about 40 minutes or until the chicken is tender. Turn the pieces halfway through cooking.

5  Remove the chicken and sauce to a warmed serving platter. Serve with freshly boiled rice.

## ~ VARIATION ~

For Curried Chicken Casserole, omit the diced pepper and cook 1½ tablespoons finely chopped fresh ginger and 1 green chilli, seeded and finely chopped, with the onion and garlic in a flame-proof casserole. In step 3, stir in the curry powder with ¼ pint (450 ml) plain yogurt; omit the tomatoes, lemon juice and water. Add the chicken pieces, cover and cook in a 325°F/170°C/Gas 3 oven for 1–1¼ hours.

# MAKING POULTRY SAUTÉS

A sauté combines frying and braising, producing particularly succulent results. It is a method suitable for pieces of poultry as well as for small whole birds such as quails and poussins.

As with frying, the poultry should be dried thoroughly with paper towels before cooking to ensure that it browns quickly and evenly.

**1 ▲** Heat a little oil, a mixture of oil and butter, or clarified butter in a heavy frying pan or sauté pan.

**2 ▲** Add the poultry and fry it over moderately high heat until it is golden brown, turning to colour evenly.

**3 ▲** Add liquid and flavourings called for in the recipe. Bring to the boil, then cover and reduce the heat to moderately low. Continue cooking gently until the poultry is done, turning the pieces or birds over once or twice.

**4 ▲** If the recipe instructs, remove the poultry from the pan and keep it warm while finishing the sauce. This can be as simple as boiling the cooking juices to reduce them or adding butter or cream for a richer result.

**Country Chicken Sauté**
Cook 6 oz (175 g) chopped bacon in 2 teaspoons oil over moderately high heat until lightly coloured. Remove and reserve. Dredge a 3½ lb (1.5 kg) chicken, cut into 8 pieces, in seasoned flour. Fry in the bacon fat until evenly browned. Add 3 tablespoons dry white wine and 8 fl oz (240 ml) poultry stock. Bring to the boil and add ½ lb (225 g) quartered mushrooms sautéed in 1 tablespoon of butter and the reserved bacon. Cover and cook over low heat for 20–25 minutes, or until the chicken is tender. *Serves 4.*

**5 ▲ Thickening cooking juices:** Thicken with equal weights of butter and flour mashed together, called 'beurre manié'. Use 1 oz (30 g) of this paste to 8 fl oz (240 ml) liquid. Whisk small pieces gradually into the boiling sauce until it is smooth and silky.

**6 ▲** Another method of thickening cooking juices is to add a mixture of cornflour and water. Use 2 teaspoons cornflour blended with 1 tablespoon water to 8 fl oz (240 ml) liquid. Boil for 2–3 minutes, whisking constantly, until the sauce is syrupy.

# Stuffed Chicken Breasts with Cream Sauce

**SERVES 4**

4 large skinless boneless chicken breasts or chicken suprêmes

2 oz (55 g) butter

3 large leeks, white and pale green parts only, thinly sliced

1 teaspoon grated lime zest

salt and pepper

8 fl oz (240 ml) chicken stock or half stock and half dry white wine

4 fl oz (120 ml) whipping or double cream

1 tablespoon lime juice

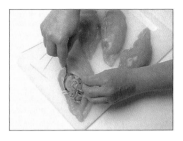

1 ▼ Cut horizontally into the thickest part of each breast to make a deep, wide pocket. Take care not to cut all the way through. Set the chicken breasts aside.

2 Melt half the butter in a large heavy frying pan over low heat. Add the leeks and lime zest and cook, stirring occasionally, for 15–20 minutes or until the leeks are very soft but not coloured.

3 Turn the leeks into a bowl and season with salt and pepper. Leave to cool. Clean the frying pan.

---

**~ VARIATION ~**

For Onion-stuffed Chicken Breasts, use 2 sweet onions, halved and thinly sliced, instead of leeks.

---

4 ▲ Divide the leeks among the chicken breasts, packing the pockets full. Secure the openings with wooden cocktail sticks.

5 Melt the remaining butter in the frying pan over moderately high heat. Add the stuffed breasts and brown lightly on both sides.

6 Add the stock and bring to the boil. Cover and simmer for about 10 minutes or until the chicken is cooked through. Turn the breasts over halfway through the cooking.

7 With a slotted spatula, remove the breasts from the pan and keep warm. Boil the cooking liquid until it is reduced by half.

8 ▼ Stir the cream into the cooking liquid and boil until reduced by about half again. Stir in the lime juice and season with salt and pepper.

9 Remove the cocktail sticks from the breasts. Cut each breast on the diagonal into ⅜ in (1 cm) slices. Pour the sauce over them and serve.

# FRYING CHICKEN

Fried chicken is justifiably popular – crisp and brown outside and tender and juicy within. It's a quick and easy cooking method that can be applied to pieces of rabbit and hare and small turkey joints too.

Dry the pieces thoroughly with paper towels before frying. If they are at all wet, they will not brown properly. If the recipe directs, lightly coat the pieces with egg and crumbs or with a batter.

**Succulent Fried Chicken**
Mix 8 fl oz (240 ml) milk with 1 beaten egg in a shallow dish. On a sheet of greaseproof paper combine 5 oz (145 g) plain flour, 1 teaspoon paprika, and some salt and pepper. One at a time, dip 8 chicken pieces in the egg mixture and turn them to coat all over. Then dip in the seasoned flour and shake off any excess. Deep-fry for 25–30 minutes, turning the pieces so they brown and cook evenly. Drain on paper towels and serve very hot. *Serves 4.*

1 ▲ **For pan-frying:** Heat oil, a mixture of oil and butter, or clarified butter in a large, heavy-based frying pan over moderately high heat. When the oil is very hot, put in the chicken pieces, skin side down. Do not crowd them or they will not brown evenly; cook in batches if necessary.

3 ▲ **For deep-frying:** Dip the pieces into a mixture of milk and beaten egg, then coat lightly with seasoned flour; allow the coating to set for 20 minutes before frying. (Or coat them with a batter just before frying.)

5 ▲ With a fish slice or tongs, lower the chicken pieces into the oil, a few at a time, without crowding them. Deep-fry until they are golden brown all over and cooked. Turn them so they colour evenly.

2 ▲ Fry until deep golden brown all over, turning the pieces so they colour evenly. Fry until all the chicken pieces are thoroughly cooked. Remove pieces of breast before drumsticks and thighs (dark meat takes longer to cook than white meat). Drain on paper towels.

4 ▲ Half fill a deep pan with vegetable oil. Heat it to 365°F (185°C). You can test the temperature with a cube of bread: if it takes 50 seconds to brown, the oil is at the right temperature.

6 ▲ Drain on paper towels and serve hot. If you want to keep a batch of fried chicken hot while you fry the rest, put it into a low oven, but don't cover it or it will become soggy.

# Chicken with Cajun Sauce

**SERVES 4**

1 × 3½ lb (1.5 kg) chicken, cut into 8 pieces

3½ oz (100 g) plain flour

salt and pepper

8 fl oz (240 ml) buttermilk or milk

vegetable oil, for frying

chopped spring onions, to garnish

FOR THE SAUCE

4 oz (115 g) lard or vegetable oil

scant 2½ oz (70 g) flour

2 onions, chopped

2–3 celery stalks, chopped

1 large green pepper, seeded and chopped

2 garlic cloves, finely chopped

8 fl oz (240 ml) passata

¾ pint (450 ml) red wine or chicken stock

8 oz (225 g) tomatoes, skinned and chopped

2 bay leaves

1 tablespoon soft brown sugar

1 teaspoon grated orange zest

½ teaspoon cayenne pepper

1  For the sauce, heat the lard or oil in a large, heavy pan and stir in the flour. Cook over moderately low heat, stirring constantly, for 15–20 minutes or until the mixture has darkened to the colour of hazelnut shells.

2 ▲  Add the onions, celery, green pepper and garlic and cook, stirring, until the vegetables are softened.

3  Stir in the remaining sauce ingredients with salt and pepper to taste. Bring to the boil, then simmer for 1 hour or until the sauce is rich and thick. Stir from time to time.

4  Meanwhile, prepare the chicken. Put the flour in a plastic bag and season with salt and pepper. Dip each piece of chicken in buttermilk, then dredge in the flour to coat lightly all over. Shake off excess flour. Set the chicken aside for 20 minutes to let the coating set before frying.

5  Heat oil 1 in (2.5 cm) deep in a large frying pan until it is very hot and starting to sizzle. Fry the chicken pieces, turning them once, for about 30 minutes or until deep golden brown all over and cooked through.

6 ▼  Drain the chicken pieces on paper towels. Add them to the sauce and sprinkle with spring onions.

~ **VARIATION** ~

For Pork Chops with Cajun Sauce, substitute 4 large loin chops. The Cajun sauce may also be served with steak, king prawns or fish.

# BONING CHICKEN AND TURKEY BREASTS

Boneless poultry breasts, both whole and halves, are widely available, but they tend to be more expensive than breasts with bone. So it is more economical to bone the breasts yourself, and it is really very easy to do. A thin-bladed boning knife is the ideal tool to use.

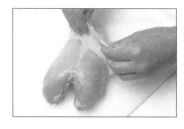

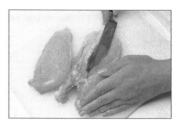

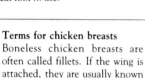

**Terms for chicken breasts**
Boneless chicken breasts are often called fillets. If the wing is attached, they are usually known as suprêmes.

**1 ▲ To take 2 boneless breasts from a whole breast:** First pull off the skin and any loose fat. Then with the knife, cut through the breast meat along both sides of the ridged top of the breastbone.

**2 ▲** With the knife at an angle, scrape the meat away from the bone down one side of the rib cage. Do this carefully so the breast meat comes away in one neat piece. Repeat on the other side. You now have 2 skinless boneless breasts.

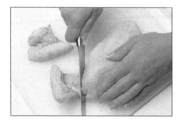

**3 ▲ To remove the meat from a breast:** If the wing is attached, cut through the ball and socket joint to separate the wing and breast. (Keep the wing for stock or another use.) Pull off the skin, if desired.

**4 ▲** Turn the breast over and scrape the meat from the bone, using short strokes and lifting away the bone as it is freed.

**5 ▲** Before cooking, remove the tendon next to the long flap or fillet on the underside of the breast. Cut it free of the meat at one end and pull it away, scraping it gently with the knife to remove it neatly.

**6 ▲** Trim any fat from the breast. Put it between 2 sheets of cling film or greaseproof paper and pound lightly with a meat mallet, the base of a saucepan or a rolling pin to flatten the breast slightly.

**7 ▲ To bone a whole breast for stuffing:** You must keep the skin intact. Set the breast skin side down and scrape the meat away from the rib cage, starting at one side and working up to the ridged top of the breastbone. Repeat on the other side.

**8 ▲** When the meat has been freed on both sides, lift up the rib cage and scrape the skin gently away from both sides of the top of the breastbone, taking care not to cut through the skin. The whole breast is now boned in one piece.

# Stuffed Turkey Breast

**SERVES 8**

1 × 4½–5 lb (2–2.25 kg) whole turkey breast, skin on, boned

salt and pepper

2 oz (55 g) butter, melted

4 tablespoons dry Madeira or dry white wine

12 fl oz (360 ml) turkey or chicken stock or water

FOR THE STUFFING

1 oz (30 g) butter

1 onion, finely chopped

8 oz (225 g) smoked ham, minced

2 oz (55 g) fresh breadcrumbs

2 tablespoons chopped fresh parsley

½ teaspoon dried thyme

2 oz (55 g) blanched almonds, coarsely chopped

1 egg, beaten to mix

**1** Preheat a 325°F/170°C/Gas 3 oven.

**2 ▲** For the stuffing, melt the butter in a frying pan and fry the onion, stirring occasionally, until soft. Tip the onion and butter into a bowl and add the ham, breadcrumbs, herbs, almonds and egg. Season to taste with salt and pepper and mix well.

**3** Lay the boned turkey breast flat, skin side down. Season with salt and pepper. Spread the stuffing over it in an even layer.

**4 ▲** Roll up the breast neatly and tie in several places with string. Use poultry skewers to secure the ends.

**5** Place the turkey breast on a rack in a roasting tin. Brush with half of the butter. Mix the remaining butter with the wine. Roast for 2–2½ hours, basting three or four times with the butter mixture. A meat thermometer should register 170°F (77°C).

**6** Remove the turkey breast to a carving board. Set aside in a warm place to rest for at least 15 minutes.

**7 ▼** Meanwhile, set the roasting tin over high heat. Add the stock or water, bring to the boil and stir to scrape up all the browned bits. Boil for 3–4 minutes. Strain and check the seasoning. Untie the breast and carve into neat slices. Serve with the sauce.

# PREPARING TURKEY ESCALOPES

Escalopes are slices cut crossways from the turkey breast. Economical and extremely versatile, they are a lean meat that cooks quickly and can be used as a substitute in most recipes that call for veal escalopes. Turkey escalopes can also be treated in much the same way as thin beef or pork steaks, or used in place of chicken breast fillets.

Slicing across the grain ensures that the escalope won't shrink or curl when it is cooked, and cutting on the diagonal gives good-sized slices.

**1 ▲** With a large sharp knife, cut the boned breast across the grain, at a slight angle, into ⅜ in (1 cm) slices.

**2 ▲** Put each slice between 2 sheets of greaseproof paper and pound lightly with the base of a pan, a meat mallet, or a rolling pin to flatten to ⅛–¼ in (3–5 mm) thickness. Be careful not to make holes in the meat.

---

# Turkey Rolls with Cranberries

**SERVES 4**

4 turkey escalopes, prepared for cooking

salt and pepper

2 tablespoons vegetable oil

4 fl oz (120 ml) cranberry juice or fruity red wine

½ teaspoon each arrowroot and water, mixed

FOR THE STUFFING

3½ oz (100 g) cranberries

6 oz (170 g) seedless red grapes

1 large red apple, quartered and cored

1 tablespoon honey

2 teaspoons finely chopped fresh ginger

½ teaspoon ground allspice

**1** For the stuffing, work the cranberries, grapes and apple in a food processor until finely chopped.

**2** Tip into a sieve placed in a bowl and drain, pressing to extract the juice. Reserve the juice. Mix the fruit with the honey, ginger and allspice.

**3** Season the turkey escalopes with salt and pepper. Divide the stuffing among them and spread it over them evenly, almost to the edges.

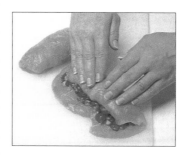

**4 ▲** Roll up each escalope, tucking in the sides, and tie in 2 or 3 places with string, or secure with wooden cocktail sticks.

**5** Heat the oil in a frying pan just large enough to accommodate the turkey rolls. Add the rolls and brown them on all sides over moderately high heat for 5–7 minutes.

**6 ▲** Add the reserved fruit juice and the cranberry juice or wine to the pan and bring to the boil. Cover and simmer for about 20 minutes or until the turkey is tender and cooked through. Turn the rolls halfway through the cooking.

**7** Remove the turkey rolls from the pan and keep warm. Boil the cooking liquid until it has reduced to about 6 fl oz (180 ml). Stir in the arrowroot mixture and boil for 2 minutes. Remove the string or sticks from the turkey rolls and cut into slices. Serve the cooking liquid as a sauce.

# MAKING POULTRY STOCK

A good home-made poultry stock is invaluable in the kitchen. It is simple and economical to make, and can be stored in the freezer for up to 6 months. If poultry giblets are available, add them (except the livers) with the wings.

### MAKES ABOUT 4 PINTS (2.5 LITRES)

2½–3 lb (1.12–1.35 kg) poultry wings, backs and necks (chicken, turkey, etc)

2 onions, unpeeled, quartered

6½ pints (4 litres) cold water

2 carrots, roughly chopped

2 celery stalks, with leaves if possible, roughly chopped

a small handful of fresh parsley

a few fresh thyme sprigs or ¼ teaspoon dried thyme

1 or 2 bay leaves

10 black peppercorns, lightly crushed

**A frugal stock**
Stock can be made from the bones and carcasses of roasted poultry, cooked with vegetables and flavourings. Save the carcasses in a plastic bag in the freezer until you have 3 or 4, then make stock. It may not have quite as rich a flavour as stock made from a whole bird or fresh wings, backs and necks, but it will still taste fresher and less salty than stock made from a cube.

**1 ▲** Combine the poultry wings, backs and necks and the onions in a stockpot. Cook over moderate heat, stirring occasionally so they colour evenly, until the poultry and onion pieces are lightly browned.

**2 ▲** Add the water and stir well to mix in the sediment on the bottom of the pot. Bring to the boil and skim off the impurities as they rise to the surface of the stock.

**3 ▲** Add the remaining ingredients. Partly cover the stockpot and gently simmer the stock for 3 hours.

**4 ▲** Strain the stock into a bowl and leave to cool, then refrigerate.

**5 ▲** When cold, remove the layer of fat that will have set on the surface.

**Stock tips**
If wished, use a whole bird for making stock instead of wings, backs and necks. A boiling fowl will give wonderful flavour and provide plenty of chicken meat to use in salads, sandwiches, soups and casseroles.

No salt is added to stock because as the stock reduces the flavour becomes concentrated and saltiness increases. Add salt to the dish in which the stock is used.

# Cream of Spring Onion Soup

**SERVES 4–6**

| |
|---|
| 1 oz (30 g) butter |
| 1 small onion, chopped |
| 5 oz (145 g) spring onions, white parts only, chopped |
| 8 oz (225 g) potatoes (2 medium-sized), peeled and chopped |
| 1 pint (600 ml) chicken stock |
| 12 fl oz (360 ml) single cream |
| salt and white pepper |
| 2 tablespoons lemon juice |
| chopped spring onion greens or fresh chives, to garnish |

**1 ▲** Melt the butter in a saucepan and add all the onions. Cover and cook over very low heat for about 10 minutes or until soft.

**2 ▲** Add the potatoes and the stock. Bring to the boil, then cover again and simmer over moderately low heat for about 30 minutes. Cool slightly.

**3** Purée the soup in a blender or in a food processor.

**4 ▼** If serving the soup hot, pour it back into the pan. Add the cream and season with salt and pepper. Reheat gently, stirring frequently. Stir in the lemon juice.

**5 ▲** If serving the soup cold, pour it into a bowl. Stir in the cream and lemon juice and season with salt and pepper. Cover the bowl and chill for at least 1 hour.

**6** Sprinkle with spring onion greens or chives before serving.

# MEAT

~

*Whether quickly grilled or stir-fried, or long-simmered for rich
flavour, meat lends itself to endless variety. With the basic
cooking methods that follow, you can choose to suit the time
available and your own preferences.*

# PREPARING MEAT FOR COOKING

You can buy meat ready for cooking from butchers and supermarkets. However, some cuts need further preparation, depending on how they are to be cooked. After stuffing, for example, a roast will need to be tied.

### How much to buy

As a general guide, when buying boneless meat that has little or no fat, allow 5–7 oz (145–200 g) per serving. For meat with bone that has a little fat at the edge, allow about 8 oz (225 g) per serving. Very bony cuts such as shin and spareribs have proportionally little meat so you will need 1 lb (450 g) per serving.

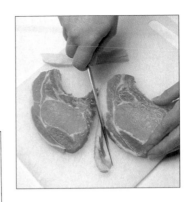

**1 ▲ To trim:** Use a sharp knife to trim skin or rind and fat from the surface. Leave a little fat on steaks to be grilled, and slash this fat at regular intervals to prevent the steak curling up during cooking. Joints to be roasted should retain a thin layer of fat about ⅛–¼ in (3–5 mm). Cut away the sinews and tough connective tissue.

**2 ▲** If you like, cut and scrape all fat and gristle from the ends of protruding bones (such as on cutlets or joints that contain rib bones). Cover the bone ends with foil to prevent charring.

**3 ▲ To chine a joint:** For large joints of meat that contain rib bones, such as rib of beef, pork loin and best end of lamb, it is a good idea to cut the chine bone (backbone) where it is joined to the rib bones, to loosen it or to remove it completely before cooking. Do this with a meat saw and sharp knife or ask your butcher to do it. Without the chine bone, the joint will be easy to carve.

**4 ▲ To bard a joint:** If a very lean piece of meat is to be roasted without a protective crust (a spice mixture, oil and crumbs or pastry, for example), it is a good idea to bard it to keep it moist. Wrap very thin slices of beef fat, pork fat or blanched bacon around the joint and tie them in place. Discard the fat before serving but keep the bacon, if liked.

**5 ▲ To tie a boned joint:** Joints that have been boned should be tied into a neat shape for roasting or pot roasting. The butcher will do this, but if you want to add a stuffing or seasoning, you will need to retie the joint yourself. Reshape it into a neat roll that is even in circumference. Use butcher's string to make ties around the circumference of the joint at 1 in (2.5 cm) intervals.

# Boned Pork Loin with Apple Cream Sauce

**SERVES 6**

1 × 3 lb (1.35 kg) boned pork loin, rolled and tied

1 tablespoon fresh thyme leaves or 1 teaspoon dried thyme

salt and pepper

fresh thyme sprigs, watercress and sliced apples, to garnish

FOR THE SAUCE

⅔ oz (20 g) butter

1 onion, chopped

2 apples, such as Granny Smiths, peeled, cored and chopped

¼ pint (150 ml) whipping or double cream

1½ teaspoons Dijon mustard

1 tablespoon creamed horseradish

**1**  Preheat a 375°F/190°C/Gas 5 oven.

**2** ▲ Untie the pork loin. Trim off the skin and most of the fat. Lay the pork out flat, skin side down. Sprinkle it with the thyme, salt and pepper and press into the meat.

~ COOK'S TIP ~

A boned joint will take longer to cook than the same weight joint with bone. This is because the bone conducts heat more readily than the flesh.

**3**  Roll up the loin again and tie it into a neat shape with string.

**4**  Put the pork loin on a rack in a small roasting tin. Roast for about 1¼–1½ hours or until well cooked.

**5** ▼  Meanwhile, for the sauce, melt the butter in a saucepan and add the onion and apples. Cook over low heat for 20–25 minutes, stirring occasionally, until very soft.

**6** ▲  Allow the apple mixture to cool slightly, then transfer it to a food processor. Add the cream, mustard and horseradish. Blend until smooth. Season with salt and pepper. Return the sauce to the pan and reheat just before serving.

**7**  When the pork is cooked, remove it from the oven to rest for about 10 minutes before carving. Garnish with thyme, watercress and apples.

# ROASTING MEAT

The dry heat of oven roasting is best suited to tender cuts of meat. If they don't have a natural marbling of fat, bard them. Alternatively, marinate the meat or baste it frequently with the roasting juices during cooking.

Meat should be at room temperature for roasting. Roast on a rack in a tin that is just a little larger than the joint. Without a rack, the base of the joint would stew and not become crisp.

There are two methods of roasting meat. For the first, the joint is seared at a high temperature and then the heat is reduced for the remainder of the cooking time. For the second method, the joint is roasted at a constant temperature throughout. Scientific studies have shown that both methods produce good results, and that it is prolonged cooking, not the method, that affects juiciness and shrinkage. So use whichever method you prefer or follow the recipe.

**Suggested roasting times**
Following the second roasting method, in a 350°F/180°C/Gas 4 oven, approximate timings in minutes per 1 lb (450 g):
Beef, rare, 20 + 20 extra*
    medium, 25 + 25 extra
    well done, 30 + 30 extra
Veal, 25 + 25 extra
Lamb, 25 + 25 extra
Pork, 35 + 35 extra
(*Prime cuts such as rib of beef and tenderloin need less time.)

**1** ▲ According to the recipe, rub the joint with oil or butter and season. If wished, for extra flavour, with the tip of a sharp knife make little slits in the meat all over the surface. Insert flavourings such as herbs, slivers of garlic, olive slices, shards of fresh ginger and so on.

**2** ▲ Insert a meat thermometer in the thickest part, not touching a bone. (An instant-read thermometer is sometimes inserted towards the end of roasting.) Roast for the suggested time, basting if necessary.

**3** ▲ Transfer the cooked meat to a carving board. Leave it to rest for 10–15 minutes before carving. During this time, make a gravy with the roasting juices (page 38), if liked.

**Roast Leg of Lamb**
Trim a 5–6 lb (2.25–2.7 kg) leg of lamb, removing almost all the fat. Cut 2–3 garlic cloves into very thin slices. Pull the leaves from 3 sprigs of fresh rosemary. Insert the garlic slices and rosemary leaves into slits in the lamb. Rub the lamb with olive oil and season with salt and pepper. Roast until cooked to your taste. *Serves 8.*

## MEAT THERMOMETER READINGS

| Beef | | Lamb | |
|---|---|---|---|
| rare | 125–130°F (52–54°C) | rare | 130–135°F (54–57°C) |
| medium-rare | 135°F (57°C) | medium | 140–145°F (60–63°C) |
| medium | 140–145°F (60–63°C) | well done | 160°F (71°C) |
| well done | 160°F (71°C) | | |
| | | Pork | |
| Veal | | medium | 150°F (66°C) |
| well done | 160°F (71°C) | well done | 160–165°F (71–74°C) |

# TESTING TO DETERMINE WHEN MEAT IS COOKED

The cooking times given in a recipe are intended to be a guideline. The shape of a cut can affect how long it takes to cook, and people have different preferences for how well cooked they like meat to be. So testing is essential.

**Natural law of roasting**
A joint will continue to cook in its own retained heat for 5–10 minutes after being removed from oven or pot, so it is a good idea to take it out when it is just below the desired thermometer reading.

**1 ▲** Large joints that are roasted or pot-roasted can be tested with a metal skewer. Insert the skewer into the thickest part and leave it for 30 seconds. Withdraw the skewer and feel it: if it is warm, the meat is rare; if it is hot, the meat is well cooked.

**2 ▲** The most reliable test is with the use of a meat thermometer, inserted in the centre of the joint, away from bones. Some instant-read thermometers are inserted at the end of cooking. Follow manufacturer's instructions. See the chart for the internal temperatures.

# COOKING METHODS AND CHOICE OF CUTS

**Roasting**
*Beef*: rib (fore), wing or prime rib, middle rib, fillet, sirloin, topside, aitchbone
*Veal*: shoulder (oyster), best end of neck, loin, fillet, breast, leg, topside (cushion)
*Lamb*: shoulder, best end of neck (crown roast), saddle, loin, breast, leg (whole or divided into fillet and knuckle)
*Pork*: shoulder (spare rib), hand and spring, blade, loin, fillet (tenderloin), leg (whole or divided into fillet and knuckle), fresh belly, spareribs. Also gammon joints and bacon collar and hock

**Pot-roasting and braising**
*Beef*: brisket, silverside, top ribs, sirloin, topside, aitchbone, chuck, flank, rump (thick flank), braising steak
*Veal*: shoulder, best end of neck, middle neck cutlets, breast
*Lamb*: shoulder, middle neck cutlets, breast, loin, leg

*Pork*: shoulder (spare rib), loin, fillet (tenderloin). Also gammon joints and bacon collar and hock

**Stewing**
*Beef*: neck (clod or sticking), blade, chuck, shin, flank, leg, skirt
*Veal*: neck, shoulder, scrag, breast, knuckle (osso buco), stewing veal or pie veal
*Lamb*: middle neck, shoulder, breast, scrag end, chump chops
*Pork*: spare rib, fillet (tenderloin), loin

**Pan-frying**
*Beef*: fillet steak (tournedos), sirloin steak (porterhouse), rump steak, T-bone steak, entrecote, chateaubriand, hamburgers
*Veal*: cutlets, loin chops, chump chops, escalopes, fillet steaks
*Lamb*: cutlets, noisettes (boned cutlets), loin chops, chump chops, leg steaks, fillet
*Pork*: loin chops, spare rib chops, cubes or slices of fillet (tenderloin).

Also streaky and back bacon rashers, gammon rashers, gammon steaks, gammon chops

**Grilling**
*Beef*: fillet steak (tournedos), sirloin steak (porterhouse), rump steak, T-bone steak, hamburgers
*Veal*: cutlets, loin chops, chump chops, fillet steaks
*Lamb*: cutlets, noisettes (boned cutlets), loin chops, chump chops, leg steaks, cubes of fillet
*Pork*: loin chops, spare rib chops, cubes or slices of fillet (tenderloin). Also streaky and back bacon rashers, gammon rashers, gammon steaks, gammon chops

**Stir-frying**
*Beef*: strips or cubes of rump steak and other steaks
*Veal*: strips of escalope
*Lamb*: strips or cubes of shoulder fillet, leg
*Pork*: strips or cubes of fillet (tenderloin)

# Making Gravy

Gravy made from the roasting juices is rich in flavour and colour. It is a traditional accompaniment for roast meat and poultry.

For a thinner sauce, an alternative method to that explained here is deglazing, where liquid is added to skimmed pan juices and boiled to reduce. This is explained on page 48.

---

**Resting a joint before carving**
Once a joint is removed from the oven or pot, it should be left in a warm place to 'rest' for 10–15 minutes. During this time, the temperature of the joint evens out, and the flesh reabsorbs most of the juices. Thus, the juices won't leak during carving.

---

**1 ▲** Spoon off most of the fat from the roasting tin. Set the tin over moderately high heat on top of the stove. When the roasting juices begin to sizzle, add flour and stir to combine well.

**2 ▲** Cook, scraping the tin well to mix in all the browned bits from the bottom, until the mixture forms a smooth brown paste. Add stock or another liquid as specified in the recipe and bring to the boil, stirring or whisking constantly. Simmer until the gravy has the right consistency, then season with salt and pepper.

---

# Rib of Beef with Shallots

### Serves 8

1 × 10 lb (4.5 kg) fore rib of beef (about 4 ribs), chined

vegetable oil

salt and pepper

1 lb (450 g) plump shallots, unpeeled

1½ tablespoons plain flour

12 fl oz (360 ml) beef stock or 8 fl oz (240 ml) beef stock and 4 fl oz (120 ml) red wine

**1** Preheat a 350°F/180°C/Gas 4 oven.

**2** If the ends of the rib bones have been left on the joint, scrape them clean, if wished. Rub any exposed bone ends with oil. Season the beef with salt and pepper. Set the joint in a roasting tin, fat side up.

**3** Roast the beef until cooked to your taste, basting often with the juices in the tin.

**4 ▲** Meanwhile, peel off the outer, papery layers of skin from the shallots, leaving at least 2 layers. Trim the root and stalk ends, if necessary.

**5** About 30 minutes before the beef has finished cooking, put the shallots into the roasting tin round the beef.

**6** When the beef is ready, transfer it to a carving board and set aside to rest for at least 15 minutes. Remove the shallots from the tin and keep warm.

**7 ▼** Spoon off all but about 2 tablespoons of fat from the roasting tin. Make gravy in the tin with the roasting sediments, flour and stock.

**8** Carve the rib of beef. Serve with the gravy, the shallots still in their skins (they slip out easily) and roast potatoes, if liked.

# BONING A LEG OF LAMB

A boned leg of lamb is much easier to carve than a joint with the bone in. By removing the bones, you can also stuff the pocket left before tying the joint into a neat shape with string.

Boning lamb and leaving the meat opened up flat (called 'butterflying' it) shortens the cooking time by about a third. A butterflied leg can be roasted, grilled or barbecued over charcoal.

Before boning, trim off all fat from the surface of the leg. The pelvic bone comprises the hip bone and the aitchbone.

**1 ▲** Set the leg pelvic bone upwards. Working from the fillet end, cut around the ball and socket joint between the hip bone and the main leg bone to free it from the meat. Cut around the pelvic bone to separate it from the meat, then remove it.

**2 ▲** Cut through the meat straight down the length of the leg bone, from the hip to the knee.

**3 ▲** Using short strokes, cut and scrape the meat away from the bone all around. Cut off the white chip of bone (the knee cap) if it is there.

**4 ▲** Continue cutting down the length of the leg bone below the knee (the shank end). Cut and scrape the meat away from the bone as before to free the bone.

**5 ▲** Lift the fillet end of the leg bone and cut around the knee to detach it from the meat. To avoid tough meat, cut out the tendons from the meat at the shank end.

**6 ▲ To butterfly:** Lay the boned leg out flat. Trim off all visible fat, then slash the thick portions of meat and open them so that the whole leg is reasonably even in thickness.

**7 ▲** Thread 2 skewers crossways through the meat at its widest part. These will keep the butterflied leg flat during cooking.

**Grilling and barbecuing meat**
These dry-heat methods of cooking are most suitable for naturally tender cuts of meat or those that have been tenderized. In grilling, meat is cooked under direct heat, either electric or gas powered; in barbecuing, meat is cooked over hot charcoal. The cooking time is determined by the heat and the distance the meat is from the heat source – normally 3 in (7.5 cm) below the grill or 4–6 in (10–15 cm) above the coals.

# Mustard-glazed Butterflied Leg of Lamb

**SERVES 6–8**

4 oz (115 g) Dijon mustard

1–2 garlic cloves, finely chopped

2 tablespoons olive oil

2 tablespoons lemon juice

2 tablespoons chopped fresh rosemary or 1 tablespoon crumbled dried rosemary

salt and pepper

1 × 5 lb (2.25 kg) leg of lamb, boned and butterflied

1 ▲ Combine the mustard, garlic, oil, lemon juice, rosemary, salt and pepper in a shallow glass or ceramic dish. Mix well together.

2 ▲ Add the leg of lamb, secured with skewers, and rub the mustard mixture all over it. Cover the dish and leave to marinate for at least 3 hours. (If the lamb is marinated in the refrigerator, let it return to room temperature before cooking.)

3 Preheat the grill or prepare a charcoal fire.

4 ▲ Place the lamb flat on the rack in the grill pan (lined with foil) or on the barbecue over the charcoal fire. Spread with any mustard mixture left in the bowl.

5 If grilling, set the lamb 4–5 in (10–12.5 cm) from the heat. Cook under the grill or over charcoal until the lamb is crusty and golden brown on the outside, 10–15 minutes on each side for rare meat, 20 minutes for medium and 25 minutes for well done.

6 Transfer the lamb to a carving board and leave it to rest for at least 10 minutes before carving into neat slices (not too thin) for serving.

# BROWNING OR SEARING MEAT

Large joints and pieces of meat to be roasted, pot-roasted or stewed are sometimes seared as the first step in their cooking. This may be done either by roasting briefly at a high temperature and then reducing the heat or by frying. The result is a browned crust that adds delicious flavour.

### Pot-roasting

This method of cooking tenderizes even the toughest cuts of meat. Prime cuts can also be pot-roasted, but cooking times are cut short – just long enough to reach the degree of cooking you like.

Depending on the desired result, meat to be pot-roasted may or may not have an initial searing.

**1 ▲ To sear by frying**: Dry the meat well with paper towels. Heat a little oil in a frying pan, flameproof casserole or roasting tin until it is very hot. Put in the meat and fry over high heat until it is well browned on all surfaces. Turn the meat using two spatulas or spoons. (Piercing with a fork would let juices escape, which would be boiled away.)

**2 ▲** If roasting, transfer the meat, in its roasting tin, to the oven. If pot-roasting, add a small amount of liquid and cover the pot tightly. If a frying pan has been used for searing, be sure to deglaze it: add some of the liquid called for in the recipe and bring to the boil, scraping up the browned bits from the bottom. Add this flavourful mixture to the pot.

---

# Pot-roast Veal with Herbs

### SERVES 6

1 tablespoon vegetable oil

1 × 3 lb (1.35 kg) boned veal shoulder, rolled and tied

4 medium onions, quartered

¼ pint (150 ml) chicken stock

a few sprigs each of fresh thyme, marjoram and rosemary or ¾ teaspoon each dried thyme, oregano and rosemary

salt and pepper

**1** Preheat a 300°F/150°C/Gas 2 oven.

**2** Heat the oil in a flameproof casserole over high heat (choose a casserole not much larger than the veal joint). Put in the veal joint and brown it, turning frequently to colour it evenly on all sides.

**3 ▼** Add the onions, stock and herbs. Season with salt and pepper. Cover tightly and transfer to the oven. Cook for 2½–3 hours.

### ~ VARIATION ~

For Pot-roast Pork with Herbs, substitute a boned pork shoulder or hand and spring.

**4 ▲** Remove the veal joint and onions and set aside on a carving board. Leave the veal to rest for at least 10 minutes before carving, discarding the strings.

**5** Skim the cooking juices to remove all fat. Bring to the boil, then strain. Taste for seasoning. Serve with the veal and onions.

# Chump Chops Braised with Carrots

**SERVES 4**

4 lamb chump chops, weighing about
  1 lb (450 g) each

4 small onions, halved

2 large celery stalks, cut into chunks

1 bay leaf

½ pint (300ml) lamb or chicken stock

2 tablespoons tomato purée

1 teaspoon Worcestershire sauce

1 tablespoon chopped fresh parsley

salt and pepper

8oz (225g) carrots, halved lengthways

---

**Emphasizing Natural Flavour**
To emphasize the natural flavours
of the ingredients rather than
those that result from browning,
the initial searing stage is omitted.

**1** Preheat the oven to 350°F/
180°C/Gas 4. Arrange the lamb
chops in a flameproof casserole,
slightly overlapping. Tuck the onions,
celery and bay leaf around the lamb.

**2** ▼ Combine stock, tomato purée,
Worcestershire sauce, parsley, salt
and pepper. Pour over the lamb.
Cover and braise in the oven 1 hour.

**3** Add the carrots and cover the pot
again. Braise until the lamb is very
tender and is pulling away from the
bone, about 1 hour longer.

**4** ▲ With a slotted spoon, transfer
the lamb chops and vegetables to a
serving platter. Skim all the fat from
the cooking liquid and discard the
bay leaf, then spoon it over the lamb
and vegetables. Serve hot.

# STEWING WITH A FRY START

Fry-start stews have a wonderful rich flavour, due greatly to the initial searing of the meat and vegetables. The long cooking period, in a seasoned liquid, produces a very tender result. Be sure to use a heavy-based pan or casserole.

**Saving the flavour**
If a different pan is used for searing the meat and vegetables, deglaze it: add wine, stock or water and bring to the boil, scraping up the browned bits from the bottom of the pan. Then add the resulting liquid to the stewpot.

**1 ▲** Cut the meat into equal-sized cubes and dry it thoroughly with paper towels. Coat lightly with flour if the recipe instructs.

**2 ▲** Heat a little oil in a frying pan or flameproof casserole until it is very hot. Add a few cubes of meat – just enough to cover the bottom of the pan without touching each other. Do not crowd the meat in the pan. If the temperature drops too much, a crisp brown crust will not form.

**3 ▲** Fry over moderately high heat until well browned on all sides. Turn the cubes so that they brown evenly, and remove them as they are done.

**4 ▲** Add the vegetables and cook, stirring occasionally, until they are well browned. Discard excess oil if the recipe instructs.

**5 ▲** Return the meat to the pan. If flour is added now, sprinkle it over the meat and vegetables and cook until it is well combined.

**6 ▲** Add liquid barely to cover and stir to mix. Add any flavourings and bring the liquid to the boil. Reduce the heat to a gentle simmer and complete the cooking as specified.

**7 ▲** If flour has not been used already, the liquid may be thickened at the end of cooking. One method is adding 'beurre manié', butter and flour paste (page 22), stirred in gradually.

**8 ▲** Alternatively, thicken with cornflour mixed with water (page 22). Or remove the meat and vegetables and boil the liquid to reduce it and to concentrate the flavour.

# Beef Stew with Dumplings

**SERVES 4**

1 oz (30 g) plain flour

salt and pepper

1½ lb (700 g) braising steak, cut into
    1½ in (4 cm) cubes

3 tablespoons vegetable oil

2 large onions, chopped

2 celery stalks, coarsely chopped

2 large carrots, thickly sliced

2 turnips, cut into cubes

6 oz (170 g) swede, cut into cubes

¾ pint (450 ml) beef stock

1 tablespoon soy sauce

1 bay leaf

1½ teaspoons fresh thyme leaves or
    ½ teaspoon dried thyme

FOR THE DUMPLINGS

5 oz (145 g) flour

2 teaspoons baking powder

½ teaspoon salt

¼ teaspoon mustard powder

¼ pint (150 ml) milk

2 tablespoons vegetable oil

**1**  Combine the flour and some salt
and pepper in a plastic bag. Add the
beef cubes, a few at a time, and toss to
coat them. Remove the cubes,
shaking off excess flour.

**2 ▲**  Heat the oil in a flameproof
casserole over moderately high heat.
Add the cubes of beef, in batches, and
brown them well on all sides. Remove
them from the casserole as they are
browned and set aside.

**3**  Add the onions, celery, carrots,
turnips and swede. Brown them all
over, stirring frequently.

**4 ▲**  Return the beef cubes to the
casserole. Add the stock, soy sauce,
bay leaf and thyme. Bring to the boil,
stirring well to mix in the browned
bits from the bottom of the pan.

**5**  Cover tightly, then reduce the heat
to very low. Simmer for about 2 hours
or until the beef is very tender.

**6**  For the dumplings, sift the dry
ingredients into a bowl. Add the milk
and oil and stir just until the dry
ingredients are bound into a soft
batter-like dough.

**7 ▲**  Uncover the casserole and bring
the stew liquid back to the boil. Drop
the dumpling dough on to the surface
of the stew in 8–10 dollops.

**8**  Cover again and simmer over low
heat for 12–15 minutes or until the
dumplings are just set and fluffy.
Serve immediately.

> **~ VARIATION ~**
>
> For Steak Pie, omit the dumplings
> and put the stew in a baking dish.
> Cover with puff pastry and bake at
> 400°F/200°C/Gas 6 for 25 minutes.

# STEWING WITH A RAW OR SWEAT START

In stews and pot-roasts where you want to emphasize the natural flavours of the ingredients rather than the flavours that result from browning, the initial searing stage is omitted.

Sweat-start stewing is a combination of two stewing methods. It doesn't use any oil or fat, relying on the fat naturally present in the meat.

**1 ▲ Raw-start stewing**: Put the meat in a casserole or other pot. Add vegetables, liquid and seasonings as specified in the recipe.

**2 ▲** If the recipe instructs, bring the liquid to the boil, then cover the pot. Continue cooking on top of the stove, or transfer to the oven.

**3 ▲ Sweat-start stewing**: Combine the meat and a little liquid in the stewpot. Cover and cook gently to draw out the meat juices.

**4 ▲** Uncover and boil the juices to reduce them to a sticky brown glaze. Continue cooking briskly to brown the meat, then remove it.

**5 ▲** Add liquid to deglaze the pot, then add vegetables and flavourings. Return the meat, stir, add more liquid and complete the cooking.

---

# Pork Hot-pot with Apples

**SERVES 4**

| |
|---|
| 1 oz (30 g) butter |
| 4 large pork loin chops, well trimmed |
| 1 small onion, thinly sliced |
| 2 apples, peeled and thinly sliced |
| 1 teaspoon sweet paprika |
| ½ tablespoon chopped fresh sage or ½ teaspoon dried sage |
| salt and pepper |
| 4 tablespoons apple juice |
| 1¼–1½ lb (575–700 g) sweet potatoes, thickly sliced |

**1** Preheat a 350°F/180°C/Gas 4 oven.

**2 ▼** Grease a baking dish with one-quarter of the butter. Arrange the chops in one layer.

**3** Scatter the onion and apples on top and sprinkle with paprika, sage, salt and pepper. Pour over the juice.

**4 ▲** Lay the potato slices over the surface, slightly overlapping them. Cover with foil or a lid. Bake for 1½ hours. Uncover and dot with the remaining butter. Continue baking, uncovered, for 20–30 minutes or until the potatoes are lightly browned.

# Lamb Stew with Peas

**SERVES 4–6**

2–2½ lb (900 g–1.12 kg) boned lamb shoulder, trimmed of excess fat and cut into 1½ in (4 cm) cubes

¾ pint (450 ml) lamb or chicken stock

1 onion, chopped

1 tablespoon chopped fresh rosemary or 1 teaspoon crumbled dried rosemary

salt and pepper

10 oz (300 g) frozen peas, thawed and drained

1 tablespoon mint jelly

**1** Put the lamb cubes and 4 fl oz (120 ml) stock in a flameproof casserole. Cover and cook over moderately low heat for about 30 minutes to draw out the juices.

**2** Remove the lid and boil the juices, stirring occasionally, until they reduce to a sticky brown glaze.

**3** ▼ Continue cooking to brown the cubes of meat well on all sides, turning the cubes so that they colour evenly. With a slotted spoon, remove the lamb cubes from the casserole and set them aside.

**4** Skim off as much fat as possible from the remaining juices, then add another 4 fl oz (120 ml) stock. Bring to the boil, stirring thoroughly to mix in all the browned bits from the bottom of the casserole.

**5** ▲ Add the onion and rosemary and cook until the onion is soft, stirring occasionally. Return the lamb cubes to the casserole with the remaining stock and season. Bring to the boil. Cover and simmer gently for about 1 hour or until the lamb is tender, adding more stock if needed.

**6** Lift out the lamb and keep warm. Skim all fat from the cooking liquid. Add the peas; simmer for 2 minutes. Stir in the mint jelly until melted. Stir in the lamb and serve hot.

*Pork Hot-pot with Apples (left), Lamb Stew with Peas*

# PAN-FRYING AND SAUTÉING

Tender cuts of meat, such as steaks and chops, slices of calf's liver and hamburgers, are ideal for cooking quickly in a heavy frying pan. And the juices left in the pan can be turned into an easy sauce.

Before pan-frying and sautéing, trim excess fat from steaks, chops, escalopes, etc, then dry them very thoroughly with paper towels.

For cooking, use a fat that can be heated to a high temperature. If using butter, an equal amount of vegetable oil will help prevent burning, or use clarified butter.

1 ▲ Heat the fat in the pan over high heat until very hot but not browning. Put in the meat, in one layer. Do not crowd the pan.

2 ▲ Fry until browned on both sides and done to your taste. If pan-frying pork or veal chops, reduce the heat to moderate once they are in the pan.

### Testing steak

A reliable way to test steak is by pressing it with your finger. When raw, it is soft and can be squashed. When cooked rare, it will be only slightly springy. When cooked medium, it will offer more resistance and drops of red juice will appear on the surface. When well done, it will be firm to the touch.

### Pan-fried Teriyaki Steak

Combine 3 tablespoons vegetable oil, 1 tablespoon each soy sauce, honey, red wine vinegar and finely chopped onion, 1 crushed garlic clove and ½ teaspoon ground ginger in a plastic bag. Add 4 rump or sirloin steaks and turn to coat well. Put the bag in a dish and marinate for 2 hours. Drain the steaks and pat dry, then pan-fry until cooked to your taste. The steaks can also be grilled. *Serves 4.*

# DEGLAZING FOR A PAN SAUCE

After pan-frying or sautéing, a simple yet delicious sauce can be made in the pan. The same method can be used to make gravy for roast meats. It is also a good way to maximize flavour in stews and casseroles.

Before deglazing, remove the meat and keep it warm. Pour or spoon off all the fat from the pan, unless the recipe calls for shallots, garlic, or the like to be softened. In that case, leave 1–2 teaspoons of fat and cook the vegetables in it.

1 ▲ Pour in the liquid called for in the recipe (wine, stock, vinegar, etc). Bring to the boil, stirring well to scrape up all the browned bits from the bottom of the pan and dissolve them in the liquid.

2 ▲ Boil over high heat for 1–2 minutes or until the liquid is almost syrupy. If the recipe instructs, enrich the sauce with cream or butter. Season to taste with salt and pepper and serve.

# Pepper Steak with Mushrooms

**Serves 4**

2 tablespoons black peppercorns, coarsely crushed

½ teaspoon hot pepper flakes (optional)

4 fillet, sirloin or rump steaks, 6–8 oz (170–225 g) each, well trimmed

3 tablespoons vegetable oil

½ oz (15 g) butter

5 oz (145 g) mushrooms, sliced

2 tablespoons Cognac or whisky

¼ pint (150 ml) whipping or double cream

salt

1 ▲ Combine the peppercorns and hot pepper flakes, if using, and press on to both sides of the steaks.

2 ▲ Heat 1 tablespoon of the oil with the butter in a heavy frying pan that is large enough to accommodate the steaks in one layer. Add the mushrooms and cook over moderate heat, stirring and turning them occasionally, for about 5 minutes or until they are wilted.

3 Increase the heat to moderately high and continue cooking until the liquid from the mushrooms has evaporated and they are lightly browned. With a slotted spoon, remove them from the pan and reserve.

4 Add the remaining oil to the frying pan. When it is very hot, add the steaks. Fry for 2 minutes on each side or until well browned. Continue cooking until done to your taste. (Test by pressing with your finger.) Remove the steaks from the pan and keep them hot.

5 ▲ Pour off all the fat from the pan. Add the Cognac and bring to the boil, stirring and scraping to mix in the browned bits from the bottom of the pan. Add the cream and bring back to the boil. Boil for 1 minute.

6 Stir in the mushrooms and reheat them. Check the seasoning, then pour this sauce over the steaks.

# STIR-FRYING

The preparation of ingredients for stir-frying often takes longer than the cooking itself. This is because all ingredients must be cut to uniform sizes so that the cooking can be accomplished quickly and evenly.

A wok is excellent for stir-frying because its high sides let you stir and toss the ingredients briskly. Use long cooking chopsticks or a wooden spatula to keep the ingredients moving around the wok.

**Stir-fried Beef with Mange-tout**
Cut 1 lb (450 g) lean boneless tender beef into very thin strips. Combine 3 tablespoons soy sauce, 2 tablespoons dry sherry, 1 tablespoon brown sugar and ½ teaspoon cornflour in a bowl. Heat 1 tablespoon vegetable oil in the hot wok. Add 1 tablespoon each finely chopped fresh ginger and garlic and stir-fry for 30 seconds. Add the beef and stir-fry for 2 minutes or until well browned. Add 8 oz (225 g) mange-tout; stir-fry for 3 minutes. Stir the soy sauce mixture until smooth, then add to the wok. Bring to the boil, stirring and tossing, and simmer just until it is thickened and smooth. Serve immediately, accompanied by freshly boiled rice. *Serves 4.*

1 ▲ Prepare all the ingredients in uniformly sized pieces following recipe instructions.

2 ▲ Heat a wok or large deep frying pan over moderately high heat. Dribble in the oil down the sides.

3 ▲ When the oil is hot (a piece of vegetable should sizzle on contact), add the ingredients in the order specified in the recipe. (Those that take longer to cook are added first.) Do not add too much to the wok at a time or the ingredients will start to steam rather than fry.

4 ▲ Fry, stirring and tossing constantly with chopsticks or a spatula, until the ingredients are just cooked: vegetables should be crisp-tender and meat and poultry tender and juicy.

5 ◄ Push the ingredients to the side of the wok or remove them. Pour liquid or sauce as specified in the recipe into the bottom. Cook and stir, then mix in the ingredients from the side. Serve immediately.

# Pork Chop Suey

**SERVES 4**

| |
|---|
| 12 oz (340 g) pork fillet (tenderloin) |
| 1½ tablespoons cornflour |
| 4 tablespoons soy sauce |
| 1 tablespoon finely chopped fresh ginger |
| ¼ pint (150 ml) beef or chicken stock |
| 4 tablespoons dry sherry |
| ½ teaspoon sugar |
| salt and pepper |
| 3 tablespoons groundnut or vegetable oil |
| 1 celery stalk, thinly sliced |
| ½ green pepper, seeded and thinly sliced |
| 8 button mushrooms, thinly sliced |
| 1 garlic clove, finely chopped |
| 1 courgette, thinly sliced |
| 4 oz (115 g) canned water chestnuts, sliced |
| 3½ oz (100 g) bean sprouts |

**1** Trim any fat from the pork, then cut it across the grain into very thin slices. (Freeze the pork for 20–30 minutes so it will be easier to slice.)

**2 ▲** Mix 1 tablespoon cornflour, half the soy sauce and the ginger in a bowl. Add the pork and stir well. Cover and marinate for 30 minutes.

**3** In another bowl, mix together the remaining cornflour and soy sauce with the stock, sherry, sugar, salt and pepper. Set aside.

**4 ▼** Heat the wok, then add half the oil. When it is hot, add the pork mixture and stir-fry over high heat for 1–2 minutes or until all the slices of pork have changed colour. Turn the pork on to a plate.

**5** Add the remaining oil to the wok. When hot, add the celery, green pepper, mushrooms and garlic. Stir-fry for 1 minute.

**6 ▲** Add the courgette, water chestnuts and bean sprouts. Stir-fry for a further 1–2 minutes or until the vegetables are tender but still crisp.

**7** Return the pork to the wok and add the sherry mixture. Cook, stirring, until the sauce boils and thickens. Serve immediately.

# PREPARING ESCALOPES

Escalopes are slices of veal from the fillet end of the leg, cut ⅜ in (1 cm) thick. They need to be pounded before cooking, to break the fibres. This tenderizes them and helps to keep them flat during cooking.

Slices of other meat or poultry may also be called escalopes. Beef slices cut from the top of the leg, to be rolled and braised ('birds' or 'olives'), are prepared in the same way.

**Pounding it out**
You can also use the base of a heavy saucepan or frying pan to pound and flatten meat escalopes. Choose a pan with a smooth base.

1 ▲ Trim any fat and gristle from around the edge of each escalope. Lay it flat between two sheets of cling film or greaseproof paper.

2 ▲ Using the smooth side of a meat mallet or the long side of a rolling pin, pound gently but firmly all over the escalope to flatten it to ⅛–¼ in (3–5 mm) thickness. It will spread out to almost twice its original size.

# Veal Escalopes with Tomato Sauce

**SERVES 4**

2½ oz (75 g) plain flour

2 tablespoons freshly grated Parmesan cheese, plus more to serve

salt and pepper

1 egg

2 tablespoons milk or water

2½–3 oz (75–85 g) fine fresh breadcrumbs

1 garlic clove, halved (optional)

8 small veal escalopes, weighing 1–1¼ lb (450–575 g), prepared for cooking

½ oz (15 g) butter

3–4 tablespoons olive oil

8 fl oz (240 ml) tomato-herb sauce (page 172)

1 Combine the flour, cheese, salt and pepper on a sheet of greaseproof paper. Lightly beat the egg with the milk or water in a shallow bowl. Spread the crumbs on another sheet of greaseproof paper.

2 If using the garlic, rub the cut sides over the veal escalopes.

3 ▼ One at a time, dip an escalope in the flour mixture to coat both sides lightly; shake off excess flour. Then dip the escalope in the egg mixture. Finally, coat on both sides with crumbs and press them on lightly to help them adhere.

4 ▲ Heat half the butter and oil in a large frying pan over moderately high heat. Add 4 of the prepared escalopes and fry for 1½ minutes on each side or until golden brown and cooked through. Remove from the pan and keep hot while you fry the remaining escalopes.

5 Top each escalope with heated tomato sauce. Serve with additional Parmesan cheese and buttered noodles, if liked.

# Beef Birds with Mustard

**SERVES 4**

8 thin slices of beef topside, weighing about 1¾lb (800g), prepared for cooking

3 tablespoons spicy brown mustard

salt and pepper

4 large pickled cucumbers, halved lengthways, or 8 medium-size

2 tablespoons vegetable oil

2 onions, thinly sliced

½pint (300ml) Guinness or beef stock

1 bay leaf

**1** Preheat a 350°F/180°C/Gas 4 oven. Select a heavy frying pan with an ovenproof handle or a flameproof casserole.

**2** Lay the slices of beef out flat on a work surface. Spread each slice with mustard, almost to the edges. Season with salt and pepper.

**3 ▼** Place a piece of cucumber along one end of each slice and roll up neatly. Tie the rolls with string or secure with wooden cocktail sticks.

**4** Heat the oil in the frying pan or casserole. Add the beef rolls and fry over moderately high heat until they are browned on all sides. Remove them from the pan and set aside.

**5** Add the onions to the pan and fry until soft and beginning to brown, stirring frequently.

**6 ▲** Return the beef rolls to the pan and add the Guinness and bay leaf. Bring to the boil over high heat.

**7** Cover the pan tightly and transfer it to the oven. Cook for 1 hour or until the beef rolls are very tender. Turn them over halfway through cooking to ensure even cooking.

**8** Remove the string or sticks and discard the bay leaf before serving. If liked, serve rice or potatoes with the beef birds.

*Veal Escalopes with Tomato Sauce (left), Beef Birds with Mustard*

# MINCING MEAT

Minced meats of all kinds are easily obtainable, but when you want something more unusual for a pâté or you want to use a particular cut of meat, well trimmed of gristle and tendons, you will mince it yourself. Also, if minced meat is to be served raw, as in steak tartare, it must be freshly prepared.

1 ◀ **With a mincer**: This produces the most uniform minced meat, and you can choose coarse or fine textures, according to which blade is used. Trim the meat well and cut it into 1½ in (4 cm) cubes or strips, then feed through the machine.

2 ▲ **With a food processor**: Trim the meat carefully (be sure to remove all gristle because a food processor will chop gristle too) and cut it into cubes. Place in the machine fitted with the metal blade and pulse.

3 ▲ In between turning the machine on and off a few times, stir the meat around so that it is evenly minced. Care must be taken not to overprocess meat to a purée, particularly if making hamburgers (they would be tough).

4 ▲ **By hand**: Trim the meat well. Using a large chef's knife, first cut the meat into cubes, then chop into smaller and smaller cubes. Continue chopping until you have the consistency you want, coarse or fine.

# Meat Loaf with Mushroom Stuffing

**SERVES 6**

| |
|---|
| 8 oz (225 g) mushrooms, coarsely chopped |
| 1 small onion, finely chopped |
| 1 oz (30 g) butter |
| 4½ oz (130 g) fresh breadcrumbs |
| 3 tablespoons chopped fresh parsley |
| 1 teaspoon dried thyme |
| 2 teaspoons bottled brown sauce |
| salt and pepper |
| 1½ lb (700 g) lean minced beef |
| 8 oz (225 g) lean minced pork |
| 5 tablespoons tomato ketchup |
| 2 eggs, beaten |

1  Preheat a 375°F/190°C/Gas 5 oven.

2  Cook the mushrooms and onion in the butter over moderate heat until soft. Turn the mixture into a bowl.

3 ▲ Add the breadcrumbs, parsley, thyme, brown sauce, salt and pepper. Mix well.

4  In another bowl, mix the beef with the pork, tomato ketchup and eggs.

5 ▲ Pack half of the meat mixture into a large loaf tin, pressing it into an even layer. Pack the mushroom mixture on top, then cover with the rest of the meat. Bake for 1¼ hours.

6  Remove from the oven and leave to stand for 15 minutes. Pour off the juices, then turn out the meat loaf on to a serving plate. Serve hot.

# Lamb Burgers with Cucumber Sauce

**Serves 4**

1½ lb (700 g) lean minced lamb

1 small onion, finely chopped

8 dried apricot halves, finely chopped

4 tablespoons pine nuts

¾ oz (25 g) fine dry breadcrumbs

2 teaspoons mild curry powder

1 egg

salt and pepper

4 pittas (pocket breads), heated and cut
   in half

For the sauce

½ cucumber, peeled and grated

½ pint (300 ml) plain yogurt

2 tablespoons chopped fresh mint

1 ▼ Combine the lamb, onion,
apricots, pine nuts, breadcrumbs,
curry powder, egg, salt and pepper in a
bowl. Mix well together with your
fingers until blended.

2 ▲ Divide into 8 portions and shape
each into a small burger. Cover and
chill for 30 minutes.

3 Meanwhile, for the sauce, squeeze
the grated cucumber in a double
thickness of paper towels to extract
excess water.

4 ▲ Mix together the cucumber,
yogurt and mint. Season to taste with
salt and pepper.

5 Preheat the grill or prepare a
charcoal fire.

6 Grill or barbecue the burgers until
they are cooked to your taste, about
10 minutes for medium. Turn them
halfway through cooking to ensure
that they brown and cook evenly.

7 Serve the burgers in the pitta
halves, with the cucumber sauce.

# Cottage Pie

**SERVES 4**

2 oz (55 g) butter

1 large onion, finely chopped

1 celery stalk, finely diced

1 large carrot, finely diced

1 lb (450 g) lean minced beef

1 tablespoon plain flour

8 fl oz (240 ml) hot beef stock

2 tablespoons chopped fresh parsley

1 tablespoon tomato purée

salt and pepper

2 lb (900 g) floury potatoes, peeled

3–4 tablespoons milk

2 teaspoons spicy brown mustard

**1** Melt ½ oz (15 g) of the butter in a frying pan over moderate heat. Add the onion, celery and carrot and cook until the onion is soft, stirring occasionally.

**2** ▲ Add the beef and fry, stirring, until it is brown and crumbly.

**3** ▲ Sprinkle the flour evenly over the surface and stir it into the meat and vegetables.

**4** ▲ Gradually add the stock, stirring well. Stir in the parsley and tomato purée. Season with salt and pepper.

**5** Bring to a simmer, then cover and cook over very low heat, stirring occasionally, for 45 minutes.

**6** Meanwhile, cook the potatoes in boiling salted water until they are tender. Drain well.

**7** Put the potatoes in a bowl and mash them. Add the remaining butter and just enough milk to make a soft fluffy texture. Season to taste with salt and pepper.

**8** Preheat a 400°F/200°C/Gas 6 oven.

**9** Stir the mustard into the beef mixture, then turn it into a baking dish. Cover with a neat layer of potatoes and seal to the sides of the dish. Mark with a fork, if liked. Bake for 20–25 minutes. Serve hot.

# COOKING BACON AND SAUSAGE

Bacon is cured meat from the fatty side (or belly) of a pig. Streaky rashers are fattier than back rashers; throughcut or middle rashers combine back and streaky. All can be used almost interchangeably in recipes. All bacon rashers are available smoked and unsmoked (or green).

Uncooked sausage – fresh or smoked – must be thoroughly cooked before eating. To test, pierce with a skewer: the juices that run out should be clear. Many precooked sausages are heated to serving temperature by poaching, braising, frying or grilling.

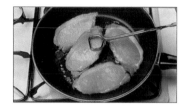

1 ▲ **To fry back bacon or gammon rashers:** Heat a little butter or oil, or other fat specified in a recipe, in a heavy frying pan. Arrange the rashers in the pan in one layer. Cook over moderate heat until lightly browned, 4–10 minutes, according to the thickness of the rashers.

2 ▲ **To fry bacon rashers:** Arrange them in a heavy unheated frying pan in one layer. Set the pan over moderately low heat. Cook the bacon, turning it occasionally, until golden brown and cooked, 8–10 minutes, according to the thickness of the rashers. Drain on paper towels.

3 ▲ **To bake or grill bacon rashers:** Arrange side by side on a rack in a shallow baking tin. Bake in a 400°F/200°C/Gas 6 oven, turning once, for 10–15 minutes or until golden brown. Or grill under a moderately high heat, turning once, for 3–8 minutes or until crisp and brown on both sides.

4 ▲ **To fry uncooked sausage patties:** Arrange in a heavy, unheated frying pan in one layer. Cook over medium-low heat until done (test with a skewer), 10–12 minutes. Turn once during cooking.

5 ▲ **To pan-braise fresh sausages:** Arrange in one layer in an unheated frying pan with 3 tablespoons water. Cover and simmer for 5–15 minutes or until cooked through. Drain. Uncover and cook until browned. Or fry, uncovered, in a little fat, turning to brown and cook evenly.

6 ▲ **To bake or grill fresh sausages:** Arrange them on a rack in a shallow baking tin. Bake in a 400°F/200°C/Gas 6 oven for about 20 minutes until cooked (test with a skewer). Or grill about 4in (10cm) from the heat until browned on all sides.

7 ▲ **To fry pork sausagemeat:** Cook in a frying pan over moderate heat until golden brown and crumbly. Stir constantly while cooking and break up with the side of a spoon or fork. Drain off excess fat.

8 ▲ **To poach frankfurters and cooked sausages:** Add them to a saucepan of boiling water. Reduce the heat, cover and simmer for 5–10 minutes or until heated through. To brown poached or fully cooked sausages, grill or fry gently.

# Sausage and Bean Casserole

**Serves 4–6**

| 12 oz (340 g) dried white haricot beans, soaked overnight |
| --- |
| 4 oz (115 g) soft light brown sugar |
| 2 teaspoons mustard powder |
| 3 oz (85 g) light molasses or treacle |
| 1 large onion, chopped |
| salt and pepper |
| 12 frankfurters or other cooked sausages, cut into 1 in (2.5 cm) pieces |

1 Drain the beans and put them in a large saucepan. Cover with plenty of fresh cold water. Bring to the boil, then simmer over low heat for about 1 hour. Drain the beans and reserve the cooking liquid.

2 Preheat a 300°F/150°C/Gas 2 oven.

3 ▲ Mix ¾ pint (450 ml) of the bean cooking liquid with the sugar, mustard and molasses or treacle.

4 ▲ Mix the beans and onion in a casserole. Add the molasses mixture and season. Cover and bake for 3 hours, stirring and adding more liquid occasionally.

5 ◀ Stir in the pieces of frankfurter or other sausage. If the beans seem dry, add a little more of the reserved cooking liquid.

6 Cover the casserole again and continue cooking for a further 1 hour, stirring occasionally. Serve hot, in the casserole.

**A selection of sausages**

Sausages are available in many forms. Some are ready to eat, but fresh sausages must be cooked thoroughly and those sold as cooked are often heated before serving. All kinds of meats are used and each country has its traditional specialities.

**Uncooked sausages** include fresh sausages and chipolatas made from pork, beef or other meat (fry, pan-braise, grill or bake); sausagemeat (fry); bockwurst and bratwurst (poach, then fry or grill); boudin blanc (poach or grill); haggis (poach); luganeghe (poach or grill); merguez (grill); Toulouse sausage (essential in cassoulet).

**Part or fully cooked sausages** include andouillette, sometimes smoked (fry or grill); black pudding (fry or grill); cotechino (poach); frankfurter (poach or grill); kielbasa, sometimes smoked (poach or slice and add to soups and stews); liverwurst (ready to eat cold); saveloy/cervelat (add to soups or bean dishes).

**Smoked and dry sausages**, all of which are ready to eat cold, include bierwurst, chorizo (which is also sold fresh), mettwurst, mortadella, peperoni (a popular pizza topping) and salami from various parts of Italy, as well as Germany, Hungary, France and Denmark.

# MAKING MEAT STOCK

The most delicious meat soups, stews, casseroles, gravies and sauces rely on a good home-made stock for success. Neither a stock cube nor a canned consommé will do if you want the best flavour. Once made, meat stock can be kept in the refrigerator for 4–5 days, or frozen for longer storage (up to 6 months).

**On the light side**
For a light meat stock, use veal bones and do not roast the bones or vegetables. Put in the pot with cold water and cook as described.

**MAKES ABOUT 3½ PINTS (2 LITRES)**

4 lb (1.8 kg) beef bones, such as shin, leg, neck and clod, or veal or lamb bones, cut into 2½ in (6 cm) pieces

2 onions, unpeeled, quartered

2 carrots, roughly chopped

2 celery stalks, with leaves if possible, roughly chopped

2 tomatoes, coarsely chopped

7½ pints (4.5 litres) cold water

a handful of parsley stalks

a few fresh thyme sprigs or ¾ teaspoon dried thyme

2 bay leaves

10 black peppercorns, lightly crushed

1 ▲   Preheat a 450°F/230°C/Gas 8 oven. Put the bones in a roasting tin or flameproof casserole and roast, turning occasionally, for 30 minutes or until they start to brown.

2 ▲   Add the onions, carrots, celery and tomatoes and baste with the fat in the tin. Roast for a further 20–30 minutes or until the bones are well browned. Stir and baste occasionally.

3 ▲   Transfer the bones and vegetables to a stockpot. Spoon off the fat from the roasting tin.

4 ▲   Add a little of the water to the roasting tin or casserole and bring to the boil on top of the stove, stirring well to scrape up any browned bits. Pour this liquid into the stockpot.

5 ▲   Add the remaining water. Bring just to the boil, skimming frequently to remove all the foam from the surface. Add the parsley, thyme, bay leaves and peppercorns.

6 ▲   Partly cover the pot and simmer the stock for 4–6 hours. The bones and vegetables should always be covered with liquid, so top up with a little boiling water from time to time if necessary.

7 ▲   Strain the stock through a sieve. Skim as much fat as possible from the surface. If possible, cool the stock and then refrigerate it; the fat will rise to the top and set in a layer that can be removed easily.

# Hearty Beef and Vegetable Soup

**SERVES 6**

8 oz (225 g) braising steak, cut into ½ in (1.5 cm) cubes

8 oz (225 g) lean boned pork shoulder, cut into ½ in (1.5 cm) cubes

3½ pints (2 litres) beef stock

1 bay leaf

12 oz (340 g) tomatoes, skinned, seeded and chopped

1 small red pepper, seeded and chopped

1 small onion, chopped

2 carrots, chopped

1 large boiling potato, peeled and diced

6 oz (170 g) fresh or thawed frozen sweetcorn kernels

1 tablespoon Worcestershire sauce

salt and pepper

**1 ▲** Put the beef and pork in a large heavy saucepan and add the stock. Bring to the boil, skimming off all the froth that rises to the surface.

**2 ▲** When the liquid is free of froth, add the bay leaf. Partly cover the pan and gently simmer over very low heat for about 1 hour.

**3 ▼** Add the tomatoes, red pepper, onion, carrots and potato. Bring back to the boil. Continue simmering, partly covered, for about 45 minutes. Stir from time to time.

**4** Add the sweetcorn and simmer for a further 20–30 minutes or until all the vegetables and meat are tender.

**5** Discard the bay leaf. Stir in the Worcestershire sauce. Taste and adjust the seasoning before serving.

~ **COOK'S TIP** ~

This soup can be made 2 or 3 days ahead. The flavour will improve.

# FISH & SEAFOOD

~

*No need to be wary of preparing fish and seafood. It is lean,*
*tasty and quick to cook – a good week-night solution as well as*
*a celebration treat. Just keep in the natural moisture and don't*
*overcook. You can even cut your own fish steaks or fillets.*

# PREPARING WHOLE FISH FOR COOKING

Most fish have scales and these should be removed before cooking unless the fish is to be filleted or the skin is to be removed before serving. Fish sold by fishmongers will normally be scaled as well as cleaned (eviscerated or gutted), but you can do this yourself, if necessary. Trimming the tail gives a whole fish a neat appearance.

All fish preparation is best done in or near the sink, with cool water running. Salt your hands for a good grip on the fish.

**1 ▲ To scale:** Grasp the tail firmly and scrape off the scales using a special fish scaler or a knife, working from the tail towards the head. Rinse the fish well. Repeat on the other side.

**2 ▲ To trim:** For flat fish to be cooked whole, use kitchen scissors to trim off the outer half of the small fin bones all round the fish.

**3 ▲** For round fish, cut the flesh on both sides of the anal and dorsal (back) fins and pull them out; the small bones attached will come out too. Trim off the other fins.

**4 ▲** If the fish is to be cooked whole, leave the fins on, or just trim them, because they help keep the shape of the fish.

**5 ▲ To trim the tail:** If the tail is to be left on, cut a neat 'V' in the centre with scissors. The fish is now ready for cooking.

# A LOOK AT FISH

In terms of shape and structure, most fish fall into one of two general categories: round fish and flat fish.

Round fish have thicker bodies and many of their bones are attached to their fins. They can be filleted or cut into steaks or cutlets, but all will contain small pin bones.

Flat fish have a flat central bone with a row of bones attached on either side. This simple bone structure makes flat fish easy to fillet. Most are too thin to cut into steaks or cutlets.

Large fish such as tuna have a thick bone running down the centre of their bodies; spiking out from this are four rows of bones that divide the flesh into quarters. These boneless 'loins' are usually sliced into steaks.

The fat content of fish is an important consideration in deciding how to cook it. Lean fish can dry out at high temperatures, so a protective coating is a good idea when frying. When grilling, marinate or baste them. Lean and moderately lean fish are best cooked by moist methods such as steaming, poaching and baking in sauce. Oily fish, however, almost baste themselves during cooking, so

they are ideal for baking, grilling and pan-frying.

Texture and flavour are also important in choosing how to prepare fish. If the flavour of the flesh is mild, it is important not to overwhelm it. But fish with rich, distinctively flavoured flesh will stand up well to spicy, pungent seasonings.

Fish that are delicate in texture need careful cooking. Pan-frying with a flour coating, steaming and gentle baking are best. However, fish with meaty, dense flesh can be cubed and put on to skewers.

# Pan-fried Trout with Olives and Capers

**SERVES 4**

4 whole trout, ¾–1 lb (340–450 g) each,
   gutted and trimmed

salt and pepper

flour, for coating

4 tablespoons vegetable oil

3 oz (85 g) butter

3 oz (85 g) black olives, sliced

3 tablespoons capers

2 tablespoons lemon juice

lemon wedges, to serve

1 ▲ Sprinkle the trout with salt and pepper. Coat them lightly with flour, shaking off any excess.

**Terms used by fishmongers**
*Cutlet:* Thickish slice cut cross-ways from the middle of a whole gutted fish.
*Escalope:* Thin slice cut on a slant from a large fillet.
*Fillet:* Boneless or nearly boneless piece cut lengthways from the sides of the fish. May or may not be skinned.
*Gutted:* Describes fish that has had its internal organs removed. Other terms used are cleaned and eviscerated.
*Steak:* Thickish slice cut cross-ways from the tail end of a whole gutted fish.

2 ▲ Heat the oil in a large frying pan over moderate heat. Add the trout and fry for 12–15 minutes or until golden on both sides and cooked.

3 Transfer the trout to a warmed serving platter and keep warm. Pour off all the oil from the pan.

4 ▼ Add the butter to the frying pan and melt it. When it starts to brown and smell nutty, stir in the olives, capers and lemon juice. Cook for 10 seconds, then pour this sauce over the fish. Serve immediately.

# BAKING FISH

Most fish are suitable for baking – whole or in fillets, cutlets or steaks. Lean fish, in particular, benefit from some protection to prevent them from drying out: choose recipes that include a stuffing or coating or bake them in a little liquid or sauce, which can also be served with the fish. All of these add extra flavour to the fish too.

Cooking in foil or paper parcels is suitable for many fish, both small whole ones and pieces (fillets, cutlets or steaks). This seals in moisture, so the effect is similar to steaming.

A good rule of thumb to calculate cooking time for fish is 10 minutes in a 425°F/220°C/Gas 7 oven for each 1 in (2.5 cm), measured at the thickest part.

1 ▲ To bake fish with liquid, pour over a small amount of stock, wine, water or other liquid as specified in the recipe, then add seasonings.

2 ▲ To bake fish in foil or paper, wrap tightly with seasonings and flavourings as specified and place the parcel on a baking sheet.

**Baked Fish Steaks**
Arrange 1½ lb (700 g) white fish steaks in a shallow baking dish. Sprinkle the fish with 2 tablespoons chopped shallot or onion and 3 tablespoons lemon juice or dry white wine. Drizzle with 1 oz (30 g) melted butter and season with salt and pepper. Bake in a 425°F/220°C/Gas 7 oven for about 10 minutes or until the fish is cooked. Pour the cooking juices over the steaks before serving. *Serves 4.*

# A SELECTION OF FISH VARIETIES

Choose the freshest fish you can find. If necessary, substitute another variety with similar qualities.

**Lean fish**

*Bream*
- round fish, saltwater
- firm, moist texture; delicate, sweet flavour
- fry, grill, bake, steam
- substitute red mullet, John Dory

*Brill*
- flat fish, saltwater
- fine texture, delicate flavour
- fry, grill, bake, steam, poach
- substitute other flat fish, such as turbot, John Dory

*Cod*
- round fish, saltwater
- flaky, tender texture; mild flavour
- grill, bake, steam, poach
- substitute haddock, halibut

*Haddock*
- round fish, saltwater
- soft, moist texture; mild flavour
- grill, bake, steam, poach
- substitute cod, halibut

*Hake*
- round fish, saltwater
- white flesh with good flavour
- grill, bake, steam, poach
- substitute cod, haddock

*Halibut*
- flat fish, saltwater
- firm, moist texture; mild, sweet flavour
- grill, bake, steam, poach
- substitute plaice, sole

*John Dory*
- flat fish, saltwater
- flaky texture; nutty sweet flavour
- poach, bake, grill, steam
- substitute brill, halibut

*Plaice*
- flat fish, saltwater
- fine texture; delicate flavour
- fry, grill, bake, steam
- substitute sole, other flat fish

*Sea bass*
- round fish, saltwater
- flaky or firm flesh; mild flavour
- grill, fry, bake
- substitute salmon, grey mullet, John Dory

# TESTING TO DETERMINE WHEN FISH IS COOKED

All seafood cooks quickly. If overcooked it becomes dry and loses its succulent quality. In the case of meaty fish such as tuna and swordfish, it can be unpleasantly chewy. It is therefore worth knowing how to judge when fish is perfectly cooked.

The flesh of raw fish and crustaceans is translucent; it becomes opaque when it is cooked.

**1 ▲** To determine whether a fish is cooked, make a small slit in the thickest part. Lift with the knife to look into the opening.

**2 ▲** The fish is ready when still very slightly translucent in the centre or near the bone (it will continue to cook when removed from the heat).

---

*Skate*
- flattened body with large fins (wings), saltwater
- flaky, well-flavoured flesh
- fry, grill, poach, steam

*Sole (Dover and lemon)*
- flat fish, saltwater
- fine texture; delicate flavour
- fry, grill, bake, poach
- substitute plaice

*Turbot*
- flat fish, saltwater
- succulent; firm yet tender; superb flavour
- bake, grill, poach, steam
- substitute brill, John Dory

**Moderately lean fish**
*Grey mullet*
- round fish, saltwater
- delicate, easily digested flesh
- fry, grill, poach, bake

*Monkfish*
- round, saltwater
- firm texture; sweet, similar to lobster
- fry, grill, bake, poach, stew
- substitute cod, halibut

*Red mullet*
- round fish, saltwater
- delicate texture with excellent flavour
- grill, bake, fry
- substitute trout

*Swordfish*
- thick central bone, saltwater
- firm, meaty texture; mild but distinctive flavour
- grill, bake, steam, poach
- substitute dogfish/rock salmon, tuna

*Trout*
- round fish, freshwater
- tender, flaky texture; delicate, rich
- fry, grill, bake
- substitute sea trout, small salmon

*Tuna*
- thick central bone, saltwater
- some varieties more oily
- firm, meaty texture; mild to strong flavour
- bake, steam, poach, grill
- substitute swordfish, dogfish/rock salmon

**Moderately oily and oily fish**
*Carp*
- round fish, freshwater
- soft, flaky texture; mild flavour
- bake, grill, fry, steam
- substitute cod, haddock

*Herring*
- round fish, saltwater
- moist and tender; rich flavour
- grill, bake, fry, souse
- substitute mackerel

*Mackerel*
- round fish, saltwater
- moist and tender or firm texture; rich, distinctive flavour
- grill, bake, fry, souse
- substitute herring

*Salmon*
- round fish, freshwater/saltwater
- flaky, tender texture; mild to rich
- bake, grill, steam, poach
- substitute large sea trout

*Sea trout/salmon trout*
- round fish, saltwater
- moist, flaky texture; mild, sweet
- grill, bake, fry
- substitute salmon, rainbow trout

# POACHING FISH

Whole fish, large and small, as well as fillets, cutlets and steaks are excellent poached because the gentle cooking gives succulent results. Poached fish can be served hot or cold, with a wide variety of sauces. The poaching liquid may be used as the basis for the sauce.

**Poaching containers**
A long rectangular fish kettle with a perforated rack enables you to lift the fish out of the liquid after cooking. You could also use a large wire rack set in a deep tin.

**1 ▲ To oven-poach small whole fish, fillets, cutlets or steaks:** Place the fish in a buttered flameproof dish that is large enough to hold the pieces comfortably. Pour in enough liquid to come two-thirds of the way up the side of the fish.

**2 ▲** Add any flavourings called for in the recipe. Press a piece of buttered greaseproof on top to keep in the moisture without sticking to the fish.

**3 ▲** Set the dish over moderate heat and bring the liquid just to the boil. Transfer the dish to a 350°F/180°C/ Gas 4 oven and poach until the fish is just cooked. To test, with the tip of a sharp knife, make a small cut into the thickest part of the fish (ideally near a bone): the flesh should be slightly translucent.

**4 ▲ To poach whole fish, fillets, cutlets or steaks on top of the stove:** Put large whole fish on the rack in a fish kettle, or set on a piece of muslin that can be used like a hammock. Small whole fish, fillets, cutlets and steaks may be poached in a fish kettle on a rack, or set directly in a wide saucepan or frying pan.

**5 ▲** Prepare the poaching liquid (salted water, milk, wine, stock or court bouillon) in the fish kettle or in a large casserole or roasting tin (or a wide saucepan or frying pan for fillets, cutlets and steaks). Set the rack in the kettle, or the muslin hammock in the casserole or tin. Add more liquid, if necessary, to cover the fish.

**6 ▲** Cover the kettle or casserole and bring the liquid just to the boil. Reduce the heat and simmer very gently until the fish is cooked.

**Poached Sole Fillets**
Oven-poach 8 skinless sole fillets, about 1½ lb (700g), each ½ in (1.5 cm) thick. Use ½ pint (300 ml) dry white wine or fish stock with 4–6 chopped spring onions, 4–6 lemon slices and a few allspice berries for flavouring. Simmer for 3–5 minutes, then remove the fish. Boil the cooking liquid until reduced to 4 tablespoons, then strain it. Season with salt and pepper. *Serves 4.*

# Poached Whole Fish with Green Mayonnaise

**SERVES 6 OR MORE**

1 whole salmon, sea trout or sea bass, weighing about 5 lb (2.25 kg), scaled if necessary, gutted and trimmed

12 fl oz (360 ml) green mayonnaise (page 180), to serve

**FOR THE COURT BOUILLON**

¾ pint (450 ml) dry white wine

about 4½ pints (3 litres) water

1 large onion, sliced

2 carrots, thinly sliced

1 celery stalk, thinly sliced

½ lemon, sliced

a few parsley sprigs

1 bay leaf

12 black peppercorns

4 allspice berries (optional)

salt

**4 ▼** Remove the kettle from the heat and lift the fish, by means of the rack or muslin hammock, out of the court bouillon. Drain well, then transfer the fish to a serving platter and leave to cool slightly.

**5 ▲** Gently peel off the skin and pull out the fins. If salmon has been used, gently scrape off the thin layer of greyish flesh. Cool completely.

**6** Serve the cooled fish with the green mayonnaise.

**1 ▲** Combine all the ingredients for the court bouillon in a fish kettle or in a large roasting tin. Bring to the boil, cover and simmer for 20 minutes.

**2** Place the fish on the kettle rack, or set it on a piece of muslin. Lower the fish into the court bouillon. The fish should be covered with liquid, so add more water if necessary.

**3** Cover and bring back to boiling point, then simmer very gently for 15–20 minutes or until just cooked.

# STEAMING FISH

This simple, moist-heat method of cooking is ideal for fish and shellfish. If you don't have a steamer, it is easy to improvise.

**Steamed Salmon with Herbs**
Line a heatproof plate with fresh herb sprigs (dill, parsley, chives etc). Set 2 portions of seasoned salmon fillet, each 1 in (2.5 cm) thick, on top. Steam Chinese-style for about 10 minutes. If liked, top with a flavoured butter (page 174) or serve with Holland-aise (page 178). *Serves 2.*

**1 ▲ Using a steamer**: Arrange the fish on the rack in the steamer and set over boiling water. Cover and steam until done.

**3 ▲ Steaming larger fish and fillets**: Arrange the fish on a rack in a roasting tin of boiling water or on a plate set on the rack. Cover tightly with foil and steam until done.

**2 ▲ Chinese-style steaming**: Arrange the fish on a heatproof plate that will fit inside a bamboo steamer or wok. Put the plate on the rack in a steamer or wok; set over boiling water. Cover and steam until done.

**4 ▲ Steaming in foil**: Wrap the fish and seasonings in foil, sealing well, and set on a rack in the steamer or in a large roasting tin of boiling water. Steam until done.

---

# CUTTING FISH STEAKS AND CUTLETS

Round fish and large flat fish such as halibut are often cut into steaks and cutlets for cooking. Steaks are cut from the tail end of the fish, while cutlets are cut from the centre. They are usually cut about 1–1½ in (2.5–4 cm) thick.

**1 ▲** With a large, sharp knife, slice the fish across, at a right angle to the backbone, into slices of the desired thickness.

**2 ▲** If necessary, cut through the backbone with kitchen scissors or a knife with a serrated blade.

# Fish Steaks with Mustard Sauce

**SERVES 4–6**

4–6 halibut or turbot steaks,
 1 in (2.5 cm) thick

salt and pepper

1½ oz (45 g) butter, melted

lemon wedges, for serving

FOR THE MUSTARD SAUCE

4 tablespoons Dijon mustard

½ pint (300 ml) double or whipping
 cream

½ teaspoon caster sugar

1 tablespoon white wine vinegar or
 lemon juice

**1** Preheat the grill. Season the fish steaks with salt and pepper. Arrange them on an oiled rack in the grill pan and brush the tops of the steaks with melted butter.

**2 ▼** Grill about 4 in (10 cm) from the heat for 4–5 minutes on each side or until cooked. Brush with more melted butter when you turn the steaks.

**3 ▲** Meanwhile, for the sauce, combine the ingredients in a saucepan and bring to the boil, whisking constantly. Simmer, whisking, until the sauce thickens. Remove from the heat and keep warm.

**4** Transfer the fish to warmed plates. Spoon over the sauce and serve immediately, with lemon wedges.

# CUTTING FISH FILLETS

Fillets are boneless pieces of fish, and for this reason are very popular. A sharp filleting knife, with its thin, flexible blade, is the tool to use for removing the fillets. Be sure to keep all the bones and trimmings for making stock.

Round fish are easy to fillet and they produce a boneless piece from each side. Large flat fish are also easy to deal with, although they are filleted slightly differently from round fish and they yield 4 narrow fillets – 2 from each side.

**Filleting small flat fish**
You can take 2 fillets from smaller flat fish (one from each side): Cut behind the head and down the sides of the fish as above, but do not make the central cut. Starting from the head end on one side and working down the fish, cut the flesh away from the rib bones until you reach the centre (the backbone). Rotate the fish and repeat on the other side to cut away the whole fillet. Turn the fish over and repeat to cut away the second whole fillet.

**1 ▲ To fillet a round fish:** Lay the fish flat, on its side. First cut off the head. With the tip of the knife, cut through the skin all along the length of the backbone.

**3 ▲** When you reach the tail, cut across to release the fillet. Repeat the procedure on the other side to remove the other fillet.

**2 ▲** Working from head to tail and holding the knife almost parallel to the fish, use short strokes to cut 1 fillet off the rib bones in one piece. Follow the slit cut along the backbone.

**4 ▲** Run your fingers over the flesh side of each fillet to locate any stray bones. Pull them out with tweezers.

**5 ▲ To fillet a flat fish:** Lay the fish flat and make a curved cut behind the head, cutting down to but not through the backbone. With the tip of the knife, slit the skin down both sides of the fish where the fin bones meet the rib bones, 'outlining' the fillets, and slit across the tail.

**6 ▲** Slit straight down the centre line of the fish, from head to tail, cutting down to the backbone. Working from the centre at the head end, cut 1 fillet neatly away from the rib bones on one side. Hold the knife blade almost parallel to the fish and use short strokes.

**7 ▲** Rotate the fish and cut away the second fillet. Turn the fish over and repeat to remove the 2 fillets on the other side. Pull out any stray bones with tweezers.

# Fish Fillets with Peppers in Paper Parcels

**SERVES 4**

| |
|---|
| 2 tablespoons olive oil |
| 1 onion, thinly sliced |
| 1 garlic clove, finely chopped |
| 2 peppers, 1 green and 1 red, seeded and cut into thin strips |
| 8 oz (225 g) tomatoes, coarsely chopped |
| 1 tablespoon chopped fresh mint |
| 2 teaspoons chopped fresh marjoram or ½ teaspoon dried oregano |
| salt and pepper |
| 4 skinless fish fillets, such as brill, bream or trout |
| 4 oz (115 g) feta cheese, crumbled |

**1** Preheat a 350°F/180°C/Gas 4 oven.

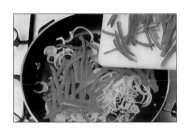

**2 ▲** Heat the oil in a frying pan and cook the onion, stirring occasionally, for 3–5 minutes or until soft. Add the garlic and peppers and fry until tender but not browned. Stir in the tomatoes and herbs. Season with salt and pepper. Remove from the heat.

**3 ▲** Cut 4 rounds of greaseproof paper, baking parchment or foil, each the size to wrap a fillet comfortably.

**4 ▲** Put a spoonful of the pepper mixture on one half of each piece of paper or foil and set a fish fillet on top. Spoon some of the remaining pepper mixture over each portion of fish. Scatter the cheese on top.

**5 ▼** Fold the paper or foil over the fish and fold the edges over several times to seal. Set the parcels on a baking sheet.

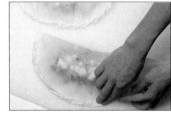

**6** Bake for 20–25 minutes or until the fish is cooked. If you used paper, you can serve the fish in the parcels, but remove fish from foil for serving.

# SKINNING FISH FILLETS

Before cooking, dark or tough skin is usually removed from fish fillets. However, if they are to be grilled, the skin helps keep the shape and should not be removed.

**Getting a grip on fish**
If you salt your fingers, you will get a better grip on the tail end so you can hold the skin taut as you cut. This is also a good way to hang on to fish while scaling.

**1 ▲** Lay the fillet flat, skin side down, tail end towards you. Make a small crossways cut through the flesh down to the skin at the tail end.

**2 ▲** Grip the bit of skin firmly and insert the knife blade so it is almost parallel to the skin, then cut the fillet away. Use a gentle sawing motion and make one continuous cut.

# Layered Fish Casserole

**SERVES 6–8**

| |
|---|
| 1¼ pints (750 ml) milk |
| 1 slice of onion |
| 2–3 sprigs of fresh parsley |
| 1 bay leaf |
| a few black peppercorns |
| 3 oz (85 g) butter |
| 2½ oz (70 g) plain flour |
| ½ teaspoon grated lemon zest |
| 1 egg, beaten to mix |
| salt and pepper |
| 5 oz (145 g) water biscuits, coarsely crushed |
| 1½ lb (700 g) skinless white fish fillets, finely diced |
| 8 oz (225 g) skinless smoked haddock or whiting fillet, cut into strips |

**1** Preheat a 350°F/180°C/Gas 4 oven.

**2** Bring the milk to the boil with the onion, herbs and peppercorns. Off the heat, let stand 20 minutes to infuse. Melt 2½ oz (70 g) of the butter, stir in the flour, then strain in the milk. Bring to the boil, whisking constantly, then simmer until thickened.

**3 ▲** Remove the pan from the heat. Add the lemon zest and egg and mix well. Season with salt and pepper.

**4 ▲** Scatter about one-third of the biscuit crumbs over the bottom of a buttered baking dish. Cover with a layer of half the diced fish. Spoon half the sauce over the fish and arrange the strips of smoked fish on top. Repeat the layers of crumbs, fish and sauce.

**5 ▼** Scatter the remaining biscuit crumbs over the surface. Dot the top with the remaining butter.

**6** Bake for about 35 minutes or until bubbling round the edges and lightly browned on top. Serve hot.

**~ VARIATION ~**

For Fish Pie, omit the biscuits and egg. Fold the diced fish into the sauce. Put half in a buttered baking dish and cover with a layer of smoked fish strips. Top with the remaining fish mixture. Cover with mashed potato, dot with butter and bake as above.

# BONING FISH FOR STUFFING OR BUTTERFLYING

Round fish, such as trout, mackerel and salmon, are normally cleaned by slitting open the belly. It is a simple step on from here to removing the backbone. This leaves a bone-free fish and a neat shape for stuffing.

When the boned fish is opened out like a book, or 'butterflied', it is approximately the same thickness throughout for even, quick cooking.

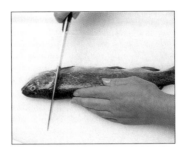

---

**Boning through the back**

An alternative boning method to the one shown here is done from the back rather than the belly. Leave the head and tail on the fish. Set the fish belly down on the work surface and use a sharp knife to slit the skin along one side of the backbone, all the way from the head to the tail. Ease the knife through the slit and work it down the side of the rib cage to detach the bones completely from the flesh. Slit the skin on the other side of the backbone and ease the knife down the rib cage to detach the flesh on that side. With scissors, snip the backbone free at head and tail ends, then lift it out along with the gills and the stomach contents.

**1 ▲** If the head has not already been removed, cut it off by slicing just behind the gills. Remove the tail completely, cutting straight across.

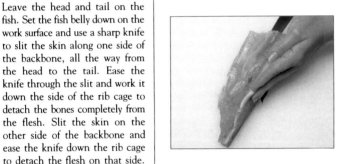

**3 ▲** If it is possible, lift out the backbone and rib cage in one piece after freeing it with the knife. If it is necessary to cut the backbone out, slide the knife under the bones along one side of the rib cage.

**2 ▲** Enlarge the belly opening. Set the fish on a board, skin side up, with the belly flaps against the board. Press firmly along the backbone to loosen it. Turn the fish over.

**4 ▲** Gently ease the knife outwards under the rib bones, away from the backbone. Repeat on the other side.

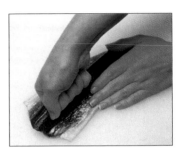

---

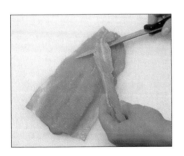

**5 ▲** Lift up the rib cage in one piece and slide the knife under the backbone, to free it from the skin.

**6 ▲** Run your fingers over the flesh to locate any other bones and pull them out with tweezers.

**7 ▲** After boning, rinse the fish under cool running water and pat dry with paper towels.

# Baked Fish Stuffed with Crab

**SERVES 4**

| |
|---|
| 4 streaky bacon rashers |
| 1 oz (30 g) butter |
| 2 oz (55 g) spring onions, chopped |
| 1 large celery stalk, diced |
| grated zest of 1 large lemon |
| 1 tablespoon chopped fresh parsley |
| 1 oz (30 g) crumbs made from day-old French or Italian bread |
| salt and pepper |
| 6–8 oz (170–225 g) white crabmeat |
| 1 egg, beaten to mix |
| 4 whole fish such as trout or red snapper, ¾–1 lb (340–450 g) each, scaled if necessary, gutted and boned for stuffing |

**1** Preheat a 375°F/190°C/Gas 5 oven.

**2** Fry the bacon rashers in the butter in a frying pan until crisp. Drain on paper towels. Chop the bacon.

**3** Pour off all but 1 tablespoon of the fat from the frying pan into a small bowl and reserve. Brush a little reserved fat over the bottom of a baking dish or roasting tin that will accommodate the fish comfortably. Set aside.

**4** ▲ Heat the fat still in the frying pan and cook the spring onions and celery, stirring occasionally, for 5–7 minutes or until soft.

**5** Mix together the vegetables, lemon zest, parsley, breadcrumbs, salt and pepper. Fold in the crabmeat and bacon. Bind with the egg.

**6** ▼ Open up each fish like a book, skin side down. Spread the stuffing over one half. Pack it down firmly, then fold over the fish and press down gently. Close the opening with cocktail sticks, if wished.

**7** ▲ Set the fish in the prepared baking dish or roasting tin. Brush the tops of the fish with a little of the reserved fat. Bake for 25–30 minutes or until the fish is cooked.

**8** Carefully transfer the fish to warmed serving plates and serve immediately.

# GRILLING FISH

The intense dry heat of this method of cooking is best used for fish with a lot of natural oil, such as salmon, mackerel and tuna. However, leaner fish can also be grilled, as long as you baste them frequently to keep them moist or cook them in a little liquid.

Always preheat the grill. If liked, line the grill pan with foil to save on washing up.

Fish can also be very successfully grilled over charcoal. Choose full-flavoured fish that will not be overwhelmed by the smoky taste. Thin pieces are easier to handle if placed in a hinged wire fish basket. Be sure to baste well during cooking to prevent the fish from drying out.

**Fish Kebabs with Lemon Butter**
Combine 2 tablespoons each melted butter and lemon juice with 1 teaspoon mustard powder and 1 finely chopped garlic clove. Cut 1½ lb (700 g) halibut, monkfish or sea bass steaks into 1 in (2.5 cm) cubes. Thread on to skewers with pieces of red pepper. Brush with the butter mixture and grill, basting frequently and turning to cook evenly, until done. *Serves 4.*

1 ▲ **To grill oilier fish**: For small whole fish, boned and butterflied fish, fillets, cutlets and steaks that are at least ½ in (1.5 cm) thick, or cubes of fish for skewers, rinse the fish and pat it dry with paper towels. Marinate the fish if the recipe instructs.

3 ▲ Set the fish under the grill, 3–4 in (7.5–10 cm) from the heat (thin pieces should be closer to the heat for a shorter time than thicker ones). Grill, basting once or twice and turning if the recipe specifies, until the fish is done.

2 ▲ Preheat the grill with the grill pan in place. When hot, lightly brush the hot pan with oil. If using foil, line it before preheating and then brush with oil when hot. Arrange the fish in the pan, in one layer, skin side down. Brush the fish with butter, oil or a basting mixture, according to the recipe instructions.

4 ▲ **To grill leaner fish**: For small whole fish, and fish steaks, cutlets and fillets that are at least ½ in (1.5 cm) thick and prepared for cooking as above, arrange in a buttered flameproof dish. Add a little liquid (wine, stock etc) just to cover the bottom of the dish. Brush the fish with butter, oil or a basting mixture, according to recipe instructions. Grill as above, without turning the fish.

# Grilled Butterflied Salmon

**SERVES 6–8**

1½ tablespoons dried juniper berries

2 teaspoons dried green peppercorns

1 teaspoon caster sugar

⅛ teaspoon salt

3 tablespoons vegetable oil

2 tablespoons lemon juice

1 × 5 lb (2.25 kg) salmon, scaled, gutted and boned for butterflying

lemon wedges, to serve

**1** Put the juniper berries and peppercorns in a spice mill or mortar and pestle and grind coarsely. Turn the ground spices into a small bowl and stir in the sugar, salt, oil and lemon juice.

**2 ▲** Open the salmon like a book, skin side down. Spread the juniper mixture evenly over the flesh. Fold the salmon closed again and place on a large plate. Cover and marinate in the refrigerator for at least 1 hour.

**3** Preheat the grill.

**4 ▼** Open up the salmon again and place it, skin side down, on an oiled baking sheet. Spoon any juniper mixture left on the plate over the fish.

**5** Grill about 4 in (10 cm) from the heat for 8–10 minutes or until the fish is cooked. Serve the fish immediately, with lemon wedges.

# COATING AND FRYING FISH

Fish to be fried is often coated with egg and crumbs, or with a batter. The coating makes a crisp crust to protect the fish and keep it moist. Many other foods – boneless chicken breasts, veal escalopes and vegetables, for example – are also egg-and-crumbed.

**Deep-fried Catfish**
Egg-and-crumb 8 catfish (or trout) fillets, using seasoned flour, egg and cornmeal. Deep-fry and serve with tartare sauce. *Serves 4.*

**1 ▲** Lightly beat egg in a shallow dish. Spread flour on a plate or sheet of greaseproof paper and season with salt and pepper or as specified. Spread crumbs (fine breadcrumbs, crushed water biscuits, etc) on another.

**3 ▲** Next dip the floured fish in the egg, turning to moisten both sides.

**2 ▲ To egg-and-crumb large pieces of fish**: Dip the fish first in the seasoned flour, turning to coat both sides lightly and evenly. Shake or brush off excess flour.

**4 ▲** Dip the fish in the crumbs, turning to coat evenly. Press to help the crumbs adhere. Shake or pat off excess crumbs. Refrigerate for at least 20 minutes to set the coating.

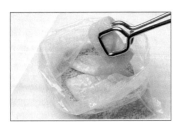

**5 ▲ To egg-and-crumb small pieces of fish** (strips of fish fillet or goujons, prawns, etc): Put the crumbs in a plastic bag. After dipping the fish in seasoned flour and egg, toss a few pieces at a time in the bag of crumbs.

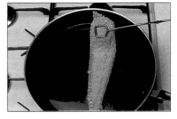

**6 ▲ To pan-fry**: Heat oil or a mixture of oil and butter in a frying pan (enough fat to coat the bottom of the pan in a thin layer or as recipe instructs). When it is very hot, put the fish in the pan, in one layer. Fry until golden brown on both sides and the fish is done. Drain on paper towels before serving.

**7 ▲ To deep-fry**: Half fill a deep pan with oil and heat it to 375°F (190°C) on a deep-frying thermometer. Gently lower the coated pieces of fish into the hot oil (frying them only a few at a time). Fry until golden brown, turning them occasionally so that they cook evenly. Remove and drain on paper towels before serving.

# Chinese-spiced Fish Fillets

**SERVES 4**

2½ oz (70 g) plain flour

1 teaspoon Chinese five-spice powder

salt and pepper

8 skinless fillets of fish such as plaice
or lemon sole, about 1¾ lb (800 g)
in total

1 egg, beaten to mix

1½–2 oz (45–55 g) fine fresh
breadcrumbs

groundnut oil, for frying

1 oz (30 g) butter

4 spring onions, cut diagonally into thin
slices

12 oz (340 g) tomatoes, seeded and diced

2 tablespoons soy sauce

**3 ▼** Drain the fillets on paper towels, then transfer to plates and keep warm. Pour off all the oil from the frying pan and wipe it out with paper towels.

**4 ▲** Melt the butter in the pan and add the spring onions and tomatoes. Cook for about 1 minute, stirring well. Stir in the soy sauce.

**5** Spoon the tomato mixture over the fish and serve immediately.

**1 ▲** Sift the flour together with the Chinese five-spice powder, salt and pepper on to a plate. Egg-and-crumb the fish fillets, dipping them first in the seasoned flour, then in beaten egg and finally in breadcrumbs.

**2** Pour oil into a large frying pan to a depth of ½ in (1.5 cm). Heat until it is very hot and starting to sizzle. Add the coated fillets, a few at a time, and fry until just cooked and golden brown on both sides, 2–3 minutes according to the thickness of the fillets. Do not crowd the pan or the temperature of the oil will drop and allow the fish to absorb too much oil.

# MAKING FISH STOCK

Fish stock is much quicker to make than meat or poultry stock. Ask your fishmonger for heads, bones and trimmings from white fish.

### MAKES ABOUT 2 PINTS (1 LITRE)

1½ lb (700 g) heads, bones and trimmings from white fish

1 onion, sliced

2 celery stalks with leaves, chopped

1 carrot, sliced

½ lemon, sliced (optional)

1 bay leaf

a few fresh parsley sprigs

6 black peppercorns

2¼ pints (1.35 litres) water

¼ pint (150 ml) dry white wine

1 ▲ Rinse the fish heads, bones and trimmings well under cold running water. Put in a stockpot with the vegetables, lemon, if using, the herbs, peppercorns, water and wine. Bring to the boil, skimming the surface frequently, then reduce the heat and simmer for 25 minutes.

2 ▲ Strain the stock without pressing down on the ingredients in the sieve. If not using immediately, leave to cool and then refrigerate. Fish stock should be used within 2 days, or it can be frozen for up to 3 months.

# Fisherman's Stew

### SERVES 4

6 streaky bacon rashers, cut into strips

½ oz (15 g) butter

1 large onion, chopped

1 garlic clove, finely chopped

2 tablespoons chopped fresh parsley

1 teaspoon fresh thyme leaves or ½ teaspoon dried thyme

1 lb (450 g) tomatoes, skinned, seeded and chopped or canned chopped tomatoes

¼ pint (150 ml) dry vermouth or white wine

¾ pint (450 ml) fish stock

10 oz (300 g) potatoes, diced

1½–2 lb (700–900 g) skinless white fish fillets, cut into large chunks

salt and pepper

1 Fry the bacon in a large saucepan over moderate heat until lightly browned but not crisp, then remove the bacon and drain on paper towels.

2 ▲ Add the butter to the pan and cook the onion, stirring occasionally, for 3–5 minutes or until soft. Add the garlic and herbs and continue cooking for 1 minute, stirring. Add the tomatoes, vermouth or wine and stock and bring to the boil.

3 Reduce the heat, cover and simmer the stew for 15 minutes. Add the potatoes, cover again and simmer for a further 10–12 minutes or until they are almost tender.

4 ▼ Add the chunks of fish and the bacon. Simmer gently, uncovered, for 5 minutes or until the fish is just cooked and the potatoes are tender. Adjust the seasoning and serve.

~ COOK'S TIP ~

For fish stock, use heads, bones and trimmings only from mild, white-fleshed fish, not from strong-flavoured oily fish.

# PEELING AND DEVEINING PRAWNS

Prawns can be cooked in their shells, but more often they are peeled first (the shells can be used to make an aromatic stock). The intestinal vein that runs down the back is removed from large prawns mainly because of its appearance, although the vein may contain grit which makes it unpleasant to eat.

Prawns in shell are sold with their heads. These are easily pulled off, and will enhance the flavour of stock made with the shells.

**1 ▲** Holding the prawn firmly in one hand, pull off the legs with the fingers of the other hand. Pull off the head above the legs.

**2 ▲** Peel the shell away from the body. When you reach the tail, hold the body and pull away the tail; the shell will come off with it. Or, you can leave the tail on the prawn and just remove the body shell.

**3 ▲** Make a shallow cut down the centre of the curved back of the prawn. Pull out the black vein with a cocktail stick or your fingers.

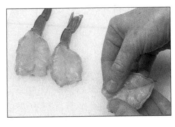

**4 ▲ To butterfly prawns:** Cut along the deveining slit to split open the prawn, without cutting all the way through. Open up the prawn flat.

**5 ▲ To devein prawns in the shell:** Insert a cocktail stick crossways in several places along the back where the shell overlaps to lift out the vein.

# Spicy Butterflied Tiger Prawns

**SERVES 4–6**

6 tablespoons olive oil

5 tablespoons orange juice

4 tablespoons lime juice

1 large garlic clove, finely chopped

1 teaspoon allspice berries, crushed

¼ teaspoon hot chilli flakes

salt and pepper

2 lb (900 g) raw tiger or king prawns, peeled, deveined and butterflied

lime wedges, to serve

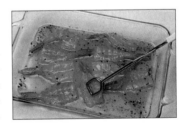

**1 ▲** Combine the oil, fruit juices, garlic, allspice, chilli flakes and seasoning in a large shallow baking dish. Add the prawns and turn to coat completely with the spiced oil.

2 Cover the dish and leave to marinate for 1 hour at room temperature or at least 2 hours in the refrigerator.

3 Preheat the grill.

4 Spread out the prawns in one layer in the baking dish, arranging them cut side up as much as possible. Grill about 4 in (10 cm) from the heat for 6–8 minutes or until the flesh becomes opaque. There is no need to turn them.

5 Serve hot, with lime wedges.

# Scallops Wrapped in Parma Ham

**SERVES 4**

24 medium-size scallops, without corals, prepared for cooking

lemon juice

8–12 slices of Parma ham, cut lengthways into 2 or 3 strips

olive oil

pepper

lemon wedges, to serve

1  Preheat the grill or prepare a charcoal fire.

2  Sprinkle the scallops with lemon juice. Wrap a strip of Parma ham around each scallop. Thread on to 8 skewers.

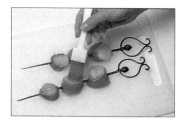

3 ▲  Brush with oil. Arrange on a baking sheet if grilling. Grill about 4 in (10 cm) from the heat, or cook over charcoal, for 3–5 minutes on each side or until the scallops are opaque.

4  Set 2 skewers on each plate. Sprinkle the scallops with freshly ground black pepper and serve with lemon wedges.

**Preparing scallops**

If they are still in the shell, use a short sturdy knife to pry open, as for clams (page 86). Discard the fringe-like membrane and dark organs. Set the red-orange coral, or roe, aside.

Pull off and discard the small piece of gristle from the side of the white meat. Rinse well.

*Spicy Butterflied Tiger Prawns (left), Scallops Wrapped in Parma Ham*

# PREPARING MUSSELS AND CLAMS

Molluscs such as mussels and clams should be eaten very fresh and must be alive when you buy them and cook them (unless they have been shelled and frozen). You can tell that they are alive if their shells are tightly closed; any shells that are open should close promptly when tapped. Any dead mussels or clams, or any with broken shells, should be discarded.

If you have collected clams yourself, let them stand in a bucket of sea water for several hours, changing the water once or twice. (Do not use fresh water because it will kill the molluscs.) Add a handful or two of cornmeal or flour to the water to help clean the clams' stomachs. Clams bought from the fishmonger will already have been purged of sand.

**Sailor's Mussels**
Prepare 7 pints (4 litres) live mussels. Steam with ½ pint (300 ml) dry white wine or fish or chicken stock, 1 small chopped onion, 1–2 crushed garlic cloves and ¾ oz (25 g) chopped fresh parsley. With a slotted spoon, transfer the opened mussels to large bowls. Add 1½ oz (45 g) butter to the cooking liquid and stir until melted, then add pepper. Pour over the mussels. *Serves 4.*

**1 ▲** Scrub the shells of mussels or clams with a stiff brush and rinse well. This can be done under cool running water.

**3 ▲ To steam:** Put a little dry white wine or water in a large pot, with flavourings as the recipe specifies. Add the mussels or clams, cover tightly and bring to the boil. Steam for 5–10 minutes or until the shells open, shaking the pot occasionally.

**5 ▲ To open a live clam or mussel:** Hold it firmly in one hand, with the hinge in your palm. Insert the side of a clam or oyster knife blade between the shell halves and work it round to cut through the hinge muscle.

**2 ▲** Before cooking mussels, pull off their 'beards' (their anchor threads) with the help of a small knife. Rinse the mussels well.

**4 ▲** Serve the mussels or clams in their shells, or shell them before using. Strain the cooking liquid (which will include all the delicious liquor from the shells) and spoon it over the mussels or clams, or use it as the basis for a sauce.

**6 ▲** Open the shell and cut the clam or mussel free of the shell. Do this over a bowl to catch all the liquor from the shell. (Clams may be eaten raw, but mussels are always cooked.)

# Phyllo Clam Puffs

**MAKES ABOUT 4½ DOZEN**

| |
|---|
| 9 sheets phyllo pastry, each about 12 × 18 in (30 × 45 cm) |
| 12 oz (340 g) full-fat soft cheese |
| 1 egg, beaten to mix |
| 6 oz (170 g) steamed clams, chopped, or well drained canned clams |
| 4 spring onions, chopped |
| 2 tablespoons chopped fresh dill |
| a few drops of Tabasco sauce |
| salt and pepper |
| 6–8 oz (170–225 g) butter, melted |

**1** Preheat a 400°F/200°C/Gas 6 oven.

**2** Stack the sheets of phyllo pastry on top of each other. Cover with a sheet of cling film to prevent drying out.

**3** ▲ Combine the soft cheese, egg, clams, spring onions, dill, Tabasco and some salt and pepper in a bowl. Mix well.

~ **COOK'S TIP** ~

Phyllo (or filo) pastry dries out very quickly and then can become too brittle to use. So when working with phyllo pastry, keep the sheets you are not using covered with cling film and a damp tea towel, and remove the sheets individually just before brushing with melted butter or oil.

**4** Lay one sheet of phyllo pastry on the work surface and brush it lightly and evenly with melted butter. Lay another sheet of phyllo pastry neatly on top and brush it also with butter. Cover with a third sheet of phyllo pastry and brush with butter.

**5** ▼ Spoon about one-third of the clam mixture in a line along one long side of the stacked phyllo pastry, about 1 in (2.5 cm) in from the edge.

**6** ▲ Fold the nearest long phyllo pastry edge over the clam filling and continue rolling up. Cut the roll across in half and put the two halves on a buttered baking sheet. Brush the rolls with melted butter.

**7** Make two more rolls in the same way and put the halves on the baking sheet. Brush them all with melted butter. Bake for 20 minutes or until golden brown and crisp.

**8** Using scissors, cut the rolls across into bite-size pieces. Serve as soon as possible, as nibbles with drinks.

# PASTA & GRAINS

~

Perfect for any occasion, simple to cook and satisfying to eat,
pasta, rice and other grains are now a mainstay of everyone's
diet. Here are plenty of ideas for cooking pasta and grains.
And try making your own pasta – it's rewarding and fun.

# COOKING PASTA

Both fresh and dried pasta are cooked in the same way. The golden rules for success are: use plenty of water and keep checking the pasta to be sure it does not overcook.

Fresh pasta will cook much more quickly than dried – in 1–4 minutes as opposed to 5 minutes or more.

**Buttered Noodles**
Cook 1 lb (450 g) fettuccine or tagliatelle (fresh or dried) until 'al dente'. Drain well and return to the pot. Add 1½–2 oz (45–55 g) butter or margarine and a good pinch of grated nutmeg. Season. Toss until the noodles are coated, then serve. *Serves 6.*

**Buttered Noodles with Herbs**
Omit the nutmeg and add ½ oz (15 g) chopped fresh herbs such as parsley, dill, basil or thyme – singly or a mixture.

**Buttered Noodles with Cheese**
Add 3 tablespoons freshly grated Parmesan cheese.

**1 ▲** Bring a very large pot of salted water to the boil: use at least 6 pints (4 litres) of water and 2 teaspoons salt to 1 lb (450 g) of pasta. Drop in the pasta all at once and stir to separate the shapes or strands.

**2 ▲** If you are cooking spaghetti, allow the ends in the water to soften slightly and then gently push in the rest as soon as you can.

**3 ▲** Bring the water back to the boil, then reduce the heat slightly and boil until the pasta is just done. For dried pasta, follow the packet instructions, but start testing as soon as you reach the minimum time given. To test, lift a piece of pasta out on a wooden fork or slotted spoon. Cut it in half. There should be no sign of opaque, uncooked pasta in the centre. Or bite it – it should be tender but still firm. In Italian, this is when it is 'al dente', or to the tooth.

**4 ▲** Drain the pasta well in a colander, shaking it vigorously to remove all excess water. Serve immediately because the pasta will continue to cook from its own heat.

**When to undercook pasta**
If you are going to cook the pasta further, by baking it in a lasagne for example, undercook it slightly at this first stage. Pasta for a salad should also be a little under-cooked, so that it will not be-come soggy when it is mixed with the dressing.

# Pasta, Bean and Vegetable Soup

**SERVES 4–6**

4 oz (115 g) dried borlotti or black-eye beans, soaked overnight

2 pints (1.2 litres) vegetable, poultry or meat stock

1 large onion, chopped

1 large garlic clove, finely chopped

2 celery stalks, chopped

½ red pepper, seeded and chopped

12 oz (340 g) tomatoes, skinned, seeded and chopped or canned chopped tomatoes

8 oz (225 g) piece of smoked bacon loin

3 oz (85 g) tiny pasta shapes for soup

2 courgettes, halved lengthways and sliced

1 tablespoon tomato purée

salt and pepper

shredded fresh basil, to garnish

**1** Drain the beans and put them in a large pot. Cover with fresh cold water and bring to the boil. Boil for 10 minutes, then drain and discard the water. Rinse the beans.

**2** Return the beans to the rinsed pot, add the stock and bring to the boil. Skim off the foam from the surface.

**3** ▲ Add the onion, garlic, celery, red pepper, tomatoes and bacon. Bring back to the boil. Cover and simmer over low heat for 1½ hours or until the beans are just tender.

**4** Lift out the bacon. Shred the meat coarsely with two forks and set aside.

**5** ▼ Add the pasta shapes, courgettes and tomato purée to the soup. Season to taste with salt and pepper. Simmer the soup, uncovered, for a further 5–8 minutes, stirring occasionally. (Check the suggested pasta cooking time on the packet.)

**6** ▲ Stir in the shredded bacon. Taste and adjust the seasoning, then serve the soup hot, sprinkled with shredded fresh basil.

# MAKING PASTA DOUGH

Pasta dough is very simple to make and, like most things, the more you do it the better the results will be. As in making pastry and bread doughs, the quantity of liquid needed can vary, according to how absorbent the flour is. The recipe here is for a basic egg pasta, with several variations.

### MAKES ABOUT 1 LB (450 G)

| |
|---|
| 10 oz (300 g) plain flour, preferably 'type 00' pasta flour |
| 1 teaspoon salt |
| 3 size-2 eggs, beaten to mix |

**1 ▲** Put the flour and salt on a work surface and make a well in the centre. Add the eggs to the well.

**2 ▲** With fingertips, gradually incorporate the flour into the eggs. When all the flour is mixed in, you should be able to gather up a pliable dough; if too moist, add more flour.

### Pasta flavourings
• For *Green Pasta*: Blanch 12 oz (340 g) spinach, Swiss chard or other green leaves, then drain well and squeeze dry. Purée or chop the greens very finely. Add with the eggs.
• For *Fresh Herb Pasta*: Finely chop 1 oz (30 g) fresh herb leaves, such as basil, flat-leaf parsley and coriander. Add with the eggs.
• For *Tomato Pasta*: Add 1½ tablespoons tomato purée with the eggs.
• For *Lemon Pasta*: Add 1½ tablespoons grated lemon zest with the eggs.
• For *Herb and Garlic Pasta*: Add ½ oz (15 g) finely chopped mixed parsley and oregano or marjoram and 1–2 finely chopped garlic cloves with the beaten eggs.
• For *Saffron Pasta*: Add ½ teaspoon ground saffron to the flour and salt or steep ½ teaspoon saffron threads in 1 tablespoon very hot water and add with the eggs through a small sieve.
• For *Wholemeal Pasta*: Substitute 2½ oz (75 g) wholemeal flour for the same quantity of plain flour.

**3 ▲** Flour the work surface. Knead the dough by pushing it away with the heel of your hand and then folding it back. Continue kneading for 8–10 minutes or until it is smooth and elastic. (Or use a pasta machine for kneading – see page 94.)

**4 ▲** Shape the dough into a ball and put it in a bowl. Cover with cling film. Leave to rest for at least 15 minutes before rolling and cutting.

### Food processor pasta dough
To mix the pasta dough in a food processor, put the flour and salt in the container. Pulse to blend. With the machine running, gradually add the eggs through the feed tube. Continue processing for 3–5 minutes or until the ingredients come together into a smooth ball of dough that is elastic.

# ROLLING AND CUTTING PASTA DOUGH BY HAND

You can roll pasta dough by hand, but it is hard work. If you intend to make pasta frequently, it may be worth buying a machine.

Divide the dough into 3 or 4 pieces. Roll and cut one piece at a time. Keep the remaining dough tightly wrapped in cling film to prevent it from drying out while you work.

**Pasta with Ham and Peas**
Cook 2 finely chopped garlic cloves in 1 oz (30 g) of butter in a saucepan for 1 minute or until softened. Add 5 oz (145 g) thawed frozen peas, 8 oz (225 g) cooked ham cut into matchstick strips, ½ pint (300 ml) whipping cream and seasoning and bring to the boil. Toss with 12 oz (340 g) fresh fettuccine, cooked and drained, and 2 oz (55 g) freshly grated Parmesan cheese. Serve at once, with additional Parmesan cheese if wished. *Serves 4.*

**Keeping fresh pasta**
If fresh noodles are not to be cooked the day they are made, allow them to dry completely. Then wrap loosely and store at room temperature for up to 4 days.

**1 ▲** Put a piece of dough on a lightly floured surface and pat it into a flat disc. Using a long rolling pin, roll out the dough in all directions, starting from the centre each time.

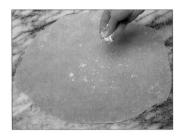

**3 ▲** For stuffed pasta shapes, use the dough immediately, while it is still malleable. If cutting noodles, sprinkle the rolled out dough with flour and leave to dry for 10–15 minutes.

**5 ▲** Uncoil the noodles with your fingers and scatter them on a floured tea towel. Leave to dry for about 5 minutes before cooking. Or wrap in cling film and refrigerate for later cooking.

**2 ▲** Continue rolling, with long even strokes, until you have a large sheet of dough that is about ⅛ in (3 mm) thick, or less for thinner noodles.

**4 ▲** To cut, roll up the sheet of dough like a flat Swiss roll. With a knife, cut across into noodles of the required width: ⅛ in (3 mm) for fettuccine, ¼ in (5 mm) for tagliatelle.

**6 ▲** To dry, leave them on the floured towel, or hang them over a broom handle, and dry for 2–3 hours. Sprinkle them with semolina to prevent them sticking together and pack loosely in a plastic bag or in a box with each layer separated.

# USING A PASTA MACHINE

A pasta machine – hand-cranked or electric – takes all the drudgery out of making fresh pasta. You are able to roll the dough paper-thin and to cut very fine noodles such as tagliolini and tagliarini – impossible by hand.

The smooth rollers on a pasta machine can be set wide apart or very close together, normally with the use of a dial. You start at the widest setting to knead the dough and then reduce the space gradually until the dough reaches the right thickness. Then a roller with blades cuts noodles of the desired width.

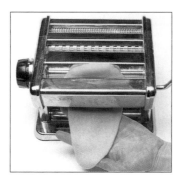

**1 ▲ To knead dough:** Flatten a piece of the dough slightly and then feed it through the machine's rollers on their widest setting.

**2 ▲** Fold the resulting strip of dough in half and feed it through again. Continue folding the dough and feeding it through until smooth and elastic, 8–10 times. (If it feels sticky, dust it with flour before continuing.)

**Lemon Pasta with Clam Sauce**
Cook 2–3 finely chopped garlic cloves in 5 tablespoons olive oil for 1 minute or until softened. Add 8 oz (225 g) steamed shelled clams, chopped if large, with 3 tablespoons of their cooking liquid, or canned baby clams (*vongole*), drained. Heat the clams through, then add 4 tablespoons chopped parsley and 2–3 tablespoons lemon juice. Toss the sauce with 12 oz (340 g) fresh lemon pasta (page 92), cooked and drained, and freshly ground pepper. Serve immediately. *Serves 4.*

**3 ▲ To roll dough:** Adjust the rollers to the next narrower setting and feed the strip of dough through again, without folding it. Narrow the rollers again and feed the strip of dough through. Continue feeding the dough through the rollers at increasingly narrow settings until it is the desired thinness. Sprinkle with flour and dry for 10–15 minutes.

**4 ▲ To cut noodles:** Set the blades on the machine to the desired width. Feed the strip of dough through the blades, letting it fall on to a floured tea towel. Dry for about 5 minutes before cooking. (Or dry completely for longer storage – see page 93.)

**Drying out**
It is important to leave the pasta dough to dry before cutting it into noodles, or they will tend to stick together. If the day is humid, this initial drying can take up to 30 minutes.

# Noodles with Tomato and Mushroom Sauce

**SERVES 2–4**

| |
|---|
| 1 oz (30 g) dried Italian mushrooms (porcini) |
| 6 fl oz (180 ml) warm water |
| 2 lb (900 g) tomatoes, peeled, seeded and chopped or drained canned tomatoes |
| ¼ teaspoon dried hot chilli flakes |
| salt and pepper |
| 3 tablespoons olive oil |
| 4 slices of pancetta or unsmoked back bacon, cut into thin strips |
| 1 large garlic clove, finely chopped |
| 12 oz (340 g) tagliatelle or fettuccine |
| freshly grated Parmesan cheese, to serve |

**1** Put the mushrooms in a bowl and cover them with the warm water. Leave to soak for 20 minutes.

**2** Meanwhile, put the tomatoes in a saucepan with the chilli flakes and seasoning. If using canned tomatoes, crush them coarsely with a fork or potato masher. Bring to the boil, reduce the heat and simmer for 30–40 minutes or until reduced to about 1¼ pints (750 ml). Stir from time to time to prevent sticking.

**3** ▲ When the mushrooms have finished soaking, lift them out and squeeze over the bowl; set aside. Carefully pour the soaking liquid into the tomatoes through a muslin-lined sieve, leaving the sandy grit in the bottom of the bowl. Simmer the tomatoes for a further 15 minutes.

**4** ▼ Meanwhile, heat 2 tablespoons of the oil in a frying pan. Add the strips of pancetta or bacon and fry until golden but not crisp. Add the garlic and mushrooms and fry for 3 minutes, stirring. Set aside.

**5** Cook the pasta in a large pot of boiling salted water until it is just tender to the bite, or 'al dente'.

**6** ▲ Add the bacon and mushroom mixture to the tomato sauce and mix well. Season with salt and pepper.

**7** Drain the pasta and return it to the pot. Add the remaining oil and toss to coat the strands. Divide among hot plates, spoon the sauce on top and serve with Parmesan cheese.

# CUTTING FLAT PASTA SHAPES

For wide noodles, like pappardelle, and for pasta for layering or rolling up, such as lasagne and cannelloni, roll the dough by hand or machine to about ⅛ in (3 mm) thickness. Lay the rolled dough strip, which will be about 4–5 in (10–12.5 cm) wide, on a lightly floured surface. Trim the sides to make them straight and square, using a sharp knife or, for pappardelle, a fluted pasta wheel. Lasagne may also be cut with a wheel for a decorative fluted edge.

1 ▲ **To make lasagne or cannelloni:** For lasagne, cut the dough strip into rectangles about 10–12 in (25–30 cm) long, or to fit your baking dish. For cannelloni, cut into rectangles about 5 × 3 in (12.5 × 7.5 cm).

2 ▲ **For pappardelle:** Cut the strip of dough into long noodles about ⅝ in (1.5 cm) wide. These noodles are traditionally cut with a fluted pasta wheel, and need not be uniform as they are meant to be rustic.

# Tuna Lasagne

### SERVES 6

1 quantity fresh pasta dough (pages 92–94), cut for lasagne, or 12 oz (340 g) oven-ready dried lasagne

½ oz (15 g) butter

1 small onion, finely chopped

1 garlic clove, finely chopped

4 oz (115 g) mushrooms, thinly sliced

4 tablespoons dry white wine (optional)

1 pint (600 ml) white sauce (page 170)

¼ pint (150 ml) whipping cream

3 tablespoons chopped parsley

salt and pepper

2 × 7 oz (200 g) cans tuna, drained

2 canned pimientos, cut into strips

2½ oz (75 g) thawed frozen peas

4 oz (115 g) mozzarella, grated

1 oz (30 g) freshly grated Parmesan cheese

1 For fresh lasagne noodles, bring a large pot of salted water to the boil. Cook the noodles, in small batches, until almost tender to the bite. For dried noodles, soak in a bowl of hot water for 3–5 minutes.

2 ▲ Lift out noodles into a colander and rinse with cold water. Lay them on a tea towel, in one layer, to drain.

3 Preheat a 350°F/180°C/Gas 4 oven.

4 ▲ Melt the butter in a saucepan. Cook the onion until soft. Add the garlic and mushrooms. Cook until they are soft, stirring occasionally.

5 Pour in the wine, if using. Boil for 1 minute. Add the white sauce, cream and parsley. Season to taste.

6 Spoon a thin layer of sauce over the bottom of a 12 × 9 in (30 × 23 cm) baking dish. Cover with a layer of lasagne noodles. Flake the tuna. Strew half of the tuna, pimiento strips, peas and mozzarella over the noodles. Spoon one-third of the remaining sauce evenly over the top and cover with another layer of lasagne noodles.

7 ▲ Repeat the layers, ending with noodles and sauce. Sprinkle with the Parmesan. Bake for 30–40 minutes or until bubbling hot and the top is lightly browned. Cut into squares and serve from the baking dish.

# MAKING RAVIOLI

The variety of stuffings for these pasta shapes is endless, and they can be dressed simply with butter, oil or cream, or with a rich sauce. Roll the dough, divided into 2 or 4 portions, as thinly as possible – no more than ¹⁄₁₆ in (1.5 mm) if you can.

---

**Making individual ravioli**
If making ravioli with hand-rolled pasta, it is easier to cut out squares or rounds from the dough rather than making them in strips. Put a mound of stuffing in the centre of each pasta shape, moisten the edges and set another one on top. Or, fold rounds into half moons.

---

**1 ▲** Lay the rolled strip of dough on a lightly floured surface. Spoon mounds of the stuffing, ½–¾ teaspoon each, in neat rows over the dough, spacing the mounds evenly about 1½ in (4 cm) apart (or according to recipe instructions).

**2 ▲** Using your fingers or a pastry brush, moisten the dough around the mounds with cold water.

**3 ▲** Lay another strip of dough carefully on top.

**4 ▲** With your fingers, press the sheets of dough together between the mounds of stuffing.

**5 ▲** Using a pasta wheel, pizza cutter or knife, cut neatly between the mounds to make squares.

**6 ▲** Crimp the edges of each ravioli with a fork or your fingers to ensure they are completely sealed.

**7 ▲** Alternatively, cut out ravioli with special cutters that are available in different shapes, or with round pastry cutters.

**8 ▲** Sprinkle the ravioli with semolina, coating them all over, to prevent them from sticking together.

# Ravioli with Cheese and Herbs

**SERVES 4–6**

8 oz (225 g) full-fat soft cheese, softened

1 garlic clove, finely chopped

1 oz (30 g) mixed herbs such as thyme, basil, chives, parsley, finely chopped

salt and pepper

1 quantity fresh pasta dough (pages 92–94), rolled by machine into 2 12 in (30 cm) strips, or divided into 4 and rolled by hand as thinly as possible

semolina, to coat

4 oz (115 g) butter

1 ▲ Mix together the soft cheese, garlic and most of the herbs. Season with salt and pepper.

2 Make the ravioli, filling them with the cheese and herb mixture. Toss the ravioli in a little semolina to coat lightly and leave to rest at room temperature for about 15 minutes.

3 ▼ Bring a large pot of salted water to the boil. Drop in the ravioli and cook for 7–9 minutes or until they are just tender to the bite. Drain well.

### ~ VARIATION ~

For Ravioli with Gorgonzola and Pine Nuts, fill the ravioli with a mixture of 4 oz (115 g) each full-fat soft cheese and crumbled gorgonzola cheese; omit the garlic and herbs. Sprinkle the cooked ravioli with 1 oz (30 g) toasted pine nuts instead of herbs.

4 ▲ Melt the butter. Toss the ravioli with the melted butter. Sprinkle with the remaining herbs and serve.

# COOKING RICE

There are many different ways to cook rice, and each has its adherents. The simplest is to cook rice in a large quantity of boiling water, then drain. However, valuable nutrients will be discarded in the water. The ways given here retain the rice's nutrients. Timings are for long-grain white rice (one part rice to two parts water).

**Rice Salad**
Steam or bake 6oz (170g) long-grain rice. While hot, dress with 6 tablespoons vinaigrette (page 182). Cool. Add 2oz (55g) each chopped spring onions, celery, radishes, cucumber and quartered black olives with another 4fl oz (120ml) vinaigrette. Combine well and sprinkle with chopped parsley. *Serves 4–6.*

**2 ▲ To sauté and steam rice (pilaf):** Heat oil, butter or a mixture of the two in a saucepan over moderate heat. Add the rice and stir to coat the grains. Sauté for 2–3 minutes, stirring constantly. Add the measured quantity of boiling salted water. Bring back to the boil, then cover and steam over very low heat until the water has been absorbed and the rice is tender.

1 ◀ **To steam rice:** Put the measured quantity of salted water in a saucepan and bring to the boil. Add the rice and stir. Bring back to the boil, then cover the pan and steam over very low heat until the rice has absorbed all the water and is tender, 15–18 minutes for white rice and 35–40 minutes for brown rice. Remove the pan from the heat and leave for 5 minutes, covered. To serve, fluff the rice with a fork.

**3 ▲ To bake rice:** Put the rice in a baking dish and add the measured quantity of boiling salted water. Cover tightly with foil or a lid and bake in a preheated 350°F/180°C/Gas 4 oven until the water has been absorbed and the rice is tender, 20–30 minutes for white rice and 35–45 for brown. Cooking time depends on many factors, including the seal of the dish.

# A LOOK AT RICE

There are thousands of varieties of rice grown all over the world, with differing flavours and aromas. But for the cook, the choice of which rice to use in a dish is based mainly on the length of the rice grain.

**Long-grain rice** has grains that are four to five times as long as they are wide. It is dry and fluffy after cooking, with the grains remaining separate. Examples of long-grain rice include: Basmati (aromatic, with a rich nutty flavour; much used in Indian cooking), brown long-grain rice (husk removed but nutritious bran layer left; texture is slightly chewy, mild nutty flavour), and white or polished long-grain rice (most widely used; mild in flavour). Long-grain rice is excellent steamed or baked, in pilafs and salads.

**Short-grain rice**, with an almost round shape, is very starchy and tends to cling together after cooking. Examples of short-grain rice include: Arborio and Carnaroli rice (used in creamy textured dishes) and glutinous or sweet rice (very sticky after cooking; used in Oriental desserts and snacks). Short-grain rice is the one to use for puddings, risotto, croquettes, sushi, stir-fried rice and moulded rice dishes.

**Medium-grain rice**, in between the other two, is more tender than long-grain rice but less moist than short-grain. It is fluffy and separate if served hot, but clumps as it cools.

# Raisin and Almond Pilaf

**SERVES 4**

1½ oz (45 g) butter

¾ oz (25 g) flaked almonds

1 small onion, finely chopped

2 oz (60 g) raisins or sultanas

8 oz (225 g) long-grain rice

1 pint (600 ml) chicken stock or water

salt and pepper

**1** Melt the butter in a saucepan. Add the almonds and fry over moderate heat, stirring, until they are golden brown. Remove the almonds with a slotted spoon, drain on paper towels and set aside.

**2** Add the onion to the saucepan and cook until soft, stirring occasionally.

**3** ▼ Stir in the raisins and rice and sauté for 2–3 minutes or until the rice looks slightly translucent.

**4** ▲ Add the stock or water. Bring to the boil, then cover the pan and steam over very low heat for 20–25 minutes or until the rice is tender and all liquid has been absorbed.

**5** Season with salt and pepper. Stir in the almonds and serve.

# MAKING RISOTTO

This Italian favourite lends itself to so many variations and, depending on the flavourings and additions, it can be served as a first course, a main dish or an accompaniment.

If possible, use a special risotto rice such as Arborio or Carnaroli, because it retains its nutty texture while giving the essential creaminess to the risotto. For best results, use well-flavoured homemade stock.

**1 ▲** In a saucepan, bring the measured quantity of stock to the boil, then reduce the heat so the liquid is kept at a gentle simmer.

**2 ▲** Heat butter, oil or a mixture of the two in a wide, heavy pan. Add chopped onion (plus garlic and/or other flavourings specified in the recipe) and cook over low heat until soft, stirring occasionally.

**Risotto with Parmesan**
Make the risotto with 2¼ pints (1.3 litres) chicken stock, 1 oz (30 g) butter, 3 tablespoons chopped onion, 1 crushed garlic clove and 12 oz (340 g) Arborio rice. Just before the risotto is ready, stir in another 1 oz (30 g) butter and 2 oz (55 g) freshly grated Parmesan cheese. Season and serve. *Serves 6.*

**3 ▲** Add the rice and stir to coat it with the fat. Sauté for 1–2 minutes over moderate heat, stirring.

**4 ▲** Add a ladleful of the simmering stock (or an initial quantity of wine, vermouth etc, if the recipe specifies) and stir well. Simmer, stirring frequently, until the rice has absorbed almost all the liquid.

**5 ◄** Add another ladleful of simmering stock and cook, stirring, until it is almost all absorbed. Continue adding the stock in this way until the grains of rice are tender but still firm to the bite ('al dente', like pasta) and the risotto is creamy but not runny. You may not need to add all the stock. Total cooking time will be about 30 minutes.

**Regulating the temperature**
During cooking, adjust the heat so that the risotto bubbles merrily, but don't let it boil fiercely or the stock will evaporate before it can be absorbed by the rice.

# Risotto with Chicken

**SERVES 4**

| |
|---|
| 2 tablespoons olive oil |
| 8 oz (225 g) skinless boneless chicken breast, cut into 1 in (2.5 cm) cubes |
| 1 onion, finely chopped |
| 1 garlic clove, finely chopped |
| ¼ teaspoon saffron strands |
| 2 oz (55 g) Parma ham, cut into thin strips |
| 1 lb (450 g) risotto rice, preferably Arborio |
| 4 fl oz (120 ml) dry white wine |
| 3 pints (1.8 litres) simmering chicken stock |
| 1 oz (30 g) butter (optional) |
| 1 oz (30 g) freshly grated Parmesan cheese, plus more to serve |
| salt and pepper |

**1 ▲** Heat the oil in a wide heavy-based pan over moderately high heat. Add the chicken cubes and cook, stirring, until they start to turn white.

**2 ▲** Reduce the heat to low and add the onion, garlic, saffron and Parma ham. Cook, stirring, until the onion is soft. Stir in the rice. Sauté for 1–2 minutes, stirring constantly.

**3 ▲** Add the wine and bring to the boil. Simmer gently until almost all the wine is absorbed.

**4** Add the simmering stock, a ladleful at a time, and cook until the rice is just tender and the risotto creamy.

**5 ▼** Add the butter, if using, and Parmesan cheese and stir in well. Season with salt and pepper to taste. Serve the risotto hot, sprinkled with more Parmesan.

# Cooking Wild Rice

Although called 'rice', this is actually an aquatic grass. Its deliciously nutty flavour and firm chewy texture make it a perfect complement to many meat and poultry dishes. It is also an excellent partner for vegetables such as courgettes, patty pan squash and mushrooms. It can be cooked like rice, by boiling or steaming, needing only a longer cooking time.

**1 ▲ To boil wild rice**: Add the rice to a large pot of boiling salted water (about four parts water to each one of rice). Bring back to a gentle boil and cook for 45–50 minutes or until the rice is tender but still firm and has begun to split open. Drain well.

**2 ▲ To steam wild rice**: Put the rice in a saucepan with the measured quantity of salted water. Bring to the boil, cover and steam over very low heat for 45–50 minutes or until tender. Cook uncovered for the last 5 minutes to evaporate excess water.

# Wild Rice and Turkey Salad

**Serves 4**

6 oz (170 g) wild rice, boiled or steamed

2 celery stalks, thinly sliced

2 oz (55 g) spring onions, chopped

4 oz (115 g) small button mushrooms, quartered

1 lb (450 g) cooked turkey breast, diced

4 fl oz (120 ml) vinaigrette dressing, made with walnut oil (page 182)

1 teaspoon fresh thyme leaves

2 pears, peeled, halved and cored

1 oz (30 g) walnut pieces, toasted

**1 ▲** Combine cooled cooked wild rice with the celery, spring onions, mushrooms and turkey in a bowl.

**2 ◀** Add the dressing and thyme and toss well together.

**3** Thinly slice the pear halves lengthways without cutting through the stalk end and spread the slices like a fan. Divide the salad among 4 plates. Garnish each with a fanned pear half and walnuts.

# PREPARING BULGAR WHEAT

Bulgar wheat, a nutritious grain, is made by steaming whole wheat berries and then drying and cracking them into very small pieces. Cook like rice, either steamed plain or as a pilaf, or soak it to rehydrate. Serve as an accompaniment or use in salads.

**Cooking simple bulgar pilaf**
Soften 1 small finely chopped onion in 1 oz (30 g) butter. Add 6 oz (170 g) bulgar wheat, ¾ pint (450 ml) chicken stock and a bay leaf. Cover and steam. Season and add 2 tablespoons chopped parsley.

**1 ▲ To steam bulgar:** Use two parts liquid to one part bulgar. Put the bulgar in a saucepan with water or other liquid such as stock, add flavourings if directed and bring to the boil. Cover and simmer over low heat for 12–15 minutes or until tender.

**2 ▲ To soak bulgar:** Put the bulgar in a sieve and rinse under cold running water until the water runs clear. Put the bulgar in a bowl, cover with fresh cold water and soak for 1 hour or until plump. Drain, pressing out all excess moisture.

# Bulgar Wheat Salad with Herbs

**SERVES 6**

| |
|---|
| 4 oz (115 g) bulgar wheat, soaked and well drained |
| 8 oz (225 g) tomatoes, seeded and diced |
| 1 small red onion, chopped |
| 3 spring onions, chopped |
| 2 oz (55 g) parsley, finely chopped |
| 4 tablespoons chopped fresh mint |
| 4 fl oz (120 ml) olive or vegetable oil |
| 5 tablespoons lemon juice |
| salt and pepper |
| black olives and mint leaves, to garnish |

**1 ▲** Combine all the ingredients in a large bowl.

**2 ◄** Stir to mix the ingredients thoroughly. Taste and adjust the seasoning if necessary.

**3** Serve the salad at room temperature, garnished with black olives and mint leaves, if liked.

# PREPARING COUSCOUS

A staple in North-African cooking, couscous is a type of tiny pasta made from semolina (which is ground from durum wheat). Its mild taste makes it the perfect accompaniment for spicy dishes, in particular the Moroccan and Tunisian stew also called couscous. It is delicious in stuffings and baked casseroles and even as a breakfast cereal.

**1 ▲ To prepare regular couscous:** Put the couscous in a sieve and rinse under cold running water until the water runs clear. Put the couscous in a bowl, cover with plenty of fresh cold water and soak for 30 minutes. Drain well in a sieve.

**2 ▲** Rub the couscous in your fingers to be sure there are no lumps, then put it in a muslin-lined colander. Set over a pan of boiling water (or over the pot containing the spicy stew) and steam, uncovered, for 30 minutes or until soft and heated through.

**Couscous Stuffing**
Prepare 6 oz (170 g) quick-cooking couscous with stock, using ¾ pint (450 ml) chicken stock, 1 oz (30 g) butter, 1 teaspoon ground cinnamon, and ½ teaspoon each ground cumin and coriander. Season with salt and pepper, then stir in 3 oz (85 g) each chopped dried apricots and sultanas. Use to stuff poussins, chicken, turkey or boned chicken pieces before roasting or pot-roasting. Makes enough to stuff 1 large chicken or 4 poussins.

**3 ▲ To prepare quick-cooking couscous with stock:** Put the stock in a saucepan, with 1 oz (30 g) butter if liked, and bring to the boil. Off the heat, gradually add the couscous and stir. Return to the boil, cover the pan, remove from the heat and leave for 5–10 minutes. Fluff the couscous with a fork. Serve hot as an accompaniment, adding seasoning and other flavourings as required, or use as a stuffing for vegetables or poultry.

**4 ▲ To prepare quick-cooking couscous with water:** Put the couscous in a bowl, cover with boiling water and soak for 20–30 minutes or until plump. Drain well. Use for salads.

**Special equipment**
A special pot (called a couscoussière) is traditionally used for cooking this grain. The bottom part of the pot is filled with a spicy stew; the perforated top part holds the couscous, where it cooks in the fragrant steam.

# Spicy Vegetable Stew with Couscous

**SERVES 4**

| |
|---|
| 1½ tablespoons vegetable oil |
| 2 large onions, cut into chunks |
| ½ teaspoon ground cumin |
| ½ teaspoon ground cinnamon |
| ¼ teaspoon turmeric |
| 12 oz (340 g) carrots, cut into chunks |
| 12 oz (340 g) white turnips, cut into chunks |
| 1½ pints (900 ml) chicken or vegetable stock or water |
| 12 oz (340 g) courgettes, cut into chunks |
| 1 red pepper, seeded and cut into large squares |
| 1½ oz (45 g) raisins |
| 12 oz (340 g) quick-cooking couscous |
| 1 oz (30 g) butter |
| 5 oz (145 g) thawed frozen peas |
| salt and pepper |

**1** Heat the oil in a large pot. Add the onions and cook until they begin to soften, stirring occasionally.

**2** Stir in the spices and cook, stirring, for 1 minute.

**3** ▲ Add the carrots, turnips and ¼ pint (150 ml) of the stock. Bring to the boil. Cover and cook for 5 minutes.

**4** ▲ Add the courgettes, red pepper and raisins. Cover again and simmer for a further 10 minutes or until the vegetables are almost tender.

**5** Meanwhile, prepare the couscous with stock, using the remaining stock and the butter.

**6** ▼ Add the peas to the vegetable stew. Cover and cook for 3–5 minutes or until all the vegetables are tender. Season with salt and pepper.

**7** Fluff the couscous and divide among hot bowls. Make a well in the centre of each and spoon in the vegetable stew.

# COOKING CORNMEAL AND POLENTA

Cornmeal, finely ground from yellow or white sweetcorn, is used as an ingredient in many American recipes – from a breakfast 'porridge' cereal through muffins, breads and dumplings. It also serves as a coating for fried foods.

Polenta is a more coarsely ground cornmeal, much used in Italian cooking. It may be served plain or mixed with butter and cheese, to take the place of rice or potatoes, or it can be cooled until firm, sliced and then fried or toasted.

**1 ▲ For cornmeal 'porridge':** Use four parts water to one part cornmeal. Bring the liquid just to the boil in a saucepan. Gradually add the cornmeal in a steady stream, stirring constantly. Do not add the cornmeal all at once or it will form lumps.

**2 ▲** Cover the pan, reduce the heat and cook gently for about 10 minutes or until very thick. Stir occasionally. Serve hot with butter, milk or maple syrup. (This can be cooled, sliced and fried like polenta.)

**Cornmeal and Cheese Topping**
Combine 12 fl oz (360 ml) milk, 1 oz (30 g) butter and ½ teaspoon salt in a saucepan. Bring just to the boil, then gradually add 2 oz (55 g) cornmeal, stirring. Cook, uncovered, for 2–3 minutes or until thick, stirring constantly. Remove from the heat and stir in 2 beaten eggs and 6 oz (170 g) grated Cheddar cheese. Spread over chilli (made with or without meat) in a baking dish, covering the chilli completely. Bake in a preheated 375°F/190°C/Gas 5 oven for 35–40 minutes or until set and lightly browned. *Serves 4.*

**3 ▲ For polenta:** Add polenta gradually to boiling liquid as for cornmeal (see above). Reduce the heat to low and simmer, uncovered, for 10–20 minutes or until thick and pulling away from the sides of the pan. Stir constantly. The polenta is now ready to be served or moulded.

**5 ▲** Cut the set polenta into shapes or slices, about ½ in (1.5 cm) thick.

**4 ▲** If to be cooled and then later fried or toasted, pour the polenta into an oiled or buttered pan or dish and leave it to cool completely.

**Polenta with Cheese**
Toast polenta slices under the grill until lightly browned on both sides. Top with slices of a strong cheese such as gorgonzola. Grill briefly until the cheese starts to melt, then serve.

# Polenta with Chicken Livers

**SERVES 8 AS A STARTER**

| |
|---|
| 1¼ pints (750 ml) chicken stock or water |
| 4½ oz (135 g) polenta |
| 2 oz (55 g) butter |
| 2 tablespoons olive oil |
| 1 lb (450 g) chicken livers, trimmed and cut in half |
| 1–2 garlic cloves, finely chopped |
| 4 tablespoons chopped parsley, preferably flat-leaf |
| 1 teaspoon chopped fresh oregano or ½ teaspoon dried oregano |
| squeeze of lemon juice |
| salt and pepper |
| 12 fl oz (360 ml) tomato sauce (page 172), heated |

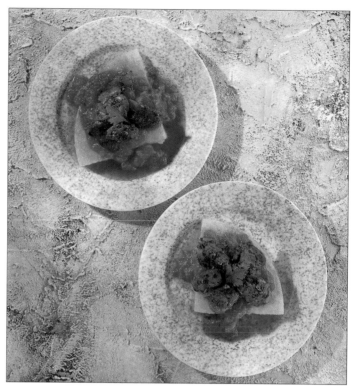

**1** Bring the stock or salted water to the boil in a large saucepan. Gradually stir in the polenta. Cook over low heat until very thick, stirring constantly.

**2 ▲** Pour the polenta into a buttered 8 in (20 cm) round pan. Set aside for at least 30 minutes to firm up.

> ~ **VARIATION** ~
>
> For Polenta with Mushrooms, use 1 lb (450 g) sliced mushrooms sautéed in 1½ oz (45 g) butter in place of the chicken livers and serve with tomato-wine sauce (page 172), if preferred.

**3 ▼** Invert the block of polenta on to a board. Cut it into 8 wedges. Fry in 1½ oz (45 g) butter until golden brown on both sides, turning once.

**4** Heat the remaining butter and the oil in a frying pan over moderately high heat. Add the livers and fry for 2–3 minutes or until they are starting to brown, turning once.

**5 ▲** Add the garlic, herbs, lemon juice and seasoning. Continue cooking for a further 1–2 minutes or until the livers are lightly browned on both sides but still pink in the centre.

**6** Put a wedge of polenta on each warmed plate. Spoon the tomato sauce over the polenta and arrange the chicken livers on top. Serve hot.

# VEGETABLES

~

*What an array of fresh vegetables we have today – good enough to be the star of the meal. Young seasonal vegetables need no dressing up, but this abundance offers the chance to try your hand at more creative preparations as well as simple ones.*

# PREPARING AND COOKING VEGETABLES

To enjoy their full flavour, fresh vegetables are often best prepared and served simply. These guidelines for vegetable preparation and cooking will help you make the most of seasonal bounty.

Serving ideas include suggested amounts of raw prepared vegetable to serve per person. Season all dishes to taste. Recipes in these sections serve 4.

## ROOTS AND BULBS
### Carrots
Naturally sweet, carrots are used in innumerable dishes, and are tasty hot and cold, raw and cooked.

**Preparation:** If they are young, there is no need to peel them; just trim the ends and scrub well. Larger carrots should be peeled. Leave whole or cut as specified. If carrots have a woody core, cut it out.

**Cooking:** *To boil,* drop into boiling salted water and simmer until just tender: 8–10 minutes for whole baby carrots, 10–20 minutes for larger whole carrots, 4–10 minutes for sliced or grated carrots. *To steam,* cook whole baby carrots, covered, over boiling water for about 10 minutes. *To braise,* cook whole baby carrots or thinly sliced carrots, with 3

tablespoons stock or water and 1 oz (30 g) butter per 1 lb (450 g), tightly covered, for about 5 minutes. Boil, uncovered, to evaporate excess liquid before serving.

**Serving ideas** (4 oz/115 g each)
- Dress hot carrots with butter and chopped fresh herbs such as parsley, chives, thyme or marjoram.
- Add a little sugar or honey and a squeeze of lemon or orange juice when braising. Or, try spices such as nutmeg, ginger or curry powder.
- Serve raw carrot sticks with a dip.

### Parsnips
Their sweet, nutty flavour makes a delicious addition to soups and stews or enjoy them on their own.

**Preparation:** Trim the ends and peel thinly. Leave small parsnips whole; cut up larger ones. If large parsnips have a woody core, cut it out.

**Cooking:** *To roast,* blanch in boiling salted water, then put in a roasting tin with butter or oil and cook in a 400°F/200°C/Gas 6 oven for about 40 minutes. Baste occasionally. *To boil,* drop into boiling salted water and simmer for 5–10 minutes or until just tender. *To fry,* blanch in boiling water

for 1–2 minutes and drain. Fry in butter for 10–12 minutes or until golden brown and tender.

**Serving ideas** (5 oz/145 g each)
- Mix 1¼ lb (600 g) boiled parsnips, 2 oz (55 g) butter and 4 tablespoons honey; cook, covered, for 5 minutes.
- Sauté sliced parsnips with sliced carrots; sprinkle with chopped herbs.
- Bake 1¼ lb (600 g) small parsnips with ¼ pint (150 ml) orange juice and 1½ oz (45 g) butter, covered, in a 350°F/180°C/Gas 4 oven for 1 hour.
- Roast blanched parsnips in the tin around a joint of beef or pork.

### Turnips
Mildly piquant, turnips go well with both sweet and savoury seasonings.

**Preparation:** Trim the ends and peel the turnips thinly.

**Cooking:** *To steam,* cook cubes, covered, over boiling water for about 15 minutes or until tender. *To boil,* drop into boiling salted water and simmer until tender: 20–30 minutes if whole, about 7 minutes if diced. *To braise,* cook thin slices, with 1 oz (30 g) butter and 5 tablespoons stock or water, in a covered pan, for 4–5 minutes.

**Serving ideas** (4 oz/115 g each)
• Mash boiled turnips with milk and butter; mix with an equal quantity of mashed carrots, parsnips or potatoes.
• Cover 1 lb (450 g) steamed turnips with 1 pint (600 ml) hot white sauce (page 170), sprinkle with breadcrumbs and grated cheese; brown under grill.
• Add 1 tablespoon sugar when braising turnips; uncover and boil to evaporate excess liquid and to caramelize the turnips.

### Swede
The orangey-yellow flesh of this root vegetable is sweet and full of flavour.

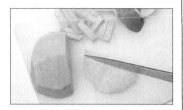

**Preparation:** Peel, removing all tough skin and roots. Cut as recipe specifies.

**Cooking:** *To boil*, put chunks into boiling salted water and simmer for 15 minutes or until tender. Do not overcook or the vegetable will be watery and mushy. *To steam*, cook slices, covered, over boiling water for 9–12 minutes or until tender. *To braise*, cook, with 1 oz (30 g) butter and 5 tablespoons stock or water per 1 lb (450 g), covered, for 5–7 minutes. *To roast*, put chunks or sticks around roasting meat and turn to coat with the dripping. Roast at 400°F/200°C/ Gas 6 for about 45 minutes.

**Serving ideas** (5 oz/145 g each)
• Braise 1¼ lb (600 g) grated swede seasoned with 1 tablespoon soft brown sugar and 1 teaspoon soy sauce.
• Mash 1¼ lb (600 g) boiled swede until smooth; beat in 2 eggs, 4 tablespoons cream, 2 tablespoons flour and ¼ teaspoon nutmeg until fluffy. Bake in a buttered dish in a 350°F/180°C/ Gas 4 oven for about 30 minutes.

### Potatoes
Boiling potatoes are moist with a waxy texture so they keep their shape when cooked. Baking potatoes are dry and starchy and their texture is more floury after cooking. In addition, there are orange- and white-fleshed sweet potatoes.

**Preparation:** If the potato skins will be eaten, scrub them well. Otherwise, peel potatoes.

**Cooking:** *To bake*, prick skins all over with a fork and bake in a 400°F/ 200°C/Gas 6 oven until tender: 1–1½ hours or 30–40 minutes for sweet potatoes. *To boil*, put into a pan of cold salted water, bring to the boil, and simmer until just tender: 10–20 minutes according to size. *To roast*, blanch peeled potatoes for 1–2 minutes; drain and pat dry. Put

around meat in a roasting tin and turn to coat with dripping; roast for 1–1½ hours, turning occasionally. *To sauté*, boil until partly cooked (in skin if specified), then fry slices or cubes in butter or oil until brown and crisp.

*To deep-fry* (chips), cut into sticks and soak in cold water for at least 30 minutes; drain and pat dry. Fry (in small batches) in oil heated to 375°F/ 190°C until beginning to colour: 3–7 minutes according to size. Drain on paper towels, then fry again for 3 minutes or until golden brown and crisp.

**Stuffed Jacket-baked Potatoes**
Cut baked potatoes in half and scoop out the centres, leaving a thin wall of flesh. Mash the scooped-out flesh with a little butter and 3 tablespoons each grated Cheddar cheese and diced cooked ham per potato. Season to taste. Fill the potato shells with the mixture, mounding it. Sprinkle the tops with grated Cheddar, then bake at 400°F/ 200°C/Gas 6 for 10–15 minutes.

**Serving ideas** (6 oz/170 g each)
- Dress boiled new potatoes with butter and chopped mixed parsley and mint or toasted pine nuts.
- Mash boiled or baked sweet potatoes with an electric mixer. Add butter to taste, orange juice to moisten and ground cinnamon. Season and beat well.

### Celeriac
The coarse knobby appearance of celeriac belies its delicate and delicious flavour.

**Preparation:** Peel off the thick skin. Do this just before cooking because celeriac discolours when cut. If serving it raw, drop the peeled root or pieces into water acidulated with lemon juice or vinegar. Cut as instructed in recipe.

**Cooking:** *To steam,* cook cubes, covered, over boiling water until tender. *To boil,* drop cubes into boiling salted water, cover and simmer until just tender: 5–15 minutes according to the size of the pieces. *To braise,* cook grated celeriac, with 2 oz (55 g) butter and 2 tablespoons stock per 1 lb (450 g), covered, for 5 minutes. Uncover and boil to evaporate excess liquid.

**Serving ideas** (4–5 oz/115–145 g each)
- Dress matchsticks of celeriac with spicy mayonnaise (page 180) and sprinkle with shredded salami.
- Boil slices of celeriac in beef stock; drain. Sprinkle with grated Parmesan cheese and serve hot.

### Onions
The onion is one of those ingredients basic to almost every savoury dish. They come in all sizes and shapes: pungent round onions and sweet mild onions, flat ones, large spherical ones (Spanish-type) and elongated Italian red ones. In addition, there are small pickling and button onions, shallots and spring onions.

**Preparation:** Peel off the papery skin. Then slice, chop, etc as the recipe specifies. For spring onions, trim the root end and cut off any wilted or discoloured green leaves. Cut as specified, using just the white bulbs or both white and green parts.

**Cooking:** *To fry,* cook chopped or sliced onions, uncovered, in butter and/or oil over moderate heat, stirring occasionally, for about 5 minutes or until soft and translucent. If directed, continue cooking until the onions are golden brown. *To slow-cook,* cook

sliced or chopped onions, covered, in butter and/or oil over low heat, stirring occasionally, for about 30 minutes or until very soft and golden. *To boil* small onions, drop into boiling salted water and simmer for 15–20 minutes or until tender.

**Serving ideas**
- Top hamburgers or steaks with slow-cooked sliced onions.
- Combine 1 lb (450 g) boiled button onions with 1½ oz (45 g) butter and 2½ oz (70 g) soft light brown sugar; cook over low heat, stirring, for about 10 minutes or until caramelized.
- Trim all but 2 in (5 cm) of green from spring onions. Stir-fry in hot oil and sprinkle with soy sauce.
- Use thin slices of sweet red onions raw in salads.
- Bake whole onions in a 425°F/ 220°C/Gas 7 oven for 45 minutes or until tender when pierced with a fork.

### Leeks
This sweet and subtle member of the onion family has myriad uses – both as a vegetable on its own and as a flavouring in soups, stews and so on.

**Preparation:** Trim the root end and the dark green leaves, leaving just the pale green and white. (Save the dark green leaves for the stockpot.) Unless the leeks are to be cooked whole, slit them open lengthways, to the centre. Put them in cold water and soak for about 20 minutes. Drain well, squeezing out the excess water. If leeks are to be sliced or chopped, do this before rinsing them thoroughly in a colander under cold running water.

**Cooking:** *To braise*, cook, with 1 oz (30 g) butter and 5 tablespoons stock or water per 1 lb (450 g), tightly covered, until just tender. *To boil*, drop into boiling salted water or stock and simmer for 10–15 minutes or until tender. *To steam*, cook in a covered steamer over boiling water, allowing 5–7 minutes for sliced or whole baby leeks.

**Serving ideas** (6 oz/170 g each)
● Boil whole leeks, then cool slightly. Marinate in a vinaigrette dressing (page 182); serve the leeks cool, not cold.
● Toss hot sliced leeks with butter and fresh herbs such as sage, tarragon, thyme or parsley.
● Wrap whole boiled leeks in slices of ham. Cover with cheese sauce (page 170), sprinkle with grated cheese and grill until the top is golden.

## FRUITING VEGETABLES
### Aubergines
The most familiar aubergines are the large ones with shiny purple skins, but there are also smaller purple ones and long, pale purple Chinese ones. All can be used interchangeably.

**Cooking:** *To grill*, brush cut surfaces with oil. Grill, 3–4 in (7.5–10 cm) from the heat, for 10 minutes or until tender and well browned; turn once and brush with oil. *To fry*, coat slices or thick sticks with flour if recipe specifies, then fry in hot oil or butter for 5 minutes on each side or until golden. *To braise*, brown slices or wedges in a little hot oil, add 4 tablespoons stock or water per 1 lb (450 g), cover and cook for 12 minutes or until tender. Add more liquid if necessary. *To bake*, prick whole aubergines all over with a fork. Bake in a 400°F/200°C/Gas 6 oven for about 20 minutes or until soft.

**Serving ideas** (5 oz/145 g each)
● Baste grilled aubergines with garlic- and herb-flavoured olive oil.
● When braising aubergines, after browning add skinned, seeded and chopped tomatoes and basil.
● Serve fried flour-coated aubergines with garlic mayonnaise (page 180).

### Courgettes
Courgettes and other thin-skinned squashes, such as pattypan, are completely edible, skin and all.

**Cooking:** *To fry*, cook sliced courgettes in butter or oil for 5–10 minutes or until tender and golden brown. *To boil*, drop into boiling salted water and simmer until tender: 10–12 minutes for whole courgettes, 3–8 minutes for slices. *To steam*, cook in a covered steamer over boiling water until tender. *To braise*, cook sliced courgettes in a covered pan, with 1 oz (30 g) butter and 5 table-spoons stock or water per 1 lb (450 g), for 4–5 minutes or until tender.

**Serving ideas** (4–5 oz/115–145 g each)
● Sauté sliced courgettes with finely chopped garlic and chopped fresh parsley and oregano.
● Cut small courgettes in half lengthways and spread cut surfaces with wholegrain mustard. Grill about 4 in (10 cm) from the heat for about 5 minutes or until tender but still firm.

### Pumpkins
Pumpkin and other squashes such as acorn and butternut, have a hard rind and central seeds and fibres that should be removed before cooking.

**Preparation:** Trim off the stalk end. Leave aubergines whole or cut according to recipe instructions.

**Preparation:** Trim the ends from courgettes. Cut as specified.

**Preparation:** Unless baking in the skin, peel pumpkin with a large, sturdy knife. Scrape away all the seeds and stringy fibres.

**Cooking:** *To steam*, cook in a covered steamer over boiling water until tender. *To bake*, cut into serving pieces, leaving on the rind, and score the flesh. Arrange cut side up in greased baking dish, dot with butter and bake in a 375°F/190°C/Gas 5 oven for 45 minutes or until tender. *To boil*, drop pieces into boiling salted water and simmer for 4–5 minutes or until tender. *To braise*, cook cubes of pumpkin as for courgettes.

**Serving ideas** (5–8 oz/145–225 g each)
• Add diced apple, a squeeze of lemon juice and 2 tablespoons soft brown sugar when braising pumpkin. If desired, spice with a little cinnamon and nutmeg or curry powder.
• Bake acorn squash halves with a knob of butter and 1 teaspoon maple syrup in each.

## LEAFY, GREEN AND OTHER VEGETABLES
### Spinach
Small tender leaves have a delicate flavour and can be used raw in salads. Large, strongly flavoured, darker leaves taste better cooked.

**Preparation:** Spinach can hide a lot of grit so needs careful rinsing. Immerse in cold water, swish round and soak

for 3–4 minutes. Then lift out the spinach and immerse in fresh cold water. Repeat, then drain in a colander. Discard any damaged or yellowed leaves. Pull off tough stalks.

**Cooking:** *To steam-boil*, put into a large pan (there should be sufficient water left on the leaves after rinsing so that no more is needed). Cook for 5–7 minutes or until just wilted, stirring occasionally to help evaporate the liquid. Drain well and press the spinach between two plates or squeeze it in your fist. *To braise*, cook, covered, with a large knob of butter until wilted. Uncover and boil to evaporate excess liquid. *To stir-fry*, cook small or shredded leaves in hot oil for 3–5 minutes or until wilted.

**Serving ideas** (5–6 oz/145–175 g each)
• Add 3–4 tablespoons double or whipping cream and a good pinch of grated nutmeg to braised spinach.
• Stir-fry chopped onion and garlic, then add spinach with halved cherry tomatoes and stir-fry for 1 minute.
• Steam-boil spinach leaves; chop finely after draining. Fry in olive oil with chopped garlic, stirring, until the garlic just starts to turn golden and the spinach is piping hot.
• Combine equal parts of chopped cooked spinach and cooked rice with butter and seasoning to taste.

### Greens
Hearty greens include those from the cabbage family – kale, spring greens, turnip leaves – as well as beet greens and Swiss chard or seakale beet. Serve alone, or in soups and stews.

**Preparation:** Discard damaged or yellowed leaves. Trim off root ends and large or coarse stalks. Leave the leaves whole or shred, according to recipe instructions. Cut leaves from stalks of Swiss chard and cook separately (the stalks take longer).

**Cooking:** *To braise*, put shredded leaves (or Swiss chard stalks) in a pan, with 1 oz (30 g) butter and 3 tablespoons stock per 1 lb (450 g). Cook, covered, until just tender. Boil, uncovered, to evaporate excess liquid. *To steam-boil*, put into a large pan (there should be sufficient water left on the leaves after rinsing so that no more is needed). Cover and cook until just wilted: 5–15 minutes according to variety. *To boil*, drop shredded leaves (or Swiss chard stalks) into boiling salted water and simmer until tender.

**Serving ideas** (8 oz/225 g each)
• Toss hot braised greens with whipping cream or soured cream and grated nutmeg; heat gently.
• Mix boiled greens with mashed potato. Shape into cakes, coat in fine breadcrumbs and fry in butter until golden brown on both sides.
• Top boiled or braised greens with crisply fried bacon and grated Gruyère cheese; grill to melt the cheese.

## Green beans

Crisp green beans are available in varying sizes, from tiny French ones ('haricots verts') to very large runner beans. French beans are stringless, whereas runner beans when mature have a stringy casing. Bobby beans are shorter and plumper than French beans. Chinese long beans are similar to runner beans, but longer.

**Preparation:** Top and tail using scissors or a knife. For older beans with strings, snap off the ends, pulling the strings from the sides as you do so. Cut large beans diagonally or sliver.

**Cooking:** *To boil*, drop into boiling salted water and simmer until just tender but still crisp and bright green: 3–15 minutes, according to size. *To steam*, cook in a covered steamer over boiling water until tender. *To braise*, cook tightly covered, with about 5 tablespoons stock or water and 1 oz (30 g) butter per 1 lb (450 g), until tender. *To stir-fry*, blanch in boiling water for 2 minutes; drain, refresh and dry. Stir-fry in hot oil for 2–3 minutes.

**Serving ideas** (4 oz/115 g each)
- Dress boiled or steamed beans with melted butter, chopped herbs and a squeeze of lemon juice.

- Add 6 tablespoons cream to 1 lb (450 g) braised beans. Cook, uncovered, stirring, until the liquid has reduced and the beans are glazed.
- Top hot beans with quickly fried shreds of Parma ham. Or, top with flaked almonds or pecan nuts lightly browned in butter.

## Peas

Mange-touts and sugar-snap peas are completely edible, pod and all. Green peas are removed from their pods for cooking; the pods weigh as much as the peas, so you need to allow twice the weight of edible-pod peas.

**Preparation:** If green peas are in the pod, split it open and pop out the peas. Top and tail mange-touts and sugar-snap peas, pulling any tough strings from the sides as you do so.

**Cooking:** *To steam*, cook in a covered steamer over boiling water until tender. *To boil*, drop into boiling salted water and simmer until tender: 5–10 minutes for peas, 1–2 minutes for mange-touts. *To braise*, cook covered, with 1 oz (30 g) butter and 4 tablespoons stock or water per 1 lb (450 g), until tender: 5–10 minutes for green peas, 2 minutes for mange-touts and sugar-snap peas.

**Serving ideas** (4 oz/115 g each)
- Add sliced spring onions, shredded lettuce and a little sugar when braising green peas.
- Stir-fry mange-touts with thinly sliced onion and mushrooms.
- Add 4 tablespoons whipping cream to 1 lb (450 g) braised sugar-snap peas and cook uncovered, stirring, until almost all liquid has evaporated.

## Broccoli

Serve this green vegetable hot or leave it to cool and use in salads. It is also excellent in stir-fries.

**Preparation:** Trim off the end of the stalk. If the rest of the stalk is to be used in the recipe, peel it. According to recipe instructions, leave the head whole or cut off the florets, or flowers, taking a little stalk with each one. Cut the remainder of the peeled stalk across into thin slices.

**Cooking:** *To steam*, cook in a covered steamer over boiling water until tender. *To boil*, drop into boiling salted water and simmer until just tender: 7–12 minutes for whole, 4–6 minutes for florets and stalks. *To braise*, cook covered, with 5 tablespoons stock or water and 1 oz (30 g) butter per 1 lb (450 g), until tender.

**Serving ideas** (5 oz/145 g each)
● Toss hot broccoli with a flavoured butter (page 174).
● Cover hot broccoli with cheese sauce (page 170), sprinkle with grated Parmesan and brown under grill.
● Blanch small broccoli florets for 1 minute; drain and refresh. Serve cold dressed with vinaigrette (page 182) and sprinkled with toasted nuts.

### Cauliflower

White or ivory cauliflower is the most widely available, although there are also green and purple varieties.

**Preparation:** Cut away the large green leaves, leaving only the tiny ones if liked. Trim the stalk level with the the head. Cut out the core. Leave the head whole, or break into florets before or after cooking.

**Cooking:** *To steam,* cook florets in a covered steamer over boiling water for 12–15 minutes. *To steam-boil,* put core down in a pan with 1 in (2.5 cm) boiling salted water and a bay leaf. Cover and cook until just tender: 15–30 minutes for whole heads, 5–9 minutes for florets. Drain well. *To braise,* cook florets, covered, with 1 oz (30 g) butter and 5 tablespoons stock or water per 1 lb (450 g), for 5–7 minutes.

**Serving ideas** (5 oz/145 g each)
● Dress hot cauliflower with butter; sprinkle with chopped fresh chives, toasted flaked almonds or chopped pecan nuts, or paprika.
● Top hot cauliflower with Hollandaise sauce (page 178).
● Coat florets in egg and crumbs, then deep-fry and serve with garlic or spicy mayonnaise (page 180).

### Cabbage

Rich in vitamins and very versatile, cabbage is good cooked or raw. The many varieties available include firm, round heads (green, white and red), looser round heads (Savoy with its crinkly leaves), and long, loose heads (pak choi and Chinese leaves or Chinese cabbage).

**Preparation:** Discard any wilted or discoloured outer leaves. Cut the heads into small wedges or halve long, loose heads. Cut out the coarse stalk from the wedges before cooking, if preferred. Or, quarter heads and shred them. Leave long, loose heads whole and cut across the leaves to shred.

**Cooking:** *To braise,* quickly blanch chopped or shredded green, Savoy or red cabbage. (There is no need to blanch Chinese leaves.) Cook, tightly covered, with about 5 tablespoons stock or water and 1 oz (30 g) butter per 1 lb (450 g), allowing 3–4 minutes for green, Savoy and Chinese leaves and 30 minutes for red cabbage (use more liquid). *To boil,* drop into boiling salted water and simmer until just tender: 6–8 minutes for wedges and 3–5 minutes for shredded green, Savoy or Chinese leaves. *To steam,* cook in a covered steamer over boiling water until tender.

**Serving ideas** (4 oz/115 g each)
● Add chopped fresh dill when braising green or Savoy cabbage.
● Blanch larger outer leaves of green or Savoy cabbage, then roll them up around a minced meat stuffing and simmer in a rich tomato sauce.
● Add sliced apples, cooked diced bacon and spices (cinnamon, nutmeg) when braising red cabbage.
● Use shredded Chinese leaves raw in tossed salads.

### Cauliflower Cheese

Cut a large cauliflower into florets and steam until just tender. Spread in a buttered gratin dish and scatter over 3 oz (85 g) sliced, sautéed mushrooms. Pour 1 pint (600 ml) cheese sauce (page 170) evenly over the top and sprinkle with a mixture of grated Cheddar and fine breadcrumbs. Brown quickly under the grill. *Serves 4.*

### Brussels sprouts

These miniature heads of cabbage are best cooked just until tender.

**Preparation:** Remove any discoloured leaves. Trim the stalks level with the heads. Cut an 'x' in the base of the stalk so that it will cook in the same time as the rest.

**Cooking:** To *braise*, put in a pan, with 5 tablespoons stock or water and 1 oz (30 g) butter per 1 lb (450 g). Cover tightly for cooking. To *boil*, drop into boiling salted water and simmer for 7–10 minutes or until just tender. To *steam*, cook in a covered steamer over boiling water for 10–12 minutes.

**Serving ideas (4–5 oz/115–145 g each)**
- Toss with butter and orange zest.
- Toss with toasted nuts, braised or poached chestnuts or canned water chestnuts.
- Cut the heads lengthways in half and blanch in boiling water for 2–3 minutes; drain and refresh. Stir-fry in hot oil with finely chopped ginger and garlic for 2–3 minutes or until tender and lightly browned.
- Shred and blanch for 2–3 minutes; drain and refresh. Add chopped onion and celery and toss with a lemony vinaigrette dressing (page 182).

### Celery

Crisp green or white celery is a popular salad ingredient and favourite flavouring in soups, stews and stuffings.

**Preparation:** Separate the stalks. Scrub with a vegetable brush under cold running water. Trim off the root end, leaves and any blemishes (keep leaves for the stockpot). If the stalks have tough strings, remove these with a vegetable peeler. Cut as specified. For celery hearts, cut in half lengthways. Trim off the leaves.

**Cooking:** To *steam-boil*, put in a pan with 1 in (2.5 cm) of boiling salted water. Cover and cook until just tender: 5–10 minutes for pieces, 10–20 minutes for celery hearts. To *braise*, cook slices, with 2 tablespoons stock or water and 1 oz (30 g) butter per 8 oz (225 g), or hearts with ½ pint (300 ml) liquid, covered: about 3 minutes for thin slices, 10–20 minutes for hearts.

**Serving ideas (4 oz/115 g each)**
- Stuff finger-length sticks of raw celery with blue cheese, flavoured soft cheese or peanut butter.
- Sprinkle braised celery with chopped walnuts and chopped parsley.
- Braise celery hearts with chopped tomatoes and tarragon or thyme.

### Mushrooms

Cultivated button and open mushrooms are widely available; you may also find fresh wild mushrooms such as shiitake and oyster.

**Preparation:** Rinse or wipe with a damp paper towel (don't immerse in water as mushrooms absorb liquid readily). Trim gritty stalks, and remove tough stalks from wild mushrooms. Small mushrooms can be left whole; larger ones are normally halved, quartered or sliced, or they may be diced or chopped. To stuff large mushrooms, pull off the stalks.

**Cooking:** To *fry*, cook in hot butter and/or oil for about 4 minutes or until tender, stirring frequently. The mushrooms will give up liquid; if the recipe specifies, continue frying until the liquid has evaporated and the mushrooms have browned. To *grill*, brush with melted butter or oil. Grill 4 in (10 cm) from the heat, turning and basting occasionally, for 5–8 minutes or until tender and browned.

**Serving ideas (4 oz/115 g each)**
- Sauté sliced mushrooms with chopped garlic and thyme.
- Top grilled mushroom caps with a pat of flavoured butter (page 174).

# PREPARING ASPARAGUS

When asparagus is young and tender, you need do nothing more than trim off the ends of the stalks. However, larger spears, with stalk ends that are tough and woody, require some further preparation.

**A standing alternative**
Asparagus spears can be cooked loose and flat in simmering water (as described below) or they can be tied into bundles and cooked standing upright in a tall pot. With the latter method, the tips are kept above the water so they cook gently in the steam.

**1 ▲** Cut off the tough, woody ends. Cut the spears so they are all about the same length.

**2 ▲** If you like, remove the skin: Lay a spear flat and hold it just below the tip. With a vegetable peeler, shave off the skin, working lengthways down the spear to the end of the stalk. Roll the spear so you can remove the skin from all sides.

# Asparagus with Ham

**SERVES 4**

1½–2 lb (700–900 g) medium-size asparagus spears, prepared for cooking

6 fl oz (180 ml) clarified butter (page 176)

2 teaspoons lemon juice

2 tablespoons chopped spring onions

1 tablespoon chopped parsley

salt and pepper

4 slices Westphalian or Parma ham

**1 ▼** Half fill a frying pan with salted water. Bring to the boil. Simmer asparagus spears for 4–5 minutes or until they are just tender. (Pierce the stalk to test.) Remove and drain well.

**2** Combine the butter, lemon juice, spring onions and parsley in a small saucepan. Season with salt and pepper to taste. Heat the mixture until lukewarm.

**3** Divide the asparagus among 4 warm plates. Drape a slice of ham over each portion. Spoon over the herb butter and serve.

# PREPARING FRESH SWEETCORN

Tender sweetcorn is a favourite, eaten on the cob or off – as kernels in soups, salad, casseroles etc. Buy the freshest sweetcorn you can find.

### Cooking corn on the cob

Bring a large pot of water to the boil and add 1 teaspoon sugar. Drop freshly prepared sweetcorn into the water. Bring back to the boil and simmer for 4–7 minutes or until just tender (test by piercing a kernel with the tip of a sharp knife). Alternatively, steam the corn with a little boiling water in a covered saucepan. Drain well before serving.

1 ▲ Just before cooking, strip off the husks and pull off all the silk. (If grilling or oven-roasting in the husk, just pull back the husks and remove the silk, then reshape.) Trim the stalk so it is level with the base.

2 ▲ **To remove the kernels**: Use a sharp knife to cut them lengthways, several rows at a time, from the cob. If the recipe specifies, after removing the kernels set each cob upright on a plate and run the blunt edge of the knife down the cob, pressing firmly, to scrape off the milky liquid.

# Sweetcorn with Courgettes and Bacon

**SERVES 4**

| 4 smoked streaky bacon rashers |
| ½ oz (15 g) butter |
| 1 onion, chopped |
| 1 small green pepper, seeded and diced |
| kernels scraped from 6 fresh sweetcorn |
| 6 oz (170 g) courgettes, diced |
| ¼ pint (150 ml) whipping cream |
| salt and pepper |

1 ▲ Fry the bacon rashers until they are crisp. Remove the rashers with tongs and drain on paper towels.

2 ◀ Add the butter, onion and pepper to the pan and fry until soft, stirring occasionally. Add the sweetcorn. Cover and cook gently for 10 minutes. Stir in the courgettes and cream. Season with salt and pepper. Cook, covered, for 10 minutes or until all the vegetables are tender. Chop the bacon and stir into the mixture. Adjust the seasoning and serve.

# SKINNING AND SEEDING TOMATOES

Some tomatoes have tough skins and seeds. In cooking, these can become separated from the flesh and can spoil the appearance and texture of a dish. In addition, some people find tomato skins indigestible, so it is often desirable to remove them. In these cases, unless a soup, sauce or other dish is sieved before serving, it is best to skin and seed the tomatoes before using them.

If the tomatoes have tender skins and they will be eaten raw, or only briefly cooked, removing the peel is less essential. However, many people prefer to skin tomatoes for eating raw as well.

**1 ▲ To skin tomatoes:** Cut a small cross in the skin at the base of each tomato. Immerse, 3 or 4 at a time, in boiling water. Once the cut skin begins to roll back, in about 10 seconds, lift the tomatoes out and immerse in iced water. Drain and peel.

**2 ▲ To seed tomatoes:** Cut out the core, then cut each tomato in half across (around the 'equator'). Gently squeeze each half and shake the seeds and juice into a bowl. Scrape out any remaining seeds with the tip of a spoon or table knife.

# Spicy Tomato Barbecue Sauce

SERVES 6

| |
|---|
| 2 tablespoons vegetable oil |
| 1 onion, finely chopped |
| 1 garlic clove, finely chopped |
| ½ pint (300 ml) passata |
| 8 oz (225 g) tomatoes, skinned, seeded and chopped |
| 4 fl oz (120 ml) cider vinegar |
| 1 tablespoon Worcestershire sauce |
| 2½ oz (70 g) soft light brown sugar |
| 2 teaspoons chilli powder, or to taste |
| 1 bay leaf |
| few drops of mesquite liquid smoke flavouring (optional) |
| salt and pepper |

**1 ▶** Heat the oil in a saucepan, add the onion and cook until soft, stirring occasionally. Stir in the garlic and cook for 30 seconds. Add the passata, tomatoes, vinegar, Worcestershire sauce, brown sugar, chilli powder, bay leaf and liquid smoke, if using. Season with salt and pepper to taste.

**2** Bring to the boil, reduce the heat, and simmer for 15 minutes, stirring from time to time. Taste and adjust the seasoning, if needed.

**3** Use as a basting sauce for grilled or barbecued hamburgers, chicken, spareribs and steak. Serve additional sauce to accompany the food.

# ROASTING AND PEELING PEPPERS

There are several methods for peeling peppers, the most basic of which is shaving off the skin with a vegetable peeler. However, because peppers have awkward curves, other methods, such as roasting, are often easier. Roasting peppers also heightens the sweetness of the flesh.

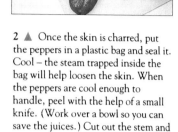

**Handling chillies**

Do not touch eyes and lips when handling chillies, and afterwards be sure to wash your hands well. Better yet, wear rubber gloves. Remove cores and seeds from chillies as for peppers.

**1** ▲ Set the peppers on a rack in a grill pan and grill close to the heat. Turn the peppers to char and blister the skin all over. Alternatively, spear each pepper on a long-handled fork and hold it over a flame – over a gas burner or charcoal fire – turning the pepper slowly so that the skin is charred and blistered on all sides.

**2** ▲ Once the skin is charred, put the peppers in a plastic bag and seal it. Cool – the steam trapped inside the bag will help loosen the skin. When the peppers are cool enough to handle, peel with the help of a small knife. (Work over a bowl so you can save the juices.) Cut out the stem and core; scrape out remaining seeds.

# Marinated Pepper Salad with Cheese

**SERVES 6**

| |
|---|
| 3 small peppers of different colours |
| 6 tablespoons olive or vegetable oil |
| 3 tablespoons fresh lime juice |
| 2 tablespoons fresh lemon juice |
| 1 teaspoon Worcestershire sauce |
| 1 small garlic clove, finely chopped (optional) |
| salt and pepper |
| 8 oz (225 g) mozzarella or firm goat's cheese, sliced |
| 2 oz (55 g) toasted walnuts, coarsely chopped, to garnish |

**1** Roast the peppers, then peel them, reserving the juices. Cut the roasted pepper flesh lengthways into strips.

**2** Combine the oil, lime and lemon juices, Worcestershire sauce and garlic, if using, in a bowl. Season to taste with salt and pepper.

**3** ◀ Add the pepper strips and juices and toss to mix thoroughly with the marinade. Cover and marinate for 1–2 hours at room temperature.

**4** To serve, arrange the pepper salad and overlapping slices of cheese on individual plates. Garnish with chopped nuts.

# PREPARING AND COOKING GLOBE ARTICHOKES

Artichokes can be served whole, with or without a stuffing, or just the meaty bottoms, or bases, may be used. Very small artichokes, 2½ in (6 cm) or less in diameter, are often called hearts; this can be confusing, as artichoke bottoms are also sometimes called hearts. These baby artichokes are best braised whole, or halved or quartered. Be sure to rub all cut surfaces with lemon juice as you work and use a stainless steel knife, to prevent darkening and discoloration.

**1 ▲ Whole artichokes**: Break off the stalk close to the base. Cut off the pointed top about one-third of the way down. Snip off the pointed end of each large outside leaf using scissors. Open up the leaves and rinse thoroughly between them.

**2 ▲ Artichoke bottoms**: Break off all the coarse outer leaves down to the pale inner leaves. Scrape off the fuzzy centre, or 'choke' (or do this after cooking) and peel away all the leaves with a stainless steel knife, leaving just the edible base or bottom.

**Artichokes with Herb Butter**
Serve boiled artichokes hot with clarified butter (page 176) mixed with freshly chopped dill and parsley or other herbs.

**3 ▲ To cook whole artichokes**: Bring a large pot of salted water to the boil. Add the juice of 1 lemon or 3–4 tablespoons vinegar. Add the prepared artichokes and put a plate on top to keep them submerged. Cover and simmer until you can pierce the stalk end easily with a fork: 15–20 minutes for small artichokes, 25–50 minutes for large artichokes.

**4 ▲** Remove and drain well, upside down. Open up the leaves so you can insert a spoon into the centre and scrape out the fuzzy choke.

**Ideas for artichokes**
• Serve boiled artichokes hot with Hollandaise sauce (page 178).
• Serve boiled artichokes cool (not chilled) with a vinaigrette dressing (page 182) or mayonnaise (page 180).
• Serve cool artichoke bottoms filled with prawn or crab mayonnaise salad.
• Boil artichoke bottoms with flavourings such as garlic, bay leaf and black peppercorns. Drain and cool, then slice and marinate in a vinaigrette dressing with chopped onion and olives.

**Eating a whole artichoke**
One by one, pull off a leaf and dip the base into the sauce. Scrape the flesh from the base of the leaf with your teeth, then discard the leaf. When you have removed all the large leaves, you will have exposed the fuzzy choke. Scrape this off and discard it. Cut the meaty bottom, or base, of the artichoke for eating with a fork.

**5 ▲ To cook artichoke bottoms**: Boil gently in salted water to cover for 15–20 minutes or until tender.

# CHOPPING VEGETABLES

In countless recipes, vegetables and other ingredients are required to be chopped to varying degrees of fineness. For most chopping, a large chef's knife should be used (be sure it is sharp). You can also use a food processor, but take care not to over-process the vegetables to a pulp.

**Cheese and Herb Dip**
Combine 8 oz (225 g) each full-fat soft cheese and cottage cheese in a food processor or blender and blend until smooth. Turn into a bowl and stir in 2 tablespoons chopped fresh dill and ¾ oz (25 g) chopped chives. Season to taste with salt and pepper. If the dip is too thick, stir in a few spoonfuls of cream or milk. Cover and chill for at least 1 hour before serving, with crudités, savoury biscuits and crisps for dipping. *Makes about 1 lb (450 g).*

**Peeling whole garlic**
If you want to peel garlic and keep the clove whole, drop it into boiling water, count to 30, then drain and rinse with cold water. The skin will slip off easily.

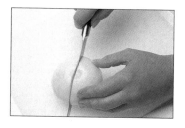

**1 ▲ To chop an onion**: Peel it, leaving on the root end to hold the onion together. Cut it in half, straight through the root.

**3 ▲** Make vertical lengthways cuts in the onion half, again not cutting the root. Then, cut across the onion to chop it, guiding the side of the knife with your knuckles. Discard the root.

**5 ▲** Crush the peeled clove again with the knife to flatten it, then begin to chop it. When it is coarsely chopped, continue chopping and crushing it until it is almost a paste. Hold the tip of the knife on the board and raise and lower the knife handle with your other hand, moving the blade back and forth over the garlic.

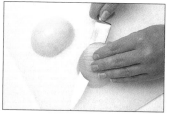

**2 ▲** Put one half flat on the work surface and hold the onion steady at the root end. With a chef's knife, make horizontal cuts in the onion half, to the root but without cutting all the way through it.

**4 ▲ To chop garlic finely**: Set a chef's knife flat on top of the clove and bang it gently with the side of your fist to crush the garlic slightly and loosen the peel. Remove the peel.

**6 ▲ To chop fresh herbs**: Hold the leaves or sprigs together in a bunch and chop coarsely, then continue chopping as for garlic (without crushing). You can also use this method of fine chopping for vegetables and fresh root ginger.

# Cubing and Dicing Vegetables

When vegetables play a starring role in a dish, they should be cut into neat shapes such as cubes or dice. This also promotes even cooking. Cubes are generally ½ in (1.5 cm) square, and dice are ⅛–¼ in (3–6 mm) square.

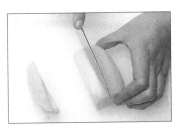 

---

**Coarsely chopping vegetables**
For coarsely chopped vegetables, follow the steps above, without shaving off curved sides. There is no need to cut uniform slices and strips. Alternatively, you can coarsely chop vegetables in a food processor by pulsing, but take care not to turn the vegetables into a purée (this can happen very quickly with juicy kinds like onions, leeks, celery and peppers).

---

**1 ▲** Peel the vegetable, if instructed. If it is long, like a carrot or celery stalk, cut it across into pieces about 3 in (7.5 cm) long. This will make cubing and dicing easier. For a neat appearance, shave off curved sides so the pieces of vegetable have straight edges. Lay the vegetable flat and cut it lengthways into uniform slices of the required thickness, guiding the side of the knife with your knuckles.

**2 ▲** Stack the slices and cut lengthways into uniform strips of the required thickness. Gather the strips together and cut across the strips into cubes or dice.

---

# Sautéed Potatoes

**Serves 4**

| |
|---|
| 1½ lb (700 g) boiling potatoes, peeled and cut into ½ in (1.5 cm) cubes |
| 3 tablespoons vegetable oil |
| 1 small onion, chopped |
| ½–1 oz (15–30 g) butter |
| salt and pepper |

**1 ▼** Put the potatoes into a saucepan and cover with cold salted water. Bring to the boil. Simmer for 1 minute, then drain well in a colander. Turn on to a tea towel and pat dry.

**2** Heat the oil in a frying pan over moderately high heat. Add the potato cubes and fry for 10 minutes or until they start to turn golden. Stir and turn the potatoes frequently so they brown evenly on all sides.

**3** Add the onion and cook, stirring, until the potatoes are just tender. Add the butter. Season with salt and pepper. Cook for a further 2 minutes, stirring constantly. Serve hot.

# CUTTING VEGETABLE MATCHSTICKS

These decorative shapes, also called 'julienne', are simple to cut yet look very special. Many other foods can also be cut into matchsticks, for example citrus zest, fresh root ginger, cooked meats, firm cheese and firm fruits such as apple.

For matchsticks, vegetables should be peeled and cut across into pieces about 2 in (5 cm) long. If necessary, cut off curved sides so the vegetable has straight edges.

**1** ▲ Lay each piece of vegetable flat and cut it lengthways into slices ⅛ in (3 mm) thick or less, guiding the side of the knife with your knuckles.

**2** ▲ Stack the vegetable slices and cut them lengthways into strips about ⅛ in (3 mm) thick or less.

# Stir-fried Vegetables

**SERVES 4**

2½ tablespoons groundnut oil

1½ tablespoons sesame seeds

2 carrots, cut into matchsticks

4 oz (115 g) French beans, blanched for 2 minutes and refreshed

6 fresh shiitake mushrooms, stalks removed and caps thinly sliced

2 thin yellow or green courgettes, cut into matchsticks

1 tablespoon soy sauce

few drops of sesame oil

**1** ▲ Heat ½ tablespoon of the oil in a hot wok or frying pan. Add the sesame seeds and cook, stirring and shaking the wok, for 1 minutes or until the seeds are golden. Turn the seeds on to paper towels to drain.

**2** ◄ Heat the remaining oil. Add the carrots and stir-fry for 2 minutes. Add the beans and mushrooms. Stir-fry for 1 minute. Add the courgettes and stir-fry for 2–3 minutes or until all the vegetables are just tender. Add the soy sauce and sesame oil with the sesame seeds. Toss well and serve.

# SHREDDING VEGETABLE HEADS

Leaf vegetables that form compact heads, such as cabbage and lettuce, are often shredded for cooking or using in a salad. A large sharp knife is essential for good results. Alternatively, you can use the appropriate blade in a food processor.

**Keep knives sharp**
Vegetable preparation is easy with sharp knives. Hone the edge regularly with a sharpening steel.

1 ▲ Cut the head in half through the core. Cut each half in half. Cut out the core from each quarter. Discard any damaged outside leaves.

2 ▲ Set each quarter flat on a cutting surface and slice across into shreds of the required thickness, guiding the side of the knife with your knuckles.

# Hot Coleslaw

**SERVES 4–6**

| 1 oz (30 g) butter |
| --- |
| 1 small firm white cabbage, finely shredded |
| 1 teaspoon caraway seeds |
| salt and pepper |
| 1 teaspoon sugar |
| 1 tablespoon cider vinegar |
| ¼ pint (150 ml) soured cream |

1 ▲ Melt the butter in a large frying pan. Add the cabbage and sprinkle with the caraway seeds. Season with salt and pepper.

2 Cook over low heat, stirring and turning the cabbage, until it is just tender and beginning to turn golden. Remove from the heat.

3 ◄ In a jug, stir together the sugar, vinegar and soured cream. Add to the cabbage, toss well to mix and serve immediately.

# SHREDDING VEGETABLE LEAVES

Individual leaves – cabbage, lettuce, spinach and other greens, and herbs such as basil – are cut into neat shreds with this method.

**A clean cut**
Leaves of very tender greens such as basil and round lettuce can turn black at the cut edge if the cut is not clean. To avoid this, be sure the knife is very sharp, and cut straight down through the roll.

**1** ▲ Stack the leaves, 6–8 at a time, and roll up tightly parallel with the central rib. If the leaves are very large, roll them up individually.

**2** ▲ With a sharp knife, slice across the roll into shreds of the required thickness, guiding the side of the knife with your knuckles.

# Chinese-style Vegetable and Noodle Soup

**SERVES 4**

2 pints (1.2 litres) vegetable or chicken stock

1 garlic clove, lightly crushed with the flat side of a knife

1 in (2.5 cm) peeled cube of fresh root ginger, cut into fine matchsticks

2 tablespoons soy sauce

1 tablespoon cider vinegar

3 oz (85 g) fresh shiitake or button mushrooms, stalks removed and thinly sliced

2 large spring onions, thinly sliced on the diagonal

1½ oz (45 g) vermicelli or other fine noodles

6 oz (170 g) Chinese leaves, shredded

a few fresh coriander leaves

**1** Pour the stock into a saucepan. Add the garlic, root ginger, soy sauce and vinegar. Bring to the boil, then cover the pan and reduce the heat to very low. Leave to simmer gently for 10 minutes. Remove the garlic clove and discard it.

**2** ◄ Add the sliced mushrooms and spring onions and bring the soup back to the boil. Simmer for 5 minutes, uncovered, stirring occasionally. Add the noodles and shredded Chinese leaves. Simmer for 3–4 minutes or until the noodles and vegetables are just tender. Stir in the coriander leaves. Simmer for a final 1 minute. Serve the soup hot.

# BLANCHING AND REFRESHING

Foods are blanched for several reasons: to loosen skins before skinning (tomatoes, peaches and nuts), to set colour and flavour (for vegetables before freezing), to reduce bitterness (in some vegetables), to firm flesh (sweetbreads), and to remove excess salt (gammon, bacon). Vegetables are often blanched as an initial cooking, when further cooking is to be done by stir-frying or a brief reheating in butter before serving, or if they are to be used in a salad. After blanching, most foods are 'refreshed' to stop them cooking any further.

**1 ▲ To blanch**: Immerse the food in a large pan of boiling water (ideally use a wire basket or sieve so the food can be lifted out easily). Bring the water back to the boil and boil for the time specified, usually 1–2 minutes. Immediately lift the food out of the water (in its basket or with a slotted spoon, or drain in a colander).

**2 ▲ To refresh**: Quickly immerse the food in iced water or hold under cold running water. If the recipe specifies, leave until it has cooled completely. Drain well.

# Broccoli, Cauliflower and Carrot Salad

**SERVES 4**

| 1 small cauliflower, cut into florets and stalks trimmed |
| 8 oz (225 g) broccoli, cut into florets and stalks trimmed |
| 2 carrots, thickly sliced |
| 5 tablespoons vegetable oil |
| 3 tablespoons chopped almonds |
| 2 tablespoons red wine vinegar |
| ½ teaspoon ground cumin |
| salt and pepper |

**1** Blanch the cauliflower, broccoli and carrots separately in boiling salted water, allowing 10 minutes for the cauliflower and 5 minutes for the broccoli and carrots. Drain well and refresh in iced water.

**2 ▶** Heat 1 tablespoon of the oil in a small frying pan. Add the almonds. Fry for about 5 minutes or until golden brown, stirring frequently. Drain on paper towels and leave to cool.

**3** Combine the remaining oil with the vinegar, cumin, salt and pepper in a large bowl. Whisk well together. Add the vegetables and toss to coat with the dressing. Scatter the almonds on top. Serve at room temperature.

# SWEATING

Sweating is a common preliminary step in vegetable cooking, particularly for onions and leeks. This process, which is essentially a form of steaming, draws out the juices and develops the vegetable's flavour.

**A matter of weight**
Be sure the pan you use for sweating has a heavy base that will conduct the heat evenly, so the vegetables don't stick and burn. It is also important that the lid be tight fitting to keep in moisture.

**1 ▲** Heat fat (usually butter) in a heavy saucepan or frying pan over low heat. Add the vegetable and stir to coat with the melted fat.

**2 ▲** Cover the pan tightly and cook gently until the vegetable is softened but not brown; onions will be translucent. This can take 10–15 minutes or longer. Stir occasionally during the cooking.

# Pasta with Courgette and Walnut Sauce

**SERVES 4**

| |
|---|
| 2½ oz (70 g) butter |
| 1 large Spanish-type onion, halved and thinly sliced |
| 1 lb (450 g) courgettes, very thinly sliced |
| 12 oz (340 g) short pasta shapes such as penne, ziti, rotini or fusilli |
| 2 oz (55 g) walnuts, coarsely chopped |
| 3 tablespoons chopped fresh parsley |
| 2 tablespoons single cream |
| salt and pepper |
| freshly grated Parmesan cheese, to serve |

**1 ▲** Melt the butter in a frying pan. Add the onion, cover and sweat for 5 minutes, then add the courgettes.

**2** Stir well, cover again and sweat until the vegetables are very soft, stirring occasionally.

**3** Meanwhile, bring a large pot of salted water to the boil. Add the pasta to the boiling water, stir and cook for 10 minutes or until it is just tender to the bite ('al dente'). Check the packet instructions for timing.

**4** While the pasta is cooking, add the walnuts, parsley and cream to the courgette mixture and stir well. Season with salt and pepper.

**5** Drain the pasta and return it to the pot. Add the courgette sauce and mix well together. Serve immediately, with freshly grated Parmesan to sprinkle on top of each portion.

# MASHING AND PURÉEING

The smooth texture of a mashed or puréed vegetable is very appealing, perhaps because it reminds us of nursery food. Vegetables to be finished this way may be first boiled, steamed, sweated or baked.

**Carrot Purée**
Thinly slice 1½lb (700g) carrots. Put them in a saucepan, cover with water and add a pinch of salt. Bring to the boil and simmer for 10–15 minutes or until tender. Drain well, then purée in a food processor. Add 1oz (30g) butter, 4 tablespoons each milk and orange juice, and ½ teaspoon ground cardamom or a pinch of grated nutmeg. Season with salt and pepper. Reheat, stirring frequently. *Serves 4.*

**Sweet Potato Purée**
Mash 1½lb (700g) boiled or baked sweet potatoes with an electric mixer. Beat in butter, 4 tablespoons orange juice and ¼ teaspoon ground cinnamon.

**1 ▲ To mash potatoes and sweet potatoes**: Mash warm, freshly cooked potatoes with a potato masher or put them through a potato ricer. With a wooden spoon, beat in butter and milk or cream, and season to taste.

**3 ▲ To purée other root vegetables or pumpkin**: Put the freshly cooked vegetable in a food processor and process until smooth, scraping down the sides of the container as necessary. Season to taste.

**2 ▲** Alternatively, beat the potatoes with an electric mixer. Do not use a food processor for puréeing starchy vegetables such as potatoes because it will make them gluey.

**4 ▲ To purée vegetables with fibres or skins** (such as asparagus or pulses): Use a vegetable mill, unless you are prepared to push the food-processor purée through a sieve.

**5 ◄ To purée greens**: Remove the stalks of leaves such as spinach or chard before cooking. Purée in a food processor. Be sure to squeeze out as much water as possible, both before and after puréeing, especially if adding cream.

# Mashed Potatoes with Celeriac

**SERVES 4**

| |
|---|
| 2 lb (900 g) baking potatoes, peeled |
| 12 oz (340 g) celeriac |
| 1½ oz (45 g) butter |
| ¼ pint (150 ml) soured cream |
| good pinch of grated nutmeg |
| salt and pepper |

1  Cut the potatoes, if large. Bring to the boil in salted water, then simmer for 20 minutes or until very tender.

2  ▲  Meanwhile, peel the celeriac, chop it coarsely and drop immediately into a pan of salted water. (If exposed to the air too long, celeriac will turn brown.) Bring to the boil, then simmer for 15–20 minutes or until very tender.

3  ▲  Drain the potatoes and return them to the saucepan. Return to very low heat for 1–2 minutes to evaporate excess moisture, shaking the pan to turn the potatoes.

4  Mash the potatoes or press through a potato ricer into a warmed bowl. Drain the celeriac and purée in a food processor. Add to the bowl.

~ **VARIATION** ~

Substitute 1 medium-size swede for the celeriac. The swede can be mashed at the same time as the potatoes.

5  ▼  Add the butter, soured cream and nutmeg. Season to taste with salt and pepper. Beat well with a wooden spoon or, for a fluffier result, with an electric mixer. Serve hot.

# MAKING VEGETABLE STOCK

Vary the ingredients for this fresh-flavoured stock according to what you have to hand. Refrigerate, covered, for up to 5 days; freeze up to 1 month.

**MAKES ABOUT 4 PINTS (2.5 LITRES)**

| |
|---|
| 2 large onions, coarsely chopped |
| 2 leeks, sliced |
| 3 garlic cloves, crushed with the flat side of a knife |
| 3 carrots, coarsely chopped |
| 4 celery stalks, coarsely chopped |
| a large strip of lemon zest |
| a handful of parsley stalks (about 12) |
| a few fresh thyme sprigs |
| 2 bay leaves |
| 4 pints (2.5 litres) water |

**1 ▲** Put the vegetables, lemon zest, herbs and water in a stockpot and bring to the boil. Skim off the foam that rises to the surface, frequently at first and then from time to time.

**2 ▲** Reduce the heat and simmer, uncovered, for 30 minutes. Strain the stock and leave it to cool.

---

# Vegetable and Herb Chowder

**SERVES 4**

| |
|---|
| 1 oz (30 g) butter |
| 1 onion, finely chopped |
| 1 leek, thinly sliced |
| 1 celery stalk, diced |
| 1 pepper, yellow or green, seeded and diced |
| 2 tablespoons chopped fresh parsley |
| 1 tablespoon plain flour |
| 2 pints (1.2 litres) vegetable stock |
| 12 oz (340 g) boiling potatoes, peeled and diced |
| a few fresh thyme sprigs or ½ teaspoon dried thyme |
| 1 bay leaf |
| 4 oz (115 g) young runner beans, thinly sliced on the diagonal |
| 4 fl oz (120 ml) milk |
| salt and pepper |

**1 ▲** Melt the butter in a heavy saucepan or flameproof casserole and add the onion, leek, celery, pepper and parsley. Cover and cook over low heat until the vegetables are soft.

**2** Add the flour and stir until well blended. Add the stock slowly, stirring to combine. Bring to the boil, stirring frequently.

**3 ▼** Add the potatoes, thyme and bay leaf. Simmer, uncovered, for about 10 minutes.

**4** Add the beans and simmer for a further 10–15 minutes or until all the vegetables are tender.

**5** Stir in the milk. Season with salt and pepper. Heat through. Before serving, discard the thyme stalks and bay leaf. Serve hot.

# PREPARING SALAD GREENS

Crisp, fresh green and variegated leaves are very appetizing. Use them as the background for a vegetable, fish, meat or fruit salad or make the leaves the focus.

### Lettuce

The four main types are: crisphead, with solid heads of tightly packed, crisp leaves (iceberg); butterhead, with looser heads of soft-textured leaves (round, 'quattro stagioni'); Cos and romaine, with elongated heads of crisp leaves; and looseleaf, with leaves that do not form a compact head ('feuilles de chêne', 'lollo rosso').

**Preparation**: Discard wilted or damaged leaves. Twist or cut out the central core. Rinse the leaves thoroughly in cold water and soak briefly to draw out any grit trapped in the folds. Drain and blot or spin dry. If the leaves are large, tear into pieces.

---

**Other salad ingredients**
To provide contrast in texture and flavour, add brightly coloured and crunchy leaves, such as red cabbage, with plain salad leaves – just a little goes a long way. Cucumber, spring onions and carrot are also appealing in a mixed salad, as are raw or lightly cooked French beans or mange-touts. Nuts or dried fruit are other tasty additions.

---

### Chicory and Endive

These have an appealing bitterness. Paler leaves are more delicate and sweet. 'Frisée' or curly endive has fine, frilly green leaves with a coarse texture. Escarole has broader, fleshier leaves with jagged edges and a firm texture. The slim leaves of chicory are white with greenish tips. Radicchio is red Italian chicory.

**Preparation**: Core the base of chicory. Discard wilted or damaged leaves. Rinse thoroughly and dry the leaves. If large, cut into pieces.

### Lamb's Lettuce

Also known as corn salad or 'mâche', this salad green has a pleasantly firm, chewy texture and mild, slightly nutty flavour. The leaves are small and may be spoon-shaped or round.

**Preparation**: Remove any wilted or damaged leaves. Trim roots. Rinse well as the leaves can be sandy.

---

### Rocket

In a salad of mixed greens, the pungent peppery, nutty taste of rocket is unmistakable and welcome. This member of the mustard family, also called 'roquette' and 'arugula', has deep green leaves with curved edges and a texture somewhat like spinach.

**Preparation**: Discard any wilted or damaged leaves. Pull off roots. Rinse thoroughly and dry on paper towels – it's best not to use a salad spinner, which could bruise the tender leaves.

### Watercress

Another member of the mustard family, the round dark green leaves have a wonderful peppery flavour that enlivens any salad, and the fresh attractive appearance of watercress makes it a popular garnish.

**Preparation**: Discard wilted or damaged leaves and snap off thick stalks. Rinse well and spin dry.

# Wilted Spinach and Bacon Salad

**SERVES 6**

| |
|---|
| 1 lb (450 g) fresh young spinach leaves |
| 8 oz (225 g) streaky bacon rashers |
| 1½ tablespoons vegetable oil |
| 4 tablespoons red wine vinegar |
| 4 tablespoons water |
| 4 teaspoons caster sugar |
| 1 teaspoon dry mustard |
| salt and pepper |
| 8 spring onions, thinly sliced |
| 6 radishes, thinly sliced |
| 2 hard-boiled eggs, coarsely grated |

**3** ▲ Combine the vinegar, water, sugar, mustard, salt and pepper in a bowl and stir until smoothly blended. Add to the fat in the frying pan. Bring the dressing to the boil, stirring.

**4** ▼ Pour the hot dressing over the spinach leaves. Sprinkle on the bacon, spring onions, radishes and eggs and toss. Serve immediately.

**1** ▲ Pull any coarse stalks from the spinach leaves and rinse well. Put the leaves in a large salad bowl.

**2** ▲ Fry the bacon rashers in the oil until crisp and brown. Remove with tongs and drain on paper towels. Chop the bacon and set aside.

# RINSING AND CRISPING SALAD GREENS

It is vital that all salad leaves be thoroughly rinsed with cold water to remove any grit or insects, as well as residues of sprays. Just as important is to dry the salad leaves well so that the dressing will not be diluted.

**Lettuce with Blue Cheese Dressing**
For each serving, use 1 small head round lettuce or Little Gem lettuce, washed and spun or blotted dry. Top with 3–4 tablespoons blue cheese dressing (page 180). Garnish with cherry tomatoes and chives, if wished.

**Salad success**
• Dress salad greens just before serving, otherwise the leaves will wilt and become unpleasantly soggy.
• Match the dressing to the greens: sharp leaves need hearty flavours, but the same dressing used on delicate greens would overpower them.
• Be imaginative with salad additions. A few blanched French beans, for instance, can lift a plain salad, especially with a sprinkling of fresh herbs.

**1 ▲** Discard any wilted, discoloured or damaged leaves. For spinach and similar greens, pull off the stalks. Pull off roots from lamb's lettuce.

**3 ▲** Put the leaves in a sink or large basin of cold water and swirl them round to wash off any dirt or insects. Leave to settle for 1–2 minutes.

**5 ▲** Alternatively, put the washed leaves in a salad spinner to spin off the water. (Do not use a salad spinner for leaves that bruise easily.)

**2 ▲** For leaves in compact or loose heads, pull them individually from the core or stalk.

**4 ▲** Lift the leaves out of the water on to a tea towel and pat dry gently with paper towels or another tea towel.

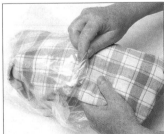

**6 ▲** Wrap the leaves loosely in a clean tea towel or paper towels and put in a large plastic bag. Refrigerate for about 1 hour. When assembling the salad, tear any large leaves into smaller pieces.

# Green Salad with Oranges and Avocado

**SERVES 4**

| |
|---|
| 1 round lettuce |
| 1 small bunch of watercress |
| a few leaves of frisée |
| 1 small bunch of rocket |
| 1 red onion, thinly sliced into rings |
| 2 seedless oranges, peeled and segmented (page 189) |
| 1 ripe avocado, peeled, stoned and cubed |
| 2 oz (55 g) walnut pieces, toasted |
| FOR THE DRESSING |
| 6 tablespoons olive oil |
| 1 tablespoon walnut oil |
| 3 tablespoons lemon juice |
| 2 tablespoons orange juice |
| 1 teaspoon grated orange zest |
| 1 teaspoon Dijon mustard |
| pinch of caster sugar |
| salt and pepper |

**1 ▲** Combine all the dressing ingredients in a bowl or screwtop jar. Whisk or shake well together.

**2 ▼** Put the rinsed and crisped salad greens in a bowl and add the onion, orange segments and avocado.

~ **VARIATION** ~

For Green Salad with Tuna and Peppers, omit oranges and walnuts. Add 1 × 7 oz (200 g) can drained, flaked tuna and 1 roasted red pepper, peeled and sliced.

**3 ▲** Add the dressing and toss the salad to combine well.

**4** Scatter the walnuts on top and serve immediately.

# PREPARING PULSES

Pulses – dried beans, peas and lentils – are a high-protein food. They keep well, making them a useful storecupboard staple. Most pulses require the same initial preparation.

**An extra safeguard**
To remove potentially harmful toxins, boil most pulses uncovered for 10 minutes before reducing the heat to a simmer for the rest of the cooking time.

**1 ▲** First rinse the pulses and pick out any small stones.

**2 ▲ To soak dried beans and peas:** Put them in a bowl, cover with plenty of cold water and soak for at least 4 hours. (Lentils do not need soaking.)

**3 ▲** A quick alternative method is to put the dried beans or peas in a large pan of water, bring to the boil and boil for 2 minutes, then leave them to soak for 1 hour.

**4 ▲** In either case, drain the pulses and rinse them well. They are now ready for cooking according to the recipe.

**5 ▲ To cook:** Put the soaked and drained beans or peas or the lentils in a pan of fresh cold water (3 parts water to 1 part pulses) and bring to the boil. Then cover the pan, reduce the heat and simmer until tender.

# A LOOK AT PULSES

Dried beans, peas and lentils range widely in colour, shape and size. Some of the most commonly available include: **haricot beans**, large to medium-sized, kidney-shaped, white; **kidney beans**, medium-sized, kidney-shaped, smooth, shiny, may be reddish-brown, black or white (when normally called cannellini beans); **flageolet**, small, oval, pale green; **black beans** (also called turtle beans), small, oval, smooth, shiny, jet-black; **borlotti beans**, medium-sized, kidney-shaped, creamy brown with red streaks; **pinto beans**, small, oval,

smooth, beige with brown specks; **black-eye beans**, small, oval, smooth, creamy colour, with small cream-centred black dot on one side; **butter beans**, large, oval/round, flattish, off-white; **chickpeas**, medium-sized, round, not smooth, beige-tan in colour; **peas**, small, round or split in half, may be grey-green or yellow; **lentils**, tiny, disc-shaped, smooth, may be brownish-green, reddish-orange or yellow.

Pulses are easy to prepare, and they can be used in many ways – in casseroles, soups, stews and salads.

The minimum soaking time for most dried pulses is 4 hours, but they can be soaked overnight if that is more convenient. Lentils do not need soaking, and it is not essential for split peas, although they may be soaked to speed cooking.

Most pulses require about 1½–2 hours' cooking time. This includes white haricot beans, borlotti beans, pinto beans, butter beans, kidney beans and chickpeas. Black-eye beans, split peas and flageolet beans require less time, about 1–1¼ hours. Lentils cook in less than 30 minutes.

# Split Pea Soup

**SERVES 4–6**

| |
|---|
| 1 oz (30 g) butter |
| 1 large onion, chopped |
| 1 large celery stalk with leaves, chopped |
| 2 carrots, chopped |
| 1 smoked gammon knuckle, 1 lb (450 g) |
| 3½ pints (2 litres) water |
| 12 oz (340 g) split peas |
| 2 tablespoons chopped fresh parsley, plus more to garnish |
| ½ teaspoon dried thyme |
| 1 bay leaf |
| about 2 tablespoons lemon juice |
| salt and pepper |

**1** ▲ Melt the butter in a large heavy-based saucepan. Add the onion, celery and carrots and cook until soft, stirring occasionally.

**2** ▲ Add the remaining ingredients. Bring to the boil, cover and simmer gently for 2 hours or until the peas are very tender.

**3** ▼ Remove the gammon knuckle. Leave it to cool slightly, then remove the skin and cut the meat from the bones. Discard skin and bones; cut the meat into chunks.

**4** ▲ Return the chunks of gammon to the soup. Discard the bay leaf. Taste and adjust the seasoning with more lemon juice, salt and pepper.

**5** Serve hot, sprinkled with parsley.

# Tuna and Black-eye Bean Salad

**SERVES 4**

5 oz (145 g) dried black-eye beans

¼ pint (150 ml) garlic vinaigrette (page 182)

1 small red onion, chopped

3 tablespoons chopped fresh parsley

1 × 7 oz (200 g) can tuna, drained

cherry tomatoes, to garnish

**2 ▲** Pour the vinaigrette dressing over the beans and mix well.

**4 ▲** Add the tuna and stir gently into the salad.

**5** Garnish with halved cherry tomatoes and serve at cool room temperature.

**1 ▲** Soak the black-eye beans for at least 4 hours. Drain, then cook in fresh water until tender. Drain well and cool slightly.

**3 ▲** Add the onion and parsley and stir to combine.

~ **VARIATION** ~

For Italian Bean Salad, use cannellini beans (canned, if liked, for quicker preparation) instead of black-eye beans.

---

# Mexican Chickpea Dip

**SERVES 6–8**

14 oz (400 g) dried chickpeas, soaked overnight, cooked and drained

4 tablespoons fromage frais

3 tablespoons lemon juice

2 tablespoons olive oil

1–2 garlic cloves, finely chopped

1–2 tablespoons tequila (optional)

4–5 tablespoons seeded and chopped green chillies (fresh or canned)

salt

¾ oz (25 g) pine nuts, to garnish

hot tortilla or corn chips, to serve

**1** Combine the chickpeas, fromage frais, lemon juice, oil, garlic and tequila in a blender or food processor. Blend until smooth.

**2 ▲** Turn into a bowl and stir in the chillies. Season with salt. Cover and chill for at least 1 hour.

**3 ▲** Toast the pine nuts in a dry frying pan over moderate heat. Serve the dip at room temperature, with the pine nuts sprinkled over the surface or stirred in, with warmed tortilla or corn chips.

*Mexican Chickpea Dip (left), Tuna and Black-eye Bean Salad*

# EGGS

~

The endlessly versatile egg lends itself to easy and exciting
suppers, starters, snacks, lunches and desserts. From fried
eggs to soufflés, the techniques for cooking eggs are essentially
simple. A little practice will give you confidence.

# BOILING EGGS

The derisive expression, 'can't boil an egg', indicates the importance of this basic cooking skill, although, to be accurate, eggs are simmered rather than boiled.

For many people, a boiled egg with toast is an everyday breakfast. But the soft-boiled egg and its cousin the coddled egg have many delicious applications. If they are to be peeled for serving, cook them for the longest time suggested below. The salt in the cooking water aids in peeling.

Hard-boiled eggs make classic salads and sandwich fillings, as well as cold first course and buffet dishes and hot main dishes.

**1 ▲ To hard-boil eggs:** Bring a pan of well-salted water to the boil. Using a slotted spoon, lower each egg into the water. Reduce the heat so the water is just simmering. Cook for 10 minutes. Immediately plunge the eggs into a bowl of iced water to cool.

**2 ▲** When the eggs are cool enough to handle, peel them. If they are not to be used immediately, keep the peeled eggs in a bowl of cold salted water. Or store the eggs, still in the shell, in the refrigerator; they will keep for up to 1 week.

**Egg, Potato and Bean Salad**
Bring a pot of salted water to the boil. Add 1 lb (450 g) small un-peeled new potatoes. Bring back to the boil and simmer for 10 minutes. Add 8 oz (225 g) French beans and simmer for 4–5 min-utes or until the potatoes and beans are just tender. Drain well in a colander and refresh under cold running water. Turn the vegetables into a large bowl. Sprinkle 4 tablespoons olive oil and 2 tablespoons balsamic vine-gar over them. Season with salt and pepper and toss well. Scatter 2 grated hard-boiled eggs and 3 tablespoons coarsely shredded mixed fresh mint and basil over the top. Serve warm or at room temperature. *Serves 4–6.*

**3 ▲ To coddle eggs:** Lower them into a pan of boiling salted water. Cover the pan and remove it from the heat. Leave for 6–8 minutes or until the eggs are done to your taste. Lift out each egg, place in an egg cup and cut off the top of the shell for serving. Or, to peel, plunge the eggs into a bowl of cold water. When they are cool enough to handle, peel carefully. To reheat for serving, immerse in a bowl of hot water for 1–2 minutes.

**Hard-boiled egg tips**
• Always cool hard-boiled eggs in iced water. The abrupt tempera-ture change helps prevent a grey layer from forming round the yolk.
• To peel hard-boiled eggs, tap them gently on a hard surface to crack the shell. Carefully peel under cold running water.

**4 ▲ To soft-boil eggs:** Bring a pan of well-salted water to the boil. Using a slotted spoon, lower each egg into the water. Reduce the heat so the water just simmers. Cook for 3–5 minutes or until the eggs are done to your taste (depending on how firm you like the white; the yolk will be runny).

**Ideas for soft-boiled and coddled eggs**
• For *Caviar-crowned Eggs:* Cut the top ¾ in (2 cm) from each egg, in its shell. Put a spoonful of soured cream and caviar on top.
• For *Smoked Salmon Eggs:* Pre-pare as above and top each with a spoonful each of soured cream and diced smoked salmon.
• Put a hot peeled egg in the centre of a bowl of cream of spinach or watercress soup.

# Caesar Salad

**Serves 6 as a starter**

6 fl oz (180 ml) salad oil, preferably olive oil

3 oz (85 g) French or Italian bread, cut into 1 in (2.5 cm) cubes

1 large garlic clove, crushed with the flat side of a knife

2 small heads of Cos lettuce, separated into leaves, rinsed and crisped

salt and pepper

2 eggs, soft-boiled for 1 minute

5 tablespoons lemon juice

2½ oz (75 g) Parmesan cheese, freshly grated

6 anchovy fillets, drained and finely chopped (optional)

---

**Ideas for hard-boiled eggs**

• For *Devilled Eggs*: Halve the eggs lengthways and scoop out the yolks. Mash the yolks with a fork and mix with enough mayonnaise to make a creamy consistency. Season with Dijon mustard, salt and pepper. Spoon or pipe the yolk mixture into the hollows in the egg white halves and sprinkle the tops with a little paprika or cayenne pepper.

• For *Herb-stuffed Eggs*: Add chopped fresh herbs such as parsley, tarragon and chives to the egg yolk and mayonnaise mixture; omit the mustard.

• For *Egg Mayonnaise*: Chop eggs. Mix with chopped spring onions or red onion to taste and a little chopped parsley. Bind with mayonnaise. Season with mustard.

• For *Eggs in Aspic*: Put cooled peeled eggs in individual ramekins and surround with chopped herbs in aspic. Refrigerate to set.

• For *Eggs in Cream Sauce*: Add quartered eggs to hot mushroom or mustard sauce (page 170). Add 6 oz (170 g) slow-cooked onions (page 114) and heat through.

**1 ▼** Heat 4 tablespoons of the oil in a large frying pan. Add the bread cubes and garlic. Fry, stirring and turning constantly, until the cubes are golden brown all over. Drain on paper towels. Discard the garlic.

**2** Tear large lettuce leaves into smaller pieces. Put all the lettuce into a large salad bowl.

**3 ▲** Add the remaining oil and season with salt and pepper. Toss the leaves to coat well.

**4** Break the eggs on top. Sprinkle with the lemon juice. Toss well again.

**5** Add the cheese and anchovies, if using. Toss gently to mix.

**6** Scatter the fried bread cubes on top and serve immediately.

# SCRAMBLING EGGS

Tender, creamy scrambled eggs are perfect for breakfast or brunch, but you can also add flavourings for a more unusual snack or supper dish.

**Ideas for scrambled eggs**
- Add chopped fresh herbs (chives, tarragon) to the eggs.
- Cook diced vegetables (onions, mushrooms, peppers) or ham in butter before adding the eggs.
- Stir in a little grated cheese or bits of full-fat soft cheese just before the eggs are ready.
- Fold peeled cooked prawns into scrambled eggs.

**1** ▲ Put the eggs in a bowl and add a little salt and pepper. Beat the eggs with a fork until they are well blended. Melt butter in a frying pan over moderately low heat (it should cover the bottom of the pan generously). Pour in the beaten eggs.

**2** ▲ Cook, scraping up and turning the eggs over, for 3–5 minutes or until they are softly set and still moist. The eggs will continue to cook after being removed from the heat, so undercook them slightly even if you prefer a firmer end result.

# Scrambled Eggs with Smoked Salmon

**SERVES 4 AS A SNACK**

| |
|---|
| 6 eggs |
| salt and pepper |
| 2 oz (55 g) butter |
| 2 tablespoons whipping cream |
| 4 tablespoons mayonnaise |
| 4 slices of pumpernickel or wholemeal bread, crusts trimmed |
| 4 oz (115 g) thinly sliced smoked salmon |
| lumpfish or salmon caviar, to garnish |

**1** ▲ Season the eggs with salt and pepper. Scramble them using half of the butter. Mix in the cream just before they have finished cooking.

**2** Remove from the heat and mix in the mayonnaise. Leave to cool.

**3** Spread the slices of bread with the remaining butter. Cover with smoked salmon, trimming it to fit. Cut in half.

**4** Divide the scrambled eggs among the plates, spreading it neatly on the smoked salmon. Top each serving with a heaped tablespoon of caviar.

# Frying Eggs

Fried eggs are a natural partner for bacon, sausages, fried tomatoes and mushrooms, and even black pudding in that great British institution – the 'cooked breakfast'.

1  Heat butter, bacon fat or oil (to generously cover the bottom) in a frying pan over moderate heat. When the fat is sizzling, break each egg and slip it into the pan.

2 ◀  Fry for 1–1½ minutes or until the egg white is just set and opaque or more firm, according to your taste. The yolk will still be runny and the base of the egg will be golden brown and crisp. The egg is ready to serve now, 'sunny side up'. Or gently turn the fried egg over with a fish slice, taking care not to break the yolk. Cook for a further 10–15 seconds or until the other side is just browned.

# Fried Eggs and Sausage on Tortillas

**Serves 4**

| |
| --- |
| 8 oz (225 g) minced pork |
| ½ small onion, finely chopped |
| 1 teaspoon chilli powder (or to taste) |
| ½ teaspoon ground cumin |
| ½ teaspoon dried oregano |
| 1 tablespoon vinegar |
| 1 garlic clove, finely chopped |
| salt and pepper |
| oil, for frying |
| 4 large fresh or canned corn tortillas |
| 4 eggs |
| 2 oz (55 g) butter or bacon fat |
| Mexican hot sauce or salsa, to serve |

1 ▲  Put the pork in a bowl and add the onion, spices, oregano, vinegar, garlic, salt and pepper. Mix well, cover and refrigerate overnight.

2 ▼  Cook the pork mixture in a large frying pan until it is browned and crumbly, stirring occasionally.

3  Meanwhile, heat 1 in (2.5 cm) oil in a wide pan to 365°F (180°C). Fry the tortillas until they are crisp and golden brown, keeping them flat. Drain on paper towels and put on a baking sheet. Keep warm in the oven.

4  Fry the eggs in the butter or bacon fat (or use oil for frying if you prefer).

5  Put a tortilla on each plate. Using a slotted spoon, divide the pork mixture among the tortillas. Top each serving with a fried egg. Serve with hot sauce or salsa.

# POACHING EGGS

The perfect poached egg has a neat oval shape, a tender white and a soft yolk. It is unbeatable on a slice of hot buttered toast, or it can be partnered with vegetables (artichoke hearts, asparagus), seafood (crab, smoked salmon) or meat (ham, bacon, steak) and dressed with a rich sauce. Use the freshest eggs possible because they will be the easiest to poach.

1  First, bring a large deep pan of water to the boil.

2 ▲  Break each egg and slip it gently into the water. Reduce the heat to low so the water just simmers. Poach for 3–4 minutes or until the eggs are done.

3 ▲  With a slotted spoon, lift out each egg and press it gently; the white should feel just firm but the yolk should still be soft.

**The clotting factor**
If your eggs are not really fresh, adding white wine vinegar to the poaching water will help the egg white to coagulate, although it will slightly flavour the egg. Use 2 tablespoons vinegar to 2 pints (1 litre) of water.

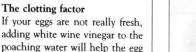

4 ◄  If there are any strings of cooked egg white, trim them off with a knife or kitchen scissors. Drain briefly on paper towels. Serve immediately, if wished. Or warm the eggs in a bowl of hot water for serving. If the eggs will be served cold, immerse them in a bowl of iced water until ready to serve. Drain and blot dry gently before serving.

# Poached Eggs Florentine

**SERVES 4**

1½ lb (700 g) spinach leaves, shredded

1 oz (30 g) butter

3–4 tablespoons whipping cream

good pinch of grated nutmeg

salt and pepper

4 eggs

½ pint (300 ml) cheese sauce made with Gruyère cheese (page 170)

1 oz (30 g) Gruyère cheese, grated

1  Preheat the grill.

2  Put the spinach in a large pan with the butter. Cover and cook until the leaves are wilted. Uncover and boil to evaporate the excess liquid.

3 ▲  Mix in the cream, nutmeg and seasoning. Poach the eggs.

4  Divide the spinach among 4 individual shallow gratin dishes or a large gratin dish. Spread it evenly and make hollows for the eggs. Set a poached egg in each hollow.

5 ▼  Spoon over cheese sauce to coat the eggs lightly. Sprinkle the grated cheese evenly over the top. Grill for 2–3 minutes or until the cheese has melted and is lightly browned. Serve immediately.

# BAKING EGGS

Baking is one of the simplest ways to cook eggs, yet it produces elegant results. The eggs can be baked individually, in buttered pots such as ramekins or small shallow dishes, or several can be baked in a large dish, on a bed of vegetables, sauce, etc.

**Ideas for baked eggs**

• Coat buttered ramekins with freshly grated Parmesan cheese. Dot eggs with butter and sprinkle each egg very lightly with Parmesan before baking.

• Put a little diced cooked ham, or a few sautéed sliced mushrooms or crisp garlic-flavoured croutons in the bottom of each buttered ramekin before breaking in the egg.

• Bake eggs on a bed of creamed spinach, mashed potato or other root vegetables, puréed broccoli or peas.

• Bake eggs on tomato sauce and roasted vegetables (page 173).

• Bake eggs in hollows made in a cooked stuffing, such as sausage stuffing for chicken (page 13) or smoked ham and almond stuffing for turkey (page 27).

• Bake potatoes, then cut off a lengthways slice from one side. Scoop out the flesh, leaving a shell 1/8–1/4 in (3–5 mm) thick. Mash the potato with butter, milk, salt and pepper. Spoon it back into the potato shells and press down firmly. Make a hollow in the top of the mashed potato in each shell and break in an egg. Dribble a little melted butter over the egg. Bake at 400°F/200°C/Gas 6 for 5–7 minutes to set the egg white.

**1 ▲ To bake in individual ramekins**: Butter the dishes and sprinkle them with salt and pepper. Break an egg into each, taking care not to pierce the yolk.

**3 ▲** Set the dishes in a baking tin. Add enough water to come halfway up the sides of the dishes. Bring to a simmer on top of the stove. Transfer to a 400°F/200°C/Gas 6 oven. Bake for 5–7 minutes or until the whites are just set and the yolks still soft.

**2 ▲** Dot the top of each egg with a few small pieces of butter, or add 1 tablespoon of whipping cream to each ramekin.

**4 ▲ To bake on a bed**: Spread a hot savoury mixture in a buttered shallow baking dish or in individual ramekins or gratin dishes. Make hollows in the mixture with the back of a spoon. Break an egg into each hollow.

**5 ◄** According to recipe instructions, dot the eggs with butter, sprinkle with cheese, drizzle with cream, etc. These toppings help to prevent the eggs from drying out during cooking. Bake until the whites are just set and the yolks are still soft.

# Eggs Baked in Ham and Potato Hash

**SERVES 6**

| |
|---|
| 2 oz (55 g) butter |
| 1 large onion, chopped |
| 12 oz (340 g) cooked ham, diced |
| 1 lb (450 g) cooked potatoes, diced |
| 4 oz (115 g) Cheddar cheese, grated |
| 2 tablespoons tomato ketchup |
| 1–2 tablespoons Worcestershire sauce |
| salt and pepper |
| 6 eggs |
| few drops of Tabasco sauce |
| chopped fresh parsley, to garnish |

1  Preheat a 325°F/170°C/Gas 3 oven.

2  Melt half of the butter in a frying pan. Cook the onion until soft, stirring occasionally.

3 ▲  Turn the onion into a bowl. Add the ham, potatoes, cheese, ketchup and Worcestershire sauce. Season with salt and pepper. Stir the mixture to combine.

4 ▲  Spread the hash in a buttered baking dish in a layer about 1 in (2.5 cm) deep. Bake for 10 minutes.

5 ▼  Make 6 hollows in the hash. Slip an egg into each.

6  Melt the remaining butter in a small pan. Season with Tabasco sauce to taste.

7 ▲  Dribble the seasoned butter over the eggs and hash.

8  Bake for 15–20 minutes or until the eggs are set and cooked to your taste. Serve immediately, in the dish, garnished with parsley.

# MAKING A ROLLED OMELETTE

The versatile rolled or folded omelette can be served plain or filled. There are also flat omelettes and soufflé omelettes. At its simplest, an omelette is made with 2 or 3 eggs, 1–2 teaspoons water, salt and pepper.

**1** ▲ Break the eggs into a bowl and add the water and some salt and pepper. Beat with a fork until just blended but not frothy.

**2** ▲ In an 8 in (20 cm) omelette pan, melt a knob of butter over moderately high heat. Tilt and rotate the pan so the bottom and sides are thoroughly coated with butter.

---

**Ideas for omelettes**
- Add 1 tablespoon chopped fresh herbs (a mixture of parsley, chives and tarragon, for example) to the beaten eggs.
- Scatter 2–3 tablespoons grated cheese (Gruyère, Cheddar) over the omelette before folding it.
- Sauté skinned, seeded and chopped tomatoes in butter for 1–2 minutes. Season with salt and pepper and stir in a little chopped fresh basil. Use to fill the omelette.
- Fill the omelette with strips of cooked ham or with Parma ham, roasted vegetables (page 173), sautéed sliced mushrooms, sautéed potatoes (page 126), buttered asparagus tips or slow-cooked onions (page 114).
- Warm left-over pasta (buttered or in sauce); if the shape is long, such as spaghetti, cut it into short pieces. If using buttered pasta, add strips of canned pimiento, sliced black olives, capers etc. Use to fill the omelette, fold and sprinkle with grated Parmesan.

**3** ▲ When the butter is foaming and just beginning to turn golden, pour in the egg mixture. Tilt and rotate the pan to spread the eggs in an even layer over the bottom.

**4** ▲ Cook for 5–10 seconds or until the omelette starts to set on the base. With a palette knife, lift the cooked base and tilt the pan so the uncooked egg mixture runs underneath on to the hot pan. Continue cooking in this way until most of the omelette is set but the top is still moist and creamy.

---

**The right pan**
Although you can use a frying pan, a special omelette pan, with its curved edge, will make folding and turning out the omelette so much easier.

**5** ▲ With the palette knife, loosen the edge of the omelette on one side and tilt the pan so that a third of the omelette folds over on to itself.

**6** ▲ Continue loosening the omelette from its folded edge, holding the pan over a warmed plate. As the omelette slides out on to the plate, tilt the pan so the omelette folds over again on itself into thirds, using the edge of the pan to guide it.

# Omelette Foo Yung

**SERVES 4**

1 tablespoon groundnut or vegetable oil

2–3 spring onions, chopped

1 celery stalk, diced

2 teaspoons finely chopped fresh ginger

1 garlic clove, finely chopped

4 oz (115 g) peeled cooked prawns

2 oz (55 g) white crabmeat

1 oz (30 g) cooked ham, diced

1½ tablespoons chopped fresh
coriander

1–2 tablespoons soy sauce, plus more
to serve

8 or 12 eggs

salt and pepper

2–3 oz (55–85 g) butter

1 Heat the oil in a frying pan over moderate heat. Add the spring onions, celery, ginger and garlic and cook for 1 minute, stirring frequently.

2 ▼ Add the prawns, crabmeat and ham. Sprinkle with the coriander and soy sauce. Reduce the heat to low and leave the mixture to heat through, stirring occasionally.

3 ▲ Meanwhile, make 4 omelettes, using 2 or 3 eggs for each. Before folding each omelette, spoon one-quarter of the prawn and crab filling over the centre. Serve hot, with more soy sauce for sprinkling.

# MAKING A FLAT OMELETTE

Called a 'frittata' in Italy and a 'tortilla' in Spain, a flat omelette is thicker than a folded omelette. It is usually cut into wedges for serving hot, warm or cold. Use a pan with a heatproof handle, or wrap the handle well in foil.

Fillings used for folded omelettes can be used in flat ones too. The quantities here will make a flat omelette to serve 4 people.

**1 ▲** Break 8 eggs into a bowl and season with salt and pepper. Beat lightly with a fork. Meanwhile, preheat the grill.

**2 ▲** In a 9–10 in (23–25 cm) frying pan with a heatproof handle, melt ½ oz (15 g) butter with 1 tablespoon oil over moderate heat. Tilt and rotate the pan to coat the bottom and sides.

---

**Flat omelette fillings**
- Prepare ½ quantity sautéed potatoes (page 126). Spread out the cooked potatoes in the frying pan. Pour the egg mixture over the potatoes. Continue cooking the flat omelette as described.
- Prepare roasted vegetables (page 173). Transfer to the frying pan and spread them out before pouring in the egg mixture. Cook the flat omelette as described.
- Roast and peel 2 peppers (page 123) and cut into thin strips. Cook in oil and butter in a frying pan over moderate heat with 1 chopped onion until very soft. Stir in some thawed frozen peas. Spread out the vegetables in the pan. Pour in the egg mixture and continue cooking as described.

---

**3 ▲** When the fat is sizzling and just beginning to turn golden, pour in the egg mixture. Tilt and rotate the pan to spread the eggs in an even layer over the bottom. Reduce the heat to low. (If the omelette has other ingredients add them now, or spread in the pan before pouring in the egg mixture.)

**4 ▲** Cook for 5–10 seconds or until the omelette starts to set on the base. With a palette knife, lift the cooked base and tilt the pan so the uncooked egg mixture runs underneath on to the hot pan. Continue cooking in this way until most of the omelette is set but the top is still moist and creamy.

---

**Flat Omelette with Ham and Cheese**
For each 8-egg omelette, scatter 4 oz (115 g) strips of cooked ham, or 2 oz (55 g) Parma ham, and 3–4 tablespoons finely chopped spring onion or red onion in the pan after pouring in the beaten egg mixture. Before transferring the omelette to the grill, sprinkle 3–4 tablespoons of freshly grated Parmesan cheese or 1½–2 oz (45–55 g) grated Cheddar or Gruyère cheese evenly over the top. Serve hot or warm. *Serves 4.*

**5 ▲** Transfer the pan to the grill, setting it about 4 in (10 cm) from the heat. Cook for 3–4 minutes or until the top is lightly browned and just set.

# MAKING A SOUFFLÉ OMELETTE

This cross between a flat omelette and a soufflé starts cooking on top of the stove and finishes in the oven. Fillings are normally sweet.

**Soufflé omelette fillings**
• Mix lightly crushed berries (raspberries, strawberries, blackberries etc) with a dash of Cognac, orange liqueur or kirsch. Use to fill the omelette. Drizzle warmed honey over the top and serve with sweetened whipped cream (page 160).
• Add 2 tablespoons orange liqueur or brandy to the egg yolks with the sugar. Fill the omelette with sweet orange segments. Sprinkle the folded omelette with icing sugar and pour on 3 tablespoons warmed orange liqueur or brandy. Set alight, and serve the omelette flaming.

**Soufflé Omelette with Peaches**
For each 4-egg omelette, spread 2 tablespoons warmed apricot, raspberry or strawberry jam over the cooked omelette and top with a peeled and thinly sliced ripe peach. After folding, sprinkle with icing sugar. Decorate with berries, if liked. *Serves 2.*

1 ▲ Separate 4 eggs. To the yolks, add 6 tablespoons caster sugar and beat until thick and pale. Preheat a 350°F/180°C/Gas 4 oven.

3 ▲ With a rubber spatula, fold the egg whites into the yolk mixture as lightly as possible, cutting down to the bottom of the bowl and turning the mixture over, while rotating the bowl at the same time.

5 ▲ Cook, without stirring, for 5 minutes or until the omelette is puffy and set round the edges but still soft in the centre. Transfer the pan to the oven. Bake for 3–5 minutes or until the top is set and lightly browned.

2 ▲ Whisk the egg whites until they hold stiff peaks. (Add a pinch of cream of tartar if not using a copper bowl.)

4 ▲ Heat a 9–10 in (23–25 cm) frying pan with an ovenproof handle over moderately high heat. Melt enough butter in the pan to cover the bottom generously. Tilt the pan to coat the bottom and sides. Pour in the egg mixture. Reduce the heat to low.

6 ▲ Spread a filling over the centre. Fold the omelette in half. Turn it on to a warmed plate and finish according to the recipe. Serve immediately.

# MAKING A SOUFFLÉ

Despite their reputation as tricky, soufflés are not difficult to make. The base for a soufflé is simply a thick sauce (sweet or savoury) or a purée. Into this, stiffly whisked egg whites are folded, and the whole is baked until it has risen and is lightly set.

Proper preparation of the dish, enabling the soufflé to 'climb' up the sides, encourages rising. Generously butter or oil the dish, including the top edge. If the recipe specifies, coat the bottom and sides with a thin layer of fine crumbs, caster sugar, etc.

**1 ▲** Separate the eggs, taking care that there is no trace of egg yolk in the whites. (It is best to separate 1 egg at a time and check each white before adding to the rest.)

**2 ▲** For a savoury soufflé, make a thick white sauce. Beat in the yolks and the soufflé flavouring. For a sweet soufflé, make a thick custard using the yolks; mix in the flavouring.

**3 ▲** In a large, scrupulously clean bowl, whisk the egg whites until they hold stiff peaks. (Any grease on the bowl or beaters will prevent maximum volume.) If not using a copper bowl, add a pinch of cream of tartar once the whites are frothy. For a sweet soufflé, add sugar once the whites hold soft peaks (the tips flop over), then continue whisking.

**4 ▲** Add one-quarter of the egg whites to the sauce base. Using a large metal spoon or a rubber spatula, stir the whites in to lighten the base. Add the remaining whites and fold them in as lightly as possible by cutting down with the spatula to the bottom of the bowl and then turning the mixture over on itself.

**5 ▲** Spoon the mixture into the prepared dish. Bake in a preheated oven until the soufflé has risen about 2 in (5 cm) above the rim of the dish and is lightly browned. Serve the soufflé immediately because it will only hold its puff out of the oven for a few minutes before it begins to deflate.

## Separating eggs

It is easier to separate the yolks and whites if eggs are cold, so take the eggs straight from the refrigerator. Tap the egg once or twice against the rim of a small bowl to crack the shell. Break open the shell and hold half in each hand. Carefully transfer the unbroken yolk from one half shell to the other several times, letting the egg white dribble into the bowl. Put the yolk in a second bowl.

## Cheese Soufflé

Butter a 2½ pint (1.5 litre) soufflé dish and coat it with fine breadcrumbs. Make ½ pint (300 ml) thick white sauce (page 170). Add 4 egg yolks and 4 oz (115 g) grated cheese (Gruyère, Cheddar, blue, or a mixture of Parmesan and Gruyère). If you like, season with 2 teaspoons Dijon mustard. Whisk 6 egg whites until stiff; fold into the sauce base. Bake in a 400°F/200°C/Gas 6 oven for 20–25 minutes. *Serves 4.*

# Amaretto Soufflé

**SERVES 6**

6 amaretti biscuits, coarsely crushed

6 tablespoons Amaretto liqueur

4 eggs, separated, plus 1 egg white

7 tablespoons caster sugar

2 tablespoons plain flour

8 fl oz (240 ml) milk

pinch of cream of tartar (if needed)

icing sugar, for decorating

1 Preheat a 400°F/200°C/Gas 6 oven. Butter a 2½ pint (1.5 litre) soufflé dish and sprinkle it with caster sugar.

2 Put the biscuits in a bowl. Sprinkle them with 2 tablespoons of the Amaretto liqueur and set aside.

3 ▲ Mix together the 4 egg yolks, 2 tablespoons of the sugar and flour.

4 ▲ Heat the milk just to the boil in a heavy saucepan. Gradually add the hot milk to the egg mixture, stirring.

5 Pour the mixture back into the pan. Set over moderately low heat and simmer gently for 3–4 minutes or until thickened, stirring constantly.

6 ▲ Add the remaining Amaretto liqueur. Remove from the heat.

7 In a scrupulously clean, grease-free bowl, whisk the 5 egg whites until they will hold soft peaks. (If not using a copper bowl, add the cream of tartar as soon as the whites are frothy.) Add the remaining sugar and continue whisking until stiff.

8 Add about one-quarter of the whites to the liqueur mixture and stir in with a rubber spatula. Add the remaining whites and fold in gently.

9 Spoon half of the mixture into the prepared soufflé dish. Cover with a layer of the moistened amaretti biscuits, then spoon the remaining soufflé mixture on top.

10 Bake for 20 minutes or until the soufflé is risen and lightly browned. Sprinkle with sifted icing sugar and serve immediately.

> ### ~ COOK'S TIP ~
>
> Some people like soufflés to be completely cooked. Others prefer a soft, creamy centre. The choice is up to you. To check how cooked the middle is, insert a thin skewer into the centre: it will come out almost clean or with moist particles clinging to it.

# MAKING SIMPLE MERINGUE

There are two types of this egg white and sugar foam: a soft meringue used as an insulating topping for pies and baked Alaska and a firm meringue that can be shaped into containers for luscious fillings.

Take care when separating the egg whites and yolks because even the smallest trace of yolk will prevent the whites from being whisked to their maximum volume. All equipment must be scrupulously clean and free of grease.

1 ▲ Put the egg whites in a large, scrupulously clean and grease-free bowl. With a whisk or electric mixer, whisk the whites until they are foamy. If not using a copper bowl, add a pinch of cream of tartar.

2 ▲ Continue whisking until the whites hold soft peaks when you lift the whisk or beaters (the tips of the peaks will flop over).

**Meringue Nests**
Make a firm meringue using 2 egg whites and 4oz (115g) caster sugar. Scoop large spoonfuls of meringue on to a baking sheet lined with baking parchment. Slightly hollow out the centre of each with the back of the spoon, to make a nest shape. Alternatively, put the meringue into a piping bag fitted with a ½in (1.5cm) plain nozzle and pipe the nest shapes. Sprinkle lightly with a little extra sugar. Dry in a 200°F/100°C/Gas low oven for 3–4 hours or until crisp and firm but not brown. Leave to cool. To serve, fill with sweetened whipped cream and fresh fruit. *Makes 4–6.*

3 ▲ **For a soft meringue:** Sprinkle the sugar over the whites, whisking constantly. Continue whisking for about 1 minute or until the meringue is glossy and holds stiff peaks when you lift the whisk or beaters. The meringue is now ready to be spread on a pie filling or used for baked Alaska.

**Sweetened whipped cream**
This is used as a topping and filling for many hot and cold desserts. Whip ½pint (300ml) chilled whipping or double cream until it starts to thicken. Add 2 tablespoons sifted icing sugar and continue whipping until the cream holds a soft peak on the beaters. If liked, the cream may be flavoured with ½ teaspoon vanilla or almond essence or 2 teaspoons brandy or liqueur, added with the sugar.

4 ▲ **For a firm meringue:** Add a little of the sugar (about 1½ teaspoons for each egg white). Continue whisking until the meringue is glossy and will hold stiff peaks.

5 ▲ Add the remaining sugar to the bowl, with any flavouring the recipe specifies. With a rubber spatula, fold the sugar into the meringue as lightly as possible by cutting down with the spatula to the bottom of the bowl and then turning the mixture over. The meringue is now ready to be shaped into containers or gâteau layers.

# Lemon Meringue Pie

**SERVES 6–8**

| |
|---|
| 9 in (23 cm) pastry case, made from shortcrust pastry (page 222) or French flan pastry (page 230), baked blind (page 232) |
| 10 oz (300 g) caster sugar |
| 1 oz (30 g) cornflour |
| pinch of salt |
| 2 teaspoons finely grated lemon zest |
| 4 fl oz (120 ml) fresh lemon juice |
| 8 fl oz (240 ml) water |
| 3 eggs, separated |
| 1½ oz (45 g) butter |
| pinch of cream of tartar (if needed) |

**1 ▼** Combine 7 oz (200 g) sugar, the cornflour, salt and lemon zest in a saucepan. Stir in the lemon juice and water until smoothly blended.

### ~ COOK'S TIP ~

Egg whites can be whisked to their greatest volume if they are at room temperature rather than cold. A copper bowl and wire balloon whisk are the best tools to use, although a stainless steel bowl and electric mixer produce very good results. Take care not to over-whisk whites (they will start to look grainy and then will separate into lumps and liquid). Using a copper bowl helps produce a stable foam that is hard to over-whisk; adding a pinch of cream of tartar has the same effect.

**2** Bring to the boil over moderately high heat, stirring constantly. Simmer for 1 minute or until thickened.

**3** Blend in the egg yolks. Cook over low heat for a further 2 minutes, stirring constantly.

**4** Remove from the heat. Add the butter and mix well.

**5 ▲** Pour the lemon filling into the pastry case. Spread it evenly and level the surface. Leave to cool completely.

**6** Preheat a 350°F/180°C/Gas 4 oven.

**7** In a scrupulously clean, grease-free bowl, whisk the egg whites until they will hold soft peaks. (If not using a copper bowl, add the cream of tartar as soon as the whites are frothy.) Add the remaining sugar and continue whisking until stiff and glossy.

**8 ▲** Spread the meringue evenly over the filling. Take care to seal it to the edges of the pastry case all round.

**9** Bake for 10–15 minutes or until the meringue is just set and lightly golden brown on the surface. Leave to cool before serving.

# MAKING A BATTER

Batters consist mainly of flour, eggs and liquid. They may be thick – for making fritters or coating food to be fried – or thin and pourable, for Yorkshire pudding, or other batter puddings, and pancakes. For a very light result, the eggs can be separated and the whites whisked and folded in.

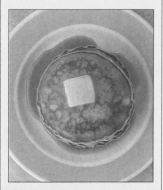

**Perfect Pancakes**
Make the batter with 6oz (170g) plain flour, 3 tablespoons sugar, 2 teaspoons baking powder, ½ teaspoon salt, 2 eggs, ½pint (300ml) milk, and 3 tablespoons melted butter. Heat a lightly oiled frying pan or griddle over a medium heat. Pour the batter on to the hot surface, using 3—4 tablespoons for each pancake; keep them well spaced. Cook until half of the bubbles on the surface have popped and the edges of the pancakes are dry. Turn the pancakes over and cook for about 1 minute until the other side is golden brown. Serve the pancakes hot, with butter and maple syrup, or a syrup of your choice. *Serves 4—6.*

**1 ▲** Sift the flour into a bowl along with other dry ingredients such as sugar, baking powder or bicarbonate of soda, salt, ground spices etc.

**3 ▲** With a wooden spoon, beat together the eggs and liquid in the well just to mix them.

**5 ▲** When the mixture is smooth, stir in the remaining liquid. Stir just until the ingredients are combined – the trick is not to overmix.

**2 ▲** Make a well in the centre of the dry ingredients and put in the eggs or egg yolks and some of the liquid.

**4 ▲** Gradually draw in some of the flour from the sides, stirring vigorously.

**6 ▲** If the recipe specifies, whisk egg whites to a soft peak and fold them into the batter (made with yolks). Do this just before using the batter.

# MAKING PANCAKES

Thin, lacy pancakes, or crêpes, are wonderfully versatile. They can be served very simply with just lemon juice and sugar, or turned into more elaborate dishes: folded and warmed in a sauce, rolled round a savoury or sweet filling, or stacked in layers with a filling.

### MAKES ABOUT 12

6 oz (170 g) plain flour

2 teaspoons caster sugar (for sweet pancakes)

2 eggs

¾ pint (450 ml) milk

about 1 oz (30 g) melted butter

### Ricotta and Peach Pancakes
Combine 1 lb (450 g) ricotta cheese, 1 oz (30 g) icing sugar, 1 teaspoon vanilla essence and 2 tablespoons brandy in a bowl. Mix well. Add 4 large ripe peaches, peeled and diced, and fold in gently. Divide the ricotta and peach mixture among 12 pancakes and spread it evenly over them. Fold each pancake in half and then in half again, into quarters. Arrange the pancakes in a buttered large oval baking dish, slightly overlapping them. Brush with 1 oz (30 g) melted butter and sprinkle generously with icing sugar. Bake in a 375°F/190°C/Gas 5 oven for 10 minutes. Serve hot, with a berry sauce (page 194) if you wish. *Serves 6.*

**1 ▲** Make the pancake batter and leave to stand for 20 minutes. Heat an 8 in (20 cm) pancake pan over moderate heat. The pan is ready when a few drops of water sprinkled on the surface jump and sizzle immediately. Grease the pan lightly with a little melted butter. Pour 3–4 tablespoons batter into the pan. Quickly tilt and rotate the pan so the batter spreads out to cover the bottom thinly and evenly; pour out any excess batter.

**3 ▲ To fill pancakes:** For folded pancakes, spread 3–4 tablespoons of filling evenly over each pancake. Fold in half then in half again, into quarters. For rolled pancakes, put 3–4 tablespoons of filling near one edge of each pancake and roll up tightly from that side. For pancake parcels, spoon 3–4 tablespoons of filling in the centre of each pancake. Fold in two opposite sides, over the filling, then fold in the other two sides. Turn the parcel over for serving. Filled pancakes are usually baked before serving, to reheat them.

**2 ▲** Cook for 30–45 seconds or until the pancake is set and small holes have appeared. If the cooking seems to be taking too long, increase the heat slightly. Lift the edge of the pancake with a palette knife; the base of the pancake should be lightly brown. Shake the pan vigorously back and forth to loosen the pancake completely, then turn or flip it over. Cook the other side for about 30 seconds. Serve or leave to cool.

**Pancake-making tips**
• Pancake batter should be the consistency of whipping cream. If the batter is at all lumpy, strain it. If it doesn't flow smoothly to make a thin pancake, add a little more liquid.
• Like most batters, pancake batter can be made in a blender or food processor. It must have time to stand before using, as more air is incorporated by this method.
• Your first pancake may well be unsuccessful because it will test the consistency of the batter and the temperature of the pan, both of which may need adjusting.
• If more convenient, pancakes can be made ahead of time. Cool, then stack them, interleaved with greaseproof, and wrap in foil. They can be refrigerated for up to 3 days or frozen for 1 month.
• A pancake pan has a flat bottom and sides that rise straight out of it without curving; these give the pancake a well-defined edge.

# MAKING CUSTARD

A home-made custard is a luscious sauce for many hot and cold puddings. It is also the basis for a very rich ice cream, which is essentially a frozen custard enriched with cream.

The secret for success is patience. Don't try to hurry the cooking of the custard by raising the heat.

**MAKES ABOUT ¾ PINT (450 ML)**

| |
|---|
| ¾ pint (450 ml) milk |
| 1 vanilla pod, split in half |
| 4 egg yolks |
| 3–4 tablespoons caster sugar, to sprinkle |

**1 ▲** Put the milk in a heavy-based saucepan. Hold the vanilla pod over the pan and scrape out the tiny black seeds into the milk. Add the split pod to the milk.

**2 ▲** Heat the milk until bubbles appear round the edge. Remove from the heat, cover and set aside to infuse for 10 minutes. Remove the split vanilla pod.

**Custard variations**
- Use 1 teaspoon vanilla essence instead of the vanilla pod. Omit steps 1 and 2, and add the essence after straining the custard.
- For *Chocolate Custard*: Add 2 oz (55 g) plain chocolate, grated, to the hot milk and sugar mixture. Stir until smooth before adding to the egg yolks.
- For *Mocha Custard*: Add 2 oz (55 g) plain chocolate, grated, and 2 teaspoons instant coffee powder or granules.
- For *Orange Custard*: Omit the vanilla pod and instead infuse the milk with the finely pared zest of 1 orange.
- For *Liqueur Custard*: Add 2–3 tablespoons brandy, kirsch or other liqueur to the custard.

**3 ▲** In a bowl, lightly beat the egg yolks with the sugar until smoothly blended and creamy. Gradually add the hot milk to the egg yolks, stirring constantly.

**4 ▲** Pour the mixture into the top of a double saucepan (or a bowl). Set over the bottom pan containing hot water. Put on a moderately low heat, so the water stays below the boil.

**Damage repair**
If the custard gets too hot and starts to curdle, remove it from the heat immediately and pour it into a bowl. Whisk vigorously for 2–3 seconds or until smooth. Then pour it back into the pan and continue cooking.

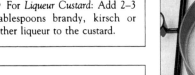

**5 ▲** Cook, stirring constantly, for 10–12 minutes or until the custard thickens to a creamy consistency that coats the spoon. Immediately remove the pan of custard from over the pan of hot water.

**6 ▲** Strain the custard into a bowl. If using cold, sprinkle a little caster sugar over the surface of the custard to help prevent a skin from forming. Set the bowl in a container of iced water and leave to cool.

# Sherry Trifle

**SERVES 6 OR MORE**

6 oz (170 g) trifle sponges, or 1 in (2.5 cm) cubes of plain Victoria sponge or coarsely crumbled sponge fingers

4 tablespoons medium sherry

4 oz (115 g) raspberry jam

10 oz (300 g) raspberries

¾ pint (450 ml) custard, flavoured with 2 tablespoons medium or sweet sherry

½ pint (300 ml) sweetened whipped cream (page 160)

toasted flaked almonds and mint leaves, to decorate

**1** Spread half of the sponges, cake cubes or sponge fingers over the bottom of a large serving bowl. (A glass bowl is best for presentation.)

**2** ▲ Sprinkle half of the sherry over the cake to moisten it. Spoon over half of the jam, dotting it evenly over the cake cubes.

**3** ▲ Reserve a few raspberries for decoration. Make a layer of half of the remaining raspberries on top.

**4** ▼ Pour over half of the custard, covering the fruit and cake. Repeat the layers. Cover and chill for at least 2 hours.

~ **VARIATIONS** ~

Use other ripe fruit in the trifle, with jam and liqueur to suit: apricots, peaches, nectarines, strawberries, etc.

**5** ▲ Before serving, spoon the sweetened whipped cream evenly over the top. To decorate, sprinkle with toasted flaked almonds and arrange the reserved raspberries and the mint leaves on the top.

# COOKING IN A BAIN-MARIE

Setting a dish in a pan of water for cooking ensures that delicate mixtures such as baked egg custards do not overheat and curdle. The pan of water, called a 'bain-marie', can be used on top of the stove or in the oven.

A double saucepan is a type of bain-marie, where the mixture for cooking is set over hot water rather than in it.

Sometimes a pan of iced water is used to protect fragile foods during cooking, such as with crème brûlée.

1 ◀ Set the dish or dishes in a roasting tin or in a wide shallow saucepan. Pour enough water into the tin to come halfway up the sides of the dish or dishes. Set the tin over moderately high heat and bring the water almost to the boil. Reduce the heat so the water is just simmering, or not moving at all, according to recipe instructions. Or transfer the dish or dishes, in the bain-marie, to the oven to finish cooking.

# Crème Brûlée Pralinée

**SERVES 6**

¾ pint (450 ml) double cream

4 egg yolks

4 oz (115 g) caster sugar

1 teaspoon vanilla essence

1 oz (30 g) pecan nuts or walnuts, finely chopped

1  Preheat a 300°F/150°C/Gas 2 oven.

2  Heat the cream in a saucepan until bubbles form round the edge.

3  Meanwhile, whisk the egg yolks with half of the sugar until the mixture is pale and creamy. Gradually stir the hot cream into the egg yolk mixture. Stir in the vanilla.

4  Strain the mixture into a jug. Pour it into 6 ramekins. Set the ramekins in a bain-marie and bring the water to the boil on top of the stove.

5  Transfer to the oven and bake for 20–25 minutes or until the custards are just set. Remove from the bain-marie and cool. Cover and chill.

6  Preheat the grill.

7  Mix together the remaining sugar and the nuts. Sprinkle over the tops of the custards in an even layer.

8 ▲ Set the ramekins in a baking tin containing iced water. Grill, about 5 in (12.5 cm) from the heat, until the sugar has melted and caramelized. Turn the ramekins for even browning. Leave to cool and set before serving.

# Making Ice Cream

At its most basic, home-made ice cream is just frozen cream, sweetened and flavoured. More often it has a custard base enriched with cream. Flavourings range from ever-popular vanilla and chocolate to fresh fruit and liqueur.

An electric ice cream machine makes light work of the arduous task of churning and freezing ice cream. Models and capacities vary, so follow manufacturer's instructions.

1 Make an egg custard, using cream or a mixture of milk and cream. For ice cream, the custard should be quite sweet. Strain and leave to cool.

2 ▶ Pour into an ice cream machine and freeze following the manufacturer's instructions. Serve as soon as possible after making. If the ice cream is left in the freezer and becomes very hard, let it soften for 20 minutes at room temperature before serving.

# Old-fashioned Chocolate Ice Cream

**Makes about 1²⁄₃ pints (1 litre)**

| 1¼ pints (750 ml) whipping cream |
| 8 fl oz (250 ml) milk |
| 1 vanilla pod, split in half |
| 5 oz (145 g) caster sugar, plus ½ teaspoon to sprinkle |
| 4 oz (115 g) plain chocolate, grated |
| 4 egg yolks |

1 Put 8 fl oz (240 ml) cream and the milk in a heavy-based saucepan with the vanilla pod. Heat until bubbles appear round the edge.

2 ▲ Add 5 oz (145 g) of the sugar and the chocolate. Heat almost to boiling point, stirring until the chocolate is melted and smooth.

3 In a bowl, lightly beat the egg yolks until smooth. Add the hot mixture to the egg yolks, stirring constantly.

4 Pour into the top of a double saucepan set over hot water. Cook, stirring, until the custard thickens enough to coat the spoon. Strain into a bowl. Stir in the remaining cream and sprinkle with the remaining sugar. Cool to room temperature.

5 Transfer to an ice cream machine and freeze.

**Ice cream variations**
- For *Vanilla Ice Cream*: Omit the chocolate.
- For *Strawberry Ice Cream*: Omit the chocolate. Mash 1 lb 2 oz (500 g) strawberries with a little lemon juice and 1 oz (30 g) sugar. Add to custard before freezing.
- For *Peach Ice Cream*: Omit the chocolate. Mash 6 large ripe peaches, peeled and stoned. Add to custard before freezing.

# SAUCES

~

A sauce can make plain food memorable, and most sauces are
quick and easy. A simple flavoured butter gives fish a lift. Or
vary a basic white sauce with cheese, mushrooms, or herbs,
and it becomes the basis for a casserole or vegetable bake.

# MAKING WHITE SAUCE

Some modern chefs consider flour-thickened sauces old-fashioned and replace them with butter sauces, vegetable purées or reduced cream. But a basic white sauce is an essential ingredient in many dishes, and lends itself to an endless variety of flavourings. This recipe makes a medium-thick sauce to coat food.

MAKES ABOUT 1 PINT (600 ML)

1½ oz (45 g) butter

1½ oz (45 g) plain flour

1 pint (600 ml) milk

good pinch of grated nutmeg

salt and pepper

**1** ▲ Melt the butter in a heavy saucepan over low heat. Remove the pan from the heat and stir in the flour to make a smooth, soft paste (called a 'roux' in French).

**2** ▲ Add about one-quarter of the milk and mix it in well with a whisk. When it is smooth, mix in the remaining milk.

### Sauce-making tips

• A whisk will blend the mixture more thoroughly than a spoon and will help avoid lumps. In the event of a lumpy sauce, push it through a fine-mesh sieve into a clean pan and then reheat it, whisking constantly.

• White sauces can be made ahead of time. Pour the sauce into a bowl or other container, dab the surface with butter and cool. Cover and refrigerate for up to 2 days. Before serving, whisk over moderate heat until boiling.

**3** ▲ Set the pan over moderately high heat and bring to the boil, whisking constantly.

**4** ▲ When the sauce bubbles and starts to thicken, reduce the heat to very low and simmer the sauce gently for 5–10 minutes, whisking well from time to time. Add the grated nutmeg and season the sauce to taste with salt and pepper. Serve the sauce hot.

### White sauce variations

• For *Thin White Sauce* to serve with meat or to use as a base for cream soups: Use 1 oz (30 g) each butter and flour.

• For *Thick White Sauce* to use as a soufflé base or to bind croquettes: Use 2 oz (55 g) each butter and flour.

• For *Blond Sauce*: Add the flour to the melted butter and cook, stirring constantly, for 1–2 minutes or until the roux is a pale beige colour. Heat the liquid and add it, off the heat. Bring to the boil, whisking, and simmer for 3–5 minutes.

• For *Velouté Sauce*: Cook the roux as for a blond sauce for 3 minutes or until it is lightly browned and smells nutty. Use hot chicken or fish stock, or a mixture of stock and wine, instead of milk.

• For *Béchamel Sauce*: Heat the milk with a slice of onion, 1 bay leaf and a few black peppercorns. Remove from the heat, cover and infuse for 20 minutes. Strain before adding to the roux, made as for a blond sauce.

• For *Cream Sauce*: Substitute cream for some of the milk.

• For *Cheese Sauce*: Stir 4–8 oz (115–225 g) grated cheese and 1–2 teaspoons spicy brown mustard into white, blond or béchamel sauce; add a pinch of cayenne pepper instead of nutmeg. Use a flavourful cheese that melts easily.

• For *Mustard Sauce*: Stir 1 tablespoon Dijon mustard and ½ teaspoon sugar into white, blond or béchamel sauce.

• For *Mushroom Sauce*: Cook 8 oz (225 g) sliced mushrooms in ½–1 oz (15–30 g) butter until soft; continue cooking until excess liquid has evaporated. Add to white, blond, béchamel, velouté or cream sauce.

# Moussaka

**Serves 4–6**

| |
|---|
| 2 aubergines, weighing about 1½ lb (700 g), trimmed and sliced across |
| about ¼ pint (150 ml) olive oil |
| 1 large onion, chopped |
| 1–2 garlic cloves, finely chopped |
| 1½ lb (700 g) minced lean lamb |
| 8 oz (225 g) tomatoes, skinned, seeded and chopped or canned chopped tomatoes |
| 2 tablespoons chopped fresh parsley |
| 1 tablespoon chopped fresh marjoram or 1 teaspoon dried oregano |
| ½ teaspoon ground cinnamon |
| 2 tablespoons tomato purée |
| salt and pepper |
| 1 pint (600 ml) hot white or blond sauce |
| 1 egg yolk |

**1** Preheat the grill.

**2** ▲ Spread out the aubergine slices on a large baking sheet and brush them with a little oil. Grill until lightly browned and beginning to soften. Turn the aubergine slices over and brush the other side with oil. Grill until lightly browned and soft.

~ **VARIATION** ~

Use left-over roast lamb or beef, finely chopped, instead of fresh minced lamb.

**3** Meanwhile, heat 2 tablespoons oil in a frying pan and cook the onion, stirring occasionally, until soft.

**4** ▲ Add the garlic and lamb and cook until the meat is browned and crumbly, stirring frequently. Stir in the tomatoes. Bring the mixture to the boil and simmer until the excess liquid has evaporated.

**5** Add the herbs, cinnamon and tomato purée. Season to taste with salt and pepper.

**6** Preheat a 375°F/190°C/Gas 5 oven.

**7** Layer the lamb mixture and aubergine slices in a baking dish, starting with meat and ending with aubergine.

**8** ▼ Mix together the sauce and egg yolk. Pour over the top layer of aubergine slices in an even layer.

**9** Bake for 30 minutes or until the sauce is golden and the moussaka is bubbling. Serve hot, in the baking dish.

# MAKING TOMATO SAUCE

Tomato sauce is a useful standby to have on hand in the refrigerator or freezer. When tomatoes are in season make a large batch. At other times of the year, use canned whole Italian plum tomatoes (drain, cut in half, scrape out seeds and chop).

### MAKES ABOUT 1 PINT (600 ML)

| |
|---|
| 1 oz (30 g) butter |
| 2 lb (900 g) tomatoes, skinned, seeded and finely chopped |
| ¼–½ teaspoon sugar |
| salt and pepper |

**1 ▲** Melt the butter in a heavy-based saucepan over low heat. Add the tomatoes and stir to mix with the butter. Cover and cook for 5 minutes.

**2 ▲** Uncover and stir in the sugar. Partly cover the pan and simmer gently, stirring occasionally, for 30 minutes or until the tomatoes have softened and the sauce is thick.

**3 ▲** Season the sauce to taste with salt and pepper. Use immediately, or cool and then refrigerate or freeze.

### Eggs Baked in Tomato Sauce

For each serving, put 1½ tablespoons of tomato sauce in a lightly buttered ramekin. Break an egg into the ramekin and sprinkle with pepper to taste and 1 tablespoon of freshly grated Parmesan or Cheddar cheese. Put the ramekins in a roasting tin and add cold water to come halfway up the sides of the ramekins. Bring to the boil on top of the stove, then transfer to a 400°F/200°C/Gas 6 oven and bake for 5–7 minutes or until the eggs are set. Serve immediately.

### Tomato sauce variations

- For *Rich Tomato Sauce*: Stir another ½–1 oz (15–30 g) butter into the sauce before serving.
- For *Smooth Tomato Sauce*: Purée in a blender or food processor.
- For *Tomato-garlic Sauce*: Use 1 tablespoon olive oil instead of butter. In a separate small pan, cook 1–2 finely chopped garlic cloves in 1 tablespoon olive oil for 1 minute. Add the garlic to the tomato sauce for the last 5 minutes of cooking.
- For *Tomato-herb Sauce*: Stir in ½–1 oz (15–30 g) chopped fresh herbs (parsley, basil, chives, thyme, oregano, marjoram – singly or a mixture of 2 or 3 at most) before serving.
- For *Italian Tomato Sauce*: Finely chop 1 onion, 1 small carrot and 1 celery stalk. Cook in 2 tablespoons olive oil until soft. Add 1–2 finely chopped garlic cloves and cook for a further 1 minute. Add the tomatoes with 1 bay leaf and 1 large sprig of fresh rosemary or ½ teaspoon crumbled dried rosemary. Continue cooking as for tomato sauce. Discard the herbs before serving.
- For *Tomato-wine Sauce*: Finely chop 3 shallots or ½ onion and cook in 1 oz (30 g) butter or 2 tablespoons olive oil until soft. Add 1 finely chopped garlic clove and cook for a further 1 minute. Stir in 4 fl oz (120 ml) dry white wine, bring to the boil and boil until almost completely evaporated. Add the tomatoes and continue cooking as for tomato sauce. For a smooth sauce, purée in a blender or food processor.
- For *Tomato-mushroom Sauce*: Fry 8 oz (225 g) sliced mushrooms in the butter until lightly browned. Add the tomatoes and cook as for tomato sauce.

# Pasta with Tomato Sauce and Roasted Vegetables

SERVES 4

1 aubergine

2 courgettes

1 large onion

2 peppers, preferably red or yellow, seeded

1 lb (450 g) tomatoes, preferably plum-type

2–3 garlic cloves, coarsely chopped

4 tablespoons olive oil

salt and pepper

½ pint (300 ml) smooth tomato sauce

2 oz (55 g) black olives, stoned and halved

¾–1 lb (340–450 g) dried pasta shapes such as rigatoni or penne

½ oz (15 g) fresh basil, shredded

1 Preheat a 475°F/240°C/Gas 9 oven.

2 ▲ Cut the aubergine, courgettes, onion, peppers and tomatoes into 1–1½ in (2.5–4 cm) chunks. Discard the tomato seeds.

3 ▲ Spread out the vegetables in a large roasting tin. Sprinkle the garlic and oil over the vegetables and stir and turn to mix evenly. Season with salt and pepper.

4 Roast the vegetables for 30 minutes or until they are soft and browned (don't worry if the edges are charred black). Stir halfway through.

5 ▼ Scrape the vegetable mixture into a saucepan. Add the tomato sauce and olives.

6 Bring a large pot of water to the boil. Add the pasta and cook until it is just tender to the bite ('al dente').

7 Meanwhile, heat the tomato and roasted vegetable sauce. Taste and adjust the seasoning.

8 Drain the pasta and return it to the pot. Add the tomato and roasted vegetable sauce and stir to mix well. Serve hot, sprinkled with the basil. If liked, serve with freshly grated Parmesan or pecorino cheese.

# MAKING FLAVOURED BUTTERS

A pat of flavoured butter melting over hot, freshly cooked vegetables, meat or seafood is an impressive finishing touch. Yet flavoured butters are so easy to make. They can be used as a spread for sandwiches or canapés, too. In addition to savoury flavoured butters, you can make sweet ones to serve with warm breads and rolls, teacakes and waffles.

**MAKES ABOUT 4 OZ (115 G)**

4 oz (115 g) butter, preferably unsalted, at room temperature

chosen flavouring (see Butter flavourings)

salt and pepper (for savoury butters)

**Butter flavourings**
- For *Herb Butter*: Use 2–4 tablespoons chopped fresh herbs (parsley, chives, tarragon, mint and so on) and a squeeze of lemon juice.
- For *Mustard Butter*: Use 1 tablespoon Dijon mustard or spicy brown mustard.
- For *Citrus Butter*: Use 2 teaspoons orange or lime juice or 1 teaspoon lemon juice and the grated zest of 1 orange, lime or lemon.
- For *Coriander-lime Butter*: Finely chop 1 oz (30 g) fresh coriander leaves. Mix into the soft butter with the grated zest and juice of 1 lime.
- For *Parsley and Lemon Butter* ('beurre maître d'hôtel'): Use 2 tablespoons chopped parsley and 1 tablespoon lemon juice.
- For *Tomato Butter*: Use 1 tablespoon tomato purée.
- For *Garlic Butter*: Use 1–2 chopped and crushed garlic cloves.
- For *Sweet Orange Butter*: Use 1–2 tablespoons icing sugar, 2 teaspoons orange juice, and the grated zest of 1 orange.
- For *Honey Butter*: Use 3 oz (85 g) honey; beat in gradually.
- For *Maple Butter*: Use 4 tablespoons maple syrup; beat in gradually.
- For *Cinnamon Butter*: Use 1–2 tablespoons icing sugar and ½ teaspoon ground cinnamon.
- For *Almond Butter*: Use 4 tablespoons finely ground almonds.

**1** ▲ **For a savoury butter:** Put the butter in a mixing bowl and beat with a wooden spoon or electric mixer until soft. Add the flavouring. Season savoury butter to taste with salt and pepper. Blend well.

**2** ▲ Transfer the butter to a piece of greaseproof paper and shape it into a neat roll, handling it as little as possible because the heat of your hands can melt it. Wrap and refrigerate until firm. Cut into discs.

**3** ▲ Alternatively, flatten with the back of a spoon or knife until it is about ¼ in (5 mm) thick. Refrigerate until firm, and stamp out small rounds or other shapes using a pastry cutter.

**4** ▲ **For a sweet butter:** Put the butter in a mixing bowl and beat with an electric mixer or wooden spoon until fluffy. Add the flavouring and blend well. Spoon into a serving bowl, cover and refrigerate until firm.

**Freezing flavoured butters**
Flavoured butters can be frozen and then used straight from the freezer. Overwrap the paper-wrapped roll in foil for storage.

# Fish Steaks with Coriander-lime Butter

**SERVES 4**

1½ lb (700 g) swordfish or tuna steak, 1 in (2.5 cm) thick, cut into 4 pieces

4 tablespoons vegetable oil

2 tablespoons lemon juice

1 tablespoon lime juice

salt and pepper

2 oz (55 g) coriander-lime butter

**1 ▲** Lay the fish steaks side by side in a shallow dish. Combine the oil, juices, salt and pepper and pour over the fish. Cover and refrigerate for 1–2 hours, turning the fish once or twice.

**2** Preheat the grill or prepare a charcoal fire in a barbecue.

**3 ▼** Drain the fish and arrange on the rack in the grill pan, or set over the hot charcoal about 5 in (12.5 cm) from the coals. Grill for 3–4 minutes or until just firm to the touch but still moist in the centre, turning the steaks over once.

~ **VARIATIONS** ~

For Salmon Steaks with Citrus Butter, lightly brush 4 salmon steaks, 1 in (2.5 cm) thick, with oil and season. Grill for 4–5 minutes on each side. Serve topped with pats of citrus butter. For Mackerel with Mustard Butter, brush 4 unskinned mackerel fillets, about 8 oz (225 g) each, with oil and season. Grill for 3–4 minutes on each side. Serve topped with pats of mustard butter.

**4 ▲** Transfer to warmed plates and top each fish steak with a pat of coriander-lime butter. Serve the fish immediately.

# MAKING CLARIFIED BUTTER

This is butter from which the milk solids have been removed. The result is a clear yellow fat that can be heated to a higher temperature than ordinary butter without burning. Thus clarified butter is an excellent fat for pan-frying. It is also used as a dip for seafood such as lobster and crab and for globe artichokes. Indian ghee is a type of clarified butter.

**MAKES ABOUT 6 OZ (170 G)**

8 oz (225 g) butter

---

**Keeping butter longer**
Since clarification removes impurities, clarified butter keeps well – several weeks in the refrigerator, longer in the freezer.

**1 ▲** Put the butter in a heavy saucepan over low heat. Melt gently. Skim off all the froth from the surface. You will then see a clear yellow layer on top of a milky layer.

**2** Carefully pour the clear fat into a bowl or jug, leaving the milky residue in the pan. Discard the milky residue, or add it to soups.

**Lobster Tail with Drawn Butter**
Drop 4 ½-lb (225-g) raw lobster tails (thawed if frozen) into a large pot of boiling salted water. Bring back to the boil. Simmer until the shells are bright red and the meat is opaque, about 8–12 minutes. Drain and serve hot, with clarified butter. *Serves 4.*

---

# Chicken Liver Pâté

**SERVES 6 OR MORE**

2 oz (55 g) butter

1 onion, finely chopped

12 oz (340 g) chicken livers, trimmed of all dark or greenish parts

4 tablespoons medium sherry

1 oz (30 g) full-fat soft cheese

1–2 tablespoons lemon juice

2 hard-boiled eggs, chopped

salt and pepper

2–3 oz (55–85 g) clarified butter

**1** Melt the butter in a frying pan. Add the onion and livers and cook until the onion is soft and the livers are lightly browned and no longer pink in the centre.

**2** Add the sherry and boil until reduced by half. Cool slightly.

**3 ▲** Turn the mixture into a food processor or blender and add the soft cheese and 1 tablespoon lemon juice. Blend until smooth.

**4** Add the hard-boiled eggs and blend briefly. Season with salt and pepper. Taste and add more lemon juice if liked.

**5 ▼** Pack the liver pâté into a mould or into individual ramekins. Smooth the surface.

**6** Spoon a layer of clarified butter over the surface of the pâté. Refrigerate until firm. Serve at room temperature, with hot toast or savoury biscuits.

# MAKING SIMPLE HOLLANDAISE SAUCE

This classic of French cuisine has a reputation for being difficult to make. It does require care: if the sauce becomes too hot, it will separate. However, a method proposed by Harold McGee of putting all the ingredients in the pan at once – rather than the traditional method of cooking the egg yolks to thicken them and then slowly beating in melted butter – lowers the chance of failure. Just take it slow and steady, and whisk constantly.

**MAKES ABOUT ½ PINT (300 ML)**

3 egg yolks

1 tablespoon lemon juice, plus more if needed

pinch of cayenne pepper

salt and pepper

8 oz (225 g) butter, preferably unsalted, cut into ½ oz (15 g) chunks

**1 ▲** Combine the egg yolks, lemon juice, cayenne, salt and pepper in a heavy saucepan. Whisk together until thoroughly blended.

**3 ▲** When all the butter has melted and has been blended into the egg yolk base, continue whisking until the sauce just thickens to a creamy consistency. Taste the sauce and add more lemon juice, salt and pepper if needed.

**2 ▲** Add the butter and set the pan over moderate heat. Whisk constantly so that as the butter melts it is blended into the egg yolks. Regulate the heat so it melts gradually.

---

**Sauce-making tips**

• If your sauce does separate into soft curds and clear butterfat, don't despair. As long as the egg yolks haven't scrambled, you can rescue the sauce. Remove the pan from the heat, add 1–2 teaspoons of water and whisk vigorously. If the sauce doesn't re-form and become creamy, put 1–2 teaspoons of water in a bowl and whisk in the separated sauce, drop by drop at first and then in a thin stream.

• Hollandaise and Béarnaise sauces can be kept warm for up to 30 minutes before serving. Set the saucepan in a bain-marie of hot water (page 166), or on a warming tray, and whisk the sauce occasionally. Alternatively, the sauce can be made 2–3 hours ahead and transferred to a wide-mouth vacuum flask to keep warm until serving time.

---

**The Hollandaise family**

• For *Mousseline Sauce*: let the sauce cool slightly, then whisk in 4 fl oz (120 ml) whipped cream.

• For *Béarnaise Sauce*: mix 5 tablespoons white wine vinegar, 2 chopped shallots, 1 tablespoon chopped fresh tarragon or 1 teaspoon dried tarragon and a little pepper in a small saucepan. Boil to reduce to about 1 tablespoon. Cool. Continue as for Hollandaise sauce, using the strained vinegar reduction in place of the lemon juice. Before serving, stir in another ½–1 tablespoon chopped fresh tarragon, if liked.

---

**Asparagus with Hollandaise Sauce**
Prepare 1½ lb (700 g) asparagus (page 120). Arrange the spears on a rack in a steamer over simmering water, cover and steam for 8–12 minutes, or simmer in a large frying pan with water just to cover for 4–5 minutes, until just tender when pierced with the tip of a knife. Transfer to warmed plates and spoon over the Hollandaise sauce. *Serves 4.*

# Eggs Benedict

**SERVES 6**

2–3 slices of ham

6 eggs

3 muffins, split in half

½ pint (300 ml) warm Hollandaise sauce

1  Preheat the grill.

2 ▲ Cut rounds from the ham about the same diameter as the muffin halves to fit neatly.

3 ▲ Arrange the ham slices on the rack in the grill pan. Grill until they are hot and golden brown.

4  Meanwhile, poach the eggs in barely simmering water for 3–4 minutes until done: the white just firm but the yolk still soft. Remove, drain and trim them if necessary. Toast the muffin halves.

5 ▼ Put a muffin half, cut side up, on each warmed plate. Arrange a slice of ham on the muffin and top with a poached egg.

6  Spoon the Hollandaise sauce over the egg and serve immediately.

~ VARIATIONS ~

If preferred, fry the ham in butter rather than grilling it. Use rashers of back bacon (1–2 per serving) instead of ham. Replace the ham with hot asparagus spears or sliced mushrooms sautéed in butter. If liked, use toasted rounds of brioche or wholemeal bread instead of muffins.

# MAKING MAYONNAISE

This cold emulsified sauce of oil and egg yolks has thousands of uses – as part of a dish or as an accompaniment, in sandwiches and in salad dressings. It can be varied by using different oils, vinegars and flavourings.

### MAKES ABOUT 12 FL OZ (360 ML)

2 egg yolks

salt and pepper

12 fl oz (360 ml) oil (vegetable, corn or olive)

1–2 tablespoons lemon juice or white wine vinegar

1–2 teaspoons Dijon mustard

**1 ▲** Put the egg yolks in a bowl and add a pinch of salt. Beat together well.

**2 ▲** Add the oil, 1–2 teaspoons at a time, beating constantly with a whisk or electric mixer.

**3 ▲** After one-quarter of the oil has been added very slowly and absorbed, beat in 1–2 teaspoons of the lemon juice or vinegar.

**4 ▲** Continue beating in the oil, in a thin, steady stream now. As the mayonnaise thickens, add another teaspoon of lemon juice or vinegar.

---

**Mayonnaise variations**
- For *Garlic Mayonnaise*: Crush 3–6 garlic cloves. Beat with the egg yolks and salt. Beat in oil (vegetable and/or olive) as above.
- For *Spicy Mayonnaise*: Increase mustard to 1 tablespoon and add ½–1 teaspoon Worcestershire sauce and a dash Tabasco sauce.
- For *Green Mayonnaise*: Combine 1 oz (30 g) each parsley sprigs and watercress sprigs in a blender or food processor. Add 3–4 chopped spring onions and 1 garlic clove. Blend until finely chopped. Add 4 fl oz (120 ml) mayonnaise and blend until smooth. Season.
- For *Blue Cheese Dressing*: Mix 8 oz (225 g) crumbled Danish blue cheese into the mayonnaise.

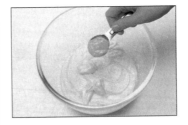

**5 ◄** When all the oil has been beaten in, add the mustard. Taste the mayonnaise and add more lemon juice or vinegar. Season with salt and pepper. If the mayonnaise is too thick, beat in a spoonful or two of water. Home-made mayonnaise will keep, covered in the refrigerator, for up to 1 week.

---

**Raw egg alert**
Eggs can harbour salmonella bacteria, so there is some risk of food poisoning if you eat raw eggs (as in home-made mayonnaise) or undercooked eggs (as in Hollandaise sauce). The elderly, infants, pregnant women and those who are ill are the most susceptible.

**Seafood Salad with Garlic Mayonnaise**
Make a bed of salad greens (green and red leaf lettuces, rocket, watercress, etc) on 4 individual plates or in large stemmed goblets. Arrange 6 oz (175 g) coarsely flaked white crabmeat and 8 oz (225 g) cooked peeled prawns on top. Spoon garlic mayonnaise over the seafood and sprinkle with a little paprika. *Serves 4.*

# Salmon Cakes with Spicy Mayonnaise

**SERVES 4**

2 boiling potatoes, about 12 oz (340 g), unpeeled

12 oz (340 g) salmon fillet, skinned and finely chopped

2–3 tablespoons chopped fresh dill

1 tablespoon lemon juice

salt and pepper

flour for coating

3 tablespoons vegetable oil

spicy mayonnaise, to serve

**1** Put the potatoes in a saucepan of boiling salted water and parboil them for 15 minutes.

**2** ▲ Meanwhile, combine the salmon, dill, lemon juice, salt and pepper in a large bowl.

**3** Drain the potatoes and leave them to cool. When they are cool enough to handle, peel them.

**4** Shred the potatoes into strips on the coarse side of a grater.

~ **COOK'S TIP** ~

The potatoes will be sticky – it is their starch that helps hold the cakes together. If necessary, you can dampen your hands a little when shaping the cakes, but do not get the cakes too wet.

**5** Add to the salmon mixture. Mix gently together with your fingers, breaking up the strips of potato as little as possible.

**6** ▼ Divide the salmon and potato mixture into 8 portions. Shape each into a compact cake, pressing well together. Flatten the cakes to about ⅜ in (1 cm) thickness.

**7** ▲ Coat the salmon cakes lightly with flour, shaking off excess.

**8** Heat the oil in a large frying pan. Add the salmon cakes and fry for 5 minutes or until crisp and golden brown on both sides.

**9** Drain the salmon cakes on paper towels, and serve with the spicy mayonnaise.

# MAKING VINAIGRETTE DRESSING

A good vinaigrette can do more than dress a salad. It can also be used to baste meat, poultry, seafood or vegetables during cooking; and it can be used as a flavouring and tenderizing marinade. The basic mixture of oil, vinegar and seasoning lends itself to many variations.

The basic vinaigrette dressing will keep in the refrigerator, in a tightly closed container, for several weeks. Add flavourings, particularly fresh herbs, just before using.

### A handy holder

If more convenient, you can make vinaigrette dressing in a screwtop jar. Combine all the ingredients in the jar, cover and shake well to mix and emulsify.

**MAKES JUST OVER 6 FL OZ (170 ML)**

3 tablespoons wine vinegar

salt and pepper

¼ pint (150 ml) vegetable oil

**1 ▲** Put the vinegar, salt and pepper in a bowl and whisk to dissolve the salt. Gradually add the oil, stirring with the whisk. Taste and adjust seasoning.

### Ideas for vinaigrette

• Use red or white wine vinegar. Or use a herb-flavoured vinegar.
• Use lemon juice instead of vinegar.
• Replace 1 tablespoon of the vinegar with wine.
• Use olive oil, or a mixture of vegetable and olive oils.
• Use 4 fl oz (120 ml) olive oil and 2 tablespoons walnut or hazelnut oil.
• Add 1–2 tablespoons Dijon mustard to the vinegar before whisking in the oil.
• Add 1 crushed garlic clove before whisking in the oil.
• Add 1–2 tablespoons chopped fresh herbs (parsley, basil, chives, thyme, etc) to the vinaigrette.

---

# Orange Chicken Salad

**SERVES 4**

3 large seedless oranges

6 oz (170 g) long-grain rice

16 fl oz (500 ml) water

salt and pepper

6 fl oz (170 ml) vinaigrette dressing, made with red wine vinegar and a mixture of olive and vegetable oils

2 teaspoons Dijon mustard

½ teaspoon caster sugar

1 lb (450 g) cooked chicken, diced

3 tablespoons scissor-snipped chives

2½ oz (75 g) toasted cashew nuts

cucumber slices, to garnish

**1** Thinly peel 1 orange, taking only the coloured part of the zest and leaving the white pith.

**2** Combine the orange zest, rice and water in a saucepan. Add a pinch of salt. Bring to the boil, then cover and steam over very low heat for 15–18 minutes or until the rice is tender and all the water has been absorbed.

**3 ▼** Peel all the oranges and cut out the segments, reserving the juice. Add the orange juice to the vinaigrette dressing. Add the mustard and sugar and whisk to combine well. Taste and add more salt and pepper if needed.

**4** When the rice is cooked, remove it from the heat and cool slightly, uncovered. Discard the orange zest.

**5** Turn the rice into a bowl and add half of the dressing. Toss well and cool completely.

**6 ▲** Add the chicken, chives, cashew nuts and orange segments to the rice with the remaining dressing. Toss gently. Serve at room temperature, garnished with cucumber.

# FRUIT, CHOCOLATE & NUTS

~

*Fruit, the focus of many desserts, and some savoury dishes as well, lends itself equally to homely or dramatic presentations. And chocolate, everyone's favourite indulgence, is easy to use – just follow a few simple rules. Nuts enhance them both.*

# PREPARING FRESH FRUIT

## PEELING AND TRIMMING FRUIT

### Citrus fruit

*To peel completely,* cut a slice from the top and from the base. Set the fruit base down on a work surface. Using a small sharp knife, cut off the peel lengthways in thick strips. Take the coloured zest and all the white pith (which has a bitter taste). Cut following the curve of the fruit.

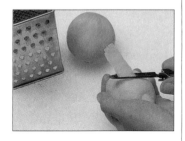

*To remove zest,* use a vegetable peeler to shave off the zest in wide strips, taking none of the white pith. Use these strips whole or cut them into fine shreds with a sharp knife, according to recipe directions. Or rub the fruit against the fine holes of a metal grater, turning the fruit so you take just the coloured zest and not the white pith. Or use a special tool, called a citrus zester, to take fine threads of zest. (Finely chop the threads as an alternative to grating.)

### Kiwi fruit

Follow citrus fruit technique, taking off the peel in thin lengthways strips.

### Apples, pears, quinces, mangoes, papayas

Use a small sharp knife or a vegetable peeler. Take off the peel in long strips, as thinly as possible.

### Peaches, apricots

Cut a cross in the base. Immerse the fruit in boiling water. Leave for 10–30 seconds (according to ripeness), then drain and immerse in iced water. The skin should slip off easily.

### Pineapple

Cut off the leafy crown. Cut a slice from the base and set the pineapple upright. With a sharp knife, cut off the peel lengthways, cutting thickly to remove the brown 'eyes' with it.

### Bananas, lychees, avocado

Make a small cut and remove the peel with your fingers.

### Passion fruit, pomegranates

Cut in half, or cut a slice off the top. With a spoon, scoop the flesh and seeds into a bowl.

### Star fruit (carambola)

Trim off the tough, darkened edges of the five segments.

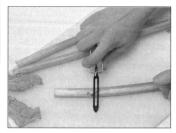

### Rhubarb

Cut off the leaves and discard them (they are poisonous). Peel off any tough skin.

***Fresh currants (red, black, white)***
Pull through the prongs of a fork to
remove the currants from the stalks.

***Fresh dates***
Squeeze gently at the stalk end to
remove the rather tough skin.

## CORING AND STONING OR
## SEEDING FRUIT

***Apples, pears, quinces***
For *whole fruit*, use an apple corer to
stamp out the whole core from stalk
end to base. Alternatively, working
up from the base, use a melon baller
to cut out the core. Leave the stalk
end intact.

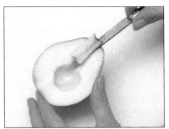

For *halves*, use a melon baller to scoop
out the core. Cut out the stalk and
base with a small sharp knife.
For *quarters*, cut out the stalk and core
with a serrated knife.

***Citrus fruit***
With the tip of a pointed knife, nick
out pips from slices or segments.

***Cherries***
Use a cherry stoner for the neatest
results.

***Peaches, apricots, nectarines, plums***
Cut the fruit in half, cutting round the
indentation. Twist the halves apart.
Lift out the stone, or lever it out with
the tip of a sharp knife.

***Fresh dates***
Cut the fruit lengthways in half and
lift out the stone. Or, if the fruit is to
be used whole, cut in from the stalk
end with a thin-bladed knife to loosen
the stone, then remove it.

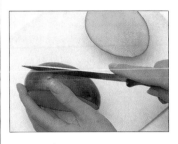

***Mangoes***
Cut lengthways on either side of the
large flat stone in the centre. Curve
the cut slightly to follow the shape of
the stone. Also cut the flesh from the
two thin ends of the stone.

***Papayas, melons***
Cut the fruit in half. Scoop out the
seeds from the central hollow, then
scrape away any fibres.

## Pineapple
*For spears and wedges*, cut out the core neatly with a sharp knife.
*For rings*, cut out the core with a small pastry cutter.

## Grapes
Cut the fruit lengthways in half. Use a small knife to nick out the pips. Alternatively, use the curved end of a sterilized hair grip.

## Gooseberries
Use scissors to trim off the stalk and flower ends.

## Star fruit (carambola), watermelon
With the tip of a pointed knife, nick out pips from slices.

## Strawberries
Use a special huller to remove leafy green top and central core. Or cut these out with a small sharp knife.

## Avocado
Cut the fruit in half lengthways. Stick the tip of a sharp knife into the stone and lever it out without damaging the surrounding flesh.

## CUTTING FRUIT

## Apples, quinces
*For rings*, remove the core and seeds with an apple corer. Set the fruit on its side and cut across into thick or thin rings, as required.

*For slices*, cut the fruit in half and remove core and seeds with a melon baller. Set one half cut side down and

cut it across into neat slices, thick or thin according to recipe directions. Or cut the fruit into quarters and remove core and seeds with a knife. Cut lengthways into neat slices.

## Pears
*For 'fans'*, cut the fruit in half and remove core and seeds with a melon baller. Set one half cut side down and cut lengthways into thin slices, not cutting all the way through at the stalk end. Gently fan out the slices so they are overlapping each other evenly. Transfer the pear fan to plate or pastry case using a palette knife.
*For slices*, follow apple technique.

### Keeping fresh colour
If exposed to the air for long, the cut flesh of some fruits and vegetables starts to turn brown. Those with a tendency to brown include apples, bananas, peaches and avocado. So if prepared fruit has to wait before being served or cooked, sprinkle the cut surfaces with lemon juice. Or you can immerse hard fruits in water and lemon juice, but do not soak or the fruit may become soggy.

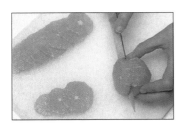

### Citrus fruit

*For slices,* using a serrated knife, cut the fruit across into neat slices.

*For segments,* hold the peeled fruit in your cupped palm, over a bowl to catch the juice. Working from the side of the fruit to the centre, slide the knife down one side of a separating membrane to free the flesh from it. Then slide the knife down the other side of that segment to free it from the membrane there. Drop the segment into the bowl. Continue cutting out the segments, folding back the membrane like the pages of a book as you work. When all the segments have been cut out, squeeze all the juice from the membrane.

### Bananas Baked with Rum

Quarter 4 bananas and put in a small baking dish. Sprinkle with a mixture of 2 oz (55 g) melted butter, 3 table-spoons soft light brown sugar, 1–2 tablespoons lemon juice and 6 table-spoons light rum or orange juice. Turn to coat. Bake at 400°F/200°C/Gas 6 for 20 minutes, basting occa-sionally. Serve with cream. *Serves 4.*

### Peaches, nectarines, apricots, plums

*For slices,* follow apple technique.

### Papayas, avocado

*For slices,* follow apple technique. Or cut the unpeeled fruit into wedges, removing the central seeds or stone. Set each wedge peel side down and slide the knife down the length to cut the flesh away from the peel.
*For fans,* follow pear technique.

### Melon

*For slices,* follow papaya technique.
*For balls,* use a melon baller.

### Mangoes

Cut the peeled flesh into slices or cubes, according to recipe directions.

### Pineapple

*For spears,* cut the peeled fruit lengthways in half and then into quarters. Cut each quarter into spears and cut out the core.
*For chunks,* cut the peeled fruit into spears. Remove the core. Cut across each spear into chunks.
*For rings,* cut the peeled fruit across into slices. Stamp out the central core from each slice using a pastry cutter.

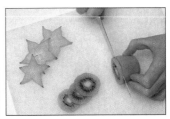

### Kiwi fruit, star fruit (carambola)

Cut the fruit across into neat slices; discard the ends.

### Banana

Cut the fruit across into neat slices. Or cut in half and then lengthways into quarters.

# PREPARING FRESH PINEAPPLE

Pineapple can be prepared in many decorative ways, apart from rings, spears and cubes.

**Tipsy Pineapple Boat**
Cut 2 small to medium-sized pineapples in half and scoop out the flesh. Cut the pineapple flesh into neat, small pieces. Put them back in the pineapple halves. Sprinkle each half with 1–2 table-spoons rum, kirsch, apricot brandy or Grand Marnier. If liked, sprinkle with a little sugar to taste. Toss the fruit to mix the liquor and sugar evenly. Cover tightly and chill for 20–30 minutes before serving. *Serves 4.*

**1 ▲ For a pineapple boat**: Trim off any browned ends from the green leaves of the crown. Trim the stalk end if necessary. With a long sharp knife, cut the pineapple lengthways in half, through the crown.

**2 ▲** Cut a thin slice from the base of each half so it has a flat surface and will not rock.

**3 ▲** With a small sharp knife, cut straight across the top and bottom of the central core in each half. Then cut lengthways at a slant on either side of the core. This will cut out the core in a V-shape.

**4 ▲** With a curved serrated grapefruit knife, cut out the flesh from each half. The boats are now ready for filling with a salad, a dessert, or with ice cream, fruit ice or sorbet.

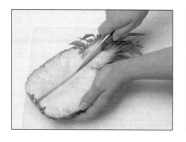

**5 ▲ For pineapple wedges**: Trim the crown and base as above. Cut the fruit lengthways in half, through the crown, and then into quarters.

**6 ▲** Cut the central core from each quarter. Slide the knife under the flesh to loosen it from the peel, but leave it in place.

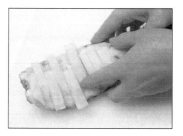

**7 ▲** Cut across the flesh on each wedge. Pull out the slices slightly in alternate directions. If desired, sprinkle the fruit lightly with sugar before serving.

# Peanut-chicken Salad in Pineapple Boats

**SERVES 4**

2 small ripe pineapples

8 oz (225 g) cooked chicken breast, cut into bite-size pieces

2 celery stalks, diced

2 oz (55 g) spring onions, white and green parts, chopped

8 oz (225 g) seedless green grapes

1½ oz (45 g) salted peanuts, coarsely chopped

FOR THE DRESSING

3 oz (85 g) smooth peanut butter

4 fl oz (120 ml) mayonnaise

2 tablespoons cream or milk

1 garlic clove, finely chopped

1 teaspoon mild curry powder

1 tablespoon apricot jam

salt and pepper

1  Make 4 pineapple boats from the pineapples. Cut the flesh removed from the boats into bite-size pieces.

2 ▲ Combine the pineapple flesh, chicken, celery, spring onions and grapes in a bowl.

~ **VARIATION** ~

For Mango-turkey Salad in Pineapple Boats, use cooked turkey breast meat instead of chicken and cubed mango flesh in place of grapes. Omit the peanuts.

3 ▼ Put all the dressing ingredients in another bowl and mix with a wooden spoon or whisk until evenly blended. Season with salt and pepper. (The dressing will be thick, but will be thinned by the juices from the pineapple.)

4 ▲ Add the dressing to the pineapple and chicken mixture. Fold together gently but thoroughly.

5  Divide the chicken salad among the pineapple boats. Sprinkle the peanuts over the top before serving.

# PREPARING MELON

Melons make attractive containers for salads, both sweet and savoury. Small melons can be used for individual servings, while large watermelons will hold salads to serve a crowd and provide a festive centrepiece at the same time!

Special tools, such as melon cutters with V- or U-shaped blades and melon ball scoops, make decorative preparation easier.

**1** ◀ **For a plain edge**: Cut the melon in half and scoop out the central seeds. Remove the flesh with a melon baller. Or cut it out with a grapefruit knife or scoop it out with a large spoon. Reserve the flesh for the salad. Continue scraping out the flesh, to leave only a thin layer.

**2** ▲ **For a zig-zag edge**: First cut a line around the circumference of the melon to ensure that your finished edge will be level. Using a sharp knife, insert it on the cut line at an angle. Continue making an angled cut about ½–2 in (1.5–5 cm) long, according to the size of the melon. Cut all the way into the centre of the melon. Remove the knife.

**3** ▲ Insert the knife at the top of the angled cut and cut back down to the line at a right angle to the first cut, forming a V. Continue cutting V-shapes in this way all round the melon. If available, a special melon cutter with a V-shaped blade will make the job easier.

**4** ▲ Lift the melon halves apart. Remove the seeds and scoop out the flesh as above.

**Watermelon Basket**
Cut a watermelon basket as directed above. Scoop out the flesh with a melon baller and nick out as many of the black pips as you can. Mix the melon balls with balls of charentais and honey-dew melon, blueberries and straw-berries. Pile the fruit in the watermelon basket for serving.

**Citrus garnishes**
The technique for preparing melons can also be used for lemons and oranges. These make attractive containers for cold and iced desserts. Another idea: cut a lemon in half with a zig-zag edge, but don't hollow out the halves. Instead, trim the base of each so it will sit flat, then dip the points of the edge in chopped parsley. Serve this instead of plain lemon wedges with fish.

**5** ▲ **For a scalloped edge**: You can do this freehand following the technique for cutting a zig-zag edge, but instead cutting curves. However, it is much easier, and the results are better, if you use a special melon cutter with a U-shaped blade.

**6 ▲ For a melon basket**: Cut a plain, zig-zag or scalloped edge, starting just off centre. Cut round the melon to a point opposite where you started.

**7 ▲** Cut up over the top of the melon and down to the point you began. Lift off the freed wedge of melon. Repeat on the other end.

**8 ▲** Cut out the flesh from under the 'handle'. Cut the flesh from the 'basket' as shown.

# Melon Salad with Herbs

**SERVES 4**

| 2 charentais melons |
| --- |
| ½ honeydew melon |
| ½ cucumber |
| 6 oz (170 g) small cherry tomatoes |
| 1½ tablespoons chopped fresh parsley |
| 1 tablespoon snipped fresh chives |
| 1 tablespoon chopped fresh mint |
| FOR THE DRESSING |
| 6 tablespoons vegetable oil |
| 2 tablespoons red wine vinegar |
| 1 teaspoon caster sugar |
| salt and pepper |

**1** Cut the charentais in half, with a plain, zig-zag or scalloped edge. Scoop out the seeds and central fibres. Using a melon baller, take small balls of flesh and put them in a bowl. Scrape most of the remaining flesh from the melon halves. Set the melon shells aside.

**2** Remove seeds and fibres from the honeydew melon. Scoop out the flesh in small balls and add to the charentais balls.

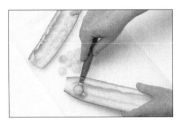

**3 ▲** Use the melon baller to make balls of cucumber, or cut into cubes.

**4** Add the cucumber to the melon balls with the cherry tomatoes.

**5** For the dressing, combine the ingredients in a screwtop jar and shake well. Add the dressing to the bowl and toss together. Cover and refrigerate the salad for 2–3 hours.

**6** Just before serving, stir in the herbs. Divide the salad among the melon shells, with all the juice.

# Making a Berry Sauce

A smooth, uncooked berry sauce, called a 'coulis' in French, has a refreshing flavour and beautiful colour. According to how much sugar you add, a berry sauce can be a sweet complement or tart contrast to a cake, pastry, ice cream or fruit dessert.

You can use fresh or frozen berries for the sauce. If using frozen berries, partially thaw them and drain on paper towels before puréeing.

**Makes about 8 fl oz (240 ml)**

1 lb (450 g) berries (raspberries, strawberries, blackberries, etc)

1–2 oz (30–55 g) icing sugar, sifted

squeeze of lemon juice (optional)

1–2 tablespoons kirsch or fruit liqueur (optional)

**1 ▲** Hull the berries if necessary. Put them in a bowl of cold water and swirl them round briefly. Scoop out and spread on paper towels. Pat dry. Purée the berries in a blender or food processor. Turn the machine on and off a few times and scrape down the bowl to be sure all the berries are evenly puréed.

**2 ▲** For raspberries, blackberries and other berries with small seeds, press the purée through a fine-mesh nylon sieve. Add icing sugar to taste, plus a little lemon juice and/or liqueur, if using (for example, raspberry liqueur – framboise – for a raspberry sauce). Stir well to dissolve the sugar completely.

---

# Iced Macaroon Cream with Raspberry Sauce

**Serves 6–8**

1¼ pints (750 ml) whipping cream

4 tablespoons brandy or orange juice

2 tablespoons caster sugar

12 crisp almond macaroons (about 4 oz/ 115 g), coarsely crushed

raspberries, to decorate

8 fl oz (240 ml) raspberry sauce, to serve

**1 ▲** Put the cream in a large bowl, preferably chilled, and whip until it starts to thicken.

**2** Add the brandy or juice and sugar. Continue whipping until the cream will hold stiff peaks.

**3 ▼** Add the macaroons and fold evenly into the cream.

~ **VARIATION** ~

Use coarsely broken meringue nests (page 160) instead of macaroons. Use almond liqueur instead of brandy or juice.

**4** Spoon into 6–8 ramekins, or a 2 pint (1.5 litre) smooth-sided mould. Press in evenly to be sure there are no air pockets. Smooth the surface. Cover and freeze until firm. (Do not freeze longer than 1 day.)

**5 ▼** To serve, dip the moulds in hot water for 5–10 seconds, then invert on to a serving plate. Lift off the moulds. Refrigerate the desserts for 15–20 minutes to soften slightly.

**6** Decorate with raspberries and serve with the sauce.

# MAKING SORBETS AND FRUIT ICES

Sorbets and fruit ices are most refreshing desserts. A fruit ice is made by freezing a sweetened fruit purée, whereas a sorbet is made from fruit juice or purée mixed with a sugar syrup. In addition, there are sorbets based on wine or liqueur. The Italian 'granita' uses the same mixture as a sorbet, but it is stirred during freezing to give it its characteristic coarse texture. A sherbet normally contains milk or cream.

## Strawberry Ice
Purée 1 lb 2 oz (500 g) strawberries with 3½ oz (100 g) caster sugar and 4 fl oz (120 ml) orange juice. Be sure the sugar has dissolved completely. Add 1 tablespoon lemon juice. Taste the mixture and add more sugar or orange or lemon juice if required. (The mixture should be highly flavoured.) Chill well, then transfer to an ice cream machine and freeze until firm. *Makes about 1 pint (600 ml).*

## Variations
• Use raspberries or blackberries instead of strawberries.
• Use 1½ lb (700 g) peeled and sliced peaches or nectarines instead of strawberries.
• Add 1–2 tablespoons of fruit liqueur (to match the fruit used).

**1 ▲ For a fruit ice:** Prepare the fruit, removing peel, stones, hulls, stalks, etc. Purée the fruit with sugar and liquid in a blender or food processor until very smooth. Be sure that the sugar has dissolved completely.

**3 ▲ For a sorbet:** If using citrus fruit, peel off strips of zest. Squeeze the juice from the fruit. Alternatively, purée fruit in a blender or food processor (first cooking if necessary).

**5 ▲** Stir in the fruit juice or purée. Strain the mixture into a bowl, if necessary, and chill well. Then transfer the mixture to an ice cream machine and freeze following the manufacturer's instructions.

**2 ▲** Add additional flavourings as directed in the recipe (alcohol, herbs, for example). If using berries with seeds (raspberries, blackberries, etc), press the purée through a fine-mesh nylon sieve. Chill the purée well. Then transfer to an ice cream machine and freeze following the manufacturer's instructions.

**4 ▲** Put the strips of zest (or other flavouring items such as vanilla pod, spices) in a saucepan with sugar and water and bring to the boil, stirring to dissolve the sugar. Leave to cool.

## Still-freezing fruit ice
If you don't have an ice cream machine, you can 'still-freeze' the fruit ice or sorbet in the freezer. Pour it into a metal tin or tray, cover and freeze until set round the edge. Turn it into a bowl and break it into small pieces. Beat with an electric mixer or in a food processor until slushy. Return to the metal tin and freeze again until set round the edge. Repeat the beating once or twice more, then freeze until firm.

# Mango Sorbet

**SERVES 6**

5 oz (145 g) sugar

6 fl oz (170 ml) water

a large strip of orange zest

1 large mango, peeled, stoned, and cubed

4 tablespoons orange juice

**1** Combine the sugar, water and orange zest in a saucepan. Bring to the boil, stirring to dissolve the sugar. Leave the sugar syrup to cool.

**2** ▼ Purée the mango with the orange juice in a blender or food processor. There should be about 16 fl oz (500 ml) of purée.

**3** ▲ Add the purée to the cooled sugar syrup and mix well. Strain. Taste the mixture (it should be well flavoured). Chill. Transfer to an ice cream machine and freeze until firm.

**Sorbet variations**
- For *Banana Sorbet*: Peel and cube 4–5 large bananas. Purée with 2 tablespoons lemon juice to make 16 fl oz (500 ml). If liked, replace the orange zest in the sugar syrup with 2–3 whole cloves, or omit the zest.
- For *Papaya Sorbet*: Peel, seed and cube 1½ lb (700 g) papaya. Purée with 3 tablespoons lime juice to make 16 fl oz (500 ml). Replace the orange zest with lime zest.
- For *Passion Fruit Sorbet*: Halve 16 or more passion fruit and scoop out the seeds and pulp (there should be about 16 fl oz/500 ml). Work in a blender or food processor until the seeds are like coarse pepper. Omit the orange juice and zest. Add the passion fruit to the sugar syrup, then press through a wire sieve before freezing.
- For *Lemon Sorbet*: Make the sugar syrup with 14 oz (400 g) sugar, 16 fl oz (500 ml) water and 2 tablespoons finely grated lemon zest. Add 6 fl oz (170 ml) fresh lemon juice. Do not strain out the zest before freezing.

# MAKING FRUIT CRUMBLE

This well-loved dessert is simple and satisfying. It consists of fruit baked with a sweet, crumbly topping. Almost any fruit can be used, and the topping mixture can be varied in many ways, according to your preferences and what you have to hand in the store-cupboard.

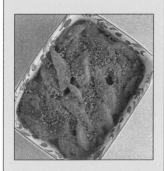

**Pear Crumble**
Make the crumble mixture with 4 oz (115 g) plain flour, 5 oz (145 g) soft light brown sugar, 1 teaspoon ground ginger and 4 oz (115 g) butter. Add 2 oz (55 g) chopped walnuts and mix lightly. Toss 1¾ lb (800 g) sliced firm pears with 2 oz (55 g) caster sugar and 1–2 tablespoons flour. Assemble the crumble and bake in a 375°F/190°C/Gas 5 oven for 30–35 minutes. *Serves 4–6.*

**Variation**
• Use apples instead of pears, and cinnamon instead of ginger.

**A freezer standby**
Fruit crumbles freeze very well and are very handy to have for an impromptu pudding. Freeze, un-cooked, in a foil container, and bake from frozen, uncovered, in • 350°F/180°C/Gas 4 oven for about 45 minutes.

**1** ▲ For the topping, combine the dry ingredients (flour and sugar plus oats or other cereal, coconut, nuts, spices, etc) in a bowl. Add the fat (butter or margarine).

**3** ▲ Prepare the fruit as directed in the recipe, by peeling, stoning or coring, slicing or cubing.

**5** ▲ Scatter the crumble mixture on top to cover the fruit in an even layer.

**2** ▲ Cut or rub the fat into the dry ingredients as if making pastry dough. Do not overmix the topping: the finished texture should be like coarse crumbs.

**4** ▲ If the recipe specifies, toss the fruit with sugar or a sweet syrup and spices. Add flour or cornflour for thickening the fruit juices, if required. Spread the fruit in a baking dish.

**6** ▲ Bake until the fruit is tender and the topping is golden brown and crisp. Serve warm, with whipped cream, soured cream, yogurt or ice cream.

# Spiced Peach Crumble

**SERVES 6**

3 lb (1.35 kg) ripe but firm peaches, peeled, stoned and sliced

4 tablespoons caster sugar

½ teaspoon ground cinnamon

1 teaspoon lemon juice

whipped cream or vanilla ice cream, for serving (optional)

FOR THE TOPPING

4 oz (115 g) plain flour

¼ teaspoon ground cinnamon

¼ teaspoon ground allspice

3 oz (85 g) rolled oats

6 oz (170 g) soft light brown sugar

4 oz (115 g) butter

1  Preheat a 375°F/190°C/Gas 5 oven.

2  ▼  For the topping, sift the flour and spices into a bowl. Add the oats and sugar and stir to combine. Cut or rub in the butter until the mixture resembles coarse crumbs.

3  Toss the peaches with the sugar, cinnamon and lemon juice. Put the fruit in an 8–9 in (20–23 cm) diameter baking dish.

4  ▲  Scatter the topping over the fruit in an even layer. Bake for 30–35 minutes. Serve warm, with whipped cream or ice cream, if liked.

~ **VARIATION** ~

Use apricots or nectarines instead of peaches. Substitute nutmeg for the cinnamon.

# MAKING A STEAMED PUDDING

Steamed puddings, many with fruit, range from light and delicate sponges to rich suet puddings, and the variety of flavourings is infinite, both sweet and savoury. Puddings may be steamed on top of the stove or in the oven. A pressure cooker can also be used. Some puddings, such as roly poly, are wrapped in greased foil rather than being cooked in a basin or mould.

First prepare the steamer. For cooking on top of the stove, you can use either a large saucepan with tight-fitting lid or a proper steamer. For oven steaming, use a deep casserole or roasting tin.

1 If using a saucepan, it is necessary to have something to help you put the pudding into the pan and then lift it out after cooking. Unless you are wrapping the pudding in a cloth (the knot at the top makes a convenient handle), use a wire steaming basket with handles or make a sling of foil. Put enough water into the saucepan or steamer to one-quarter fill it, and bring to the boil. Boil water in the kettle too.

2 ▲ Generously butter the pudding basin or mould(s). Put a disc of buttered greaseproof paper in the bottom. Make the pudding mixture. Turn it into the basin or mould(s), which should be about two-thirds full.

3 ▲ Cover the basin or mould(s). This must be done carefully so that the steam from the boiling water does not fall on to the pudding, thus making it soggy. First lay a disc of buttered greaseproof paper on top.

4 ▲ To cover with foil, lay a piece of foil on another sheet of paper. Holding the paper and foil together, fold a 1 in (2.5 cm) pleat across the centre (the pleat will allow for the pudding rising above the basin rim).

5 ▲ Smooth the paper and foil down over the edge. Wrap a piece of string twice around the basin, just below the rim, and tie firmly. Trim off the corners with scissors.

6 ▲ To cover with a cloth, use a square of cotton that is about three times larger than the top of the basin or mould(s). Lay it over the buttered paper, pleat and tie with string as above. Bring the corners of the cloth up over the top and tie opposite ones together into knots.

7 ▲ Lower the basin or mould(s) into the boiling water in the saucepan or steamer, or arrange in the roasting tin. Pour enough boiling water into the pan or tin to come halfway up the sides of the basin or mould(s).

8 Cover tightly with a lid or foil. Set over a moderately low heat on top of the stove or put into a preheated 350°F/180°C/Gas 4 oven. The water in the steamer should simmer but not boil up over the top of the pudding. Steam for the required time, topping up with more boiling water as needed. (With oven steaming you will need to replenish the water less often as there is much less evaporation.) When cooked, remove the basin or mould(s) from the water and cool for a few minutes. Remove the covering, set a serving plate, inverted, on top of the basin or mould(s) and, holding them firmly together, turn them over. Lift off the mould and serve.

# Apple and Kumquat Sponge Puddings

**SERVES 8**

5 oz (145 g) butter, at room temperature

6 oz (170 g) cooking apples, peeled and thinly sliced

3 oz (85 g) kumquats, thinly sliced

5 oz (145 g) golden caster sugar

2 eggs

4 oz (115 g) self-raising flour

FOR THE SAUCE

3 oz (85 g) kumquats, thinly sliced

3 oz (85 g) caster sugar

8 fl oz (240 ml) water

¼ pint (150 ml) crème fraîche

1 teaspoon cornflour mixed with 2 teaspoons water

lemon juice to taste

**1** Prepare the steamer. Butter eight ¼ pint (150 ml) dariole moulds or ramekins and put a disc of buttered greaseproof paper on the bottom of each one.

**2 ▲** Melt 1 oz (30 g) butter in a frying pan. Add the apples, kumquats and 1 oz (30 g) sugar and cook over moderate heat for 5–8 minutes or until the apples start to soften and the sugar begins to caramelize. Remove from the heat and leave to cool.

**3** Meanwhile, cream the remaining butter with the remaining sugar until the mixture is pale and fluffy. Add the eggs, one at a time, beating well after each addition. Fold in the flour.

**4 ▼** Divide the apple and kumquat mixture among the prepared moulds. Top with the sponge mixture.

**5** Cover the moulds and put into the steamer. Steam on top of the stove for 45 minutes. If oven-steaming, cook for 30 minutes.

**6** For the sauce, put the kumquats, sugar and water in a frying pan and bring to the boil, stirring to dissolve the sugar. Simmer for 5 minutes.

**7 ▲** Stir in the crème fraîche and bring back to the boil, stirring.

**8** Remove from the heat and whisk in the cornflour mixture. Return the pan to the heat and simmer gently for 2 minutes, stirring. Add lemon juice to taste.

**9** Turn out the puddings and serve hot, with the sauce.

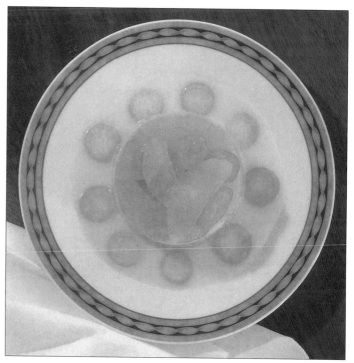

# MELTING CHOCOLATE

If chocolate is overheated, it can burn or develop a grainy texture, so care must be taken when melting it. If the chocolate is being melted with butter or a large quantity of liquid, this can be done in a heavy-based pan over moderately low heat. When melting chocolate alone, use a bain-marie or microwave oven as described here.

For the richest, most intense chocolate flavour in cakes, biscuits and confectionery, use a chocolate that contains a lot of cocoa solids (the pure chocolate essence) and cocoa butter (a natural vegetable fat) rather than vegetable oil. Check the labels, and choose chocolate with at least 50 per cent cocoa solids. The more bitter it is – with less sugar content – the more chocolatey it will taste.

You can find good-quality 'luxury' chocolate in many large supermarkets now, or buy French or Belgian chocolate from a delicatessen.

**Spiced Mocha Drink**
Melt 6oz (170g) milk chocolate with 4fl oz (120ml) single cream. Add 1¼ pints (750ml) hot black coffee and ¼ teaspoon ground cinnamon. Whisk until foamy. Serve hot with a dollop of whipped cream, or cool and chill, then serve over ice. *Serves 4.*

**1 ▲ In a bain-marie**: First, cut the chocolate into small pieces with a sharp knife to enable it to melt quickly and evenly.

**3 ▲** According to the recipe instructions, add liquid such as milk, cream, coffee or water, or a fat such as butter.

**5 ▲ In a microwave oven**: Arrange the chocolate in a glass container and melt it in a microwave oven (consult manufacturer's handbook for timings).

**2 ▲** Put the chocolate in a double saucepan or a bowl set over a saucepan of almost simmering water. The base of the bowl should not touch the water.

**4 ▲** Heat gently until the chocolate is melted and smooth, stirring occasionally. Remove from the heat.

**Moisture problems**
If any steam from boiling water gets into the chocolate while melting, it can turn into a solid mass. If this happens, stir in a little fat, about 1 teaspoon to each 1oz (30g) of chocolate.

# Bittersweet Chocolate Sauce

**MAKES ABOUT 12 FL OZ (340 ML)**

3 tablespoons sugar

4 fl oz (120 ml) water

6 oz (170 g) dark Continental chocolate, chopped into small pieces

1 oz (30 g) unsalted butter, diced

4–6 tablespoons single cream

½ teaspoon vanilla essence

---

~ **VARIATION** ~

If preferred, use 1–2 tablespoons orange liqueur instead of vanilla.

---

**1** Combine the sugar and water in a heavy-based saucepan. Bring to the boil, stirring to dissolve the sugar.

**2** ▲ Add the chocolate and butter and remove the pan from the heat.

**3** ▲ Stir until the mixture is smooth, then stir in the cream and vanilla essence. Serve the sauce warm, over ice cream, profiteroles, etc.

# Chocolate Truffles

**MAKES ABOUT 24**

8 oz (225 g) bittersweet or good plain chocolate, chopped into small pieces

6 tablespoons double cream

cocoa powder

**1 ▲** Put the chocolate in a bowl set over a pan of hot water or in the top of a double saucepan. Heat until melted and smooth, stirring occasionally.

**2 ▼** Remove from the pan of hot water. Add the cream and stir well. Leave to cool.

**3** Cover and refrigerate for 35 minutes or until the mixture is just firm enough to hold its shape.

**4** Sift a layer of cocoa powder on to a plate or shallow dish.

**5 ▲** Take a heaped teaspoonful of the chocolate mixture and shape it into a ball.

**6 ▲** Roll in the cocoa to coat all over in an even layer. Shake off excess cocoa. Set the truffle on a tray.

**7** Continue shaping and coating the remaining truffles, setting them on the tray in a single layer, not touching each other.

**8** Cover and refrigerate. Remove from the refrigerator 15 minutes before serving.

> ~ **VARIATIONS** ~
>
> For Liqueur-flavoured Truffles, add 2 tablespoons cherry or apricot brandy or orange liqueur. For Coated Truffles, roll the truffles in finely chopped toasted hazelnuts or other nuts, or in finely grated chocolate instead of cocoa powder.

# Chocolate Nut Cake

**SERVES 6–8**

6 oz (170 g) good plain chocolate, chopped into small pieces

4 oz (115 g) butter, preferably unsalted

7 oz (200 g) caster sugar

4 eggs, separated

4 oz (115 g) unsalted macadamia nuts or almonds, freshly ground

1 oz (30 g) plain flour

pinch of cream of tartar (if needed)

cocoa powder, to dust

sweetened whipped cream (page 160)

**1** Preheat a 325°F/170°C/Gas 3 oven. Grease a 9 in (23 cm) round cake tin and line the bottom with greased paper. Dust the cake tin with cocoa powder and shake out excess.

**2** Combine the chocolate and butter in a heavy-based saucepan. Set over moderately low heat and stir until melted and smooth. Leave to cool.

**3 ▲** Whisk together the sugar and egg yolks until pale and thick.

**4 ▲** Add the chocolate mixture, nuts and flour and beat in gently.

**5** In another large bowl, scrupulously clean and grease-free, and using clean beaters, whisk the egg whites until they will hold stiff peaks. (If not using a copper bowl, add the cream of tartar when the whites are frothy.)

**6 ▲** Lighten the chocolate mixture by gently mixing in about one-quarter of the whites. It is not necessary to blend thoroughly.

**7 ▲** Add the remaining whites and fold them in gently but thoroughly using a rubber spatula.

**8** Pour the mixture into the prepared tin. Bake for 1–1¼ hours or until a skewer inserted into the centre of the cake comes out clean. Cool in the tin for 10 minutes, then turn out on to a wire rack to cool completely.

**9** Dust the cake with cocoa powder. Serve with sweetened whipped cream.

# PREPARING NUTS

Nuts are enjoyed as a snack or with drinks, as well as being an important ingredient or garnish in many dishes, from breakfast cereals and breads to salads, main dishes, vegetable and grain accompaniments, and desserts.

Some nuts may be bought complete with their brown, papery skins. The skin often has a bitter taste and so should be removed before the nuts are used. The flavour of all nuts is improved by toasting; this makes them appealingly crisp too.

**1 ▲ To skin almonds and pistachios**: Put the nuts in a bowl and cover with boiling water. Leave for 2 minutes. (This is known as blanching.) Drain the nuts and cool slightly, then squeeze or rub each nut with your fingers to remove the skins.

**2 ▲ To skin hazelnuts and brazils**: Spread the nuts on a baking sheet. Toast in a 350°F/180°C/Gas 4 oven for 10–15 minutes to dry the skins. Wrap the nuts in a rough tea towel and rub to remove the skin. Pick off any bits of skin still adhering to the nuts.

**Spicy Cocktail Nuts**
Combine 3 tablespoons corn oil, 2 halved garlic cloves and 1 teaspoon dried hot red pepper flakes in a saucepan. Heat for 1 minute, stirring. Discard the garlic. Add 8oz (225g) mixed nuts, such as blanched almonds, walnuts, skinned peanuts, blanched hazelnuts, and stir well. Add salt to taste. Pour the mixture on to a baking sheet and bake in a 300°F/150°C/Gas 2 oven for about 20 minutes, stirring occasionally. Drain the nuts on paper towels and leave to cool before serving.

**3 ▲ To oven-toast or grill nuts**: Spread the nuts on a baking sheet. Toast in a 350°F/180°C/Gas 4 oven or under a moderate grill, until golden brown and smelling nutty. Stir the nuts occasionally.

**4 ▲ To fry-toast nuts**: Put the nuts in a frying pan, with no fat. Toast over moderate heat until golden brown. Stir constantly and watch carefully because nuts scorch easily.

**5 ▲ To grind nuts**: Using a nut mill or a clean coffee grinder, grind a small batch of nuts at a time so that you can be sure of getting an even texture. As soon as the nuts have a fine texture, stop grinding: if overworked, they will turn to a paste.

**6 ▲** You can also grind nuts in a food processor, but it is not as easy to get an even texture, and thus there is more risk of overworking the nuts to a paste. To prevent this, grind the nuts with some of the sugar or flour called for in the recipe.

# Bread Pudding with Pecan Nuts

**SERVES 6**

14 fl oz (400 ml) milk

14 fl oz (400 ml) single or whipping
  cream

5 oz (145 g) caster sugar

3 eggs, beaten to mix

2 teaspoons grated orange zest

1 teaspoon vanilla essence

24 slices of day-old French bread, ½ in
  (1.5 cm) thick

3 oz (85 g) toasted pecan nuts, chopped

icing sugar, for sprinkling

whipped cream or soured cream and
  maple syrup, to serve

1 ▲ Put 12 fl oz (360 ml) each of the
milk and cream in a saucepan. Add
the sugar. Warm over low heat,
stirring to dissolve the sugar. Remove
from the heat and cool. Add the eggs,
orange zest and vanilla and mix well.

2 ▲ Arrange half of the bread slices
in a buttered 9–10 in (23–25 cm)
baking dish. Scatter two-thirds of the
pecans over the bread. Arrange the
remaining bread slices on top and
scatter on the rest of the pecans.

3 ▼ Pour the egg mixture evenly
over the bread slices. Soak for 30
minutes. Press the top layer of bread
down into the liquid once or twice.

4 Preheat a 350°F/180°C/Gas 4 oven.

5 If the top layer of bread slices looks
dry and all the liquid has been
absorbed, moisten with the remaining
milk and cream.

6 ▲ Set the baking dish in a roasting
tin. Add enough water to the tin to
come halfway up the sides of the dish.
Bring the water to the boil.

7 Transfer to the oven. Bake for 40
minutes or until the pudding is set and
golden brown on top. Sprinkle the top
of the pudding with sifted icing sugar
and serve warm, with whipped cream
or soured cream and maple syrup, if
you like.

# BREADS

~

*The enticing aroma of fresh bread baking is enough to lure anyone to the kitchen, and the enjoyment of teabreads, home-made loaves and bread rolls is even better than the anticipation. You can make your own pizza dough, too.*

# MAKING TEABREADS AND MUFFINS

These sorts of bread are very quick and easy to make. The raising agent reacts quickly with moisture and heat to make the breads and muffins rise, without the need for a rising (or proving) period before baking.

The raising agent is usually bicarbonate of soda or baking powder, which is a mixture of bicarbonate of soda and an acid salt such as cream of tartar. Many recipes use self-raising flour which conveniently includes a raising agent. Remember that the raising agent will start to work as soon as it comes into contact with liquid, so don't mix the dry and liquid ingredients until just before you are ready to fill the tin or tins and bake.

**1 ▲ For muffins:** Combine the dry ingredients in a bowl. It is a good idea to sift the flour with the raising agent, salt and any spices to mix them evenly. Add the liquid ingredients and stir just until the dry ingredients are moistened; the mixture will not be smooth. Do not overmix attempting to remove all the lumps. If you do, the muffins will be tough and will have air holes in them.

**2 ▲** Divide the mixture evenly among the greased muffin tins or deep bun tins lined with paper cases, filling them about two-thirds full. Bake until golden brown and a wooden skewer inserted in the centre comes out clean. To prevent soggy bottoms, remove the muffins immediately from the tins to a wire rack. Cool, and serve warm or at room temperature.

**Crunchy Muesli Muffins**
Make the mixture from 5 oz (145 g) plain flour, 2½ teaspoons baking powder, 2 tablespoons caster sugar, 8 fl oz (240 ml) milk, 2 oz (55 g) melted butter or corn oil, and 1 egg, adding 7 oz (200 g) toasted oat cereal with raisins to the dry ingredients. Pour into muffin tins or deep bun tins. Bake in a 200°C/400°F/Gas 6 oven for 20 minutes or until golden brown. *Makes 10.*

**3 ▲ For fruit and/or nut teabreads:**
Method 1: Stir together all the liquid ingredients. Add the dry ingredients and beat just until smoothly blended. Method 2: Beat the butter with the sugar until the mixture is light and fluffy. Beat in the eggs followed by the other liquid ingredients. Stir in the dry ingredients. Pour the mixture into a prepared tin (typically a loaf tin). Bake until a wooden skewer inserted in the centre comes out clean. If the bread is browning too quickly, cover the top with foil.

**4 ▲** Cool in the tin for 5 minutes, then turn out on to a wire rack to cool completely. A lengthways crack on the surface is characteristic of teabreads. For easier slicing, wrap the bread in greaseproof paper and overwrap in foil, then store overnight at room temperature.

# Banana Bread

**MAKES 1 LOAF**

| |
|---|
| 7 oz (200 g) plain flour |
| 2¼ teaspoons baking powder |
| ½ teaspoon salt |
| ¾ teaspoon ground cinnamon (optional) |
| 4 tablespoons wheat germ |
| 2½ oz (75 g) butter or margarine, at room temperature |
| 4 oz (115 g) caster sugar |
| ¾ teaspoon grated lemon zest |
| 3 ripe bananas, mashed |
| 2 eggs, beaten to mix |

**1** Preheat a 350°F/180°C/Gas 4 oven. Grease and flour an 8½ × 4½ in (21 × 11 cm) loaf tin.

**2 ▲** Sift the flour, baking powder, salt and cinnamon, if using, into a bowl. Stir in the wheat germ.

**3 ▲** In another bowl, combine the butter or margarine with the sugar and lemon zest. Beat until the mixture is light and fluffy.

**4 ▲** Add the mashed bananas and eggs and mix well.

**5** Add the dry ingredients and blend quickly and evenly.

~ **VARIATION** ~

For Banana Walnut Bread, add 2–3 oz (55–85 g) finely chopped walnuts with the dry ingredients.

**6 ▼** Spoon into the prepared loaf tin. Bake for 50–60 minutes or until a wooden skewer inserted in the centre comes out clean.

**7** Cool in the pan for about 5 minutes, then turn out on to a wire rack to cool completely.

# MAKING SCONES

Scone dough may be rolled out and cut into shapes for baking in the oven or cooking on a griddle. To ensure light, well risen scones, do not handle the dough too much and do not roll it out too thinly.

**2 ▲** Add the fat (butter, margarine, vegetable fat, etc). With a pastry blender or two knives used scissor-fashion, cut the fat into the dry ingredients until the mixture resembles fine crumbs, or rub in the fat with your fingertips.

**3 ▲** Add the liquid ingredients (milk, cream, buttermilk, eggs). Stir with a fork until the dry ingredients are thoroughly moistened and will come together in a ball of fairly soft dough in the centre of the bowl.

**1** Sift the dry ingredients into a bowl (flour, baking powder with or without bicarbonate of soda, salt, sugar, ground spices, etc).

**4 ▲** Turn the dough on to a lightly floured surface. Knead it very lightly, folding and pressing, to mix evenly – about 30 seconds. Roll or pat out the dough to ¾in (2 cm) thickness.

**5 ▲ For oven-baked scones**: With a floured, sharp-edged cutter, cut out rounds or other shapes. Or cut diamond shapes or triangles with a floured knife. Arrange on an ungreased baking sheet, not touching. Brush the tops with beaten egg, milk or cream if the recipe specifies. Bake until risen and golden brown.

**Baking Powder Scones**
Make the scone dough using 10oz (300g) flour, 1 tablespoon baking powder, ½ teaspoon salt, 4oz (115g) chilled butter and 4–6fl oz (150–175ml) milk. Roll or pat out the dough and cut out 2in (5cm) rounds. Bake the scones in a preheated 450°F/ 230°C/Gas 8 oven for 10–12 minutes. *Makes about 10.*

**6 ▲ For drop biscuits**: Add the liquid ingredients, using more than for a rolled-out dough. Stir with a fork until evenly mixed. Using a floured spoon, drop scoops of batter onto an ungreased baking sheet, leaving space around each biscuit. Bake until puffed and golden brown.

**Cutting tips**
• Be sure the cutter or knife is sharp so that the edges of the scone shapes are not compressed; this would inhibit rising.
• Cut the shapes close together so that you won't have to reroll the dough more than once.
• If necessary, a short, sturdy drinking glass can be pressed into service as a cutter. Flour the rim well and do not press too hard.

# American Berry Shortcake

**Serves 8**

| |
|---|
| ½ pint (300 ml) whipping cream |
| 1 oz (30 g) icing sugar, sifted |
| 1½ lb (700 g) strawberries or mixed berries, halved or sliced if large |
| 2 oz (55 g) caster sugar, or to taste |
| For the shortcake |
| 10 oz (300 g) plain flour |
| 2 teaspoons baking powder |
| 2½ oz (75 g) caster sugar |
| 4 oz (115 g) butter |
| 5 tablespoons milk |
| 1 size-1 egg |

**1** Preheat a 450°F/230°C/Gas 8 oven. Grease an 8 in (20 cm) round cake tin.

**2** For the shortcake, sift the flour, baking powder and sugar into a bowl. Add the butter and rub in until the mixture resembles fine crumbs. Combine the milk and egg. Add to the crumb mixture and stir just until evenly mixed to a soft dough.

**3** Put the dough in the prepared tin and pat out to an even layer. Bake for 15–20 minutes or until a wooden skewer inserted in the centre comes out clean. Leave to cool slightly.

**4 ▲** Whip the cream until it starts to thicken. Add the icing sugar and continue whipping until the cream will hold soft peaks.

**5** Put the berries in a bowl. Sprinkle with the caster sugar and toss together lightly. Cover and set aside for the berries to give up some juice.

**6 ▼** Remove the cooled shortcake from the tin. With a long, serrated knife, split the shortcake horizontally into two equal layers.

**7 ▲** Put the bottom layer on a serving plate. Top with half of the berries and most of the cream. Set the second layer on top and press down gently. Spoon the remaining berries over the top layer (or serve them separately) and add the remaining cream in small, decorative dollops.

# MAKING YEAST DOUGH

Making bread is a very enjoyable and satisfying culinary experience – with no other preparation do you have such 'hands-on' contact. And from the kneading through to the shaping of the risen (or proven) dough, you are working with a living organism, yeast, not a chemical raising agent. You can use either fresh yeast or dried yeast, which is available in an easy-blend variety too.

**Everyday White Bread**
Sift 1½lb (700g) strong plain flour into a large bowl with 1½ teaspoons salt and 1 tablespoon caster sugar. Stir in 2 teaspoons easy-blend dried yeast. Make a well in the centre and add ¾ pint (450ml) mixed warm water and milk and 1oz (30g) melted and cooled butter. Mix to a soft dough, adding more flour or liquid if necessary, then knead until smooth and elastic. Leave to rise until doubled in bulk. Knock back the dough to deflate. Divide it in half and shape each piece into a loaf, tucking the ends under. Put in 2 greased 8½ × 4½ in (21 × 11 cm) loaf tins. Leave in a warm place to rise for 30–45 minutes. Glaze the tops of the loaves with 1 egg beaten with 1 tablespoon milk. Bake in a 450°F/230°C/Gas 8 oven for 30–35 minutes. *Makes 2 loaves.*

**1 ▲** If using ordinary dried yeast, put it in a small bowl, add some of the warm liquid (105–110°F/40–43°C) called for in the recipe and whisk with a fork until dissolved. Add a little sugar if the recipe specifies.

**2 ▲** Sift the flour into a large warm bowl (with other dry ingredients such as salt). Make a well in the centre and add the yeast mixture plus any other liquid ingredients.

**3 ▲** Using your fingers or a spoon, *gradually draw the flour into the* liquids. Mix until all the flour is incorporated and the dough pulls away from the sides of the bowl. If the dough feels too soft and wet, work in a little more flour. If it doesn't come together, add a little more liquid.

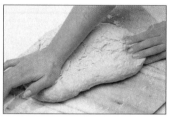

**4 ▲** Turn the dough on to a lightly floured surface. Fold the dough over on to itself towards you and then press it down away from you with the heels of your hands. Rotate the dough slightly and fold and press it again. Knead until the dough looks satiny and feels elastic, about 10 minutes.

**5 ▲** Shape the dough into a ball. Put it in a lightly greased bowl and turn the dough to grease all over. Cover the bowl with a towel or cling film. Set it aside in a warm, draught-free place (about 80°F/27°C).

**6 ▲** Leave to rise until about doubled in bulk, 1–1½ hours. To test if it is sufficiently risen, press a finger about 1 in (2.5 cm) into the dough and withdraw it quickly; the indentation should remain.

**7** ▲ Gently punch the centre of the dough with your fist to deflate it and fold the edges to the centre. Turn the dough on to a lightly floured surface and knead it again for 2–3 minutes. If instructed, shape the dough into a ball again and rise a second time.

**8** ▲ Shape the dough into loaves, rolls or other shapes as instructed. Put into prepared tins or on to baking sheets. Cover and leave to rise in a warm place for ¾–1 hour. If the recipe instructs, glaze the loaves or rolls.

**9** ▲ Bake in the centre of a heated oven until well risen and golden brown. To test, tip the loaf out of the tin and tap the base with your knuckle. If it sounds hollow, like a drum, it is fully cooked. Immediately transfer to a wire rack for cooling.

# SHAPING ROLLS

A basket of freshly baked bread rolls, in decorative shapes, is a delightful accompaniment for soups or salads. After shaping, arrange the rolls on a baking sheet, leaving space around each roll for spreading, and leave to rise for 30 minutes before baking.

**Working with yeast**

Easy-blend (or fast-action) is the most readily available dried yeast. Unlike ordinary dried yeast, there is no need to mix it with liquid. Just combine it with the flour and other dry ingredients and then add the warm liquids.

If using fresh yeast, allow ½ oz (15 g) to each 1 tablespoon dried. Crumble it into a small bowl, add warm liquid and mash with a fork until blended.

If you are in any doubt about the freshness of ordinary dried or fresh yeast, set the mixture aside in a warm place; after 10 minutes or so it should be foamy. If it isn't, discard it.

**1** ▲ **For Parker House rolls**: Roll out the risen dough to ¼ in (5 mm) thickness and cut out 2½–3 in (6–7 cm) rounds using a floured cutter. Brush the rounds with melted butter. Fold them in half, slightly off-centre so the top overlaps the bottom. Press the folded edge firmly. Arrange the rolls on a greased baking sheet.

**2** ▲ **For crescent rolls**: Roll out the risen dough to a large round ¼ in (5 mm) thick. Brush with melted butter. With a sharp knife, cut into wedges that are 2½–3 in (6–7 cm) at their wide end. Roll up each wedge, from the wide end. Set the rolls on a greased baking sheet, placing the points underneath.

**3** ◀ **For bowknot rolls**: Divide the risen dough into pieces. Roll each with your palms on a lightly floured surface to make ropes that are about ½ in (1.5 cm) thick. Divide the ropes into 9 in (27 cm) lengths. Tie each rope loosely into a knot, tucking the ends under. Arrange the rolls on a greased baking sheet.

# Two-tone Bread

**MAKES 2 LOAVES**

| |
|---|
| 1½ tablespoons dried yeast |
| 4 fl oz (120 ml) warm water |
| 2¼ oz (70 g) caster sugar |
| about 1½ lb (700 g) strong plain flour |
| ½ tablespoon salt |
| 1 pint (600 ml) warm milk |
| 2½ oz (75 g) butter or margarine, melted and cooled |
| 3 tablespoons treacle or molasses |
| 10 oz (300 g) strong plain wholemeal flour |

**1** Dissolve the yeast in the water with 1 teaspoon of the sugar.

**2** Sift 12 oz (360 g) of the white flour, the remaining sugar and salt into a large warm bowl. Make a well in the centre and put in the yeast, milk and butter or margarine. Gradually draw the flour into the liquids and mix to a smooth soft batter.

**3** ▲ Divide the batter in half and put one portion in another bowl. To the first half add 10 oz (300 g) white flour and mix together to a soft dough. If necessary, add a little more flour or warm water.

**4** Turn the dough on to a lightly floured surface and knead until it is smooth and elastic. Shape into a ball. Put it in a greased bowl and rotate to grease the dough all over. Cover the bowl with a towel or cling film.

**5** ▲ To the second portion of batter add the treacle and wholemeal flour. Mix to combine well. Add enough of the remaining white flour to make a soft dough. Turn on to a lightly floured surface and knead until smooth and elastic. Shape into a ball, put in a greased bowl and cover.

**6** Leave the dough to rise in a warm place for about 1–1¼ hours until doubled in bulk. Grease two 8½ × 4½ in (21 × 11 cm) loaf tins.

**7** Knock back the dough to deflate it. Divide each ball in half. On a lightly floured surface, roll out half of the light dough to a rectangle about 12 × 8 in (30 × 20 cm). Roll out half of the dark dough to a rectangle of the same size.

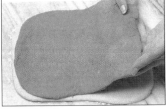

**8** ▲ Set the dark dough rectangle atop the light one. Roll up tightly from a short side. Set in a greased tin. Repeat with the remaining dark and light doughs. Cover the tins and leave the dough to rise for about ¾–1 hour until doubled in bulk.

**9** Preheat a 425°F/220°C/Gas 7 oven. Bake the loaves for 30–35 minutes.

# Cinnamon and Walnut Buns

**MAKES ABOUT 24**

| |
|---|
| 2 tablespoons dried yeast |
| 4 fl oz (120 ml) warm water |
| about 2 lb (900 g) strong plain flour |
| 4 tablespoons caster sugar |
| 2 teaspoons salt |
| 12 fl oz (360 ml) warm milk |
| 5½ oz (160 g) butter or margarine, melted and cooled |
| 2 eggs, beaten |
| 1½ teaspoons grated orange zest |
| 6 oz (170 g) icing sugar, sifted |
| 3–4 tablespoons orange juice |
| FOR THE FILLING |
| 3½ oz (100 g) caster sugar |
| 2 oz (55 g) walnuts, finely chopped |
| 1½ teaspoons ground cinnamon |

**1** Dissolve the yeast in the water.

**2** Sift the flour, caster sugar and salt into a large warm bowl. Make a well in the centre and put in the yeast mixture, milk, half of the butter, the eggs and grated orange zest.

**3** Gradually draw the flour into the liquids and mix until the dough pulls away from the sides of the bowl. If the dough feels too soft and wet, work in a little more flour.

**4** Turn the dough on to a lightly floured surface and knead until satiny smooth and elastic. Shape into a ball. Put it in a greased bowl and rotate to grease the dough all over. Cover the bowl and leave the dough to rise in a warm place until doubled in bulk. Grease two 9–10 in (23–25 cm) round cake tins.

**5** With your fist gently knock back the dough to deflate it. Divide it in half. On a lightly floured surface, roll out one piece of dough to a 12 × 8 in (30 × 20 cm) rectangle.

**6 ▲** For the filling, put the sugar, chopped nuts and cinnamon into a bowl. Mix the ingredients together until well combined.

**7 ▲** Brush the dough with half the remaining melted butter. Sprinkle half of the filling evenly over the surface. Roll up tightly from a long side and pinch the seam to seal it.

**8 ▲** With a sharp knife, cut the roll across into 1 in (2.5 cm) pieces. Arrange the pieces, cut side down, in one of the prepared tins. Repeat with the second portion of dough and the remaining melted butter and filling.

**9** Cover the tins and leave the buns to rise in a warm place until very puffy, about 30 minutes. Preheat a 375°F/190°C/Gas 5 oven.

**10** Bake the buns for 30–40 minutes or until golden. Transfer to a wire rack to cool.

**11** Stir the icing sugar with enough orange juice to make a smooth icing of pourable consistency. Drizzle the icing over the buns and leave to set.

# MAKING PIZZA DOUGH

The range of toppings for a pizza is virtually limitless. Although you can buy pizza bases, it's very easy to make your own at home, and takes much less time than you would expect.

### MAKES A 14 in (35 cm) PIZZA BASE

| |
| --- |
| 2 teaspoons dried yeast |
| 6 fl oz (180 ml) warm water |
| 11½ oz (315 g) strong plain flour |
| 1 teaspoon salt |
| 1½ tablespoons olive oil |

**1 ▲** Put the yeast in a small bowl, add 4 tablespoons of the water and soak for 1 minute. Whisk lightly with a fork until dissolved.

**2 ▲** Sift the flour and salt into a large warm bowl. Make a well in the centre and add the yeast mixture, olive oil and remaining warm water.

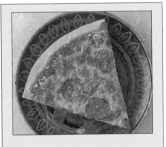

**Tomato and Mozzarella Pizza**
Spread ½ pint (300 ml) tomato-garlic sauce (page 172) over the pizza base, not quite to the edges. Scatter 4 oz (115 g) grated mozzarella cheese evenly over the sauce (plus thinly sliced pepperoni or salami if liked). Sprinkle over freshly grated Parmesan cheese and then add a drizzle of olive oil. Bake in a 475°F/240°C/Gas 9 oven for 15–20 minutes.

**3 ▲** Using your fingers, gradually draw the flour into the liquids. Continue mixing until all the flour is incorporated and the dough will just hold together.

**4 ▲** Turn the dough on to a lightly floured surface. Knead it until it is smooth and silky, about 5 minutes. Shape the dough into a ball. Put it in an oiled bowl and rotate to coat the surface evenly with oil.

**Food processor pizza dough**
Combine the flour, salt, yeast mixture and olive oil in the processor container. Process briefly, then add the rest of the warm water. Work until the dough begins to form a ball. Process 3–4 minutes to knead the dough, then knead it by hand for 2–3 minutes.

**5 ▲** Cover the bowl with cling film. Set aside in a warm place to rise about 1 hour until doubled in bulk. Turn the dough on to the lightly floured surface again. Gently knock back to deflate it, then knead lightly until smooth.

**6 ▲** Roll out the dough into a round or square about ¼ in (5 mm) thick. Transfer it to a lightly oiled metal pizza tin or baking sheet. Add the topping as specified in the recipe. Bake until the pizza crust is puffy and well browned. Serve hot.

# Goat's Cheese, Basil and Olive Pizza

**SERVES 2–4**

½ pint (300 ml) tomato-garlic sauce (page 172)

14 in (35 cm) pizza base

3 tomatoes, preferably plum-type, sliced

6 oz (170 g) firm goat's cheese, cut into small cubes or crumbled

½ oz (15 g) fresh basil leaves

18 large black olives, preferably Kalamata

2 tablespoons freshly grated Parmesan cheese

2 tablespoons olive oil

**1** Preheat a 475°F/240°C/Gas 9 oven.

**2 ▲** Spread the tomato sauce over the pizza base, not quite to the edges. Arrange the tomato slices on top.

**3** Scatter the goat's cheese evenly over the tomato slices, followed by the basil leaves, torn if large, and olives.

**~ COOK'S TIP ~**

A stoneware pizza baking brick or stone will give a pizza a very crisp crust, similar to restaurant pizza. A flat terracotta tile will give the same result. The pizza is assembled on a semolina-dusted wooden paddle, and then slid on to the preheated stone for baking.

**4 ▼** Sprinkle with the Parmesan and then the olive oil.

**5** Bake for 15–20 minutes or until the pizza crust is puffy and well browned and the topping is golden brown.

**~ VARIATIONS ~**

For Tuna Pizza, spread with tomato-herb sauce (page 172), then add thinly sliced spring onions and 7 oz (200 g) drained flaked canned tuna. Make a lattice of anchovy fillets on top and put a black olive in each space. Sprinkle generously with grated Parmesan and Gruyère and drizzle with olive oil. For Mushroom Pizza, spread with tomato-garlic sauce and scatter 8 oz (225 g) sliced mushrooms on top. Sprinkle with 4 oz (115 g) grated mozzarella, plus Parmesan and olive oil.

# Pastry & Cakes

~

*A reputation for good cooking is often built on pastries and cakes. A solid grounding in the basic skills takes the mystery out of shortcrust and choux pastry, sponge cakes and Swiss rolls, and helps you enjoy the creativity of beautiful baking.*

# MAKING SHORTCRUST PASTRY

A meltingly short, crumbly pastry sets off any filling to perfection, whether sweet or savoury. The pastry dough can be made with half butter or margarine and half white vegetable fat or with all one kind of fat.

### FOR A 9 IN (23 CM) PASTRY CASE

| |
| --- |
| 8 oz (225 g) plain flour |
| ¼ teaspoon salt |
| 4 oz (115 g) fat, chilled and diced |
| 3–4 tablespoons iced water |

**1 ▲** Sift the flour and salt into a bowl. Add the fat. Cut the fat into the flour or rub it in with your fingertips until the mixture is crumb-like.

**2 ▲** Sprinkle 3 tablespoons water over the mixture. With a fork, toss gently to mix and moisten it.

**3 ▲** Press the dough into a ball. If it is too dry to form a dough, add the remaining water.

**4 ▲** Wrap the ball of dough with cling film or greaseproof paper and refrigerate it for at least 30 minutes.

---

### Pastry making tips

• It helps if the fat is cold and firm, particularly if making the dough in a food processor. Cold fat has less chance of warming and softening too much when it is being rubbed into the flour, resulting in an oily pastry. Use block margarine rather than the soft tub-type.

• When rubbing the fat into the flour, if it begins to soften and feel oily, put the bowl in the refrigerator to chill for 20–30 minutes. Then continue making the dough.

• Liquids used should be ice-cold so that they will not soften or melt the fat.

• Take care when adding the water: start with the smaller amount (added all at once, not in a dribble), and add more only if the mixture will not come together into a dough. Too much water will result in tough pastry.

• When gathering the mixture together into a ball of dough, handle it as little as possible: overworked pastry will be tough.

• To avoid shrinkage, refrigerate the pastry dough before rolling out and baking. This 'resting time' will allow any elasticity developed during mixing to relax.

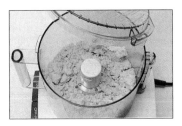

**5 ▲ To make pastry in a food processor**: Combine the flour, salt and cubed fat in the work bowl. Process, turning the machine on and off, just until the mixture is crumbly. Add the iced water and process again briefly – just until the dough starts to pull away from the sides of the bowl. It should still look crumbly. Remove the dough from the processor and gather it into a ball. Wrap and refrigerate.

### Shortcrust pastry variations

• For *Nut Shortcrust*: Add 1 oz (30 g) finely chopped walnuts or pecan nuts to the flour mixture.

• For *Rich Shortcrust*: Use 8 oz (225 g) flour and 6 oz (170 g) fat (preferably all butter), plus 1 tablespoon caster sugar if making a sweet pie. Bind with 1 egg yolk and 2–3 tablespoons water.

• For a *Two-crust Pie*, increase the proportions for these pastries by 50%, thus the amounts needed for basic shortcrust pastry are: 12 oz (340 g) flour, ½ teaspoon salt, 6 oz (170 g) fat, 5–6 tablespoons water. For Nut Shortcrust, as above with 2 oz (55 g) nuts. For Rich Shortcrust, as above but using 9 oz (260 g) fat, 4–5 tablespoons water and 1 egg yolk.

# Sweet Potato Pie

### SERVES 6–8

| |
|---|
| 1½ pounds (675g) sweet potatoes, unpeeled |
| 6oz (170g) firmly packed light brown sugar |
| 2 eggs, separated |
| pinch of salt |
| 1 teaspoon ground cinnamon |
| ½ teaspoon ground ginger |
| ¼ teaspoon grated nutmeg |
| 6fl oz (175ml) whipping cream |
| pinch of cream of tartar (if needed) |
| 9 inch (23cm) pie shell made from plain pastry |

**1** Put the sweet potatoes in a saucepan of boiling water. Simmer until tender, 20–25 minutes. Drain and let cool. When the sweet potatoes are cool enough to handle, peel them.

**2 ▲** Pureé the sweet potatoes in a blender or food processor; there should be 12fl oz (350ml) of pureé. Preheat the oven to 375°F/190°C/Gas 5.

**3 ▲** Combine the pureé, sugar, egg yolks, salt and spices in a bowl. Stir well to dissolve the sugar. Add the cream and stir to mix.

**4** In another bowl, completely clean and greasefree, beat the egg whites until they will hold a soft peak (the tips will just flop over). If not using a copper bowl, add the cream of tartar when the whites are frothy.

**5 ▼** Stir one-quarter of the whites into the potato mixture to lighten it. Fold in the remaining whites with a metal spoon or rubber spatula.

**6** Pour the filling into the pie shell and spread it out evenly. Bake until the filling is set and lightly golden brown and the pastry is golden, 40–45 minutes. The filling will rise during baking but will fall again when the pie cools. Serve warm or at room temperature. If desired, the pie can be accompanied by ice cream or sweetened whipped cream.

---

### ~ VARIATION ~

For Pumpkin Pie, use fresh or canned pumpkin instead of sweet potatoes.

---

# ROLLING OUT AND LINING A TIN

A neat pastry case that doesn't distort or shrink in baking is the desired result. The key to success is handling the dough gently. Use the method here for lining a round pie or tart tin that is about 2 in (5 cm) deep.

Remove the chilled dough from the refrigerator and allow it to soften slightly at room temperature. Unwrap and put it on a lightly floured surface. Flatten the dough into a neat, round disc. Lightly flour the rolling pin.

**Rolling out and lining tips**
- Reflour the surface and rolling pin if the dough starts to stick.
- Should the dough tear, patch with a piece of moistened dough.
- When rolling out and lining the pie or tart tin, do not stretch the dough. It will only shrink back during baking, spoiling the shape of the pastry case.
- Once or twice during rolling out, gently push in the edges of the dough with your cupped palms, to keep the circular shape.
- A pastry scraper will help lift the dough from the work surface, to wrap it around the rolling pin.
- Tins made from heat-resistant glass or dull-finish metal such as heavyweight aluminium will give a crisp crust.
- When finishing the edge, be sure to hook the dough over the rim all the way round or to press the dough firmly to the rim. This will prevent the dough pulling away should it start to shrink.
- If covering a pie dish, roll the dough to a round or oval 2 in (5 cm) larger than the dish. Cut a 1 in (2.5 cm) strip from the outside and lay this on the moistened rim of the dish. Brush the strip with water and lay the sheet of dough on top. Press edges to seal, then trim even with the rim. Knock up the edge with a knife.

**1 ▲** Using even pressure, start rolling out the dough, working from the centre to the edge each time and easing the pressure slightly as you reach the edge.

**2 ▲** Lift up the dough and give it a quarter turn from time to time during the rolling. This will prevent the dough sticking to the surface, and will help keep the thickness even.

**3 ▲** Continue rolling out until the dough circle is about 2 in (5 cm) larger all round than the tin. The dough will be about ⅛ in (3 mm) thick.

**4 ▲** Set the rolling pin on the dough, near one side of the circle. Fold the outside edge of dough over the pin, then roll the pin over the dough to wrap the dough round it. Do this gently and loosely.

**5 ▲** Hold the pin over the tin and gently unroll the dough so it drapes into the tin, centring it as much as possible.

**6 ▲** With your fingertips, lift and ease the dough into the tin, gently pressing it over the bottom and up the side. Turn excess dough over the rim and trim it with a knife or scissors, depending on the edge to be made.

# FINISHING THE EDGE

**1 ▲ For a forked edge:** Trim the dough even with the rim and press it flat. Firmly and evenly press the prongs of a fork all round the edge. If the fork sticks, dip it in flour.

**2 ▲ For a crimped edge:** Trim the dough to leave an overhang of about ½ in (1.5 cm) all round. Fold the extra dough under. Put the knuckle or tip of the index finger of one of your hands inside the edge, pointing directly out. With the thumb and index finger of your other hand, pinch the dough edge around your index finger into a 'V' shape. Continue all round the edge.

**3 ▲ For a ruffled edge:** Trim the dough to leave an overhang of about ½ in (1.5 cm) all round. Fold the extra dough under. Hold the thumb and index finger of one of your hands about 1 in (2.5 cm) apart, inside the edge, pointing directly out. With the index finger of your other hand, gently pull the dough between them, to the end of the rim. Continue all the way round the edge.

**Apple and Cherry Crumble Pie**
Mix together 12 oz (340 g) peeled, cored and sliced Granny Smith apples, 10 oz (300 g) stoned cherries and 4 oz (115 g) soft light brown sugar. Put into a 9 in (23 cm) pastry case. For the topping, combine 4 oz (115 g) plain flour, 4 oz (115 g) soft light brown sugar and 1 teaspoon ground cinnamon. Rub in 3 oz (85 g) butter until the mixture resembles coarse crumbs. Sprinkle over the fruit. Bake in a 375°F/190°C/Gas 5 oven for about 45 minutes or until golden. *Serves* 6.

**4 ▲ For a cutout edge:** Trim the dough even with the rim and press it flat on the rim. With a small pastry cutter, cut out decorative shapes from the dough trimmings. Moisten the edge of the pastry case and press the cutouts in place, overlapping them slightly if you like.

**5 ▲ For a ribbon edge:** Trim the dough even with the rim and press it flat on the rim. Cut long strips about ¾ in (2 cm) wide from the dough trimmings. Moisten the edge and press one end of a strip on to it. Twist the strip gently and press it on to the edge again. Continue all the way round the edge.

# MAKING A TWO-CRUST PIE

Two succulent pastry layers enveloping a sweet filling – what could be nicer? Use the same method for making small pies, such as mince pices.

**American-style Apple Pie**
Combine 2 lb (900 g) peeled, cored and thinly sliced Granny Smith apples, 1 tablespoon plain flour, 3½ oz (100 g) caster sugar and ¾ teaspoon mixed spice. Toss to coat the fruit evenly with the sugar and flour. Use to fill the two-crust pie. Bake in a 375°F/190°C/ Gas 5 oven for about 45 minutes or until the pastry is golden brown and the fruit is tender (test with a skewer through a slit in the top crust). Cool on a rack.

**1 ▲** Roll out half of the pastry dough on a floured surface and line a pie tin that is about 2 in (5 cm) deep. Trim the dough even with the rim.

**3 ▲** Roll out a second piece of dough to a circle that is about 1 in (2.5 cm) larger all round than the tin. Roll it up around the rolling pin and unroll over the pie. Press the edges together.

**5 ▲** Fold the overhang of the lid under the edge of the case. Press the two together gently and evenly to seal. Finish the edge as wished.

**2 ▲** Put in the filling. Brush the edge of the pastry case evenly with water to moisten it.

**4 ▲** Trim the edge of the lid to leave a ½ in (1.5 cm) overhang. Cut slits or a design in the centre. These will act as steam vents during baking.

**6 ▲** Brush the top of the pie with milk or cream for a shiny finish. Or brush with 1 egg yolk mixed with 1 teaspoon water for a glazed golden brown finish. Or brush with water and then sprinkle with caster sugar or cinnamon and sugar for a sugary crust.

**7 ▲** If you like, cut out decorative shapes from the dough trimmings, rolled out as thinly as possible. Moisten the cutouts with a little water and press them on to the top. Glaze the decorations before baking.

# Blueberry Pie

## SERVES 6–8

basic or rich shortcrust for a two-crust
    pie (page 222, shortcrust variations)

1¼ lb (575 g) blueberries

5½ oz (160 g) caster sugar

3 tablespoons plain flour

1 teaspoon grated orange zest

¼ teaspoon grated nutmeg

2 tablespoons orange juice

1 teaspoon lemon juice

1  Preheat a 375°F/190°C/Gas 5 oven.

2 ▲  Roll out half of the pastry and
use to line a 9 in (23 cm) pie tin that is
about 2 in (5 cm) deep.

3 ▲  Combine the blueberries, 5 oz
(145 g) of the sugar, the flour, orange
zest and nutmeg in a bowl. Toss the
mixture gently to coat the fruit evenly
with the dry ingredients.

4 ▼  Pour the blueberry mixture into
the pastry case and spread it evenly.
Sprinkle over the citrus juices.

5  Roll out the remaining pastry
and cover the pie. Cut out small
decorative shapes or cut 2–3 slits for
steam vents. Finish the edge.

6 ▲  Brush the top lightly with water
and sprinkle evenly with the
remaining caster sugar.

7  Bake for about 45 minutes or until
the pastry is golden brown. Serve
warm or at room temperature.

# MAKING A LATTICE TOP

A woven pastry lattice is a very attractive finish for a pie. Prepare shortcrust for a two-crust pie.

Roll out half of the pastry dough and line the pie tin. Trim the dough to leave a ½ in (1.5 cm) overhang all round. Put in the filling. Roll out the second piece of dough into a circle that is about 2 in (5 cm) larger all round than the pie tin.

**Apricot Lattice Pie**
Toss together 2¼ lb (1 kg) peeled, stoned and thinly sliced apricots, 2 tablespoons plain flour and 3½ oz (100 g) sugar. Fill the pastry case and make a lattice top. Glaze with milk and bake in a 375°F/190°C/Gas 5 oven for about 45 minutes or until the pastry is golden and the filling is bubbling. Cool on a wire rack.

**1 ▲** With the help of a ruler, cut neat straight strips of dough that are about ½ in (1.5 cm) wide, using a knife or fluted pastry wheel.

**2 ▲ For a square woven lattice:** Lay half of the strips across the pie filling, keeping them neatly parallel and spacing them evenly.

**3 ▲** Fold back every other strip from the centre. Lay another strip across the centre, on the flat strips, at right angles to them. Lay the folded strips flat again.

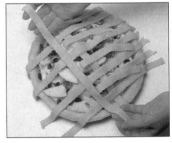

**4 ▲** Now fold back those strips that were not folded the first time. Lay another strip across those that are flat now, spacing this new strip evenly from the centre strip.

**5 ▲** Continue folding the strips in this way until half of the lattice is completed. Repeat on the other half of the pie.

**6 ▲** Trim the ends of the strips even with the rim of the pie tin. Moisten the edge of the pastry case and press the strips gently to it to seal. Finish the edge.

**7 ▲ For a diamond lattice:** Weave as above, laying the intersecting strips diagonally instead of at right angles. Or lay half the strips over the filling and the remaining strips on top.

# Walnut and Pear Lattice Pie

**SERVES 6–8**

nut shortcrust for a two-crust pie (page 222, pastry variations), using walnuts

2 lb (900 g) pears, peeled, cored and thinly sliced

2 oz (55 g) caster sugar

1 oz (30 g) plain flour

½ teaspoon grated lemon zest

1 oz (30 g) raisins or sultanas

1 oz (30 g) walnuts, chopped

½ teaspoon ground cinnamon

2 oz (55 g) icing sugar

1 tablespoon lemon juice

about 2 teaspoons cold water

**1** Preheat a 375°F/190°C/Gas 5 oven.

**2** Roll out half of the pastry dough and use to line a 9 in (23 cm) tin that is about 2 in (5 cm) deep.

**3** ▲ Combine the pears, caster sugar, flour and lemon zest in a bowl. Toss gently until the fruit is evenly coated with the dry ingredients. Mix in the raisins, nuts and cinnamon.

~ **COOK'S TIP** ~

For a simple cutout lattice top, roll out the dough for the top into a circle. Using a small pastry cutter, cut out shapes in a pattern, spacing them evenly and not too close together.

**4** ▲ Put the pear filling into the pastry case and spread it evenly.

**5** Roll out the remaining pastry dough and use to make a lattice top.

**6** Bake for 55 minutes or until the pastry is golden brown.

**7** Combine the icing sugar, lemon juice and water in a bowl and stir until smoothly blended.

**8** ▼ Remove the pie from the oven. Drizzle the icing sugar glaze evenly over the top of the pie, on pastry and filling. Leave the pie to cool, set on a wire rack, before serving.

# Making French Flan Pastry

The pastry for tarts, flans and quiches is made with butter or margarine, giving a rich and crumbly result. The more fat used, the richer the pastry will be – almost like a biscuit dough – and the harder to roll out. If you have difficulty rolling it, you can press it into the tin instead, or roll it out between sheets of cling film. Flan pastry, like shortcrust, can be made by hand or in a food processor. Tips for making, handling and using shortcrust pastry apply equally to French flan pastry.

**For a 9 in (23 cm) flan case**

| |
| --- |
| 7 oz (200 g) plain flour |
| ½ teaspoon salt |
| 4 oz (115 g) butter or margarine, chilled |
| 1 egg yolk |
| ¼ teaspoon lemon juice |
| 2–3 tablespoons iced water |

**1** ▲ Sift the flour and salt into a bowl. Add the butter or margarine. Rub into the flour until the mixture resembles fine crumbs.

**2** ▲ In a small bowl, mix the egg yolk, lemon juice and 2 tablespoons water. Add to the flour mixture. With a fork, toss gently to mix and moisten.

**3** ▲ Press the dough into a rough ball. If it is too dry to come together, add the remaining water. Turn on to the work surface or a pastry board.

**4** ▲ With the heel of your hand, push small portions of dough away from you, smearing them on the surface.

**Flan pastry variations**
- For *Sweet Flan Pastry:* Reduce the amount of salt to ¼ teaspoon; add 1 tablespoon caster sugar with the flour.
- For *Rich Flan Pastry:* Use 7 oz (200 g) flour, ½ teaspoon salt, 5 oz (145 g) butter, 2 egg yolks, and 1–2 tablespoons water.
- For *Rich Sweet Flan Pastry:* Make rich flan pastry, adding 3 tablespoons caster sugar with the flour and, if liked, ½ teaspoon vanilla essence with the egg yolks.

**5** ▲ Continue mixing the dough in this way until it feels pliable and can be peeled easily off the surface.

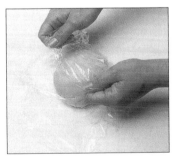

**6** ▲ Press the dough into a smooth ball. Wrap in cling film and chill for at least 30 minutes.

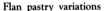

# LINING A FLAN TIN OR RING

A flan tin is shallow, with no rim. Its straight sides (smooth or fluted) give a tart or flan the traditional shape. The most useful tins have removable bases, making it very easy to turn out a tart. Flan rings are straight-sided metal rings that are set on a baking sheet.

In addition to flan tins and rings, there are porcelain quiche dishes and small, individual tartlet tins, both plain and fluted.

**Pecan Nut Tartlets**
Line six 4 in (10 cm) tartlet tins with flan pastry. Place 1 oz (30 g) pecan nut halves in each. In a bowl, beat 3 eggs to mix. Add 1 oz (30 g) melted butter, 10 oz (300 g) golden syrup and ½ teaspoon vanilla essence. Sift together 4 oz (115 g) caster sugar and 1 tablespoon plain flour. Add to the egg mixture and stir until evenly blended. Fill the tartlet cases and leave until the nuts rise to the surface. Bake in a 350°F/ 180°C/Gas 4 oven for 35–40 minutes or until a knife inserted near the centre comes out clean. Cool in the tins for 15 minutes, then turn on to a wire rack.

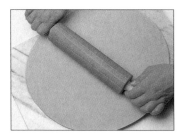

**1 ▲** Remove the chilled dough from the refrigerator and let it soften slightly at room temperature. Roll out to a circle about 2 in (5 cm) larger all round than the tin or ring. It will be about ⅛ in (3 mm) thick.

**3 ▲** With your fingertips, ease the dough into the tin or ring, gently pressing it smoothly over the bottom, without stretching it.

**5 ▲** Roll the rolling pin over the top of the tin or ring to cut off excess dough. Smooth the cut edge and press it against the side of the tin or ring, if necessary, to keep it in place.

**2 ▲** Roll up the dough round the rolling pin, then unroll it over the tin or ring, draping it gently.

**4 ▲** Fold the overhanging dough down inside the tin or ring, to thicken the side of the pastry case. Smooth and press the side of the case against the side of the tin or ring.

**6 ▲ For tartlet tins**: Arrange them close together and unroll the dough over them, draping it loosely. Roll the rolling pin over the top to cut off excess pastry. Press into the bottom and sides of the tins.

# BAKING BLIND

Baked custard and cream fillings can make pastry soggy, so the cases for these flans and tarts are often given an initial baking before the filling is added and the final baking is done. Such pre-baking is referred to as baking 'blind'. The technique is also used for pastry cases that are to be filled with an uncooked or precooked mixture.

The purpose of using weights is to prevent the bottom of the pastry case from rising too much and becoming distorted, thus keeping its neat shape.

**1 ▲** Set the pie or flan tin, or flan ring, on a sheet of greaseproof paper or foil. Draw or mark around its base. Cut out a circle about 3 in (7.5 cm) larger all round than the drawn or marked one.

**2 ▲** Roll out the pastry dough and use to line the tin or ring set on a baking sheet. Prick the bottom of the pastry case all over with a fork.

**Fresh Strawberry Flan**
Make the case using sweet flan pastry or rich sweet flan pastry (page 230). Bake it blind fully, then cool. Beat 14 oz (400 g) full-fat soft cheese with 1¾ oz (50 g) caster sugar, 1 egg yolk and 4 tablespoons whipping cream until smooth. Fold in 1 stiffly whisked egg white. Pour into the case and spread evenly. Bake at 350°F/180°C/Gas 4 for 15–20 minutes or until the filling is softly set; it will set further as it cools. When cool, arrange halved strawberries on top in concentric circles. Melt 5 oz (145 g) redcurrant jelly and brush over the berries to glaze them. Leave to cool before serving. *Serves* 6.

**3 ▲** Lay the circle of greaseproof paper or foil in the pastry case and press it smoothly over the bottom and up the side.

**4 ▲** Put enough dried beans or baking beans in the case to cover the bottom thickly.

**5 ▲ For partially baked pastry:** Bake the case in a 400°F/200°C/Gas 6 oven for 15–20 minutes or until it is slightly dry and set. Remove the paper or foil and beans. The pastry is now ready to be filled and baked further.

**6 ▲ For fully baked pastry:** After baking for 15 minutes, remove the paper or foil and beans. Prick the bottom again with a fork. Return to the oven and bake for 5–10 minutes or until golden brown. Cool completely before adding the filling.

# Quiche Lorraine

**SERVES 6**

8 oz (225 g) smoked streaky bacon
  rashers, chopped

9 in (23 cm) flan case, partially baked
  blind

3 eggs

2 egg yolks

12 fl oz (360 ml) whipping cream

4 fl oz (120 ml) milk

salt and pepper

1   Preheat a 200°C/400°F/Gas 6 oven.

2 ▲ Fry the bacon in a frying pan
until it is crisp and golden brown.
Drain the bacon on paper towels.

3 ▲ Scatter the bacon in the
partially baked flan case.

4   In a bowl, whisk together the eggs,
egg yolks, cream and milk. Season
with salt and pepper.

5 ▼ Pour the egg mixture into the
flan case.

6   Bake for 35–40 minutes or until the
filling is set and golden brown and the
pastry is golden. Serve warm or at
room temperature.

~ **VARIATIONS** ~

Add 3 oz (85 g) grated Gruyère
cheese with the bacon. Replace
the bacon with diced cooked ham,
if desired. For a vegetarian quiche,
omit the bacon. Slice 1 lb (450 g)
courgettes and fry in a little oil
until lightly browned on both sides.
Drain on paper towels, then
arrange in the flan case. Scatter
2 oz (55 g) grated cheese on top.
Make the egg mixture with 4 eggs,
8 fl oz (240 ml) cream, 4
tablespoons milk, ⅛ teaspoon
grated nutmeg, salt and pepper.

# MAKING A BISCUIT CASE

A biscuit case is one of the simplest bases to make, and the variations in flavouring are almost endless. Crumbs from any dry biscuit can be used, both sweet and savoury. You can also use breadcrumbs and cake crumbs. Most biscuit cases are sweet, to hold sweet fillings, but there are also unsweetened biscuit cases for savoury cheesecakes.

**MAKES AN 8–9 IN (20–23 CM) CASE**

8 oz (225 g) biscuits (see below), crushed

4 oz (115 g) butter, melted

3–4 tablespoons caster sugar (optional)

**1 ▲** Combine the biscuits, melted butter and sugar, plus other flavourings, if using. Stir well to mix.

**2 ▲** Turn the biscuit mixture into a buttered 8 in (20 cm) springform cake tin or 9 in (23 cm) tart tin. Spread it over the bottom and up the side.

**Biscuit case flavourings**
• Use digestive biscuits. Sweeten with sugar to taste, if liked. Add 1 teaspoon ground cinnamon or ginger or mixed spice or ½ teaspoon grated nutmeg.
• Use digestive biscuits and sweeten with sugar to taste, if liked. Add 1 teaspoon grated lemon zest or 2 teaspoons grated orange zest.
• Use 7 oz (200 g) digestive biscuits and 1½ oz (45 g) ground or finely chopped nuts (almonds, hazelnuts, pecan nuts or walnuts).
• Use ginger nuts, shortbread, almond butter biscuits, amaretti biscuits or crisp almond macaroons. No sugar is needed.
• Use water biscuits or other cheese biscuits, without adding sugar, for a savoury filling.

**3 ▲** With the back of a large spoon or your fingers, press the biscuit mixture firmly against the tin, to pack the crumbs into a solid crust.

**4 ▲** According to the recipe, refrigerate the case to set it, usually at least 1 hour. Or bake the case in a 350°F/180°C/Gas 4 oven for 8–10 minutes; cool before filling.

**Crushing the biscuits**
To make fine crumbs, break the biscuits into small pieces. Put them, a small batch at a time, in a heavy plastic bag and roll over them with a rolling pin. Or grind them finely in a blender or food processor.

**Easy Chocolate Tart**
Prepare the biscuit case using ginger biscuits and pressing it into a 9 in (23 cm) tin. Bake and cool. Melt 6 oz (170 g) plain chocolate with 4 tablespoons milk; cool. Whip ¾ pint (450 ml) double or whipping cream until thick. Fold into the cooled chocolate. Spread evenly in the case. Cover and refrigerate until firm. Just before serving, garnish with chocolate curls or grated chocolate. *Serves 6.*

# Rich Orange Cheesecake

**SERVES 8**

1½ lb (700 g) full-fat soft cheese, at room temperature

7 oz (200 g) caster sugar

2 tablespoons plain flour

3 eggs

4 oz (115 g) butter, melted

1 teaspoon vanilla essence

1 tablespoon grated orange zest

8 in (20 cm) biscuit case, made with digestive biscuits and orange zest, chilled

4 sweet oranges, peeled and segmented

squeeze of lemon juice

1–2 tablespoons orange liqueur (optional)

1 Preheat a 300°F/150°C/Gas 2 oven.

2 ▲ Combine the soft cheese, sugar and flour in a bowl. Beat until the mixture is light and fluffy.

3 ▲ Add the eggs, butter, vanilla essence and orange zest and beat until smoothly blended.

4 ▲ Pour the filling into the biscuit case. Set the springform tin on a baking sheet.

5 Bake for 1–1¼ hours or until the filling is gently set (it will continue to firm up as it cools). If the top browns too quickly, cover with foil. Turn off the oven and open the door.

6 Leave the cheesecake to cool in the oven. When it is cold, cover and refrigerate overnight.

7 Mix together the orange segments, lemon juice and liqueur, if using. Serve with the cheesecake.

~ **VARIATIONS** ~

For Lemon Cheesecake, use 1½ teaspoons lemon zest instead of orange in the filling. For a lighter cheesecake, use a mixture of ricotta or curd cheese and full-fat soft cheese, worked in a food processor until smooth.

# MAKING CHOUX PASTRY

Unlike other pastries, where the fat is rubbed into the flour, with choux pastry the butter is melted with water and then the flour is added, followed by eggs. The result is more of a paste than a pastry. It is easy to make, but care must be taken in measuring the ingredients.

**FOR 18 PROFITEROLES OR 12 ECLAIRS**

| |
|---|
| 4 oz (115 g) butter, cut into small pieces |
| 8 fl oz (240 ml) water |
| 2 teaspoons caster sugar (optional) |
| ¼ teaspoon salt |
| 5 oz (145 g) plain flour |
| 4 eggs, beaten to mix |

**Shaping choux pastry**
- For *large puffs*: Use two large spoons dipped in water. Drop the paste in 2–2½ in (5–6 cm) wide blobs on the paper-lined baking sheet, leaving 1½ in (4 cm) between each. Neaten the blobs as much as possible. Alternatively, for well-shaped puffs, pipe the paste using a piping bag fitted with a ¾ in (2 cm) plain nozzle.
- For *profiteroles*: Use two small spoons or a piping bag fitted with a ½ in (1.5 cm) nozzle and shape 1 in (2.5 cm) blobs.
- For *éclairs*: Use a piping bag fitted with a ¾ in (2 cm) nozzle. Pipe strips 4–5 in (10–12 cm) long.
- For a *ring*: draw a 12 in (30 cm) circle on the paper. Spoon the paste in large blobs on the circle to make a ring. Or pipe two rings round the circle and a third on top.

**Baking times for choux pastry**
Bake large puffs and éclairs 30–35 minutes, profiteroles 20–25 minutes, rings 40–45 minutes.

**1** ▲ Combine the butter, water, sugar, if using, and salt in a large heavy-based saucepan. Bring to the boil over moderately high heat, stirring occasionally.

**3** ▲ Return the pan to moderate heat and cook, stirring, until the mixture will form a ball, pulling away from the side of the pan. This will take about 1 minute. Remove from the heat again and allow to cool for 3–5 minutes.

**5** ▲ While still warm, shape large choux puffs, éclairs, profiteroles or large rings on a baking sheet lined with baking parchment.

**2** ▲ As soon as the mixture is boiling, remove the pan from the heat. Add the flour all at once and beat vigorously with a wooden spoon to mix the flour into the liquid.

**4** ▲ Add a little of the beaten egg and beat well with the spoon or an electric mixer to incorporate. Add a little more egg and beat in well. Continue beating in the eggs until the mixture becomes a smooth, shiny paste thick enough to hold its shape.

**6** ▲ Glaze with 1 egg beaten with 1 teaspoon cold water. Put into a 425°F/ 220°C/Gas 7 oven, then reduce the heat to 400°F/200°C/Gas 6. Bake until puffed and golden brown.

7 ▶ When baked (see baking times, left) use the tip of a knife to make a slit in the side of each puff or éclair, or several around a ring, to let the steam inside escape. Return to the turned-off oven and dry out for 5–10 minutes. Cool on a wire rack. Shortly before serving, split the pastries open horizontally and fill as desired.

**Fillings for choux pastry**
• Fill sweet choux with sweetened whipped cream (page 160), ice cream or sweetened chestnut purée. Serve with bittersweet chocolate sauce (page 203).
• Fill savoury choux with cheese sauce or creamed chicken.

# Hot Cheddar Puffs

**MAKES ABOUT 28 APPETIZER PUFFS**

2 oz (55 g) butter, cut into pieces

8 fl oz (240 ml) water

½ teaspoon salt

5 oz (145 g) plain flour

¼ teaspoon mustard powder

good pinch of hot paprika

2 oz (55 g) mature Cheddar cheese, grated

4 eggs, beaten

1 egg beaten with 1 teaspoon cold water, to glaze

FOR THE FILLING

8 oz (225 g) full-fat soft cheese, at room temperature

2 tablespoons spicy fruit sauce

4 tablespoons diced canned pimiento

2 tablespoons chopped black olives

1 Preheat a 425°F/220°C/Gas 7 oven.

2 Make the choux pastry, adding the mustard and paprika with the flour and beating in the cheese before the eggs. Shape into small puffs on a baking sheet lined with baking parchment. Brush with the egg glaze.

3 Put in the oven and reduce the temperature to 400°F/200°C/Gas 6. Bake for 20–25 minutes or until risen, golden brown and crisp.

4 ▲ Meanwhile, for the filling, beat the soft cheese with the spicy fruit sauce until well blended. Mix in the pimiento and olives.

5 Cut a slit in the side of each puff and return to the turned-off oven to dry out for about 10 minutes.

6 ▼ While the puffs are still warm, fill them with the cheese filling, piping or spooning it carefully into the slit cut in the side of each puff. Serve the Cheddar puffs warm.

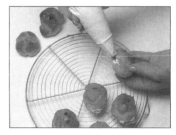

# MAKING A BUTTER CAKE

The butter cake, with its tender crumb and moist flavour, is always popular. It is rich enough to be served plain, with just a dusting of icing sugar (as with pound cake), or it can be layered and iced.

To make a butter cake, the fat and sugar are creamed together before the eggs and dry ingredients are added. The fat (butter or margarine) should be soft enough to be beaten, so if necessary remove it from the fridge and let it stand at room temperature for 30 minutes. For best results, the eggs should be at room temperature, too.

**1 ▲** Sift the flour with the salt, raising agent(s) and any other dry ingredients, such as spices or cocoa powder. Set aside.

**2 ▲** Put the fat in a large, deep bowl and beat with an electric mixer at medium speed, or a wooden spoon, until the texture is soft and pliable.

**Pound Cake**
Make the batter using ½ lb (225g) butter, 14oz (400g) sugar, 4 eggs, 12oz (375g) flour, ¼ teaspoon salt, ½ teaspoon baking powder, ½ pint (300ml) milk, ½ teaspoon vanilla extract and 1 teaspoon almond extract. Pour into a greased and floured 8½ x 4½ in (21 x 11 cm) loaf tin. Bake in a preheated 350°F/ 180°C/Gas 4 oven for 1½ hours. Cool in the tin 15 minutes, then unmould on to a wire rack to cool completely.

**3 ▲** Add the sugar to the creamed fat gradually. With the mixer at medium-high speed, beat it into the fat until the mixture is pale and very fluffy. The sugar should be completely incorporated. This will take 4–5 minutes. During this process, air will be beaten into the mixture, which will help the cake to rise.

**4 ▲** Add the eggs or egg yolks, one at a time, beating well after each addition (about 45 seconds). Scrape the bowl often so all the ingredients are evenly combined. When adding the eggs, the mixture may begin to curdle, especially if the eggs are cold. If this happens, add 1 tablespoon of the measured flour.

**5 ▲** Add the dry ingredients to the mixture, beating at low speed just until smoothly combined. Or fold in with a large metal spoon.

**6 ▲** If the recipe calls for any liquid, add it in small portions alternately with portions of the dry ingredients.

**7 ▲** If the recipe specifies, whisk egg whites separately until frothy, add sugar and continue whisking until stiff peaks form. Fold into the mixture.

**8 ▲** Pour the mixture into a cake tin or tins, prepared according to the recipe, and bake as specified.

**9 ▲** To test creamed-method cakes, insert a metal skewer or wooden cocktail stick into the centre; it should come out clean.

# MAKING AMERICAN FROSTING

This fluffy white frosting has an attractive gloss and a texture like meringue. It is a delicious filling and icing for sandwich cakes.

**MAKES ENOUGH TO FILL AND ICE A 9 IN (23 CM) SANDWICH CAKE**

| |
|---|
| 10 oz (300 g) sugar |
| ¼ teaspoon cream of tartar |
| 2 egg whites |
| 4 tablespoons cold water |
| 1 tablespoon liquid glucose |
| 2 teaspoons vanilla essence |

**1 ▲** Combine the sugar, cream of tartar, egg whites, water and glucose in a large heatproof bowl or the top of a double saucepan. Stir just to mix.

**2 ▲** Set the bowl over a saucepan of boiling water. The base of the bowl should not touch the water.

**3 ▲** Beat with a hand-held electric mixer at high speed for about 7 minutes or until the frosting is thick and white and will form stiff peaks.

**4 ▲** Remove from the heat. Add the vanilla and continue beating for about 3 minutes or until the frosting has cooled slightly. Use immediately.

**Frosting variations**

For *Orange Frosting*: Use orange juice instead of water and add 1 teaspoon grated orange zest. Reduce the vanilla to ½ teaspoon.

For *Lemon Frosting*: Use 2 tablespoons each lemon juice and water and add ½ teaspoon grated lemon zest. Reduce the vanilla to ½ teaspoon.

# Coconut Lime Gâteau

**SERVES 8 OR MORE**

8 oz (225 g) plain flour

2½ teaspoons baking powder

¼ teaspoon salt

8 oz (225 g) butter, at room temperature

8 oz (225 g) caster sugar

grated zest of 2 limes

4 eggs

4 tablespoons fresh lime juice (from about 2 limes)

3 oz (85 g) desiccated coconut

1 recipe quantity American frosting (page 239)

**1** Preheat a 350°F/180°C/Gas 4 oven. Grease two 9 in (23 cm) sandwich tins and line the bottoms with greased greaseproof paper.

**2** Sift together the flour, baking powder and salt.

**3** In a large bowl, beat the butter until it is soft and pliable. Add the sugar and lime zest and beat until the mixture is pale and fluffy. Beat in the eggs, one at a time.

**4** ▲ Using a wooden spoon fold in the sifted dry ingredients in small portions, alternating with the lime juice. When the mixture is smooth, stir in two-thirds of the coconut.

**5** ▲ Divide the mixture between the prepared tins and spread it evenly to the sides. Bake for 30–35 minutes (test with a skewer).

**6** ▲ Remove the cakes from the oven and set them, in their tins, on a wire rack. Cool for 10 minutes. Then turn out and peel off the lining paper. Cool completely on the rack.

**7** ▲ Spread the remaining coconut in another cake tin. Bake until golden brown, stirring occasionally. Watch carefully so that the coconut does not get too dark. Cool.

**8** ▲ Put one of the cakes, base up, on a serving plate. Spread a layer of frosting evenly over the cake.

**9** ▲ Set the second layer on top, base down. Spread the remaining frosting all over the top and round the sides of the cake.

**10** ▲ Scatter the toasted coconut over the top of the cake and leave to set before serving.

# MAKING CAKES BY THE ALL-IN-ONE METHOD

Many cakes are made by an easy all-in-one method where all the ingredients are combined in a bowl and beaten thoroughly. The mixture can also be made in a food processor, but take care not to over-process. A refinement on the all-in-one method is to separate the eggs and make the mixture with the yolks. The whites are whisked separately and then folded in.

**1 ▲** Sift the dry ingredients (flour, salt, raising agent, spices and so on) into a bowl.

**2 ▲** Add the liquid ingredients (eggs, melted or soft fat, milk, fruit juices and so on) and beat until smooth, with an electric mixer for speed. Pour into the prepared tins and bake as specified in the recipe.

---

# MAKING SIMPLE BUTTERCREAM

Quick to make and easy to spread, buttercream is ideal for all kinds of cakes, from simple ones to gâteaux. The basic buttercream can be varied with many other flavours, and it can be tinted with food colouring, too.

**MAKES ENOUGH TO COVER THE TOP AND SIDE OF A 7–8 IN (17–20 CM) CAKE**

| |
|---|
| 4 oz (115 g) butter, preferably unsalted, at room temperature |
| 8 oz (225 g) icing sugar, sifted |
| 1 teaspoon vanilla essence |
| about 2 tablespoons milk |

**1 ▲** Put the butter in a deep mixing bowl and beat it with an electric mixer at medium speed, or a wooden spoon, until it is soft and pliable.

**2 ▲** Gradually add the icing sugar and beat at medium-high speed. Continue beating until the mixture is pale and fluffy.

**Buttercream variations**

- For *Orange or Lemon Buttercream*, grate the zest from 1 small orange or ½ lemon; squeeze the juice. Beat in the zest with the sugar; use the juice instead of the vanilla and milk.
- For *Chocolate Buttercream*, add 4 tablespoons cocoa powder, beating it in with the sugar. Increase the milk to 3–4 tablespoons.

- For *Mocha Buttercream*: Warm the milk and dissolve 1 teaspoon instant coffee powder in it; cool and use to make chocolate buttercream, adding more milk if needed.
- For *Coffee Buttercream*, warm the milk and dissolve 1 tablespoon of instant coffee powder in it; cool before adding to the buttercream.

**3 ▲** Add the vanilla essence and 1 tablespoon milk. Beat until smooth and of a spreading consistency. If it is too thick, beat in more milk. If too thin, beat in more sugar.

# Chocolate Fairy Cakes

**MAKES 24**

4 oz (115 g) good-quality plain chocolate, cut into small pieces

1 tablespoon water

10 oz (300 g) plain flour

1 teaspoon baking powder

½ teaspoon bicarbonate of soda

pinch of salt

10 oz (300 g) caster sugar

6 oz (170 g) butter or margarine, at room temperature

¼ pint (150 ml) milk

1 teaspoon vanilla essence

3 eggs

1 recipe quantity buttercream, flavoured to taste

**1** Preheat a 350°F/180°C/Gas 4 oven. Grease and flour 24 deep bun tins, about 2¾ in (6.5 cm) in diameter, or use paper cases in the tins.

**2 ▲** Put the chocolate and water in a bowl set over a pan of almost simmering water. Heat until melted and smooth, stirring. Remove from the heat and leave to cool.

**3** Sift the flour, baking powder, bicarbonate of soda, salt and sugar into a large bowl. Add the chocolate mixture, butter, milk and vanilla essence.

**4 ▲** With an electric mixer on medium-low speed, beat until smoothly blended. Increase the speed to high and beat for 2 minutes. Add the eggs and beat for 2 minutes.

**5** Divide the mixture evenly among the prepared bun tins.

**6** Bake for 20–25 minutes or until a skewer inserted into the centre of a cake comes out clean. Cool in the tins for 10 minutes, then turn out to cool completely on a wire rack.

**7 ▼** Ice the top of each cake with buttercream, swirling it into a peak in the centre.

# MAKING A CLASSIC WHISKED SPONGE

The classic whisked sponge contains no fat and no raising agents – just eggs, sugar and flour. The light, airy texture of the finished cake depends on the large quantity of air beaten into the mixture.

Sometimes the eggs are separated for a whisked sponge and sometimes the cake is enriched with butter. American angel food cake uses egg whites only.

A whisked sponge can be simply dusted with icing or caster sugar, filled with sweetened whipped cream, a fruit jam or fresh fruit, or used to make a Swiss roll.

If you use a table-top electric mixer to beat the eggs and sugar, or if using separated eggs, there is no need to set the bowl over a pan of simmering water.

**Whisked Sponge**
Make the mixture using 4 whole eggs, 5 oz (145 g) caster sugar and 4 oz (115 g) plain flour. Pour into a greased, bottom-lined and floured 9 in (23 cm) round cake tin. Bake in a 350°F/180°C/Gas 4 oven for 25–30 minutes Cool in the tin for 10 minutes, then turn out on to a wire rack and cool completely. Before serving, peel off the lining paper. Dust the top lightly with sifted icing sugar.

**1 ▲** In a heatproof bowl, combine the eggs (at room temperature) and sugar. Set the bowl over a saucepan of simmering water; the base of the bowl should not touch the water.

**3 ▲** Lift out the beaters; the mixture on the beaters should trail back on to the surface of the remaining mixture in the bowl to make a ribbon that holds it shape.

**5 ▲** Sift the flour and fold it into the mixture, cutting in to the bottom of the bowl with a rubber spatula or large metal spoon and turning the mixture over, working gently yet thoroughly to retain the volume of the whisked egg and sugar mixture.

**2 ▲** Beat with a hand-held electric mixer at medium-high speed, or a rotary beater or whisk, until the mixture is very thick and pale – about 10 minutes.

**4 ▲** Remove the bowl from over the pan of water and continue beating for 2–3 minutes or until the mixture is cool.

**6 ▲** Pour the mixture into the prepared tin or tins and bake as directed in the recipe. To test a whisked sponge, press the centre lightly with your fingertip: the cake should spring back.

# Lemon Sponge Cake with Cream Cheese Icing

**SERVES 8 OR MORE**

4 eggs

5 oz (150g) granulated sugar

1 teaspoon grated lemon rind

3¼ oz (100 g) self-raising flour

FOR THE ICING

6oz (175g) cream cheese, at
room temperature

2oz (50g) butter, at room
temperature

1lb (450g) icing sugar

3–4 tablespoons fresh lemon juice

**1** Preheat the oven to 350°F/180°C/
Gas 4. Grease, line the bottom, and
flour a 9 inch (23cm) cake tin.

**2** Put the eggs and sugar in a large
bowl (over a saucepan of just
simmering water if not using an
electric mixer). Beat until the
mixture is thick and pale. Remove
the bowl from the pan of water and
continue beating until the mixture
is cool. Beat in the lemon rind.

**3** Sift the flour and fold it into the
mixture with a rubber spatula.
Pour the mixture into the prepared
tin. Bake 35–40 minutes. Let cool.

**4** ▲ For the icing, beat the cream
cheese with the butter until smooth.
Gradually beat in the sugar. Beat
in enough lemon juice to make
a fluffy icing that has a smooth
spreadable consistency.

**5** ▼ When the cake is cold, cut it
into two layers, holding it steady
with one hand on top. (First, wrap
a piece of string around the cake,
at the point where you want to cut.
When it is level, pull it taut to make
an indentation in the cake side to
follow while slicing. Remove the
string before slicing. )

**6** ▲ Cover the bottom cake layer
with a layer of icing.

**7** Put the second layer on top.
Cover the cake with the remaining
cream cheese icing, smoothing the
top layer decoratively.

# PREPARING CAKE TINS

Instructions vary from recipe to recipe for preparing cake tins. Some are simply greased, some are greased and floured, some are lined with baking parchment or greased greaseproof paper. The preparation required depends on the type of cake mixture and the length of the baking time. Proper preparation aids turning out.

**Flavourful coatings**
Some cake recipes specify that the greased tin be coated with sugar, cocoa powder or ground nuts. Follow the method for flouring.

**1 ▲ To grease a tin**: Use butter, margarine, or a mild or flavourless oil. If using butter or margarine, hold a small piece in a paper towel (or use your fingers), and rub it all over the bottom and up the side of the tin to make a thin, even coating. If using oil, brush it on with a pastry brush.

**2 ▲ To flour a tin**: Put a small scoopful of flour in the centre of the greased tin. Tip and rotate the tin so that the flour spreads and coats all over the bottom and up the side. Turn the tin over and shake out excess flour, tapping the base of the tin to dislodge any pockets of flour.

**3 ▲ To line the bottom of a tin**: Set the tin on the sheet of paper and draw round the base. Cut out this circle, square or rectangle, cutting just inside the drawn line. Press the paper smoothly on to the bottom of the tin.

**4 ▲ To line the sides of a tin** (for rich mixtures and fruit cakes): Cut a strip of paper long enough to wrap round the outside of the tin and overlap by 1½ in (4 cm). The strip should be wide enough to extend 1 in (2.5 cm) above the rim of the tin.

**5 ▲** Fold the strip lengthways at the 1 in (2.5 cm) point and crease firmly. With scissors, snip at regular intervals along the 1 in (2.5 cm) fold, from the edge to the crease. Line the side of the tin, with the snipped part of the strip on the bottom.

**6 ▲** For square and rectangular cake tins, fold the paper and crease it with your fingernail to fit snugly into the corners of the tin. Then press the bottom paper lining into place.

**7 ▲** If the recipe specifies, grease the paper before you put it in the tin. If the tin is to be floured, do this after the paper is in place.

**8 ▲ To line bun and muffin tins**: Use paper liners of the required size. Or grease and flour the tins.

**9 ▲ To line a Swiss roll tin**: Cut a rectangle of paper 2 in (5 cm) larger all round than the tin. Grease the bottom of the tin lightly to prevent the paper from slipping.

**10 ▲** Lay the paper evenly in the tin. With a table knife, press the paper into the angle all round the bottom of the tin, creasing the paper firmly but not cutting it.

**11 ▲** With scissors, snip the paper in the corners, from top to bottom, so it will fit neatly into them. Grease the paper according to recipe instructions, unless using baking parchment.

---

# USING SEPARATED EGGS FOR A WHISKED SPONGE

This version of whisked sponge is easier to make than the classic one that uses whole eggs, but the results are no less light and delicious. There is no need to set the bowl over a pan of simmering water for whisking, although if you are using a balloon whisk rather than an electric mixer or rotary beater you may want to do so to speed up the thickening of the egg yolk and sugar mixture and to increase its volume. Bowls and beaters used with egg whites must be scrupulously clean.

**1 ▲** Separate the eggs, taking care that there is no trace of yolk with the whites. Put the yolks and whites in separate large bowls.

**2 ▲** Add most of the sugar to the yolks. With a hand-held or table-top electric mixer, whisk at medium-high speed until the mixture is very thick and pale. Lift out the beaters: the mixture on the beaters should trail back on to the surface of the remaining mixture in the bowl to make a ribbon that holds its shape.

**3 ▲** Whisk the egg whites until they form soft peaks (if not using a copper bowl, add a pinch of cream of tartar once the whites are frothy). Add the remaining sugar and continue whisking until the whites will form stiff peaks.

**4 ▲** With a rubber spatula, fold the sifted flour into the egg yolk mixture, then fold in the whisked egg whites. Fold gently but thoroughly. Pour the mixture into the prepared tin and bake as instructed.

**A Genoese sponge**
This whisked sponge, made with whole or separated eggs, is more rich and trickier to make, as melted butter is folded in just before pouring into the tin.

# MAKING A SWISS ROLL

A rolled sponge reveals an attractive spiral of filling when it is sliced. The filling may be sweetened whipped cream (page 160), ice cream (page 167), fruit jam or buttercream (page 242).

The whisked sponge mixture can be made using whole or separated eggs (pages 244 or 247), as preferred.

Line the tin with greaseproof paper or baking parchment, grease the paper and dust with flour.

**Chocolate Ice Cream Roll**
Make the sponge mixture using 4 eggs, separated, 4oz (115g) caster sugar and 4oz (115g) plain flour sifted with 3 tablespoons cocoa powder. Pour into a prepared 15 × 10in (37.5 × 25cm) Swiss roll tin. Bake in a 375°F/190°C/Gas 5 oven for about 15 minutes. Turn out, roll up and cool. When cold, unroll the cake and spread with 1 pint (600ml) softened vanilla or chocolate ice cream. Roll up the cake again, wrap in foil and freeze until firm. About 30 minutes before serving, transfer the cake to the refrigerator. Sprinkle with caster or icing sugar before serving. If desired, serve with warm bittersweet chocolate sauce (page 203). *Serves 8.*

**1 ▲** Pour the mixture into the prepared tin and spread it evenly into the corners with a palette knife. Bake as specified in the recipe.

**3 ▲** Carefully peel off the lining paper from the cake. If necessary, trim off any crisp edges from the side of the cake.

**5 ▲** Remove the towel and unroll the cake. Lift off the paper. Spread the chosen filling over the cake.

**2 ▲** Spread a tea towel flat and lay a sheet of baking parchment on top. Sprinkle the paper evenly, as specified, with caster or icing sugar, cocoa or a sugar and spice mixture. Invert the cake on to the paper.

**4 ▲** Carefully roll up the cake, with the paper inside, starting from a short side. Wrap the towel round the cake roll and leave to cool on a wire rack.

**6 ▲** Roll up the cake again, using the paper to help move it forward. Sprinkle with sugar or ice the cake, as the recipe specifies.

# Yule Log Cake

**SERVES 8 OR MORE**

4 eggs, separated

5 oz (145 g) caster sugar

1 teaspoon vanilla essence

pinch of cream of tartar (if needed)

4 oz (115 g) plain flour, sifted

8 fl oz (240 ml) whipping cream

10 oz (300 g) plain or bittersweet chocolate, chopped

2 tablespoons rum or Cognac

1 Preheat a 375°F/190°C/Gas 5 oven. Grease, line and flour a 16 × 11 in (40 × 28 cm) Swiss roll tin.

2 Put the egg yolks in a large bowl. Reserve 2 tablespoons sugar; add the remainder to the egg yolks. Whisk until pale and thick. Add the vanilla.

3 In another bowl, scrupulously clean and grease-free, whisk the egg whites (with the cream of tartar if not using a copper bowl) until they will hold soft peaks. Add the reserved sugar and continue whisking until the whites are glossy and will hold stiff peaks.

4 Gently fold half the flour into the egg yolk mixture. Add one-quarter of the egg whites and fold in to lighten the mixture. Fold in the remaining flour, then the remaining egg whites.

5 ▲ Spread the mixture in the prepared tin. Bake for 15 minutes.

6 Turn on to paper sprinkled with caster sugar. Roll up and cool.

7 Bring the cream to the boil in a small saucepan. Put the chocolate in a bowl, add the cream and stir until the chocolate has melted.

8 ▲ Beat the chocolate mixture until it is fluffy and has thickened to a spreading consistency. Spoon one-third of the chocolate mixture into another bowl. Mix in rum or Cognac.

9 Unroll the cake. Spread the rum and chocolate mixture evenly over the surface. Roll up the cake again.

10 Cut off about one-quarter of the cake, at an angle. Place it against the side of the larger piece of cake, to resemble a branch from a tree trunk.

11 ▼ Spread the remaining chocolate mixture all over the cake. Mark with the prongs of a fork to resemble bark. Before serving, add small Christmas decorations and sprigs of holly if liked, and dust with a little icing sugar 'snow'

# MAKING CAKES BY THE MELTING METHOD

Cakes made by the melting method are wonderfully moist and keep quite well. Ingredients such as sugar, syrup (treacle, honey, golden syrup) and fat are warmed together until melted and smoothly combined before being added to the dry ingredients.

**1 ▲** Sift the dry ingredients (such as flour, raising agent, salt, ground spices) into a large bowl.

**2 ▲** Put the sugar and/or syrup and fat in a saucepan with any other ingredients specified in the recipe. Warm over a low heat, stirring occasionally, until the fat has melted and sugar dissolved. The mixture should not boil.

**Fruit Cake**
Sift 8 oz (225 g) self-raising flour, a pinch of salt and 1 teaspoon mixed spice. Melt together 4 oz (115 g) butter or margarine, 4 oz (115 g) soft light brown sugar, ¼ pint (150 ml) water and the grated zest and juice of 1 orange. When smooth, add 4 oz (115 g) each sultanas, currants and raisins and simmer gently for about 10 minutes, stirring occasionally. Cool. Add the fruit mixture to the dry ingredients. Add 2 oz (55 g) each chopped glacé cherries and chopped mixed peel, 1 tablespoon orange marmalade and 2 beaten eggs. Mix thoroughly. Pour into a greased and lined 8 in (20 cm) round cake tin. Bake at 325°F/170°C/Gas 3 for 1½ hours or until firm and golden; a skewer inserted in the centre should come out clean. Cool in the tin for 30 minutes before turning out on to a wire rack.

**3 ▲** If recipe instructs, warm fruit in the syrup mixture. Remove from the heat and leave to cool slightly (if too hot, it will not combine well with dry ingredients).

**5 ▲** If called for in the recipe, stir in fruit and/or nuts (if these have not been warmed in the syrup). Turn the cake mixture into a lined tin and bake according to the recipe.

**4 ▲** Make a well in the centre of the dry ingredients and pour in the cooled melted mixture. Add beaten eggs and any other liquid ingredients (milk, water, etc) and beat to a smooth, thick batter.

**Maturing for flavour**
Melting-method cakes taste best if they are allowed to 'mature' before serving. After the cake has cooled completely, wrap it in greaseproof paper and then overwrap in foil. Keep it in a cool place for 1–2 days before cutting into slices.

# Rich Sticky Gingerbread

**MAKES AN 8IN (20CM) SQUARE CAKE**

8oz (225g) plain flour

pinch of salt

1 teaspoon bicarbonate of soda

2 teaspoons ground ginger

1 teaspoon mixed spice

4oz (115g) butter or margarine

4oz (115g) golden syrup

4oz (115g) black treacle

2oz (55g) soft dark brown sugar

2 eggs, beaten

4fl oz (120ml) milk

4oz (115g) sultanas or chopped stem
ginger (optional)

FOR THE ICING (OPTIONAL)

4oz (115g) icing sugar

about 4 teaspoons water

**1 ▲** Preheat a 350°F/180°C/Gas 4
oven. Grease and line an 8in (20cm)
square cake tin.

**2 ▲** Sift the flour, salt, bicarbonate
of soda and spices into a bowl.

**3** Put the butter or margarine, golden
syrup, treacle and brown sugar in a
saucepan and warm over a gentle
heat, stirring occasionally, until the
fat has melted and the mixture is
smooth. Remove from the heat and
leave to cool slightly.

**4 ▼** Make a well in the centre of the
dry ingredients and add the melted
mixture, the beaten eggs and milk.
Beat with a wooden spoon until the
mixture is smooth. Add the sultanas
or ginger, if using.

**5** Turn the cake mixture into the
prepared tin. Bake for about 1 hour.
To test if the gingerbread is done,
press it lightly in the centre; it should
spring back. Allow to cool in the tin
for 5 minutes before turning out on to
a wire rack to cool completely.

**6 ▲** If icing the gingerbread, sift the
icing sugar into a bowl and add 3
teaspoons of the water. Stir to mix,
then add more water 1 teaspoon at a
time until the icing is smooth and has
a pouring consistency. Pour the icing
over the gingerbread and leave to set
before serving.

# INTRODUCTION

~

Complete creative cooking means putting together varied, tempting meals throughout the week and having friends and relatives over for dinner without stress. It used to mean rummaging through notebooks and clippings to find that special grandmother's recipe for beef stew or a neighbour's traditional chocolate cake.

In preparing this book we have brought together such favourite old recipes and also added new ideas, which reflect the increasing availability of exotic and speciality ingredients and the evolution of the way we eat. And each recipe is brought to life, every step of the way, in pictures.

It's easy to learn basic cooking know-how with the help of this book. With pictures to guide you at every stage, even a beginner can cook meals with confidence. For the experienced cook, the step-by-step photographs serve as memory joggers. You will practically be able to cook at a glance from a treasury of over 200 recipes.

To start off a meal or sit down to a simple one, there are chunky soups and cold ones, plus sandwiches to eat with both hands, and appetizers both plain and fancy. The seafood recipes take full advantage of the increasingly wide variety of fish and shellfish available locally. For many people, meat and poultry are the heart of a meal, and the choice here includes long-simmering as well as speedy dishes. An increasing trend towards grains and fresh produce is reflected here, with recipes for pasta, pizza, beans and vegetables well represented. Time set aside for baking may seem a luxury these days, but with the steps simply laid out, it requires only a small amount of effort to fill the kitchen with mouth-watering smells.

Here is creative family cooking in all its variety. In the category of snug, winter night's fare we have chosen such standbys as macaroni cheese, traditional chicken potpie and peach cobbler. Sometimes we put a twist on the basics, offering baby chickens with cranberry sauce, cheeseburgers with spicy avocado relish, and hazelnut sundaes with hot fudge sauce. International dishes are also given fair showing, with Mexican chicken, jambalaya, pork with sauerkraut and Spanish omelette just some of the favourites to be found here.

The only thing that's missing in *The Complete Creative Cook* are the aromas. Still, there's no substitute for experience. Only you know the quirks of your oven and how to get the best from your utensils. Setting out all the ingredients before beginning is just sound culinary practice. Even perfect technique won't remedy a lack of flavour, so good ingredients are essential to good cooking. Stay in tune with the seasons, choosing fruits and vegetables at their peak. And remember to taste and adjust the seasoning, if necessary, before serving.

Our hectic schedules leave us less time in the kitchen these days, but we hope this book rekindles the pleasures of family cooking. Homemade food will make a comeback in your house with the help of *The Complete Creative Cook.*

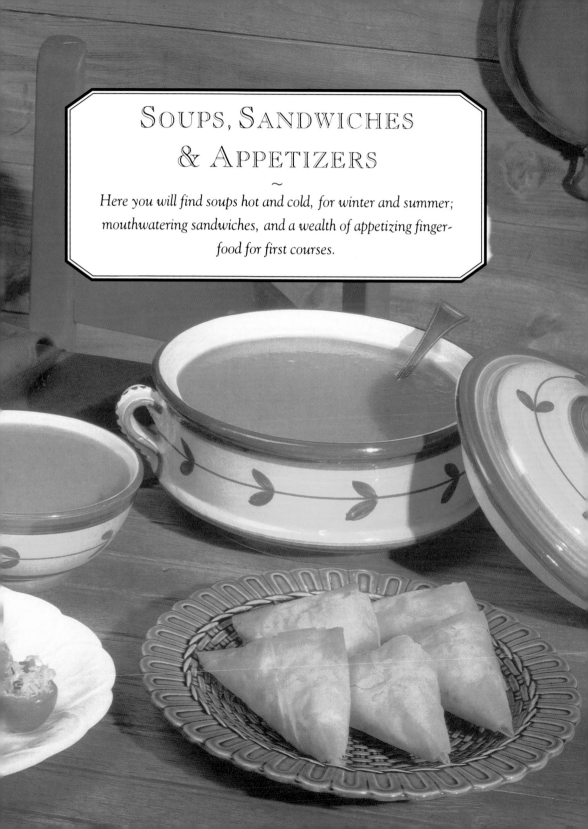

# SOUPS, SANDWICHES & APPETIZERS

~

*Here you will find soups hot and cold, for winter and summer;
mouthwatering sandwiches, and a wealth of appetizing finger-
food for first courses.*

# Warming Winter Vegetable Soup

**SERVES 8**

1 medium-size head of Savoy cabbage, quartered and cored

2 tbsp vegetable oil

4 carrots, thinly sliced

2 celery sticks, thinly sliced

2 parsnips, diced

2½ pt (1.5 litres) chicken stock

3 medium-size potatoes, diced

2 courgettes, sliced

1 small red pepper, seeded and diced

1 small cauliflower, stems trimmed and separated into florets

2 tomatoes, seeded and diced

½ tsp fresh thyme leaves, or ¼ tsp dried thyme

2 tbsp chopped fresh parsley

salt and pepper

1  Slice the cabbage quarters into thin strips across the leaves.

2 ▲ Heat the oil in a large saucepan. Add the cabbage, carrots, celery and parsnips and cook 10–15 minutes over medium heat, stirring frequently.

3  Stir the stock into the vegetables and bring to the boil. Skim off any foam that rises to the top.

4 ▲ Add the potatoes, courgettes, pepper, cauliflower and tomatoes with the herbs, and salt and pepper to taste. Bring back to the boil. Reduce the heat to low, cover the pan, and simmer until the vegetables are tender, 15–20 minutes.

---

# Traditional Tomato Soup

**SERVES 4**

1 oz (30 g) butter or margarine

1 onion, chopped

2 lb (900 g) tomatoes, quartered

2 carrots, chopped

16 fl oz (500 ml) chicken stock

2 tbsp chopped fresh parsley

½ tsp fresh thyme leaves, or ¼ tsp dried thyme

3 fl oz (85 ml) whipping cream (optional)

salt and pepper

~ COOK'S TIP ~

Canned Italian plum tomatoes are ideal for this soup.

1  Melt the butter or margarine in a large saucepan. Add the onion and cook until softened, about 5 minutes.

2 ▲ Stir in the tomatoes, carrots, chicken stock, parsley and thyme. Bring to the boil. Reduce the heat to low, cover the pan, and simmer until tender, 15–20 minutes.

3 ▼ Purée the soup in a vegetable mill. Return the puréed soup to the saucepan.

4  Stir in the cream, if using, and reheat gently. Season with salt and pepper. Ladle into warmed soup bowls and serve hot, sprinkled with a little more thyme, if you wish.

*Warming Winter Vegetable Soup (top), Traditional Tomato Soup*

# Carrot Soup

**SERVES 6**

| |
|---|
| 1 oz (30 g) butter or margarine |
| 1 onion, chopped |
| 1 celery stick, chopped |
| 1 medium-sized potato, chopped |
| 1½ lb (700 g) carrots, chopped |
| 2 tsp grated fresh root ginger |
| 2 pt (1.25 litres) chicken stock |
| 3 fl oz (85 ml) whipping cream |
| ¼ teaspoon grated nutmeg |
| salt and pepper |

**1 ▼** Combine the butter or margarine, onion and celery and cook until softened, about 5 minutes.

**2** Stir in the potato, carrots, ginger and stock. Bring to the boil. Reduce the heat to low, cover the pan and simmer 20 minutes.

**3 ▲** Pour the soup into a food processor or blender and process until smooth. Alternatively, use a vegetable mill to purée the soup. Return the soup to the pan. Stir in the cream and nutmeg and add salt and pepper to taste. Reheat gently for serving.

# Minty Pea Soup

**SERVES 6**

| |
|---|
| 1 oz (30 g) butter or margarine |
| 1 onion, chopped |
| 1 small head of lettuce, shredded |
| 2 lb (900 g) shelled fresh green peas or frozen peas, thawed |
| 2½ pt (1.5 litres) chicken stock |
| 3 tbsp chopped fresh mint |
| salt and pepper |
| 6 fl oz (175 ml) whipping cream |
| fresh mint sprigs, for garnishing |

~ **VARIATION** ~

To serve cold, refrigerate the puréed soup until thoroughly chilled, 3–4 hours. Stir all the cream into the soup just before serving, or keep some to swirl over each serving.

**1 ▲** Melt the butter or margarine in a large saucepan. Add the onion and cook until softened, about 5 minutes.

**2 ▲** Stir in the lettuce, peas, stock and mint. Bring to the boil. Reduce the heat to low, cover the pan and simmer 15 minutes.

**3** Pour the soup into a blender or food processor and process until smooth. Alternatively, purée the soup in a vegetable mill. Return the puréed soup to the pan. Season to taste.

**4 ▲** Stir in two-thirds of the cream and reheat gently. Ladle into bowls and serve with the remaining cream. For a decorative effect, pour a scant tablespoon of cream in a spiral design into the centre of each serving, or stir it in and garnish with sprigs of mint.

*Carrot Soup (top), Minty Pea Soup*

# Chilled Avocado and Courgette Soup

### SERVES 6

1¾ pt (1 litre) chicken stock

1 lb (450 g) courgettes, sliced

2 large, very ripe avocados

3 tbsp fresh lemon juice

6 fl oz (175 ml) plain yogurt

2 tsp Worcestershire sauce

½ tsp chilli powder

⅛ tsp sugar

dash of chilli sauce

salt

**1** In a large saucepan, bring the chicken stock to the boil.

**2 ▲** Add the courgettes and simmer until soft, 10–15 minutes. Let cool.

**3 ▲** Peel the avocados. Remove and discard the stones. Cut the flesh into chunks and put in a food processor or blender. Add the lemon juice and process until smooth.

**4 ▲** Using a slotted spoon, transfer the courgettes to the food processor or blender; reserve the stock. Process the courgettes with the avocado purée.

**5 ▲** Pour the avocado-courgette purée into a bowl. Stir in the reserved stock. Add two-thirds of the yogurt, the Worcestershire sauce, chilli powder, sugar, chilli sauce and salt to taste. Mix well. Cover tightly and chill 3–4 hours.

**6** To serve, ladle the soup into bowls. Swirl the remaining yogurt on the surface.

# Chicken Soup with Noodles

**SERVES 8**

| |
|---|
| 1 × 3 lb (1.35 kg) chicken, cut in pieces |
| 2 onions, quartered |
| 1 parsnip, quartered |
| 2 carrots, quartered |
| ½ tsp salt |
| 1 bay leaf |
| 2 allspice berries |
| 4 black peppercorns |
| 4¾ pt (3 litres) water |
| 3 oz (85 g) very thin egg noodles |
| sprigs of fresh dill, for garnishing |

**1 ▲** In a large saucepan, combine the chicken pieces, onions, parsnip, carrots, salt, bay leaf, allspice berries and peppercorns.

**2 ▲** Add the water to the pan and bring to the boil, skimming frequently.

**3** Reduce the heat to low and simmer 1½ hours, skimming occasionally.

**4** Strain the broth through a fine-mesh strainer into a bowl. Cool then refrigerate overnight.

**5 ▲** When the chicken pieces are cool enough to handle, remove the meat from the bones. Discard the bones, skin, vegetables and flavourings. Chop the chicken meat and refrigerate overnight.

**6** Remove the solidified fat from the surface of the chilled broth. Pour the broth into a saucepan and bring to the boil. Taste the broth; if a more concentrated flavour is wanted, boil 10 minutes to reduce slightly.

**7 ▲** Add the chicken meat and noodles to the broth and cook until the noodles are tender, about 8 minutes (check packet instructions for timing). Serve hot, garnished with dill sprigs.

# Green Bean Soup with Parmesan Cheese

**SERVES 4**

1 oz (30 g) butter or margarine

8 oz (225 g) green beans, trimmed

1 garlic clove, crushed

16 fl oz (500 ml) vegetable stock

salt and pepper

2 oz (55 g) Parmesan cheese

2 fl oz (65 ml) single cream

2 tbsp chopped fresh parsley

**1** Melt the butter or margarine in a medium saucepan. Add the green beans and garlic and cook 2–3 minutes over medium heat, stirring frequently.

**2 ▲** Stir in the stock and season with salt and pepper. Bring to the boil. Reduce the heat and simmer, uncovered, until the beans are tender, 10–15 minutes.

**3 ▼** Pour the soup into a blender or food processor and process until smooth. Alternatively, purée the soup in a food mill. Return to the pan. Stir in the grated cheese and cream. Sprinkle with the parsley and serve.

# Hearty Lentil Soup

**SERVES 6**

6 oz (175 g) brown lentils

1¾ pt (1 litre) chicken stock

8 fl oz (250 ml) water

2 fl oz (65 ml) dry red wine

1½ lb (700 g) ripe tomatoes, peeled, seeded and chopped, or 14 oz (400 g) canned chopped tomatoes

1 carrot, sliced

1 onion, chopped

1 celery stick, sliced

1 garlic clove, crushed

¼ tsp ground coriander

2 tsp chopped fresh basil, or ½ tsp dried basil

1 bay leaf

6 tbsp freshly grated Parmesan cheese

**1 ▲** Rinse the lentils and discard any discoloured ones and any grit.

**2 ▲** Combine the lentils, stock, water, wine, tomatoes, carrot, onion, celery and garlic in a large saucepan. Add the coriander, basil and bay leaf.

**3 ▼** Bring to the boil, reduce the heat to low, cover and simmer until the lentils are just tender, 20–25 minutes, stirring occasionally.

**4** Discard the bay leaf. Ladle the soup into 6 soup bowls and sprinkle each with 1 tablespoon of the cheese.

~ **VARIATION** ~

For a more substantial soup, add about 4 oz (115 g) finely chopped cooked ham for the last 10 minutes of cooking.

*Green Bean Soup with Parmesan Cheese (top), Hearty Lentil Soup*

# Spicy Mixed Bean Soup

**SERVES 8**

12 oz (350 g) dried black or red kidney beans, soaked overnight

3½ pt (2 litres) water

6 garlic cloves, crushed

12 oz (350 g) dried haricot or white beans, soaked overnight

6 tbsp balsamic or white wine vinegar

4 chilli peppers, seeded and chopped

6 spring onions, finely chopped

juice of 1 lime or lemon

2 fl oz (65 ml) olive oil

3 tbsp chopped fresh coriander, plus more for garnishing

salt and pepper

**1** Drain and rinse the black or red kidney beans. Place them in a large saucepan with half the water and garlic. Bring to the boil. Reduce the heat to low, cover and simmer until the beans are soft, about 1½ hours.

**2** Drain and rinse the white beans. Put them in another saucepan with the remaining water and garlic. Bring to a boil, cover and simmer until soft, about 1 hour.

**3 ▲** Purée the cooked haricot or white beans in a food processor or blender. Stir in the vinegar, chilli peppers and half the spring onions. Return to the saucepan and reheat gently.

**4** Purée the other cooked beans. Return to the saucepan and stir in the lime or lemon juice, olive oil, coriander and the remaining spring onions. Reheat gently.

**5 ▲** Season both soups with salt and pepper. To serve, place a ladleful of each puréed soup in each soup bowl, side by side. Swirl the two soups together with a cocktail stick. If liked, garnish with extra chopped fresh coriander.

# Warming Autumn Soup

**SERVES 4**

1 oz (30 g) butter or margarine

2 small onions, finely chopped

1 lb (450 g) butternut squash or pumpkin, peeled, seeded and cubed

2 pt (1.25 litres) chicken stock

8 oz (225 g) potatoes, cubed

1 tsp paprika

4 fl oz (125 ml) whipping cream (optional)

salt and pepper

1½ tbsp chopped fresh chives, plus whole chives, for garnishing

**1** Melt the butter or margarine in a large saucepan. Add the onions and cook until soft, about 5 minutes.

**2 ▲** Add the squash or pumpkin, stock, potatoes and paprika. Bring to the boil. Reduce the heat to low, cover the pan and simmer until the vegetables are soft, about 35 minutes.

**3** Pour the soup into a food processor or blender and process until smooth. Return the soup to the pan and stir in the cream, if using. Season with salt and pepper. Reheat gently.

**4 ▲** Stir in the chopped chives just before serving. If liked, garnish each serving with a few whole chives.

*Spicy Mixed Bean Soup (top), Warming Autumn Soup*

# Mozzarella Cheese and Tomato Sandwiches

**SERVES 4**

4 small round white bread rolls

4 fl oz (125 ml) freshly made or bottled
   pesto sauce

8 oz (225 g) Mozzarella cheese, thinly
   sliced

4 medium tomatoes, thinly sliced

3 tbsp olive oil

fresh basil leaves, for garnishing

**1** With a serrated knife, cut each roll
open in half. Spread 1 tablespoon of
pesto sauce over the cut side of each
half.

**2 ▲** Arrange alternating slices of
Mozzarella cheese and tomato on the
bottom half of each roll.

**3 ▲** Drizzle the olive oil over the
cheese and tomatoes.

**4** Replace the top half of each roll;
garnish with basil leaves, if you wish.

---

# Greek Salad in Pitta Bread

**SERVES 6**

½ small head of iceberg lettuce, cut in
   fine strips across the leaves

½ cucumber, diced

9 cherry tomatoes, halved

2 spring onions, finely chopped

4 oz (115 g) feta cheese, crumbled

8 black olives, stoned and chopped

6 oval pitta breads, cut in half crosswise

FOR THE DRESSING

1 small garlic clove, crushed

⅛ tsp salt

1 tsp fresh lemon juice

2 tbsp olive oil

1 tsp chopped fresh mint

pepper

**1 ▲** In a bowl, combine the lettuce,
cucumber, tomatoes, spring onions,
feta cheese and olives.

**2 ▲** For the dressing, combine all
the ingredients in a small screwtop jar
and shake well to mix.

**3 ▲** Pour the dressing over the salad
and toss together.

**4 ▲** Gently open the pitta bread
halves. Fill the pockets with the salad.
Serve immediately.

*Mozzarella Cheese and Tomato Sandwiches (top), Greek Salad in Pitta Bread*

# Club Sandwiches

**SERVES 4**

8 rashers of bacon

12 slices of white bread, toasted

4 fl oz (125 ml) mayonnaise

4–8 oz (115–225 g) cooked chicken breast meat, sliced

8 large lettuce leaves

salt and pepper

1 beef tomato, cut across in 4 slices

1 ▼ In a heavy frying pan, fry the bacon until crisp and the fat is rendered. Drain on kitchen paper.

2 Lay 4 slices of toast on a flat surface. Spread them with some of the mayonnaise.

3 ▲ Top each slice with one-quarter of the chicken and a lettuce leaf. Season with salt and pepper.

4 ▲ Spread 4 of the remaining toast slices with mayonnaise. Lay them on top of the lettuce.

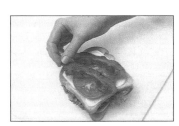

5 ▲ Top each sandwich with a slice of tomato, 2 rashers of bacon and another lettuce leaf.

6 Spread the remaining slices of toast with the rest of the mayonnaise. Place them on top of the sandwiches, mayonnaise-side down.

7 Cut each sandwich into 4 triangles and secure each triangle with a cocktail stick.

# Chilli Hot Dogs

**SERVES 6**

6 frankfurters

6 large finger rolls, split open

1 oz (30 g) butter or margarine

1½ oz (45 g) Cheddar cheese, grated

1½ oz (45 g) red onion, chopped

FOR THE CHILLI

2 tbsp corn oil

1 small onion, chopped

½ green pepper, seeded and chopped

8 oz (225 g) minced beef

8 fl oz (250 ml) fresh tomatoes, blanched, skinned, cooked and sieved

3 oz (85 g) drained canned red kidney beans

2 tsp chilli powder, or to taste

salt and pepper

3 ▼ Stir in the sieved tomatoes, beans, chilli powder and salt and pepper to taste. Cover the pan and simmer 10 minutes.

4 Meanwhile, put the frankfurters in a saucepan and cover with cold water. Bring to the boil. Remove from the heat, cover and let stand 5 minutes.

5 ▲ Spread both sides of each finger roll with the butter or margarine. Fry in a hot frying pan until golden brown on both sides.

6 To serve, put a frankfurter in each bun. Top with chilli and sprinkle with cheese and onion. Serve immediately.

1 ▲ For the chilli, heat the oil in a frying pan. Add the onion and green pepper and cook until softened, about 5 minutes.

2 ▲ Add the beef and cook until well browned, stirring frequently and breaking up lumps with the side of a wooden spatula.

# Fried Cheddar and Chutney Sandwiches

**SERVES 4**

| |
|---|
| 1½ oz (45 g) butter or margarine |
| 3 large garlic cloves, crushed |
| 3 fl oz (85 ml) homemade or bottled mango chutney |
| 8 slices of white bread |
| 8 oz (225 g) Cheddar cheese, grated |

**2 ▲** Spread the chutney on 4 slices of bread.

**4 ▲** Brush both sides of each sandwich with the garlic butter.

**5** Fry the sandwiches in a hot frying pan over a medium heat until golden brown, about 2 minutes on each side. Serve immediately.

**1 ▲** Melt the butter or margarine in a small saucepan. Add the garlic and cook until softened but not brown, about 2 minutes, stirring. Remove from the heat.

**3 ▲** Divide the cheese among the 4 bread slices, spreading it evenly. Top with the remaining bread slices.

> **~ COOK'S TIP ~**
>
> Well-aged mature cheddar cheese works best in combination with the strong flavours of the chutney and garlic.

---

# Tuna and Tomato Rolls

**SERVES 4**

| |
|---|
| 2 × 7 oz (200 g) cans tuna fish, drained |
| 2 tbsp finely chopped black olives |
| 2 fl oz (65 ml) finely chopped drained sun-dried tomatoes preserved in oil |
| 3 spring onions, finely chopped |
| 4 round white bread rolls, split open |
| 1 handful rocket or small lettuce leaves |
| FOR THE DRESSING |
| 1½ tbsp red wine vinegar |
| 5 tbsp olive oil |
| 3 tbsp chopped fresh basil |
| salt and pepper |

**1 ▼** For the dressing, combine the vinegar and oil in a mixing bowl. Whisk until an emulsion is formed. Stir in the basil. Season with salt and pepper.

**2** Add the tuna, olives, sun-dried tomatoes and spring onions and stir.

**3 ▲** Divide the tuna mixture among the rolls. Top with the rocket or lettuce leaves and replace the tops of the rolls, pressing them on firmly.

*Fried Cheddar and Chutney Sandwiches (top), Tuna and Tomato Rolls*

# Roast Beef and Horseradish Open Sandwiches

**SERVES 4**

4 slices of pumpernickel or rye bread

12 oz (350 g) roast beef, thinly sliced

salt and pepper

4 tbsp mayonnaise

1½ tbsp prepared horseradish

2 small tomatoes, seeded and chopped

2–2 tbsp finely chopped pickled gherkin

fresh dill sprigs, for garnishing

1 ▲ Lay the slices of pumpernickel or rye bread on a flat surface. Divide the slices of roast beef between the bread, folding the slices in half, if large. Season with salt and pepper.

2  In a small bowl, combine the mayonnaise and horseradish. Stir in the tomatoes and pickled gherkin.

3 ▲ Spoon the horseradish mayonnaise onto the beef. Garnish with dill sprigs and serve.

# Roast Pork and Coleslaw Rolls

**SERVES 6**

6 fl oz (175 ml) mayonnaise

2 tbsp tomato ketchup

¼–½ tsp cayenne pepper

1 tbsp light brown sugar

1 lb (450 g) roast pork, thinly sliced

1 lb (450 g) green or white cabbage, cut into wedges

2 carrots, finely grated

1 small green pepper, seeded and diced

½ small red onion, finely chopped

12 small round white bread rolls, split open

~ **VARIATIONS** ~

Instead of roast pork, substitute cooked ham or turkey, and prepare as above. As an alternative, try tuna in place of meat.

1 ▲ In a bowl, combine the mayonnaise, ketchup, cayenne and brown sugar. Stir well.

2  Stack the slices of roast pork. With a sharp knife, cut them into matchstick strips.

3  Remove the cores from the cabbage wedges. Lay them on a chopping board and cut into fine strips across the leaves.

4 ▲ Add the pork, cabbage, carrots, green pepper and red onion to the mayonnaise mixture. Toss to mix.

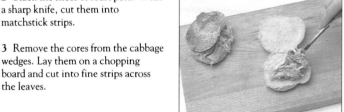

5 ▲ Fill the split bread rolls with the pork and coleslaw mixure.

*Roast Beef and Horseradish Open Sandwiches (top), Roast Pork and Coleslaw Rolls*

# Baked Potatoes with Cheesy Topping

**MAKES 20**

20 small new potatoes

2 fl oz (65 ml) vegetable oil

coarse salt

4 fl oz (125 ml) soured cream

1 oz (30 g) blue cheese, crumbled

2 tbsp chopped fresh chives

**1** Preheat a 350°F/180°C/Gas 4 oven.

**2** Wash and dry the potatoes. Pour the oil into a bowl. Add the potatoes and toss to coat well with oil.

**3** ▼ Dip the potatoes in the coarse salt to coat lightly. Spread out the potatoes on a baking sheet. Bake until tender, 45–50 minutes.

**4** ▲ In a small bowl, combine the soured cream and blue cheese.

**5** ▲ Cut a cross in the top of each potato. Press with your fingers to open the potatoes.

**6** ▲ Top each potato with a dollop of the cheese mixture. Sprinkle with chives and serve immediately.

# Avocado Dip with Spicy Tortilla Chips

**SERVES 10**

| |
|---|
| 2 very ripe avocados |
| 2 shallots or spring onions, chopped |
| 2 tbsp fresh lime juice |
| 1 tsp salt |
| 2 tsp chilli powder |
| 1 medium-size tomato, seeded and chopped |

FOR THE TORTILLA CHIPS

| |
|---|
| 3 tbsp corn oil |
| 1½ tsp ground cumin |
| 1 tsp salt |
| 9 × 6 in (15 cm) corn tortillas, each cut in 6 triangles |

**1** Preheat a 300°F/150°C/Gas 2 oven.

**2 ▲** For the tortilla chips, combine the oil, cumin and salt in a bowl.

**3 ▲** Spread the tortilla triangles on 2 baking sheets. Brush the seasoned oil on both sides. Bake until they are crisp and golden, about 20 minutes, turning once or twice and brushing with the seasoned oil. Let cool.

**4 ▼** Peel the avocados, discard the stones, and chop the flesh. In a food processor or blender, combine the avocados, shallots or spring onions, lime juice, salt and chilli powder. Process until smooth.

**5 ▲** Transfer the mixture to a bowl. Gently stir in the chopped tomato.

**6** Serve the avocado dip in a bowl in the centre of a platter, surrounded with the tortilla chips.

# Pancakes with Soured Cream and Salmon

**Makes 25**

8 oz (225 g) salmon fillet, skinned

juice of 1 lime or lemon

2 fl oz (65 ml) extra-virgin olive oil

pinch salt

3 tbsp chopped fresh dill

5 fl oz (150 ml) soured cream

¼ avocado, peeled and diced

3 tbsp chopped fresh chives

fresh dill sprigs, for garnishing

**For the pancakes**

3 oz (85 g) buckwheat flour

2 tsp caster sugar

1 egg

4 fl oz (125 ml) milk

1 oz (30 g) butter or margarine, melted

½ tsp cream of tartar

¼ tsp bicarbonate of soda

1 tbsp water

**1 ▲** With a long, sharp knife, slice the salmon as thinly as possible. Place the slices, in one layer, in a large non-metallic dish.

~ **COOK'S TIP** ~

For easy entertaining, make the pancakes early in the day and store, covered. To serve, arrange them on a baking tray, and reheat in a preheated 400°F/200°C/Gas 6 oven until hot, 3–4 minutes.

**2 ▲** In a small bowl, combine the lime juice, olive oil, salt and chopped dill. Pour the mixture over the salmon. Cover tightly and refrigerate several hours or overnight.

**3 ▲** For the pancakes, combine the buckwheat flour and sugar in a mixing bowl. Set aside.

**4 ▲** In a small bowl, beat together the egg, milk and butter or margarine. Gradually stir the egg mixture into the flour mixture. Stir in the cream of tartar, bicarbonate of soda and water.

**5 ▲** Cover the bowl and let the batter stand 1 hour.

**6** With a sharp knife, cut the marinated salmon in thin strips.

**7 ▲** To cook the pancakes, heat a heavy non-stick frying pan. Using a large spoon, drop the batter into the pan to make small pancakes about 2 in (5 cm) in diameter. When bubbles appear on the surface, turn over. Cook until the other side is golden brown, 1–2 minutes longer. Transfer the pancakes to a plate and continue until all the batter is used.

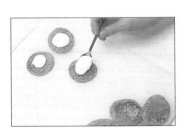

**8 ▲** To serve, place a teaspoon of soured cream on each pancake and top with the marinated salmon. Sprinkle with the diced avocado and chives and garnish with dill sprigs.

# Smoked Salmon Buns

**MAKES 25**

2 oz (55 g) cornmeal or polenta

1 oz (30 g) plain flour

½ tsp baking powder

⅛ tsp salt

1 tbsp sugar

1 egg

4 fl oz (125 ml) buttermilk

2 fl oz (65 ml) single cream

2½ oz (70 g) smoked salmon, cut in fine strips

1  Preheat a 400°F/200°C/Gas 6 oven. Grease 1–2 small bun trays.

2  In a mixing bowl, combine the cornmeal, flour, baking powder, salt and sugar. Set aside.

3 ▼  In another bowl, mix together the egg, buttermilk and cream. Gradually add the egg mixture to the cornmeal mixture, stirring quickly until just combined.

4 ▲  Stir the smoked salmon strips into the bun mixture.

5  Fill the small bun trays three-quarters full with the bun mixture. Bake until slightly risen and golden brown, 18–20 minutes. Let cool 5 minutes in the trays on a wire rack before unmoulding.

# Spicy Mexican Snack Cups

**MAKES 30**

14 oz (400 g) canned black or red kidney beans, rinsed and drained

2 tomatoes, seeded and diced

1 garlic clove, crushed

1 shallot or ½ small onion, minced

1 chilli pepper, seeded and chopped

1 tsp finely grated lime or lemon rind

1 tbsp olive oil

2 tbsp fresh lime or lemon juice

2 tsp maple syrup

salt and pepper

3 tbsp chopped fresh coriander

**FOR THE CUPS**

10 × 6 in (15 cm) corn tortillas

3–4 tbsp corn oil, for brushing

1  Preheat a 400°F/200°C/Gas 6 oven.

2 ▼  For the cups, using a 2 in (5 cm) round pastry cutter, cut 3 rounds from each tortilla, pressing firmly to cut through. Discard the tortilla trimmings. Brush both sides of each tortilla round with oil.

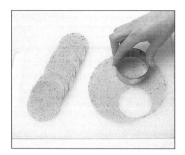

3  Press the tortilla rounds into small bun trays. Bake until crisp, about 6 minutes. Let cool on a wire rack.

4 ▲  In a mixing bowl, combine the beans, tomatoes, garlic, shallot or onion, chilli pepper, lime rind, oil, lime juice and maple syrup. Stir in salt and pepper to taste.

5  Place a spoonful of the bean and tomato mixture in each cup. Sprinkle with the chopped coriander just before serving.

*Smoked Salmon Buns (top), Spicy Mexican Snack Cups*

# Cheesy Twists with Fruit Sauce

**MAKES 12**

6 large sheets of frozen filo pastry, thawed

4 oz (115 g) butter or margarine, melted

8 oz (225 g) Brie cheese, finely diced

FOR THE SAUCE

3 oz (85 g) cranberries or redcurrants

2 tbsp light brown sugar

**1** For the sauce, combine the cranberries or redcurrants and sugar in a small saucepan with just enough water to cover. Bring to the boil and simmer until the fruit 'pop', about 3 minutes, stirring.

**2 ▼** Pour the fruit mixture into a blender or food processor and process until finely chopped. Press it through a fine-mesh nylon sieve into a bowl. Taste and add more sugar if needed. Set aside.

**3** Preheat a 450°F/230°C/Gas 8 oven.

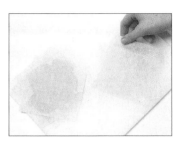

**4 ▲** To make the cheesy twists, cut the filo pastry into 36 × 5 in (13 cm) squares. Lay one pastry square on a flat surface and brush with some of the butter or margarine. Lay a second pastry square on top, placing it so the corners are not on top of each other. Brush with butter. Lay a third pastry square on top, again placing it so the corners are not on top of the others, thus forming a 12-pointed star.

**5** Put a heaped tablespoon of the diced cheese in the centre of each pastry star.

**6 ▲** Bring the points of each pastry star up over the cheese and twist to close securely. Fold back the tips of the points.

**7** Arrange the twists on a baking tray. Bake until the pastry is crisp and golden brown, 10–15 minutes.

**8** Meanwhile, gently reheat the fruit sauce. Serve the cheese twists hot with the sauce.

# Spicy Bean Snacks

**SERVES 8**

| |
|---|
| 2 tbsp vegetable oil |
| 2 onions, chopped |
| 2 garlic cloves, chopped |
| 3 chilli peppers, seeded and chopped |
| 1½ tbsp mild chilli powder |
| 1 × 16 oz (450 g) can red kidney beans, drained and liquid reserved |
| 3 tbsp chopped fresh coriander |
| nacho chips (fried tortilla rounds) or tortilla chips, for serving |
| 8 oz (225 g) Cheddar cheese, grated |
| 3 oz (85 g) stoned black olives, thinly sliced |
| fresh coriander sprigs, for garnishing |

1  Preheat a 425°F/220°C/Gas 7 oven.

2  ▼  Heat the oil in a frying pan. Add the onions, garlic and chilli peppers and cook until soft, about 5 minutes. Add the chilli powder and cook 1 minute more.

~ **VARIATION** ~

To serve as a bean dip, stir in the cheese and olives. Transfer the bean mixture to a round earthenware dish. Bake until the cheese melts and browns slightly, 10–15 minutes. Garnish with coriander, and serve with tortilla chips for dipping.

3  ▲  Stir the beans into the onion mixture with 4 fl oz (125 ml) of the reserved can liquid. Cook until thickened, about 10 minutes, mashing the beans with a fork from time to time. Remove the pan from the heat and stir in the chopped coriander.

4  ▼  Put a little of the bean mixture on each nacho chip. Top each nacho with a little cheese and a slice of olive. Arrange on a baking tray.

5  Bake until the cheese has melted and is beginning to brown, 5–10 minutes. Serve immediately. Garnish with coriander, if liked.

# Cheese and Spinach Pastry Delights

**SERVES 20**

2 tbsp olive oil

2 shallots or 1 small onion, finely
  chopped

1 lb (450 g) frozen spinach, thawed

4 oz (115 g) feta cheese, crumbled

2 oz (55 g) chopped walnuts

¼ tsp grated nutmeg

salt and pepper

4 large sheets frozen filo pastry, thawed

4 oz (115 g) butter or margarine, melted

1   Preheat a 400°F/200°C/Gas 6 oven.

**2 ▲** Heat the olive oil in a frying
pan. Add the shallots or onion and
cook until softened, about 5 minutes.

**3 ▲** A handful at a time, squeeze all
the liquid out of the spinach. Add the
spinach to the shallots or onion.
Increase the heat to high and cook,
stirring, until all excess moisture has
evaporated, about 5 minutes.

**4 ▲** Transfer the spinach mixture to
a bowl. Let cool. Stir in the feta and
walnuts. Season with nutmeg, salt and
pepper.

**5 ▲** Lay a filo sheet on a flat surface.
(Keep the remaining filo covered with
a damp tea towel to prevent it drying
out.) Brush with some of the butter or
margarine. Lay a second filo sheet on
top of the first. With scissors, cut the
layered filo pastry lengthwise into 3 in
(8 cm) wide strips.

### ~ VARIATION ~

For an alternative filling, omit the
spinach and shallots. Use 12 oz
(350 g) crumbled goat cheese,
instead of the feta cheese, and 2 oz
(55 g) toasted pine kernels instead
of the walnuts. Mix the cheese
with the olive oil and 1 tablespoon
chopped fresh basil.

**6 ▲** Place a tablespoonful of the
spinach mixture at the end of one strip
of filo pastry.

**7 ▲** Fold a bottom corner of the
pastry over the filling to form a
triangle, then continue folding over
the pastry strip to the other end. Fill
and shape the triangles until all the
ingredients are used.

**8 ▲** Set the triangles on baking
sheets and brush with butter. Bake the
filo triangles until they are crispy and
golden brown, about 10 minutes.
Serve hot.

# Potato Pancakes with a Tangy Dip

**MAKES 40**

| |
|---|
| 2 tbsp butter or margarine |
| 1 shallot, finely chopped |
| 1 egg |
| 8 oz (225 g) potatoes |
| salt and pepper |
| oil for frying |
| FOR THE DIP |
| 4 oz (115 g) cream cheese |
| 2 tbsp soured cream |
| 1 tsp finely grated lemon rind |
| 1 tbsp fresh lemon juice |
| 1 tbsp chopped fresh chives |

**1** Melt the butter or margarine in a small frying pan. Add the shallot and cook until softened, about 3 minutes. Set aside and let cool.

**2** Beat the egg in a large mixing bowl until light and frothy.

**3** Coarsely grate the potatoes. Add them to the bowl and mix with the egg until completely coated. Season generously with salt and pepper. Add the shallot and mix well.

**4** ▼ For the tangy dip, combine the cream cheese and soured cream in a bowl. Beat until smooth. Add the lemon rind and juice and the chives. Set aside.

**5** ▲ Heat ¼ in (5 mm) of oil in a frying pan. Drop teaspoonfuls of the potato mixture into the hot oil and press them with the back of a spoon to make flat rounds. Fry until well browned, 2–3 minutes on each side. Drain on kitchen paper and keep warm. Fry the remaining pancakes.

**6** Serve the pancakes hot, with the dip either spooned on top or served in a separate bowl.

# Cherry Tomatoes Stuffed with Crab

**MAKES 40**

| |
|---|
| 4 oz (115 g) crab meat |
| 1 tsp chilli sauce |
| ¼ tsp Dijon mustard |
| 2 tbsp mayonnaise |
| ½ tsp Worcestershire sauce |
| 2 spring onions, finely chopped |
| 1 tbsp chopped fresh basil |
| 1 tbsp chopped fresh chives |
| 40 cherry tomatoes |
| salt |

**1** In a mixing bowl, combine the crab meat, chilli sauce, mustard, mayonnaise, Worcestershire sauce, spring onions and herbs. Mix well. Cover and refrigerate until needed.

**2** ▲ Using a serrated knife, cut a very thin slice from the stem end of each tomato. Carefully scoop out the pulp and seeds with the tip of a teaspoon.

**3** Sprinkle the insides of the tomato shells lightly with salt. Invert them on kitchen paper and let them drain 15 minutes.

**4** ▲ Using a small spoon, stuff the tomatoes with the crab, mounding the filling slightly on top. Serve cold.

*Potato Pancakes with a Tangy Dip (top), Cherry Tomatoes Stuffed with Crab*

# FISH & SEAFOOD

~

*Whether fresh from the sea, or frozen or canned, fish and
seafood make nutritious and easy-to-prepare dishes. The
recipes here offer exciting ideas, from rich stews and stir-fries
to tasty kebabs and grilled steaks.*

# Fish with Orange and Caper Sauce

**SERVES 4**

2 fl oz (65 ml) fresh orange juice

1 tsp soy sauce

2 tbsp olive oil

4 × 8 oz (225 g) swordfish or other firm, white fish steaks

salt and pepper

1½ oz (45 g) cold butter or margarine, cut into pieces

2 tbsp capers in vinegar

1 tbsp chopped fresh parsley

**1** In a small bowl, combine the orange juice, soy sauce and 1 tablespoon of the olive oil. Whisk to mix.

**2** Lay the fish steaks in a shallow baking dish. Pour the orange-soy mixture over them and sprinkle with salt and pepper.

**3** Heat the remaining tablespoon of olive oil in a heavy frying pan over a medium-high heat.

**4** ▲ Drain the fish steaks, reserving the marinade. Add the steaks to the frying pan and cook until the fish flakes easily when tested with a fork, 3–4 minutes on each side, basting occasionally with the reserved marinade. Transfer the fish steaks to a warmed serving platter.

**5** ▲ Pour the reserved marinade into the pan and cook 1 minute, stirring to mix in the cooking juices. Add the butter or margarine, capers with their vinegar, and parsley. Cook until the butter has melted and the sauce is slightly syrupy.

**6** Pour the sauce over the fish steaks and serve immediately.

# Tuna with Oriental Dressing

**SERVES 6**

6 tuna steaks (about 2 lb/900 g)

FOR THE DRESSING

1 in (2.5 cm) piece of fresh root ginger, peeled and finely grated

2 spring onions, thinly sliced

2 tbsp chopped fresh chives

grated rind and juice of 1 lime or lemon

2 tbsp dry sherry

1 tbsp soy sauce

4 fl oz (125 ml) olive oil

salt and pepper

**1** ▲ For the dressing, combine the ginger, spring onions, chives, lime rind and juice, sherry and soy sauce. Add the olive oil and whisk to mix. Season and set aside.

**2** Preheat the grill. Sprinkle the tuna steaks with salt and pepper.

**3** ▼ Arrange the tuna steaks on the rack in the grill pan. Grill about 3 in (8 cm) from the heat for about 5 minutes on each side, until the fish flakes easily when tested with a fork.

**4** Arrange the cooked fish on a warmed serving platter or individual plates. Spoon the dressing over the fish and serve.

*Fish with Orange and Caper Sauce (top), Tuna with Oriental Dressing*

# Crispy Cod Steaks with Tomato Sauce

**SERVES 4**

3 tbsp cornmeal, or polenta

½ tsp salt

¼ tsp hot chilli powder

4 cod steaks, each 1 in (2.5 cm) thick (about 1½ lb/700 g)

2 tbsp vegetable oil

fresh basil sprigs, for garnishing

**FOR THE TOMATO SAUCE**

2 tbsp olive oil

1 shallot, or ½ small onion, finely chopped

1 garlic clove, crushed

1 lb (450 g) ripe tomatoes, chopped, or 1 16 oz (450 g) can chopped tomatoes

⅛ tsp sugar

2 fl oz (65 ml) dry white wine

2 tbsp chopped fresh basil, or ½ tsp dried basil

salt and pepper

**1** For the sauce, heat the oil in a saucepan. Add the shallot or onion and the garlic and cook until soft, about 5 minutes. Stir in the tomatoes, sugar, wine and basil. Bring to a boil. Simmer until thickened, 10–15 minutes.

**2** ▲ Work the sauce through a vegetable mill or sieve until smooth. Return it to the pan. Season with salt and pepper. Set aside.

**3** ▲ Combine the cornmeal or polenta, salt and chilli powder on a sheet of greaseproof paper.

**4** ▲ Rinse the cod steaks, then dip them on both sides into the cornmeal mixture, patting gently until evenly coated.

**5** ▲ Heat the oil in a large frying pan. Add the cod steaks and cook until golden brown and the flesh will flake easily when tested with a fork, about 5 minutes on each side. Cook in batches if necessary. Meanwhile, reheat the tomato sauce.

**6** Garnish the cod steaks with basil sprigs and serve with the tomato sauce.

# Spicy Fish Steaks

**SERVES 4**

| |
|---|
| 1 tsp onion powder |
| 1 tsp garlic salt |
| 2 tsp paprika |
| 1 tsp ground cumin |
| 1 tsp mustard powder |
| 1 tsp cayenne |
| 2 tsp dried thyme |
| 2 tsp dried oregano |
| ½ tsp salt |
| 1 tsp pepper |
| 4 swordfish steaks, or other firm fleshed fish (about 1½ lb/700 g) |
| 2 oz (55 g) butter or margarine, melted |
| dill sprigs, for garnishing |

**1** In a small bowl, combine all the spices, herbs and seasonings.

**2 ▲** Brush both sides of the fish steaks with some of the melted butter or margarine.

**3 ▲** Coat both sides of the fish steaks with the seasoning mixture, rubbing it in well.

**4** Heat a large heavy frying pan until a drop of water sprinkled on the surface sizzles, about 5 minutes.

**5 ▲** Drizzle 2 teaspoons of the remaining butter or margarine over the fish steaks. Add the steaks to the frying pan, butter-side down, and cook until the underside is blackened, 2–3 minutes.

**6 ▲** Drizzle another 2 teaspoons of melted butter or margarine over the fish, then turn the steaks over. Cook until the second side is blackened and the fish flakes easily when tested with a fork, 2–3 minutes more.

**7** Transfer the fish to warmed plates, garnish with dill and drizzle with the remaining butter or margarine.

# Grilled Salmon with Lime Butter

**SERVES 4**

4 salmon steaks (about 1½ lb/700 g)

salt and pepper

**FOR THE LIME BUTTER**

2 oz (55 g) butter or margarine, at room temperature

1 tbsp chopped fresh coriander, or 1 tsp dried coriander

1 tsp finely grated lime rind

1 tbsp fresh lime juice

1 For the lime butter, combine the butter or margarine, coriander and lime rind and juice in a bowl. Mix well with a fork.

2 ▲ Transfer the lime butter to a piece of greaseproof paper and shape into a log. Roll in the paper until smooth and round. Refrigerate until firm, about 1 hour.

3 Preheat the grill.

4 ▼ Sprinkle the salmon steaks with salt and pepper. Arrange them on the rack in the grill pan. Grill about 3 in (8 cm) from the heat, 5 minutes on each side.

5 Unwrap the lime butter and cut into 4 pieces. Top each salmon steak with a pat of lime butter and serve.

# Fish Fillets with Citrus Sauce

**SERVES 6**

½–1 oz (15–30 g) butter or margarine, melted

2 lb (900 g) sole fillets

salt and pepper

1 tsp grated lemon rind

1 tsp grated orange rind

2 tbsp fresh orange juice

3 fl oz (85 ml) whipping cream

1 tbsp chopped fresh basil

fresh basil sprigs, for garnishing

1 Preheat a 350°F/180°C/Gas 4 oven. Generously grease a large baking dish with the butter or margarine.

~ **VARIATION** ~

Use an equal amount of grapefruit rind and juice to replace the lemon and orange.

2 ▲ Lay the fish fillets skin-side down in the baking dish, in one layer. Sprinkle with salt and pepper.

3 ▲ In a small bowl, combine the lemon and orange rinds and orange juice. Pour the mixture over the fish.

4 Bake until the fish flakes easily when tested with a fork, 15–20 minutes. Transfer the fish to a warmed serving platter.

5 ▲ Strain the juices from the baking dish into a small saucepan. Stir in the cream and chopped basil. Boil until thickened, about 5 minutes.

6 Spoon the citrus sauce over the fish fillets. Garnish with basil sprigs and serve.

*Grilled Salmon with Lime Butter (top), Fish Fillets with Citrus Sauce*

# Sweet and Spicy Salmon Fillets

**SERVES 6**

2 lb (900 g) salmon fillet, cut in 6 pieces

4 fl oz (125 ml) honey

2 fl oz (65 ml) soy sauce

juice of 1 lime or lemon

1 tbsp sesame oil

¼ tsp crushed dried chilli pepper

¼ tsp crushed black peppercorns

~ COOK'S TIP ~

The acid in the citrus juice begins to 'cook' the fish, so grilling on one side only is sufficient.

1 Place the salmon pieces skin-side down in a large baking dish, in one layer.

2 ▲ In a bowl, combine the honey, soy sauce, lime or lemon juice, sesame oil, crushed chilli pepper and peppercorns.

3 ▲ Pour the mixture over the fish. Cover and let marinate 30 minutes.

4 Preheat the grill. Remove the fish from the marinade and arrange on the rack in the grill pan, skin-side down. Grill about 3 in (8 cm) from the heat until the fish flakes easily when tested with a fork, 6–8 minutes.

# Cod Steaks with Pepper Crust

**SERVES 4**

1 tsp each pink, white and green peppercorns

1½ oz (45 g) butter or margarine

4 cod steaks, each 1 in (2.5 cm) thick (about 1 lb/450 g)

salt

4 fl oz (125 ml) fish stock

4 fl oz (125 ml) whipping cream

3 tbsp chopped fresh chives

1 ▼ Wrap the peppercorns in a tea towel or heavy plastic bag and crush with a rolling pin.

2 Melt the butter or margarine in a large frying pan. Remove from the heat. Brush the cod steaks with some of the butter or margarine.

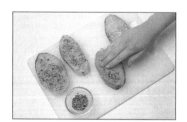

3 ▲ Press the crushed peppercorns onto both sides of the cod steaks. Season with salt.

4 Heat the frying pan. Add the cod steaks and cook over medium-low heat until the fish flakes easily when tested with a fork, about 4 minutes on each side. Transfer the steaks to a warmed serving platter.

5 ▲ Add the stock and cream to the frying pan and bring to the boil, stirring well. Boil until reduced by half, about 5 minutes. Remove from the heat and stir in the chives.

6 Pour the sauce over the fish and serve immediately.

~ COOK'S TIP ~

If pink and green peppercorns are not available, use 1½ tsps each of white and black peppercorns.

*Sweet and Spicy Salmon Fillets (top), Cod Steaks with Pepper Crust*

# Breaded Fish with Tartare Sauce

**SERVES 4**

2 oz (55 g) dry breadcrumbs

1 tsp dried oregano

½ tsp cayenne pepper

8 fl oz (250 ml) milk

2 tsp salt

4 pieces of cod fillet (about 1½ lb/ 700 g)

1½ oz (45 g) butter or margarine, melted

FOR THE TARTARE SAUCE

4 fl oz (125 ml) mayonnaise

½ tsp Dijon mustard

1–2 pickled gherkins, finely chopped

1 tbsp drained capers, chopped

1 tsp chopped fresh parsley

1 tsp chopped fresh chives

1 tsp chopped fresh tarragon

salt and pepper

1  Preheat a 450°F/230°C/Gas 8 oven. Grease a shallow ovenproof baking dish.

2 ▲ Combine the breadcrumbs, oregano and cayenne on a plate and blend together. Mix the milk with the salt in a bowl, stirring well to dissolve the salt.

3 ▲ Dip the pieces of cod fillet in the milk, then transfer to the plate and coat with the breadcrumb mixture.

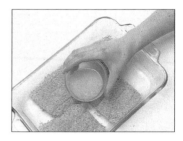

4 ▲ Arrange the coated fish in the prepared baking dish, in one layer. Drizzle the melted butter or margarine over the fish.

5  Bake until the fish flakes easily when tested with a fork, about 10–15 minutes.

6 ▲ Meanwhile, for the tartare sauce, combine all the ingredients in a small bowl. Stir gently to mix well.

7  Serve the fish hot, accompanied by the tartare sauce.

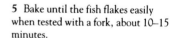

# Stuffed Sole

**SERVES 4**

8 skinless sole fillets (about 1 lb/450 g)

½ oz (15 g) butter or margarine, cut into 8 pieces

2 fl oz (65 ml) dry white wine

paprika, for garnishing

FOR THE STUFFING

1 oz (30 g) butter or margarine

1 small onion, finely chopped

1 handful of fresh spinach leaves, shredded

2 tbsp pine kernels, toasted

2 tbsp raisins

2 tbsp fresh breadcrumbs

⅛ tsp ground cinnamon

salt and pepper

1  Preheat a 400°F/200°C/Gas 6 oven. Butter a shallow baking dish.

2 ▲ For the stuffing, melt the butter or margarine in a small saucepan. Add the onion and cook over medium heat until softened, about 5 minutes. Stir in the spinach and cook, stirring constantly, until the spinach wilts and renders its liquid.

~ **VARIATION** ~

Use plaice instead of sole in this recipe, or try stuffing fillets of lean freshwater fish such as trout or perch.

3  Add the pine kernels, raisins, breadcrumbs, cinnamon and a little salt and pepper. Raise the heat and cook until most of the liquid has evaporated, stirring constantly. Remove from the heat.

4 ▲ Sprinkle the sole fillets with salt and pepper. Place a spoonful of the spinach stuffing at one end of each fillet. Roll up and secure with a wooden cocktail stick, if necessary.

5 ▲ Place the sole rolls in the prepared baking dish. Put a small piece of butter or margarine on each roll. Pour the wine over the fish. Cover the baking dish with foil and bake until the fish flakes easily when tested with a fork, about 15 minutes.

6  Serve on warmed plates with a little of the cooking juices spooned over the fish. Garnish with paprika, if wished.

# Fish Fillets with Orange and Tomato Sauce

**SERVES 4**

3 tbsp plain flour

salt and pepper

4 fillets of firm white fish such as cod,
sea bass, sole etc (about 1½ lb/700 g)

½ oz (15 g) butter or margarine

2 tbsp olive oil

1 onion, sliced

2 garlic cloves, chopped

¼ tsp ground cumin

1¼ lb (575 g) tomatoes, peeled, seeded
and chopped, or 14 oz (400 g) canned
chopped tomatoes

4 fl oz (125 ml) fresh orange juice

orange wedges, for garnishing

**1** ▼ Put the flour on a plate and
season with salt and pepper. Coat the
fish fillets lightly with the seasoned
flour, shaking off any excess.

**2** Heat the butter or margarine and
half the oil in a large frying pan. Add
the fish fillets to the pan and cook
until golden brown and the flesh
flakes easily when tested with a fork,
about 3 minutes on each side.

**3** ▲ When the fish is cooked,
transfer to a warmed serving platter.
Cover with foil and keep warm while
making the sauce.

**4** ▲ Heat the remaining oil in the
pan. Add the onion and garlic and
cook until softened, about 5 minutes.

**5** ▲ Stir in the cumin, tomatoes and
orange juice. Bring to the boil and
cook until thickened, about 10
minutes, stirring frequently.

**6** Garnish the fish with orange
wedges. Pass the sauce separately.

# Baked Trout

**SERVES 4**

| |
|---|
| 1 oz (30 g) butter or margarine |
| 1 onion, chopped |
| 1 celery stick, diced |
| 2 slices of fresh bread, cut in ½ in (1 cm) cubes |
| 1 tbsp fresh thyme, or 1 tsp dried thyme |
| salt and pepper |
| 4 trout, cleaned (each about 8 oz/225 g) |
| 8 rashers of bacon, rinded |
| celery leaves or parsley, for garnishing |

1  Preheat a 450°F/230°C/Gas 8 oven.

4 ▲  Stuff each trout with the bread mixture, dividing it evenly between the fish. If necessary, secure the openings with wooden cocktail sticks.

5 ▼  Wrap 2 bacon rashers around each stuffed trout. Arrange in a baking dish, in one layer.

6  Bake until the fish flakes easily when tested with a fork and the bacon is crisp, 35–40 minutes. Serve garnished with celery leaves or sprigs of parsley.

2 ▲  Melt the butter or margarine in a frying pan. Add the onion and celery and cook until softened, about 5 minutes. Remove the pan from the heat. Add the bread cubes and thyme, and season with salt and pepper to taste. Stir to mix well.

3 ▲  Season the cavity of each trout with salt and pepper.

# Halibut with Fruity Sauce

**SERVES 4**

| |
|---|
| 4 halibut steaks (about 1½ lb/700 g) |
| 1 oz (30 g) butter or margarine, melted |
| salt and pepper |
| fresh mint sprigs, for garnishing |

FOR THE SAUCE

| |
|---|
| 2½ oz (70 g) fresh pineapple, finely diced |
| 2 tbsp diced red pepper |
| 1 tbsp finely chopped red onion |
| finely grated rind of 1 lemon |
| 1 tbsp lemon juice |
| 1 tsp honey |
| 2 tbsp chopped fresh mint |

1 For the sauce, combine the pineapple, red pepper, red onion, lemon rind and juice and honey in a small bowl. Stir to mix. Cover with cling film and refrigerate for 30 minutes.

2 Preheat the grill.

3 ▲ Brush the halibut with butter or margarine and sprinkle with salt and pepper. Arrange on the rack in the grill pan, buttered-side up.

4 Grill the steaks about 3 in (8 cm) from the heat, turning once and brushing with the remaining butter or margarine, about 5 minutes on each side. Transfer to warmed serving plates.

5 ▲ Stir the chopped mint into the sauce. Garnish the halibut with mint sprigs and serve with the sauce.

---

# Thick and Creamy Fish Stew

**SERVES 4**

| |
|---|
| 3 thick-cut rashers of bacon, cut into small pieces |
| 1 large onion, chopped |
| 2 large potatoes, cut in ¾ in (2 cm) cubes (about 1½ lb/700 g) |
| salt and pepper |
| 1¾ pt (1 litre) fish stock |
| 1 lb (450 g) skinless haddock or cod fillet, cut into 1 in (2.5 cm) cubes |
| 2 tbsp chopped fresh parsley |
| 1 tbsp chopped fresh chives |
| 8 fl oz (250 ml) whipping cream or milk |

1 Fry the bacon in a deep saucepan until the fat is rendered. Add the onion and potatoes and cook over a low heat, without browning, about 10 minutes. Season to taste with salt and pepper.

2 ▲ Pour off excess fat from the pan. Add the fish stock to the pan and bring to the boil. Simmer until the vegetables are tender, 15–20 minutes.

3 ▲ Stir in the cubes of fish, the parsley and chives. Simmer until the fish is just cooked, 3–4 minutes.

4 Stir the cream or milk into the chowder and reheat gently. Season to taste and serve immediately.

*Halibut with Fruity Sauce (top), Thick and Creamy Fish Stew*

# Crab Cakes

**SERVES 3 OR 6**

1 lb (450 g) fresh white crab meat

1 egg, well beaten

1 tsp Dijon mustard

2 tsp prepared horseradish

2 tsp Worcestershire sauce

8 spring onions, finely chopped

3 tbsp chopped fresh parsley

3 oz (85 g) fresh breadcrumbs

salt and pepper

1 tbsp whipping cream (optional)

2 oz (55 g) dry breadcrumbs

1½ oz (45 g) butter or margarine

lemon wedges, for serving

1 In a mixing bowl, combine the crab meat, egg, mustard, horseradish, Worcestershire sauce, spring onions, parsley, fresh breadcrumbs and seasoning. Mix gently, leaving the pieces of crab meat as large as possible. If the mixture is too dry to hold together, add the cream.

2 ▲ Divide the crab mixture into 6 portions and shape.

3 ▲ Put the dry breadcrumbs on a plate. Coat the crab cakes on both sides with the breadcrumbs.

4 Melt the butter or margarine in a frying pan. Fry the crab cakes until golden, about 3 minutes on each side. Add more fat if necessary.

5 Serve 1 or 2 per person, with lemon wedges.

# Baked Stuffed Crab

**SERVES 4**

4 freshly cooked crabs

1 celery stick, diced

1 spring onion, finely chopped

1 small fresh green chilli pepper, seeded and finely chopped

3 fl oz (85 ml) mayonnaise

2 tbsp fresh lemon juice

1 tbsp chopped fresh chives

salt and pepper

1 oz (30 g) fresh breadcrumbs

2 oz (55 g) Cheddar cheese, grated

1 oz (30 g) butter or margarine, melted

parsley sprigs, for garnishing

1 Preheat a 375°F/190°C/Gas 5 oven.

2 ▼ Pull the claws and legs from each crab. Separate the body from the shell. Scoop out the meat from the shell. Discard the feathery gills and the intestines; remove the meat and coral from the body. Crack the claws and remove the meat.

3 Scrub the shells. Cut into the seam on the underside with scissors. The inner part of the shell should break off cleanly along the seam, enlarging the opening. Rinse the shells and dry them well.

4 In a bowl, combine the crab meat, celery, spring onion, chilli pepper, mayonnaise, lemon juice and chives. Season with salt and pepper to taste and mix well.

5 In another bowl, toss together the breadcrumbs, cheese, and melted butter or margarine.

6 ▲ Pile the crab mixture into the shells. Sprinkle with the cheese mixture. Bake until golden brown, about 20 minutes. Serve hot, garnished with parsley sprigs.

*Crab Cakes (top), Baked Stuffed Crab*

# Paella

**SERVES 6**

4 tbsp olive oil

10 oz (300 g) short-grain rice

1 large onion, chopped

1 red pepper, seeded and chopped

12 oz (350 g) squid, cleaned and cut into rings (optional)

18 fl oz (500 ml) fish or chicken stock

4 fl oz (125 ml) dry white wine

½ tsp saffron strands

1 large garlic clove, crushed

8 fl oz (250 ml) canned chopped tomatoes

1 bay leaf

¼ tsp finely grated lemon rind

4 oz (115 g) chorizo or other spicy cooked sausage, cut into ¼ in (5 mm) slices

salt and pepper

7 oz (200 g) fresh or frozen green peas

12 oz (350 g) monkfish, skinned and cut into 1 in (2.5 cm) pieces

24 mussels, well scrubbed

12 raw or cooked prawns, peeled and deveined

**1 ▼** Heat the oil in a large frying pan or paella pan. Add the rice and cook over a medium-high heat until it begins to colour, stirring frequently.

**2 ▲** Stir in the onion and pepper and cook 2–3 minutes longer.

**3 ▲** Add the squid, if using, and cook, stirring occasionally, until it is lightly browned.

**4** Stir in the stock, wine, saffron, and garlic. Bring to the boil.

**5 ▲** Add the tomatoes, bay leaf, lemon rind, and sausage. Season with salt and pepper. Return to the boil, then reduce the heat. Cover and simmer until the rice has absorbed most of the liquid, about 15 minutes.

**6 ▲** Add the peas, monkfish and mussels to the rice. Push the mussels down into the rice.

**7 ▲** Gently stir in the prawns. Cover and continue cooking until the mussels have opened and the rice is tender, about 5 minutes. Raw prawns should have turned bright pink.

**8** Taste and adjust the seasoning. Serve immediately in a heated serving dish or from the paella pan, if using.

~ COOK'S TIP ~

This recipe can be doubled to feed a crowd. Be sure to use a larger pan, such as a wide shallow flameproof casserole. The final simmering, after the pan has been covered (step 5), can be done in a preheated 375°F/190°C/Gas 5 oven. If using a paella pan, cover with foil.

# Seafood and Vegetable Stir-Fry

**SERVES 4**

1 lb (450 g) rice vermicelli

2 tbsp oil drained from sun-dried tomatoes

4 fl oz (125 ml) sun-dried tomatoes preserved in oil, drained and sliced

4 spring onions, cut diagonally in ½ in (1 cm) lengths

2 large carrots, cut in thin sticks

1 courgette, cut in thin sticks

8 oz (225 g) raw prawns, peeled and deveined, or cooked peeled prawns

8 oz (225 g) scallops, shelled

1 in (2.5 cm) piece of fresh root ginger, peeled and finely grated

3 tbsp fresh lemon juice

3 tbsp chopped fresh basil, or 1 tsp dried basil

salt and pepper

1 ▲ Bring a large saucepan of water to the boil. Add the rice vermicelli and cook until tender (check packet instructions for timing). Drain, rinse with boiling water, and drain again thoroughly. Keep warm.

2 ▲ Heat the oil in a wok over high heat. Add the tomatoes, spring onions and carrots and stir-fry 5 minutes.

3 ▲ Add the courgette, raw prawns, scallops and grated ginger. Stir-fry 3 minutes.

4 ▲ Add the lemon juice, basil and salt and pepper to taste and stir well. Add the cooked prawns, if using. Stir-fry until the prawns are all pink and hot, about 2 more minutes.

5 Serve on the rice vermicelli.

# Chunky Seafood Stew

**SERVES 6**

| |
|---|
| 3 tbsp olive oil |
| 2 large onions, chopped |
| 1 small green pepper, seeded and sliced |
| 3 carrots, chopped |
| 3 garlic cloves, crushed |
| 2 tbsp tomato purée |
| 2 × 14 oz (400 g) cans chopped tomatoes |
| 3 tbsp chopped fresh parsley |
| 1 tsp fresh thyme, or ¼ tsp dried thyme |
| 1 tbsp chopped fresh basil, or 1 tsp dried basil |
| 4 fl oz (125 ml) dry white wine |
| 1 lb (450 g) raw prawns, peeled and deveined, or cooked peeled prawns |
| 3 lb (1.35 kg) mussels or clams (in shells), or a mixture of both, thoroughly cleaned |
| 2 lb (900 g) halibut or other firm, white fish fillets, cut in 2–3 in (5–8 cm) pieces |
| 12 fl oz (375 ml) fish stock or water |
| salt and pepper |
| extra chopped fresh herbs, for garnishing |

1 ▲ Heat the oil in a flameproof casserole. Add the onions, green pepper, carrots and garlic and cook until tender, about 5 minutes.

2 Add the tomato purée, canned tomatoes, herbs and wine and stir well to combine. Bring to the boil and simmer 20 minutes.

3 ▲ Add the raw prawns, mussels, clams, fish pieces and stock or water. Season with salt and pepper.

4 ▲ Bring back to the boil, then simmer until the prawns turn pink, the fish flakes easily and the mussels and clams open, 5–6 minutes. Add cooked prawns for last 2 minutes.

5 Serve in large soup plates, garnished with chopped herbs.

# Spicy Tomato Prawns

**SERVES 4**

2 oz (55 g) butter or margarine

3 garlic cloves, crushed

1 large onion, finely chopped

1 green pepper, seeded and diced

2 sticks celery, chopped

16 fl oz (450 ml) canned chopped
   tomatoes

1 tsp sugar

2 tsp salt

1 bay leaf

1½ tsp fresh thyme leaves, or ½ tsp
   dried thyme

¼ tsp cayenne pepper

2 lb (900 g) raw prawns, peeled and
   deveined, or cooked peeled prawns

½ tsp grated lemon rind

2 tbsp fresh lemon juice

pepper

**1** Heat the butter or margarine in a
flameproof casserole. Add the garlic,
onion, pepper and celery and cook
until softened, about 5 minutes.

**2 ▲** Add the tomatoes, sugar, salt,
bay leaf, thyme and cayenne. Bring to
the boil. Reduce the heat and simmer
10 minutes.

**3 ▲** Stir in the prawns, lemon rind
and juice and pepper to taste. Cover
and simmer until raw prawns turn
pink, about 5 minutes, or until cooked
prawns are hot, about 2 minutes.

**4** Serve immediately on a bed of
freshly cooked rice.

---

# Prawns in Creamy Mustard Sauce

**SERVES 4**

2 oz (55 g) butter or margarine

2 lb (900 g) raw prawns, peeled and
   deveined, or cooked peeled prawns

1 small onion, finely chopped

4 spring onions, cut diagonally in ⅛ in
   (3 mm) lengths

2 tbsp fresh lemon juice

4 fl oz (125 ml) dry white wine

4 fl oz (125 ml) whipping cream

2 tbsp whole-grain mustard

salt and pepper

**1** Melt half the butter or margarine in
a frying pan over high heat. Add raw
prawns, if using, and cook until they
turn pink and opaque, about 2
minutes, stirring constantly. Remove
with a slotted spoon and set aside.

**2** Melt the remaining butter or
margarine in the frying pan. Add the
onion and spring onions and cook
until softened, 3–4 minutes, stirring
frequently.

**3 ▲** Stir in the lemon juice and
wine. Bring to the boil, scraping the
bottom of the pan with a wooden
spoon to mix in the cooking juices.

**4 ▲** Add the cream. Simmer until
the mixture thickens, 3–4 minutes,
stirring frequently. Stir in the
mustard.

**5** Return the fried prawns to the pan
and reheat briefly. Add cooked
prawns at this stage and heat through,
about 2 minutes. Season with salt and
pepper and serve.

*Spicy Tomato Prawns (top), Prawns in Creamy Mustard Sauce*

# Special Occasion Seafood Platter

**SERVES 6**

salt

6 × 1 lb (450 g) lobsters, fresh, frozen and thawed, or cooked

2 lb (900 g) button onions, peeled

2 lb (900 g) small red potatoes

3 dozen small hard-shelled clams, or mussels, thoroughly cleaned

6 sweetcorn cobs, trimmed

8 oz (225 g) butter or margarine

3 tbsp chopped fresh chives

**1** Put 1 in (2.5 cm) of salted water in the bottom of a deep pan. Put the fresh lobsters on top. Cooked lobsters should be steamed with 1 in (2.5 cm) of salted water in a separate pan 5 minutes only to heat through.

**2** Add the onions and potatoes. Cover the pan tightly and bring the water to the boil.

**3** ▲ After 10 minutes, add the clams or mussels and the sweetcorn cobs. Cover again and cook until the lobster shells are red and the potatoes are tender, 15–20 minutes longer.

**4** ▲ Meanwhile, in a small saucepan melt the butter or margarine and stir in the chives.

**5** Serve the lobsters and clams or mussels with the vegetables, accompanied by the chive butter.

# Seafood Kebabs

**SERVES 4**

16 scallops, shelled, or frozen and thawed

½ tsp ground ginger

1 × 8 oz (225 g) can pineapple chunks in juice, drained and juice reserved

1 small fresh red chilli pepper, seeded and chopped

grated rind and juice of 1 lime or lemon

16 mange-tout

16 cherry tomatoes

8 baby courgettes, halved

**1** Put the scallops in a bowl. Add the ginger, the juice from the pineapple, the chilli pepper and lime or lemon rind and juice and stir well. Cover and let marinate at room temperature about 20 minutes, or 2 hours in the refrigerator.

**2** Preheat the grill.

**3** ▲ Drain the scallops, reserving their marinade. Wrap a mange-tout around a scallop and thread onto 1 of 4 skewers. Thread on a cherry tomato, a piece of courgette, and a piece of pineapple, followed by another mange-tout-wrapped scallop. Repeat until all the ingredients have been used.

**4** ▲ Lay the kebabs in the grill pan and brush with the reserved marinade.

**5** Grill about 3 in (8 cm) from the heat, brushing frequently with the marinade and turning occasionally, until the scallops are opaque, 4–5 minutes.

**6** Serve immediately, on a bed of cooked rice, if wished.

# Meat & Poultry

~

*The wide range of different meats – beef, lamb and pork, as well as chicken and turkey – lends itself to endless variations. Ring the changes with these delicious recipes, from traditional grills and roasts to exotically spicy dishes.*

# Layered Meat and Fruit Loaf

**SERVES 6**

1½ lb (700 g) minced beef

8 oz (225 g) minced pork

2 eggs, lightly beaten

2 oz (55 g) fresh breadcrumbs

¼ tsp ground cinnamon

salt and pepper

FOR THE STUFFING

½ oz (15 g) butter or margarine

1 small onion, chopped

1½ oz (45 g) chopped dried figs

1½ oz (45 g) chopped dried apricots

1½ oz (45 g) sultanas

1 oz (30 g) pine kernels

4 fl oz (125 ml) dry white wine

2 tbsp chopped fresh parsley

1 Preheat a 350°F/180°C/Gas 4 oven.

2 ▼ For the stuffing, melt the butter or margarine in a small frying pan. Add the onion and cook until softened, about 5 minutes. Stir in the figs, apricots, raisins, pine kernels and wine. Bring to the boil and boil to evaporate the liquid, about 5 minutes. Remove from the heat and stir in the parsley. Set aside.

3 In a bowl, mix together the beef, pork, eggs, breadcrumbs, cinnamon and a little salt and pepper.

4 ▲ Press half of the meat mixture in a 9 × 5 in (23 × 13 cm) loaf tin. Spoon the stuffing over the meat. Spread the remaining meat mixture on top and press down gently.

5 Cover the tin with foil. Bake 1¼ hours. Pour off any excess fat from the tin. Let the meat loaf cool slightly before serving.

# Steak with Spicy Mushroom Sauce

**SERVES 4**

2½ oz (70 g) butter or margarine

1 lb (450 g) mushrooms, quartered

1 shallot or ½ small onion, finely chopped

3 tbsp chopped fresh parsley

salt and pepper

4 sirloin steaks, each about 1 in (2.5 cm) thick

1 onion, thinly sliced

⅛ tsp crushed dried chilli pepper

⅛ tsp cayenne pepper

dash of chilli sauce

2 tsp Worcestershire sauce

2 tsp sugar

5 fl oz (150 ml) brandy

8 fl oz (250 ml) beef stock

1 ▼ Melt 1 oz (30 g) of the butter or margarine in a frying pan. Add the mushrooms and shallot and cook until softened, about 5 minutes. Drain off the excess liquid. Sprinkle the mushrooms with the parsley and a little salt and pepper. Set aside.

2 Preheat the grill. Sprinkle the steaks with salt and pepper and arrange them on the rack in the grill pan. Set aside.

3 Melt the remaining butter or margarine in a saucepan. Add the onion and cook until softened, about 5 minutes. Stir in the dried chilli pepper, cayenne, chilli sauce, Worcestershire sauce, sugar and brandy. Bring to the boil and boil until the sauce is reduced by half.

4 Meanwhile, grill the steaks about 3 in (8 cm) from the heat, 5 minutes on each side for medium-rare, 8 minutes on each side for medium.

5 While the steaks are cooking, add the stock to the sauce and boil again to reduce by half. Season to taste with salt and pepper. Stir in the cooked mushrooms.

6 Transfer the steaks to heated plates and spoon the sauce on top.

*Layered Meat and Fruit Loaf (top), Steak with Spicy Mushroom Sauce*

# Cheeseburgers with Spicy Avocado Relish

**SERVES 6**

2 lb (900 g) minced beef

salt and pepper

6 slices of Gruyère or Cheddar cheese

6 hamburger buns with sesame seeds, split and toasted

2 large tomatoes, sliced

FOR THE AVOCADO RELISH

1 large ripe avocado

1 spring onion, chopped

2 tsp fresh lemon juice

1 tsp chilli powder

2 tbsp chopped fresh tomato

1 To make the relish, peel the avocado, discard the stone, and mash the flesh with a fork. Stir in the spring onion, lemon juice, chilli powder, and chopped tomato. Set aside.

2 Preheat the grill.

3 ▼ Handling the beef as little as possible, divide it into 6 equal portions. Shape each portion into a burger ¾ in (2 cm) thick and season.

4 Arrange the burgers on the rack in the grill pan. Grill about 3 in (8 cm) from the heat, 5 minutes on each side for medium-rare, 8 minutes on each side for well-done.

5 ▲ Top each hamburger with a slice of cheese and grill until melted, about 30 seconds.

6 Place a hamburger in each toasted bun. Top with a slice of tomato and a spoonful of avocado relish and serve.

# Chilli con Carne

**SERVES 8**

3 tbsp vegetable oil

1 large onion, chopped

2 lb (900 g) minced beef

4 garlic cloves, crushed

1 tbsp light brown sugar

2–3 tbsp chilli powder

1 tsp ground cumin

1 tsp each salt and pepper

1 × 5 oz (140 g) can tomato purée

8 fl oz (250 ml) beer

15 fl oz (450 ml) fresh tomatoes, blanched, skinned, cooked and sieved

12 oz (350 g) cooked or canned red kidney beans, rinsed and drained

FOR SERVING

1 lb (450 g) spaghetti, broken in half

8 fl oz (250 ml) soured cream

8 oz (225 g) Cheddar or Gruyère cheese, grated

1 Heat the oil in a deep saucepan and cook the onion until softened, about 5 minutes. Add the beef and cook until browned, breaking up the meat with the side of a spoon.

2 ▼ Stir in the garlic, brown sugar, chilli powder, cumin, salt and pepper. Add the tomato purée, beer and sieved tomatoes and stir to mix. Bring to the boil. Reduce the heat, cover, and simmer 50 minutes.

3 ▲ Stir in the kidney beans and simmer 5 minutes longer, uncovered.

4 Meanwhile, cook the spaghetti in a large pot of boiling salted water until just tender (check packet instructions for cooking time). Drain.

5 To serve, put the spaghetti into a warmed bowl. Ladle the chilli over the spaghetti and top with some of the soured cream and grated cheese. Serve the remaining soured cream and cheese separately.

*Cheeseburgers with Spicy Avocado Relish (top), Chilli con Carne*

# Old-Fashioned Beef Stew

**SERVES 6**

| |
|---|
| 3 tbsp vegetable oil |
| 1 large onion, sliced |
| 2 carrots, chopped |
| 1 celery stick, chopped |
| 1 oz (30 g) plain flour |
| 3 tbsp paprika |
| 2 lb (900 g) braising steak, cubed |
| 2 tbsp tomato purée |
| 8 fl oz (250 ml) red wine |
| 15 fl oz (450 ml) beef stock |
| 1 sprig of fresh thyme, or 1 tsp dried thyme |
| 1 bay leaf |
| salt and pepper |
| 3 medium potatoes, cut into 1½ in (3 cm) pieces |
| 3 oz (85 g) button mushrooms, quartered |

1 Preheat a 375°F/190°C/Gas 5 oven.

2 ▼ Heat half the oil in a large flameproof casserole. Add the onion, carrots and celery and cook until softened, about 5 minutes. Remove the vegetables with a slotted spoon and set aside.

3 ▲ Combine the flour and paprika in a plastic bag. Add the beef cubes and shake to coat them with the seasoned flour.

4 Heat the remaining oil in the casserole. Add the beef cubes and brown well on all sides, about 10 minutes.

5 Return the vegetables to the casserole. Stir in the tomato purée, red wine, stock, herbs and seasoning. Bring to the boil.

6 ▲ Stir in the potatoes. Cover the casserole and transfer it to the oven. Cook 1 hour.

7 Stir in the mushrooms and continue cooking until the beef is very tender, about 30 minutes longer. Discard the bay leaf before serving.

# Beef and Vegetable Stir-Fry

**Serves 4**

2–3 tsp chilli powder

1 tsp ground cumin

½ tsp dried oregano

salt and pepper

1 lb (450 g) topside of beef, cut into thin strips

2 tbsp vegetable oil

5 spring onions, cut diagonally into 1 in (2.5 cm) lengths

1 small green pepper, seeded and thinly sliced

1 small red pepper, seeded and thinly sliced

1 small yellow pepper, seeded and thinly sliced

4 oz (115 g) baby corn cobs, halved lengthwise, or 8 oz (225 g) canned sweetcorn, drained

4 garlic cloves, crushed

2 tbsp fresh lime or lemon juice

2 tbsp chopped fresh coriander

**1** ▼ In a medium bowl, combine the spices, oregano and a little salt and pepper. Rub the mixture into the beef strips.

**2** Heat half the oil in a wok or large frying pan over high heat. Add the beef strips and stir-fry until well browned on all sides, 3–4 minutes. Remove the beef from the wok with a slotted spoon and keep hot.

**3** ▲ Heat the remaining oil in the wok and add the spring onions, peppers, sweetcorn and garlic. Stir-fry until the vegetables are just tender, about 3 minutes.

**4** ▼ Return the beef to the wok and toss briefly to mix with the vegetables and heat it through. Stir in the lime or lemon juice and coriander and serve.

# Boiled Beef Platter

**SERVES 6**

2–2½ lb (about 1 kg) salted brisket

1 tsp black peppercorns

2 bay leaves

1 small swede, about 1 lb (450 g), cut into pieces

8 button onions

8 small red potatoes

3 carrots, cut into sticks

1 small head of green cabbage, cut into 6 wedges

FOR THE SAUCE

3 fl oz (85 ml) red wine vinegar

2 oz (55 g) sugar

1 tbsp mustard powder

about 2 oz (55 g) butter or margarine

salt and pepper

1  Put the brisket in a large pan. Add the peppercorns and bay leaves and cover with water. Bring to the boil. Reduce the heat and simmer until the beef is almost tender, about 2 hours.

2 ▼  Add the swede, onions, potatoes and carrots. Bring the liquid back to the boil, then reduce the heat and cover the pan. Simmer 10 minutes.

3  Add the cabbage wedges. Cover and cook 15 minutes longer.

4  With a slotted spoon, remove the meat and vegetables from the pan and keep them hot. Reserve 12 fl oz (350 ml) of the cooking liquid.

5 ▲  For the sauce, combine the reserved cooking liquid, vinegar, sugar and mustard in a small saucepan. Bring to the boil, then reduce the heat and simmer until thickened, about 5 minutes. Remove the pan from the heat and swirl in the butter or margarine. Season to taste with salt and pepper.

6  Slice the beef and arrange with the vegetables on a warmed platter. Serve with the sauce in a sauceboat.

# Steak Sandwiches with Onions

**SERVES 3**

3 pieces thinly cut rump steak (about 1 lb/450 g)

salt and pepper

1 oz (30 g) butter or margarine

2 tbsp vegetable oil

1 large onion, thinly sliced into rings

1 long French stick, split in half lengthwise, and cut into 3 sections

Dijon mustard, for serving

1  Sprinkle the steaks generously with salt and pepper.

2 ▲  Heat the butter or margarine and half the oil in a frying pan. Add the onion and cook until browned and crispy, about 8 minutes. Remove the onion with a slotted spoon and drain on kitchen paper. Add the remaining oil to the pan.

3 ▼  Add the steaks to the frying pan and cook until well browned, about 3 minutes, turning once.

4  Divide the steak and onions among the bottom halves of the bread sections, and put on the tops. Serve on warmed plates with mustard.

*Boiled Beef Platter (top), Steak Sandwiches with Onions*

# Pork with Mustard and Pepper Sauce

**SERVES 4**

2 pork fillets, each about 12 oz (350 g)

1 oz (30 g) butter or margarine

1 tbsp olive oil

1 tbsp red wine vinegar

1 tbsp whole-grain mustard

3 tbsp whipping cream

1 tbsp green peppercorns in brine, drained

pinch salt

1  Cut the pork fillets across into 1 in (2.5 cm) thick slices.

2 ▼  Heat the butter or margarine and oil in a frying pan. Add the slices of pork and fry until browned and cooked through, 5–8 minutes on each side. Transfer the pork to a warmed serving plate and keep hot.

3 ▼  Add the vinegar and mustard to the pan and cook 1 minute, stirring with a wooden spoon to loosen any particles attached to the bottom.

4  Stir in the cream, peppercorns and salt. Boil 1 minute. Pour the sauce over the pork and serve immediately.

# Pork Chops with Apple and Potato

**SERVES 6**

15 fl oz (450 ml) apple juice

8 oz (225 g) baking potatoes, peeled and cut into ½ in (1 cm) slices

8 oz (225 g) sweet potatoes, or swede, peeled and cut into ½ in (1 cm) slices

1 lb (450 g) apples, peeled, cored, and cut into ½ in (1 cm) slices

salt and pepper

1½ oz (45 g) plain flour

6 pork chops, cut 1 in (2.5 cm) thick, trimmed of excess fat

2 oz (55 g) butter or margarine

3 tbsp vegetable oil

6 fresh sage leaves

1  Preheat a 350°F/180°C/Gas 4 oven. Grease a 13 × 9 in (33 × 23 cm) baking dish.

2  In a small saucepan, bring the apple juice to the boil.

3 ▼  Arrange a row of baking-potato slices at a short end of the prepared dish. Arrange a row of sweet-potato slices next to the first row, slightly overlapping it, and then a row of apple slices. Repeat the alternating overlapping rows to fill the dish. Sprinkle with salt and pepper.

4  Pour the apple juice over the potato and apple slices. Cover the dish with foil and bake 40 minutes.

5 ▲  Meanwhile, season the flour with salt and pepper. Coat the chops with the seasoned flour, shaking off any excess. Melt the butter or margarine with the oil in a frying pan. Fry the chops until well browned, about 5 minutes on each side.

6  Uncover the baking dish. Arrange the chops on top of the potatoes and apples. Put a sage leaf on each chop.

7  Return to the oven, uncovered, and cook until the potatoes and pork chops are tender and most of the liquid is absorbed, about 1 hour.

*Pork with Mustard and Pepper Sauce (top), Pork Chops with Apple and Potato*

# Pork Chops with Sauerkraut

**SERVES 6**

6 rashers of bacon, coarsely chopped

3 tbsp plain flour

salt and pepper

6 boned loin pork chops

2 tsp light brown sugar

1 garlic clove, crushed

1½ lb (700 g) sauerkraut, rinsed

1 tsp juniper berries

1 tsp black peppercorns

8 fl oz (250 ml) beer

8 fl oz (250 ml) chicken stock

1  Preheat a 350°F/180°C/Gas 4 oven.

2 ▼  In a frying pan, fry the bacon until just beginning to brown. With a slotted spoon, transfer the bacon to a casserole dish.

3 ▲  Season the flour with salt and pepper. Coat the pork chops with the seasoned flour, shaking off any excess. Brown the chops in the bacon fat, about 5 minutes on each side. Remove and drain on kitchen paper.

4 ▲  Add the brown sugar and garlic to the fat in the frying pan and cook, stirring, for 3 minutes. Add the sauerkraut, juniper berries and peppercorns.

5 ▲  Transfer the sauerkraut mixture to the casserole and mix with the bacon. Lay the pork chops on top. Pour the beer and chicken stock over the chops.

6  Place the casserole in the oven and cook until the chops are very tender, 45–55 minutes.

# Barbecued Spareribs

**Serves 4**

3 lb (1.35 kg) meaty pork spareribs

4 fl oz (125 ml) vegetable oil

½ tsp paprika

For the sauce

3 oz (85 g) light brown sugar

2 tsp mustard powder

1 tsp salt

⅛ tsp pepper

½ tsp ground ginger

4 fl oz (125 ml) fresh tomatoes, skinned, cooked and sieved

4 fl oz (125 ml) orange juice

1 small onion, finely chopped

1 garlic clove, crushed

2 tbsp chopped fresh parsley

1 tbsp Worcestershire sauce

**1 ▲** Preheat a 375°F/190°C/Gas 5 oven. Arrange the ribs in one layer in a roasting tin.

**2 ▲** In a small bowl, combine the oil and paprika. Brush the mixture over the spareribs. Bake until the ribs are slightly crisp, 55–60 minutes.

**3 ▼** Combine the sauce ingredients in a saucepan and bring to the boil. Simmer 5 minutes, stirring occasionally.

**4 ▲** Pour off the fat from the roasting tin. Brush the ribs with half of the sauce and bake 20 minutes. Turn the ribs over and brush with the remaining sauce. Bake 20 minutes longer. Cut into sections for serving.

# Spicy Pork on Tortilla Pancakes

### SERVES 4

| |
|---|
| 1 garlic clove, crushed |
| 2 tbsp vegetable oil |
| 3 fl oz (85 ml) fresh lime juice |
| 3 tbsp Worcestershire sauce |
| ⅛ tsp pepper |
| 1¼ lb (575 g) pork cutlets, cut lengthwise into ⅜ in (1 cm) strips |
| 1 large ripe avocado |
| 4 tbsp finely chopped fresh coriander leaves |
| 8 corn tortillas |
| 1 onion, sliced |
| 1 green pepper, seeded and sliced |
| black olives, for garnishing |

### FOR THE SALSA

| |
|---|
| 8 oz (225 g) drained canned sweetcorn, or frozen sweetcorn, thawed |
| 1 small red pepper, seeded and finely chopped |
| 1 small red onion, thinly sliced |
| 1 tsp honey |
| juice of 1 lime or lemon |

**1 ▼** In a medium bowl, combine the garlic, 1 tablespoon of the oil, the lime juice, Worcestershire sauce and pepper. Add the pork strips and toss to coat. Let marinate 10–20 minutes, stirring the strips at least once.

**2 ▲** Meanwhile, combine all the ingredients for the salsa in a bowl and mix well. Set aside.

**3 ▲** Cut the avocado in half and remove the stone. Scrape the flesh into a bowl and mash it with a fork. Stir in the chopped coriander.

**4 ▲** Preheat the oven to 350°F/ 180°C/Gas 4. Wrap the corn tortillas in foil and heat them in the oven for 10 minutes.

**5 ▲** Meanwhile, heat the remaining oil in a frying pan. Add the onion and green pepper slices and cook until softened, about 5 minutes.

**6 ▲** Add the pork strips to the frying pan and fry briskly, turning occasionally, until cooked and browned, about 5 minutes.

**7 ▲** To serve, place a spoonful of the avocado on each of the heated tortillas. Top with some of the pork mixture and a spoonful of the salsa. Garnish with an olive, and serve with more salsa, if wished.

# Baked Sausages and Beans with Crispy Topping

**SERVES 6**

12 oz (350 g) dried haricot or white beans, soaked overnight and drained

1 onion, stuck with 4 cloves

1½ oz (45 g) butter or margarine

1 lb (450 g) pork link sausages

1 lb (450 g) garlic sausage, cut into ½ in (1 cm) slices

4 oz (115 g) bacon, chopped

1 large onion, finely chopped

2 garlic cloves, crushed

1 × 16 oz (450 g) can chopped tomatoes

5 oz (140 g) can tomato purée

2 fl oz (65 ml) maple syrup

2 tbsp dark brown sugar

½ tsp mustard powder

¼ tsp salt

pepper

1 oz (30 g) fresh breadcrumbs

**1 ▲** Put the beans in a saucepan and cover with fresh cold water. Add the clove-studded onion. Bring to the boil and boil until the beans are just tender, about 1 hour. Drain the beans. Discard the onion.

**2** Preheat a 350°F/180°C/Gas 4 oven.

**3 ▲** Melt half of the butter or margarine in a large flameproof casserole. Add the sausages, bacon, onion and garlic and fry until the bacon and sausages are well browned.

**4 ▲** Stir in the beans, tomatoes, tomato purée, maple syrup, brown sugar, mustard, salt and pepper to taste. Bring to the boil.

**5 ▲** Sprinkle the breadcrumbs over the surface and dot with the remaining butter or margarine.

**6** Transfer the casserole to the oven and bake until most of liquid has been absorbed by the beans and the top is crisp, about 1 hour.

# Jambalaya

**SERVES 6**

2 tbsp vegetable oil

4 skinless boneless chicken breast halves, cut into chunks

1 lb (450 g) spicy cooked sausage, sliced

6 oz (170 g) smoked ham, cubed

1 large onion, chopped

2 celery sticks, chopped

2 green peppers, seeded and chopped

3 garlic cloves, crushed

8 fl oz (250 ml) canned chopped tomatoes

16 fl oz (450 ml) chicken stock

1 tsp cayenne pepper

1 sprig of fresh thyme, or ¼ tsp dried thyme

2 sprigs of flat-leaved parsley

1 bay leaf

10 oz (300 g) rice

salt and pepper

4 spring onions, finely chopped

1 ▼  Heat the oil in a large frying pan. Add the chicken chunks and sausage slices and cook until well browned, about 5 minutes. Stir in the ham cubes and cook 5 minutes longer.

2  Add the onion, celery, peppers, garlic, tomatoes, stock, cayenne, thyme, parsley and bay leaf to the frying pan. Bring to the boil, stirring well.

3 ▲  Stir in the rice, and add salt and and pepper to taste. When the liquid returns to the boil, reduce the heat and cover the pan tightly. Simmer 10 minutes.

4  Remove the pan from the heat and, without removing the lid, set aside for 20 minutes, to let the rice finish cooking.

5 ▲  Discard the bay leaf. Scatter the chopped spring onions on top of the jambalaya just before serving.

# Ham and Asparagus with Cheese Sauce

**SERVES 4**

24 asparagus spears

1½ oz (45 g) butter or margarine

3 tbsp plain flour

12 fl oz (350 ml) milk

4 oz (115 g) Gruyère or Cheddar cheese, grated

⅛ tsp grated nutmeg

salt and pepper

12 thin slices of cooked ham or Parma ham

1 Trim any tough stalk ends from the asparagus. Bring a wide shallow pan of salted water to the boil. Add the asparagus and simmer until barely tender, 5–7 minutes. Drain the asparagus in a colander, rinse with cold water and spread out on kitchen paper to dry.

2 Preheat the grill. Grease a 13 × 9 in (33 × 23 cm) baking dish.

3 Melt the butter or margarine in a saucepan. Add the flour and cook 2 minutes, stirring. Stir in the milk. Bring to the boil, stirring constantly, and simmer until thickened, about 5 minutes.

4 ▲ Add three-quarters of the cheese to the sauce. Season to taste with nutmeg, salt and pepper. Keep warm.

5 ▲ Wrap a pair of asparagus spears in each slice of ham. Arrange in the prepared baking dish, in one layer.

6 Pour the sauce over the ham and asparagus rolls and sprinkle the remaining cheese on top. Grill about 3 in (8 cm) from the heat until bubbling and golden brown, about 5 minutes. Serve hot.

# Gammon Steaks with Raisin Sauce

**SERVES 4**

2 oz (55 g) raisins

8 fl oz (250 ml) warm water

½ tsp instant coffee

1 tsp cornflour

1½ oz (45 g) butter or margarine

4 gammon steaks, about 4 oz (115 g) each, trimmed of excess fat

2 tsp dark brown sugar

2 tsp cider vinegar

2 tsp soy sauce

> ~ **VARIATION** ~
>
> For a richer sauce, substitute an equal quantity of chopped prunes for the raisins.

1 ▼ In a small bowl, soak the raisins in half of the water to plump them, about 10 minutes.

2 Stir the coffee and cornflour into the remaining water until smooth.

3 Melt the butter or margarine in a large frying pan. Add the gammon steaks and cook over a medium-low heat until lightly browned, about 5 minutes on each side.

4 ▲ Transfer the cooked steaks to a heated serving dish.

5 Drain the raisins and add them to the frying pan. Stir the coffee mixture to recombine it, then add to the pan with the sugar, vinegar and soy sauce. Bring to the boil and simmer until slightly thickened, about 3 minutes, stirring constantly.

6 Spoon the raisin sauce over the gammon steaks and serve.

*Ham and Asparagus with Cheese Sauce (top), Gammon Steaks with Raisin Sauce*

# Lamb Chops with Basil Sauce

**Serves 4**

small bunch of fresh basil leaves

1 oz (30 g) pine kernels

2 garlic cloves

1 oz (30 g) Parmesan cheese, diced

4 fl oz (125 ml) extra-virgin olive oil

salt and pepper

4 lamb sirloin or chump chops, about
    8 oz (225 g) each

fresh basil sprigs, for garnishing

**1** In a food processor or blender, combine the basil, pine kernels, garlic and Parmesan cheese. Process until the ingredients are finely chopped. Gradually pour in the olive oil in a thin stream. Season to taste with salt and pepper. The sauce should be thin and creamy. Alternatively, use a mortar and pestle to make the sauce.

**2 ▼** Put the lamb chops in a shallow dish that will hold them comfortably side by side. Pour the basil sauce over the chops. Turn to coat on both sides. Let marinate 1 hour.

**3** Preheat the grill. Brush the rack in the grill pan with olive oil.

**4 ▲** Transfer the chops to the grill rack. Grill about 3 in (8 cm) from the heat until well browned and cooked to taste, about 15 minutes, turning once. Serve garnished with fresh basil sprigs.

# Lamb and Bean Stew

**Serves 6**

9 oz (250 g) dried red kidney beans,
    soaked overnight and drained

2 tbsp vegetable oil

2 lb (900 g) lean boned lamb, cut into
    1½ in (3 cm) cubes

1 large onion, chopped

1 bay leaf

1¼ pt (750 ml) chicken stock

1 garlic clove, crushed

salt and pepper

**1** Put the beans in a large pot. Cover with fresh water, bring to the boil and boil 10 minutes. Reduce the heat and simmer 30 minutes, then drain.

**2** Meanwhile, heat the oil in another large pot. Add the lamb cubes and fry until browned all over. Remove the lamb with a slotted spoon and reserve until needed.

**3 ▼** Add the onion to the hot oil and cook until softened, about 5 minutes.

**4 ▲** Return the lamb cubes to the pot and add the drained beans, bay leaf, stock, garlic and salt and pepper to taste. Bring to the boil. Reduce the heat, cover and simmer 1¼ hours, or until the lamb and beans are tender.

**5** Discard the bay leaf and adjust the seasoning before serving.

*Lamb Chops with Basil Sauce (top), Lamb and Bean Stew*

# Special Lamb Chops

SERVES 4

8 lamb rib chops

salt and pepper

1 egg

1 tsp Dijon mustard

3 tbsp fine dry breadcrumbs

3 tbsp sesame seeds

2 tbsp plain flour

1 oz (30 g) butter or margarine

1 tbsp vegetable oil

1 ▼ If necessary, trim any excess fat from the chops. With a small knife, scrape all the meat and fat off the top 2 in (5 cm) of the bone in each chop. Sprinkle the chops generously with salt and pepper.

2 ▲ In a bowl, beat the egg and mustard together. Pour into a shallow dish. In another dish, mix the breadcrumbs and sesame seeds. Place the flour in a third dish.

3 ▲ Coat each chop with flour, shaking off any excess. Dip in the egg and mustard mixture and then coat with the breadcrumb mixture, pressing it on the meat to get an even coating. Refrigerate 15 minutes.

4 ▲ Heat the butter or margarine and oil in a frying pan. Add the chops and fry over medium heat until crisp and golden and cooked to taste, 4–5 minutes on each side, turning gently with tongs.

# Roast Rack of Lamb

**SERVES 4**

| |
|---|
| 2 racks of lamb, each with 8 chops, ends of bones scraped clean |
| 3 tbsp Dijon mustard |
| 1½ tbsp chopped fresh rosemary, or 1 tbsp dried rosemary |
| salt and pepper |
| 2 oz (55 g) fine dry breadcrumbs |
| 3 tbsp chopped fresh parsley |
| 4 garlic cloves, crushed |
| 2 fl oz (65 ml) olive oil |
| 4 oz (115 g) butter or margarine |
| 8 fl oz (250 ml) chicken stock |

**1**  Preheat a 425°F/220°C/Gas 7 oven.

**2 ▲**  Brush the meaty side of the racks with the mustard. Sprinkle with the rosemary, salt and pepper.

**3 ▲**  In a bowl, mix the breadcrumbs with the parsley, garlic and half of the olive oil. Press this mixture evenly over the mustard on the racks of lamb. Wrap the scraped bone ends with foil. Put the racks in a roasting tin.

**4**  In a small saucepan, melt half the butter or margarine. Stir in the remaining olive oil. Drizzle this mixture over the racks of lamb.

**5**  Roast the racks of lamb, allowing 40 minutes for medium-rare meat and 50 minutes for medium.

**6**  Transfer the racks to a warmed serving platter, arranging them so the scraped ends of the bones are interlocked. Cover loosely with foil and set aside.

**7**  Pour the stock into the roasting tin and bring to the boil, scraping the bottom of the tin with a wooden spoon to mix in all the cooking juices. Remove from the heat and swirl in the remaining butter or margarine. Pour the gravy into a warmed sauceboat.

**8**  To serve, carve each rack by cutting down between the chop bones, or cut down after every 2 bones for double chops.

# Lamb Kebabs

**SERVES 4**

1 lb (450 g) boned leg of lamb, cut into 1 in (2.5 cm) cubes

3 medium courgettes, cut into ½ in (1 cm) slices

3 tbsp mint jelly

2 tbsp fresh lemon juice

2 tbsp olive oil

1 tbsp chopped fresh mint

---

~ VARIATION ~

Substitute an equal quantity of orange marmalade for the mint jelly. Instead of fresh mint, use 2 teaspoons of grated orange rind.

---

1 Preheat the grill.

2 Thread the cubes of lamb and slices of courgette alternately onto metal or wooden skewers.

3 ▲ Combine the mint jelly, lemon juice, olive oil and chopped mint in a small saucepan. Stir over low heat until the jelly melts.

4 ▼ Brush the lamb and courgettes with the mint glaze. Lay them on the rack in the grill pan.

5 Cook under the grill, about 3 in (8 cm) from the heat, until browned and cooked to taste, 10–12 minutes, turning the skewers frequently. Serve on a bed of rice, if wished.

---

# Lamb Burgers with Cucumber and Mint

**SERVES 4**

1½ lb (700 g) minced lamb

1 medium onion, finely chopped

1 tbsp paprika

2 tbsp chopped fresh parsley

2 tbsp chopped fresh mint, or 1 tbsp dried mint

salt and pepper

4 hamburger buns with sesame seeds, split open

**FOR THE RELISH**

1 large cucumber, thinly sliced

1 small red onion, thinly sliced

3 tbsp fresh lime or lemon juice

2 tbsp vegetable oil

4 tbsp chopped fresh mint, or 2 tbsp dried mint

2 spring onions, finely chopped

1 To make the relish, combine the cucumber, red onion, lime or lemon juice, oil, mint and spring onions in a non-metallic bowl. Cover the mixture and refrigerate at least 2 hours.

2 ▲ In a bowl, combine the lamb, onion, paprika, parsley, mint and a little salt and pepper. Mix thoroughly.

3 Preheat the grill.

4 ▲ Divide the lamb mixture into 4 equal portions and shape each into a burger 1 in (2.5 cm) thick.

5 Grill the burgers, about 3 in (8 cm) from the heat, allowing 5 minutes on each side for medium and 8 minutes on each side for well-done. At the same time, toast the cut surfaces of the buns briefly under the grill.

6 Serve the lamb burgers in the buns, with the cucumber and mint relish.

*Lamb Kebabs (top), Lamb Burgers with Cucumber and Mint*

# Chicken Breasts with Prunes and Almonds

**SERVES 4**

1 oz (30 g) butter or margarine

1 tbsp vegetable oil

about 2½ lb (1.2 kg) chicken breast halves

1¼ pt (750 ml) chicken stock

4 oz (115 g) raisins

1 tbsp fresh thyme, or 1 tsp dried thyme

3 fresh sage leaves, chopped

3 tbsp chopped fresh parsley

1 tbsp chopped fresh marjoram, or 1 tsp dried marjoram

2 oz (55 g) fresh breadcrumbs

2 oz (55 g) ground almonds

12 prunes, stoned

4–6 whole cloves

½ tsp ground mace

pinch of saffron strands, crumbled

salt and pepper

1½ oz (45 g) flaked almonds, toasted

1 ▼ Melt the butter or margarine with the oil in a frying pan. Add the chicken and brown 10 minutes, turning once. Transfer the chicken pieces to a large pot.

~ COOK'S TIP ~

For ground almonds, chop whole or flaked almonds in a food processor until powdery.

2 ▲ Pour the stock into the pot and bring to the boil. Add all the remaining ingredients, except the toasted almonds, and stir well to mix. Simmer 45 minutes.

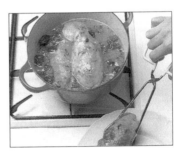

3 ▲ With tongs, remove the chicken from the pot and let cool. Bring the cooking liquid back to the boil and boil until well reduced, about 10 minutes, stirring frequently.

4 ▲ Remove the bones from the chicken and return the meat to the sauce. Heat through. Serve sprinkled with the toasted almonds.

# Spicy Fried Chicken

**SERVES 4**

| 4 fl oz (125 ml) buttermilk |
| 3 lb (1.35 kg) chicken pieces |
| vegetable oil, for frying |
| 2 oz (55 g) plain flour |
| 1 tbsp paprika |
| ¼ tsp pepper |
| 1 tbsp water |

1 ▼ Pour the buttermilk into a large bowl and add the chicken pieces. Stir to coat, then set aside for 5 minutes.

2 Heat ¼ in (5 mm) of oil in a large frying pan over medium-high heat. Do not let the oil overheat.

3 ▲ In a bowl or plastic bag, combine the flour, paprika and pepper. One by one, lift the chicken pieces out of the buttermilk and dip into the flour to coat all over, shaking off any excess.

4 ▼ Add the chicken pieces to the hot oil and fry until lightly browned, about 10 minutes, turning over halfway through cooking time.

5 ▲ Reduce the heat to low and add the water to the frying pan. Cover and cook 30 minutes, turning the pieces over at 10-minute intervals. Uncover the pan and continue cooking until the chicken is very tender and the coating is crisp, about 15 minutes, turning every 5 minutes. Serve hot.

# Roast Chicken

**SERVES 4**

| |
| --- |
| 1 × 3½ lb (1.6 kg) chicken |
| 2 tbsp clear honey |
| 1 tbsp brandy |
| 1½ tbsp plain flour |
| 5 fl oz (165 ml) chicken stock |
| FOR THE STUFFING |
| 2 shallots or 1 small onion, chopped |
| 4 rashers of bacon, chopped |
| 1½ oz (45 g) button mushrooms, diced |
| 1 tbsp butter or margarine |
| 2 thick slices of white bread, diced |
| 1 tbsp chopped fresh parsley |
| salt and pepper |

**1 ▼** For the stuffing, gently fry the shallots, bacon and mushrooms in a frying pan for 5 minutes. With a slotted spoon, transfer them to a bowl.

**2** Pour off all but 2 tablespoons of bacon fat from the pan. Add the butter or margarine to the pan and fry the bread until golden brown. Add the bread to the bacon mixture. Stir in the parsley and salt and pepper to taste. Let cool.

**3** Preheat a 350°F/180°C/Gas 4 oven.

**4 ▲** Pack the stuffing into the body cavity of the chicken. Truss it with string, or secure with small skewers, to keep it in a neat shape.

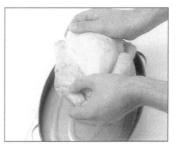

**5 ▲** Transfer the chicken to a roasting tin which just holds it comfortably.

**6 ▲** Mix the honey with the brandy. Brush half of the mixture over the chicken. Roast until the chicken is thoroughly cooked, about 1 hour 20 minutes. Baste the chicken frequently with the remaining honey mixture during roasting.

**7 ▲** Transfer the chicken to a warmed serving platter. Cover with foil and set aside.

**8 ▲** Strain the cooking juices into a measuring jug. Set aside to let the fat rise to the surface then skim it off.

**9 ▲** Stir the flour into the sediments in the roasting tin. Add the skimmed juices and the stock. Boil rapidly until the gravy has thickened, stirring constantly.

**10** Pour the gravy into a warmed sauceboat and serve with the chicken.

# Chicken and Bacon Rolls

**SERVES 4**

16 rashers of bacon

8 chicken thighs, skin removed

**FOR THE MARINADE**

finely grated rind and juice of 1 orange

finely grated rind and juice of 1 lime or
    lemon

5 garlic cloves, crushed

1 tbsp chilli powder

1 tbsp paprika

1 tsp ground cumin

½ tsp dried oregano

1 tbsp olive oil

1 For the marinade, combine the
citrus rind and juice, garlic, chilli
powder, paprika, cumin, oregano and
olive oil in a bowl.

2 ▲ Wrap 2 rashers of bacon around
each chicken thigh in a cross shape.
Secure with wooden cocktail sticks.
Arrange the wrapped chicken thighs
in a baking dish.

3 Pour the marinade over the
chicken, cover, and let marinate
1 hour at room temperature or several
hours in the refrigerator.

4 Preheat a 375°F/190°C/Gas 5 oven.

5 ▼ Put the baking dish in the oven
and bake until the chicken is cooked
through and the bacon is crisp, about
40 minutes for small thighs and 1 hour
for large thighs. Skim excess fat from
the sauce before serving. Rice is a
good accompaniment because there is
plenty of sauce.

# Hot and Spicy Chicken Drumsticks

**SERVES 4**

2 tbsp vegetable oil

8 chicken drumsticks, about 3 lb
    (1.35 kg)

1 medium onion, chopped

4 fl oz (125 ml) water

3 tbsp Dijon mustard

1 tbsp grated horseradish

1 tbsp Worcestershire sauce

1 tsp light brown sugar

¼ tsp salt

parsley sprigs, for garnishing

1 Heat the oil in a frying pan. Add
the chicken drumsticks and brown
them on all sides. With a spatula or
tongs, remove the drumsticks from the
pan and drain on kitchen paper.

2 ▲ Add the onion to the hot oil
and cook until softened, about 5
minutes. Return the chicken to the
pan. Stir in the water, mustard,
horseradish, Worcestershire sauce,
brown sugar and salt, and bring to the
boil.

3 Reduce the heat to low. Cover the
pan and simmer until the chicken is
very tender, about 45 minutes, stirring
occasionally.

4 ▼ Transfer the drumsticks to a
warmed serving dish. Skim any fat off
the cooking juices. Pour the juices
over the chicken. Garnish with
parsley and serve.

*Chicken and Bacon Rolls (top), Hot and Spicy Chicken Drumsticks*

# Baby Chickens with Cranberry Sauce

**SERVES 4**

4 poussins or spring chickens, with
  giblets, each about 1 lb (450 g)

1½ oz (45 g) butter or margarine

salt and pepper

1 onion, quartered

2 fl oz (65 ml) port

5½ fl oz (170 ml) chicken stock

2 tbsp honey

5 oz (140 g) fresh cranberries

~ **COOK'S TIP** ~

If fresh cranberries are not
available, use bottled cranberry
sauce and omit the honey.

1  Preheat a 450°F/230°C/Gas 8 oven.

2 ▼  Smear the chickens on all sides
with 1 oz (30 g) of the butter or
margarine. Arrange them, on their
sides, in a roasting tin in which they
will fit comfortably. Sprinkle them
with salt and pepper. Add the onion
quarters to the tin. Chop the giblets
and livers and arrange them around
the chickens.

3 ▲  Roast 20 minutes, basting often
with the melted fat in the tin. Turn
the chickens onto their other sides
and roast 20 minutes longer, basting
often. Turn them breast up and
continue roasting until they are
cooked through, about 15 minutes.
Transfer to a warmed serving dish.
Cover with foil and set aside.

4  Skim any fat off the juices in the
roasting tin. Put the tin on top of the
stove and bring the juices to the boil.
Add the port and bring back to the
boil, stirring well to dislodge any
particles sticking to the bottom of
the tin.

5 ▲  Strain the sauce into a small
saucepan. Add the stock, bring to the
boil, and boil until reduced by half.
Stir in the honey and cranberries.
Simmer until the cranberries pop,
about 3 minutes.

6  Remove the pan from the heat and
swirl in the remaining butter or
margarine. Season to taste, pour the
sauce into a sauceboat and serve with
the chickens.

# Barbecued Chicken

**SERVES 4**

3 tbsp vegetable oil

1 large onion, chopped

6 fl oz (175 ml) tomato ketchup

6 fl oz (175 ml) water

2½ tbsp fresh lemon juice

1½ tbsp grated horseradish

1 tbsp light brown sugar

1 tbsp French mustard

3 lb (1.35 kg) chicken pieces

1  Preheat a 350°F/180°C/Gas 4 oven.

2 ▲ Heat 1 tablespoon of the oil in a saucepan. Add the onion and cook until softened, about 5 minutes. Stir in the ketchup, water, lemon juice, horseradish, brown sugar and mustard and bring to the boil. Reduce the heat and simmer the sauce 10 minutes, stirring occasionally.

3 ▲ Heat the remaining oil in a heavy frying pan. Add the chicken pieces and brown on all sides. Drain the chicken pieces on kitchen paper.

4 ▼ Transfer the chicken pieces to an 11 × 9 in (28 × 23 cm) baking dish and pour the sauce over the top.

5 ▲ Bake until the chicken is cooked and tender, about 1¼ hours, basting occasionally. Alternatively, barbecue over a medium heat for 40–50 minutes, turning once and brushing frequently with the sauce.

# Traditional Chicken Pie

**SERVES 6**

| |
|---|
| 2 oz (55 g) butter or margarine |
| 1 medium onion, chopped |
| 3 carrots, cut into ½ in (1 cm) dice |
| 1 parsnip, cut into ½ in (1 cm) dice |
| 3 tbsp plain flour |
| 12 fl oz (350 ml) chicken stock |
| 3 fl oz (85 ml) medium sherry |
| 3 fl oz (85 ml) dry white wine |
| 6 fl oz (175 ml) whipping cream |
| 3½ oz (100 g) frozen peas, thawed |
| 12 oz (350 g) cooked chicken meat, in chunks |
| 1 tsp dried thyme |
| 1 tbsp finely chopped fresh parsley |
| salt and pepper |
| FOR THE PASTRY |
| 5½ oz (165 g) plain flour |
| ½ tsp salt |
| 4 oz (115 g) lard or vegetable fat |
| 2–3 tbsp iced water |
| 1 egg |
| 2 tbsp milk |

**1 ▲** For the pastry, sift the flour and salt into a mixing bowl. Using a pastry blender, cut in the fat until the mixture resembles coarse breadcrumbs. Sprinkle in the water, 1 tablespoon at a time, tossing lightly with a fork until the dough forms a ball. Dust with flour, wrap and refrigerate until required.

**2** Preheat a 400°F/200°C/Gas 6 oven.

**3 ▲** Heat half of the butter or margarine in a saucepan. Add the onion, carrots and parsnip and cook until softened, about 10 minutes. Remove the vegetables from the pan with a slotted spoon.

**4 ▲** Melt the remaining butter or margarine in the saucepan. Add the flour and cook 5 minutes, stirring constantly. Stir in the stock, sherry and white wine. Bring the sauce to the boil, and continue boiling for 1 minute, stirring constantly.

**5 ▲** Add the cream, peas, chicken, thyme and parsley to the sauce. Season to taste with salt and pepper. Simmer 1 minute, stirring.

**6 ▼** Transfer the chicken mixture to a 3½ pt (2 litre) shallow baking dish.

**7** On a lightly floured surface, roll out the pastry to ½ in (1 cm) thickness. Lay the pastry over the baking dish and trim off the excess. Dampen the rim of the dish. With a fork, press the pastry to the rim to seal.

**8** Cut decorative shapes from the pastry trimmings.

**9 ▲** Lightly whisk the egg with the milk. Brush the pastry all over with the egg wash. Arrange the pastry shapes in an attractive design on top. Brush again with the egg wash. Make 1 or 2 holes in the crust so steam can escape during baking.

**10** Bake the pie until the pastry is golden brown, about 35 minutes. Serve hot.

# Chicken with Sweet Potatoes

**SERVES 6**

grated rind and juice of 1 large navel orange

3 fl oz (85 ml) soy sauce

1 in (2.5 cm) piece of fresh root ginger, peeled and finely grated

¼ tsp pepper

2½ lb (1.2 kg) chicken pieces

2 oz (55 g) flour

3 tbsp corn oil

1 oz (30 g) butter or margarine

2 lb (900 g) sweet potatoes, peeled and cut into 1 in (2.5 cm) pieces

1½ oz (45 g) light brown sugar

**1 ▲** In a plastic bag, combine the orange rind and juice, soy sauce, root ginger and pepper. Add the chicken pieces. Put the bag in a mixing bowl (this will keep the chicken immersed in the marinade), and seal. Let marinate in the refrigerator overnight.

**2** Preheat a 425°F/220°C/gas 7 oven.

**3 ▼** Drain the chicken, reserving the marinade. Coat the pieces with flour, shaking off any excess.

**4** Heat 2 tablespoons of the oil in a frying pan. Add the chicken pieces and brown on all sides. Drain.

**5** Put the remaining oil and the butter or margarine in a 12 × 9 in (30 × 23 cm) baking dish. Heat in the oven for a few minutes.

**6 ▲** Put the potato pieces in the bottom of the dish, tossing well to coat with the butter and oil. Arrange the chicken pieces in a single layer on top of the potatoes. Cover with foil and bake for 40 minutes.

**7** Mix the reserved marinade with the brown sugar. Remove the foil from the baking dish and pour the marinade mixture over the chicken and potatoes. Bake uncovered until the chicken and potatoes are cooked through and tender, about 20 minutes.

# Mexican Chicken

**SERVES 4**

| |
|---|
| 1 × 3 lb (1.35 kg) chicken |
| 1 tsp salt |
| 12 taco shells |
| 1 small head of iceberg lettuce, shredded |
| 6 oz (170 g) tomatoes, chopped |
| 8 fl oz (250 ml) soured cream |
| 4 oz (115 g) Cheddar cheese, grated |

FOR THE SAUCE

| |
|---|
| 8 fl oz (250 ml) fresh tomatoes, skinned, cooked and sieved |
| 1–2 garlic cloves, crushed |
| ½ tsp cider vinegar |
| ½ tsp dried oregano |
| ½ tsp ground cumin |
| 1–2 tbsp mild chilli powder |

**1** Put the chicken in a large pot and add the salt and enough water to cover. Bring to the boil. Reduce the heat and simmer until the chicken is thoroughly cooked, about 45 minutes. Remove the chicken and let cool. Reserve 4 fl oz (125 ml) of the chicken stock for the sauce.

**2** ▲ Remove the chicken meat from the bones, discarding all skin. Chop the meat coarsely.

**3** For the sauce, combine all the ingredients with the stock in a saucepan and bring to the boil. Stir in the chicken meat. Simmer until the sauce thickens considerably, about 20 minutes, stirring occasionally.

**4** Preheat a 350°F/180°C/Gas 4 oven.

**5** ▲ Spread out the taco shells on 2 baking trays. Heat in the oven for 7 minutes.

**6** Meanwhile, put the shredded lettuce, chopped tomatoes, soured cream and grated cheese in individual serving dishes.

**7** ▲ To serve, spoon a little of the chicken mixture into each taco shell. Garnish with the lettuce, tomatoes, soured cream and cheese.

# Roast Turkey with Middle-Eastern Stuffing

**SERVES 12**

| |
|---|
| 1 12 lb (5.5 kg) turkey, with giblets |
| 6 oz (170 g) softened butter |
| salt and pepper |
| 1 lemon, quartered |
| 2 onions, quartered |
| 16 fl oz (500 ml) cold water |
| 6 small aubergines (optional) |
| 1 tbsp cornflour |
| parsley sprigs, for garnishing |

**FOR THE STUFFING**

| |
|---|
| 1 oz (30 g) pine kernels |
| 6 oz (170 g) couscous |
| 12 fl oz (375 ml) boiling water |
| 1 oz (30 g) butter or margarine |
| 6 spring onions, chopped |
| 1 red pepper, seeded and chopped |
| 1½ oz (45 g) raisins |
| ½ tsp ground cumin |
| 3 tbsp chopped fresh parsley |
| 1 tbsp fresh lemon juice |

**1** Preheat a 325°F/165°C/gas 3 oven. Put the pine kernels on a baking sheet in the oven until golden brown, about 5–10 minutes, stirring occasionally.

**2** For the stuffing, put the couscous into a large bowl and pour the boiling water over it. Let stand 10 minutes.

**3 ▲** Add the pine kernels to the couscous with the rest of the stuffing ingredients. Mix with a fork to keep the grains of couscous separate.

**4** Rinse the turkey inside and out with cold water. Pat dry. Gently slide your hand under the breast skin and loosen it from the meat.

**5 ▲** Spread two-thirds of the softened butter under the skin all over the breast meat.

**6** Fill the neck end of the turkey with stuffing, without packing it down. Reserve any remaining stuffing to serve separately. Sew the neck flap with a trussing needle and thread, or secure with poultry pins.

**7 ▲** Sprinkle the body cavity with salt and pepper. Put the quartered lemon and one of the onions inside. Tie the legs together with string.

**8** Smear the remaining butter all over the turkey. Wrap it loosely in foil and set in a roasting pan. Roast, allowing 25 minutes per pound (55 minutes per kg). Remove the foil for the last 30 minutes of roasting. To test if cooked, pierce the thigh with the tip of a sharp knife; the juices that run out should be clear.

**9 ▲** Meanwhile, put the giblets in a saucepan with the remaining onion and the water. Bring to a boil, simmer 1 hour, then strain.

**10** If using, halve the aubergines and steam until tender, about 10 minutes. Scoop out the inside, leaving a thick shell, and fill with the remaining stuffing. Alternatively, serve the remaining stuffing separately.

**11** When the turkey is done, transfer it to a warmed serving platter. Cover with foil and let rest 30 minutes.

**12 ▲** Skim the fat off the drippings in the roasting pan. Stir the cornflour into a little of the giblet stock until smooth. Add the remaining giblet stock to the roasting pan, then stir in the cornflour mixture. Bring to the boil, scraping the bottom of the pan well with a wooden spoon. Simmer 15 minutes. Strain the gravy and adjust the seasoning.

**13** Garnish the turkey with the stuffed aubergines, if using, and parsley sprigs, and serve the gravy in a warmed sauceboat.

# Hot Turkey Sandwich

**SERVES 4**

2 oz (55 g) butter or margarine

½ small onion, finely chopped

8 oz (225 g) button mushrooms, quartered

1¼ lb (575 g) roast turkey breast

4 thick slices of wholewheat bread

16 fl oz (450 ml) thick turkey gravy

parsley sprigs, for garnishing

**1** Melt half the butter or margarine in a frying pan. Add the onion and cook until softened, about 5 minutes.

~ **VARIATION** ~

If preferred, the sandwich bread may be toasted and buttered.

**2** Add the mushrooms and cook until the moisture they render has evaporated, about 5 minutes, stirring occasionally.

**3** ▲ Meanwhile, skin the turkey breast, and carve into 4 thick slices.

**4** In a saucepan, reheat the turkey gravy. Stir in the onion and mushroom mixture.

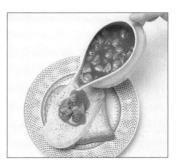

**5** ▲ Spread the slices of bread with the remaining butter or margarine. Set a slice on each of 4 plates and top with the turkey slices. Pour the mushroom gravy over the turkey and serve hot, garnished with parsley.

# Leftover Turkey Casserole

**SERVES 6**

4 fl oz (125 ml) vegetable oil

4 eggs

16 fl oz (450 ml) milk

4 oz (115 g) plain flour

salt and pepper

1½ lb (700 g) cooked turkey meat, cubed

4 fl oz (125 ml) thick plain yoghurt

3 oz (85 g) cornflakes, crushed

**1** Preheat a 425°F/220°C/Gas 7 oven.

**2** Pour the oil into a 13 × 9 in (33 × 23 cm) baking dish. Heat in the oven about 10 minutes.

**3** Meanwhile, beat the eggs in a mixing bowl. Add the milk. Sift in the flour and add a little salt and pepper. Mix until the batter is smooth. Set aside.

**4** ▲ Coat the turkey cubes in the yoghurt, then roll in the crushed cornflakes to coat all over.

**5** ▲ Remove the baking dish from the oven and pour in the prepared batter. Arrange the turkey pieces on top. Return to the oven and bake until the batter is set and golden, 35–40 minutes. Serve hot.

*Hot Turkey Sandwich (top), Leftover Turkey Casserole*

# Turkey Kiev

**SERVES 4**

| |
|---|
| 4 turkey cutlets (boneless slices of breast), each about 6 oz (175 g) |
| salt and pepper |
| 4 oz (115 g) butter or margarine, chilled |
| 1 tsp grated orange rind |
| 2 tbsp chopped fresh chives |
| plain flour, for dredging |
| 3 eggs, beaten |
| 4 oz (115 g) fine dry breadcrumbs |
| vegetable oil, for frying |
| orange wedges and parsley, for garnishing |

**1** ▼ Place each cutlet between 2 sheets of greaseproof paper. With the flat side of a meat mallet, beat until about ¼ in (5 mm) thick, being careful not to split the meat. Remove the greaseproof paper. Sprinkle the cutlets with salt and pepper.

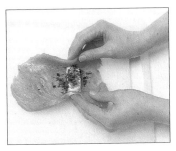

**2** ▲ Cut the butter or margarine into 4 finger-shaped pieces. Place a piece crosswise in the middle of a cutlet. Sprinkle with a little orange rind and chives.

**3** ▲ Fold in the 2 long sides of the cutlet, then roll up from a short end. Secure with wooden cocktail sticks. Repeat with the remaining cutlets.

**4** Dredge each roll lightly with flour, shaking off any excess. Dip in the beaten eggs, then roll in the breadcrumbs to coat evenly. Refrigerate 1 hour to set the breadcrumb coating.

**5** Pour enough oil into a frying pan to make a ½ in (1 cm) layer and heat. Add the breaded turkey rolls to the hot oil and fry until crisp and golden on all sides, 15–20 minutes, turning gently with tongs.

**6** Remove the cocktail sticks before serving. Garnish with orange wedges and parsley.

# Turkey Breasts with Lemon and Sage

**SERVES 4**

4 turkey cutlets (boneless slices of breast), each about 6 oz (175 g)

salt and pepper

1 tbsp grated lemon rind

1 tbsp chopped fresh sage, or 1 tsp dried sage

2 fl oz (65 ml) fresh lemon juice

6 tbsp vegetable oil

4 oz (115 g) fine dry breadcrumbs

fresh sage leaves, for garnishing

lemon slices, for garnishing

**1** Place each cutlet between 2 sheets of greaseproof paper. With the flat side of a meat mallet, beat until about ¼ in (5 mm) thick, being careful not to split the meat. Remove the greaseproof paper. Sprinkle the cutlets with salt and pepper.

**2 ▲** In a small bowl, combine the lemon rind, sage, lemon juice and 2 tablespoons of the oil. Stir well to mix.

> ~ **VARIATION** ~
>
> For a delicious alternative, substitute fresh tarragon leaves for the sage.

**3 ▼** Arrange the turkey cutlets, in one layer, in 1 or 2 shallow baking dishes. Divide the lemon mixture evenly between the dishes and rub well into the turkey. Let marinate 20 minutes.

**4 ▲** Heat the remaining oil in a frying pan. Dredge the turkey breasts in the breadcrumbs, shaking off the excess. Fry in the hot oil until golden brown, about 2 minutes on each side. Serve garnished with sage leaves and lemon slices.

# Turkey Chilli

**SERVES 8**

2 tbsp vegetable oil

1 medium onion, halved and thinly sliced

1 green pepper, seeded and diced

3 garlic cloves, crushed

2 lb (900 g) minced turkey

2–3 tbsp mild chilli powder

1½ tsp ground cumin

1 tsp dried oregano

1 × 16 oz (450 g) can chopped tomatoes

2 tbsp tomato purée

8 fl oz (250 ml) chicken stock

1 × 16 oz (450 g) can red kidney beans, drained and rinsed

¼ tsp salt

**1** Heat the oil in a large saucepan over a medium heat. Add the onion, green pepper and garlic and cook until softened, about 5 minutes, stirring frequently.

**2 ▼** Add the turkey and cook until it is lightly browned, about 5 minutes longer, stirring to break up the meat.

**3 ▼** Stir in the chilli powder, cumin and oregano. Add the tomatoes, tomato purée, chicken stock, kidney beans and salt, and stir well.

**4** Bring to the boil, then reduce the heat and simmer 30 minutes, stirring occasionally. Serve the chilli with boiled rice.

# Turkey and Pasta Bake

**SERVES 4**

2½ oz (70 g) butter or margarine

8 oz (225 g) mushrooms, thinly sliced

1 oz (30 g) plain flour

14 fl oz (400 ml) milk

16 fl oz (450 ml) chicken stock

2 fl oz (65 ml) dry white wine

10 oz (300 g) spaghetti

12 oz (350 g) chopped cooked turkey meat

5 oz (140 g) frozen peas, thawed and drained

2½ oz (70 g) Parmesan cheese, freshly grated

salt and pepper

1 oz (30 g) fine fresh breadcrumbs

**1** Preheat a 375°F/190°C/Gas 5 oven. Grease a shallow 5 pt (3 litre) baking dish.

**2 ▲** Melt 2 oz (55 g) of the butter or margarine in a medium saucepan. Add the mushrooms and cook 5 minutes, stirring frequently. Stir in the flour and cook 3 minutes, stirring constantly. Pour in the milk, stock and white wine and bring to the boil, stirring. Reduce the heat and simmer 5 minutes.

**3** Meanwhile, cook the spaghetti in a large pan of boiling salted water until just tender (see pack instructions for suggested cooking time). Drain.

**4 ▼** Transfer the spaghetti to a mixing bowl. Pour in the mushroom sauce and mix well. Stir in the turkey, peas, half of the Parmesan and salt and pepper to taste. Transfer the mixture to the baking dish.

**5** In a small bowl, combine the remaining Parmesan with the breadcrumbs. Sprinkle evenly over the turkey mixture. Dot with the remaining butter or margarine, cut into pieces. Bake until bubbling and golden, 30–40 minutes. Serve hot, in the baking dish.

*Turkey Chilli (top), Turkey and Pasta Bake*

# PASTA, PIZZA & GRAINS

~

*Versatile pasta and grains – rice, couscous, and bulgur wheat*
*– star in the recipes here, with a myriad of tasty sauces and*
*flavourings, for first courses or main dishes. And there are*
*pizzas with mouthwatering toppings.*

# Spicy Cheese Lasagne

**SERVES 8**

8 oz (225 g) lasagne

2 oz (55 g) butter or margarine

1 large onion, finely chopped

3 garlic cloves, crushed

1½ tbsp chopped green chilli pepper

2 oz (55 g) plain flour

1¾ pt (1 litre) milk

1¼ pt (750 ml) canned chopped
  tomatoes

1 large courgette, sliced

½ tsp crushed dried chilli pepper

salt and pepper

12 oz (350 g) Cheddar cheese, grated

**1** Preheat a 375°F/190°C/Gas 5 oven.
Grease a 13 × 9 in (33 × 23 cm) dish.

**2** Put the lasagne sheets, one at a
time, in a bowl of hot water, and let
soak for 10–15 minutes.

**3** ▲ Melt the butter or margarine in
a large saucepan. Add the onion,
garlic and chopped chilli and cook
until softened, about 5 minutes.

**4** Stir in the flour and cook 3
minutes, stirring constantly. Pour in
the milk and bring to the boil,
stirring. Reduce the heat to low and
simmer gently until thickened, about
5 minutes, stirring occasionally.

**5** Stir the tomatoes, courgettes, and
dried chilli pepper into the sauce.
Season with salt and pepper.

**6** Spoon a little of the sauce into the
prepared baking dish and spread it out
evenly over the bottom. Cover with a
layer of lasagne.

**7** ▲ Add one-third of the remaining
sauce and one-third of the cheese.
Repeat the layers until all the
ingredients are used.

**8** Bake until the top is golden and
bubbling, about 45 minutes. Serve
hot, in the dish.

# Spaghetti with Rich Tomato Sauce

**SERVES 4**

12 oz (350 g) spaghetti

4 garlic cloves, crushed

10–15 sun-dried tomatoes preserved in
  oil, drained and chopped

5 oz (140 g) black olives, stoned

4 fl oz (125 ml) extra-virgin olive oil

3 beef tomatoes, peeled, seeded and
  chopped

3 tbsp capers, drained

3 tbsp chopped fresh basil, plus leaves
  for garnishing, or 1 tsp dried basil

salt and pepper

**1** Cook the spaghetti in a large pan of
boiling salted water until just tender
to the bite (check packet instructions
for timing). Drain well.

**2** ▲ In a food processor or blender,
combine the garlic, sun-dried
tomatoes and half the olives. Process
until finely chopped.

**3** With the motor running, slowly
add the olive oil. Continue processing
until thickened.

**4** ▼ Transfer the mixture to a mixing
bowl. Stir in the fresh tomatoes,
capers and basil. Season with salt and
pepper to taste.

**5** Return the spaghetti to the
saucepan and add the tomato sauce.
Toss well. Serve immediately,
garnished with the remaining olives
and fresh basil leaves, if wished.

*Spicy Cheese Lasagne (top), Spaghetti with Rich Tomato Sauce*

# Pasta with Fresh Basil Sauce

**SERVES 4**

about 2 oz (55 g) chopped fresh basil

about 1 oz (30 g) chopped fresh parsley

1½ oz (45 g) Parmesan cheese, freshly grated

2 garlic cloves

2 oz (55 g) butter or margarine, at room temperature

2 fl oz (65 ml) extra-virgin olive oil

salt

12 oz (350 g) mixed green and white fettucine or tagliatelle

2 oz (55 g) pine kernels, toasted

fresh basil leaves, for garnishing

1 ▲ In a food processor or blender, combine the basil, parsley, Parmesan and garlic. Process until finely chopped.

2 Add the butter or margarine and process to mix well.

3 ▼ With the machine running, slowly add the olive oil. Season with salt to taste.

4 Cook the pasta in a large pan of boiling salted water until just tender (check packet instructions for timing). Drain well.

5 Toss the hot pasta with the basil sauce. Sprinkle with the pine kernels, garnish with basil and serve.

---

# Pasta Quills with Cheesy Aubergine Sauce

**SERVES 6**

1¼ lb (575 g) aubergine, cut into ½ in (1 cm) cubes

salt and pepper

3 tbsp olive oil

½ oz (15 g) butter or margarine

1 garlic clove, chopped

16 fl oz (450 ml) canned chopped tomatoes

12 oz (350 g) pasta quills (penne)

4 oz (115 g) firm goat cheese, cubed

3 tbsp shredded fresh basil, or 1 tsp dried basil

1 Put the aubergine cubes in a large colander and sprinkle them lightly with salt. Let drain at least 30 minutes.

2 Rinse the aubergine under cold water and drain well. Dry on kitchen paper.

3 Heat the oil and butter or margarine in a large saucepan. Add the aubergine and fry until just golden on all sides, stirring frequently.

4 ▲ Stir in the garlic and tomatoes. Simmer until thickened, about 15 minutes. Season with salt and pepper.

5 ▲ Cook the pasta quills in a large pan of boiling salted water until just tender (check packet instructions for timing). Drain well and transfer to a warmed serving bowl.

6 Add the aubergine sauce, goat cheese and basil to the pasta and toss well together. Serve immediately.

*Pasta with Fresh Basil Sauce (top), Pasta Quills with Cheesy Aubergine Sauce*

# Pasta with Chicken and Sausage Sauce

**SERVES 4**

3 tbsp olive oil

1 lb (450 g) skinless boneless chicken breasts, cut into ½ in (1 cm) pieces

3 small spicy cooked sausages, cut diagonally into ½ in (1 cm) slices

salt and pepper

6 spring onions, cut diagonally into ¼ in (5 mm) lengths

10 sun-dried tomatoes preserved in oil, drained and chopped

8 fl oz (250 ml) canned chopped tomatoes

1 medium-sized courgette, cut diagonally into ¼ in (5 mm) slices

12 oz (350 g) bow-tie pasta (farfalle)

**1 ▼** Heat the olive oil in a frying pan. Add the chicken and sausage pieces with a little salt and pepper and cook until browned, about 10 minutes. With a slotted spoon, remove the chicken and sausage from the pan and drain on kitchen paper.

**2 ▲** Add the spring onions and sun-dried tomatoes to the pan and cook until softened, about 5 minutes.

**3 ▲** Stir in the canned tomatoes and cook until thickened, about 5 minutes.

**4 ▲** Add the courgette and return the chicken and sausage to the pan. Cook 5 minutes longer.

**5** Cook the pasta in a large pan of boiling salted water until just tender (check packet instructions for timing). Drain well.

**6** Serve the pasta with the chicken and sausage sauce.

# Pasta with Spinach, Bacon and Mushrooms

**SERVES 4**

6 rashers of bacon, cut in small pieces

½ small onion, finely chopped

8 oz (225 g) small mushrooms, quartered

1 lb (450 g) fresh spinach leaves, stems removed

¼ tsp grated nutmeg

salt and pepper

12 oz (350 g) pasta shells

2 tbsp freshly grated Parmesan cheese

**1 ▼** In a frying pan, cook the bacon until it is browned and the fat is rendered. Drain the bacon on kitchen paper, then put it in a bowl.

**2** Add the onion to the bacon fat in the pan and cook until softened, about 5 minutes.

**3 ▲** Add the mushrooms to the pan and cook until lightly browned, about 5 minutes, stirring frequently. With a slotted spoon, transfer the onion and mushrooms to the bacon in the bowl. Pour off the bacon fat from the frying pan.

**4 ▼** Add the spinach to the pan and cook over a medium heat until wilted, stirring constantly.

**5** Sprinkle with the nutmeg. Raise the heat to high and cook briskly, stirring to evaporate excess liquid from the spinach. Transfer the spinach to a board and chop it coarsely. Return it to the pan.

**6 ▲** Return the bacon, mushrooms and onion to the pan and stir to mix with the spinach. Season with salt and pepper. Set aside.

**7** Cook the pasta in a large pan of boiling salted water until just tender (check packet instructions for timing). Just before the pasta is ready, reheat the spinach mixture.

**8** Drain the pasta well and return to the saucepan. Add the spinach mixture and toss well to mix. Sprinkle with Parmesan cheese before serving.

# Pasta Spirals with Spicy Sausage

**SERVES 4**

3 tbsp olive oil

1 lb (450 g) chorizo or other spicy cooked sausages, cut diagonally in ½ in (1 cm) slices

1 onion, chopped

1 garlic clove, crushed

2 red peppers, seeded and sliced

12 oz (350 g) drained canned sweetcorn, or frozen sweetcorn, thawed

salt and pepper

12 oz (350 g) pasta spirals (fusilli)

1 tbsp chopped fresh basil, or ½ tsp dried basil

fresh basil leaves, for garnishing

1 Heat 1 tablespoon of the oil in a frying pan. Add the sausage slices and brown them on both sides.

2 Remove the sausage from the pan with a slotted spoon and drain on kitchen paper.

3 ▲ Heat the remaining oil in the pan and add the onion, garlic and peppers. Cook until softened, about 5 minutes, stirring frequently.

4 ▲ Stir the sausage and sweetcorn into the pepper mixture and heat through, about 5 minutes. Season with salt and pepper.

5 Cook the pasta in boiling salted water until just tender (check packet instructions for timing). Drain well and return to the pan.

6 Add the sausage sauce and basil to the pasta. Toss together well, garnish with basil and serve immediately.

# Pasta with Tomato and Lime Sauce

**SERVES 4**

1 lb (450 g) very ripe tomatoes, peeled and chopped

1 small bunch of tender, young rocket or spinach leaves

4 garlic cloves, crushed

grated rind of ½ lime

juice of 2 limes

¼ tsp chilli sauce

12 oz (350 g) thin spaghetti (capellini)

2 fl oz (65 ml) olive oil

salt and pepper

freshly grated Parmesan cheese, for serving

1 ▼ Combine the tomatoes, rocket, garlic, lime rind and juice and chilli sauce. Stir well to mix. Set aside for 20–30 minutes.

2 Cook the pasta in boiling salted water until just tender (check packet instructions for timing). Drain and return to the pan.

3 ▲ Add the olive oil and tomato and lime sauce to the pasta. Toss well together. Season with salt and pepper. Add Parmesan cheese to taste, toss again and serve.

*Pasta Spirals with Spicy Sausage (top), Pasta with Tomato and Lime Sauce*

# Macaroni Cheese

**SERVES 4**

4 oz (115 g) macaroni

2 oz (55 g) butter or margarine

1 oz (30 g) plain flour

1 pt (575 ml) milk

6 oz (170 g) Cheddar cheese, grated

3 tbsp finely chopped fresh parsley

salt and pepper

3½ oz (100 g) dry breadcrumbs

1½ oz (45 g) Parmesan cheese, freshly
grated

1 Preheat a 350°F/180°C/Gas 4 oven.
Grease a 10 in (25 cm) gratin dish.

2 Cook the macaroni in boiling salted
water until just tender (check packet
instructions for timing). Drain well.

3 Melt the butter or margarine in a
saucepan. Add the flour and cook 2
minutes, stirring. Stir in the milk.
Bring to a boil, stirring constantly,
and simmer until thickened, about 5
minutes.

4 ▲ Remove the pan from the heat.
Add the macaroni, Cheddar cheese
and parsley to the sauce and mix well.
Season with salt and pepper.

5 Transfer the mixture to the
prepared gratin dish, spreading it out
evenly with a spoon.

6 ▲ Toss together the breadcrumbs
and Parmesan cheese with a fork.
Sprinkle over the macaroni.

7 Bake until the top is golden brown
and the macaroni mixture is bubbling,
30–35 minutes.

# Noodle and Vegetable Bake

**SERVES 10**

1 lb (450 g) egg noodles

3 oz (85 g) butter or margarine

1 onion, chopped

3 garlic cloves, chopped

3 carrots, grated

12 oz (350 g) small mushrooms,
quartered

3 eggs, beaten

12 oz (350 g) cottage cheese

8 fl oz (250 ml) soured cream

2 courgettes, finely chopped in a food
processor

3 tbsp chopped fresh basil, or 1 tbsp
dried basil

salt and pepper

fresh basil leaves, for garnishing

1 Preheat a 350°F/180°C/Gas 4 oven.
Grease a 13 × 9 in (33 × 23 cm)
baking dish.

2 Cook the pasta in boiling salted
water until just tender (check packet
instructions for timing). Drain and
rinse with cold water. Transfer to a
mixing bowl.

3 Melt two-thirds of the butter or
margarine in a frying pan. Add the
onion, garlic and carrots and cook
until tender, about 10 minutes,
stirring frequently.

4 ▲ Stir in the mushrooms and cook
5 minutes longer. Add the vegetables
to the noodles in the mixing bowl.

5 In a small bowl, combine the eggs,
cottage cheese, soured cream,
courgettes, basil and salt and pepper
to taste. Mix well.

6 ▲ Add the cottage cheese mixture
to the noodles and mix well. Transfer
to the prepared baking dish. Dot the
top with the remaining butter or
margarine.

7 Cover the dish with foil. Bake until
the casserole is set, about 1 hour.
Serve hot, in the baking dish,
garnished with basil leaves.

*Macaroni Cheese (top), Noodle and Vegetable Bake*

# Baked Seafood Pasta

**SERVES 6**

8 oz (225 g) egg noodles

2½ oz (70 g) butter or margarine

1 oz (30 g) flour

16 fl oz (500 ml) milk

½ tsp mustard powder

1 tsp fresh lemon juice

1 tbsp tomato purée

salt and pepper

2 tbsp minced onion

2 oz (55 g) finely diced celery

4 oz (125 g) small mushrooms, sliced

8 oz (225 g) cooked peeled shrimps

8 oz (225 g) crab meat

1 tbsp chopped fresh dill

fresh dill sprigs, for garnishing

1  Preheat a 350°F/180°C/gas 4 oven. Generously butter a 3½ pt (2 litre) baking dish.

2  Cook the noodles in a large pan of boiling salted water until just tender to the bite (check packet instructions for timing). Drain well.

3  ▲ While the pasta is cooking, make a white sauce. Melt 1½ oz (45 g) of the butter or margarine in a saucepan. Add the flour and cook 2 minutes, stirring. Stir in the milk. Bring to the boil, stirring constantly, and simmer until thickened, about 5 minutes.

4  ▲ Add the mustard, lemon juice and tomato purée to the sauce and mix well. Season to taste with salt and pepper. Set aside.

5  ▲ Melt the remaining butter or margarine in a frying pan. Add the onion, celery and mushrooms. Cook until softened, about 5 minutes.

6  ▲ In a mixing bowl, combine the pasta, sauce, vegetables, shrimps, crab meat and dill. Stir well to mix.

7  Pour the mixture into the prepared baking dish. Bake until piping hot and the top is lightly browned, 30–40 minutes. Garnish with dill sprigs, if wished.

# Pasta-Stuffed Peppers

| |
|---|
| 6 rashers of bacon, chopped |
| 1 small onion, chopped |
| 12 fl oz (350 ml) canned chopped tomatoes |
| ⅛ tsp crushed dried chilli peppers |
| 2 oz (55 g) macaroni |
| 6 oz (170 g) Mozzarella cheese, diced |
| 12 black olives, stoned and thinly sliced |
| salt and pepper |
| 2 large red peppers |
| 2 large yellow peppers |
| 2 tbsp olive oil |

1  Preheat a 350°F/180°C/Gas 4 oven. Grease an 8 in (20 cm) baking dish.

2 ▲ In a frying pan, cook the bacon until browned and the fat is rendered. Drain the bacon on kitchen paper.

3  Add the onion to the bacon fat in the pan and cook until softened, about 5 minutes. Pour off excess fat.

4 ▲ Stir in the tomatoes and dried chilli peppers. Cook over high heat until thickened, about 10 minutes.

5  Meanwhile, cook the pasta in a large pan of boiling salted water until just tender (check packet instructions for timing). Drain well.

6 ▲ Put the pasta in a mixing bowl and add the bacon, tomato sauce, Mozzarella cheese and olives. Toss well to mix. Season to taste.

7  Cut the stem end off each pepper; reserve these 'lids'. Remove the seeds from inside the peppers and cut out the white ribs.

8 ▲ Divide the pasta mixture evenly among the peppers. Put on the "lids". Brush the peppers all over with the olive oil and set them in the prepared baking dish.

9  Cover the dish with foil and bake 30 minutes. Remove the foil and bake until the peppers are tender, 25–30 minutes longer.

# Broccoli and Goat Cheese Pizza

**SERVES 2–3**

| |
|---|
| 8 oz (225 g) broccoli florets |
| 2 tbsp cornmeal, or polenta |
| 4 fl oz (125 ml) fresh tomatoes, skinned, cooked and sieved |
| 6 cherry tomatoes, halved |
| 12 black olives, stoned |
| 4 oz (115 g) goat cheese, cut into pieces |
| 1½ oz (45 g) Parmesan cheese, grated |
| 1 tbsp olive oil |

FOR THE PIZZA DOUGH

| |
|---|
| 8–9 oz (225–250 g) plain flour |
| 1 package active dry yeast (¼ oz/7.5 g) |
| ⅛ tsp sugar |
| 5 fl oz (150 ml) tepid water |
| 2 tbsp olive oil |
| ½ tsp salt |

**1** For the pizza dough, combine 3 oz (85 g) of the flour, the yeast and sugar in a food processor. With the motor running, pour in the water. Turn the motor off. Add the oil, 5 oz (140 g) of the remaining flour and the salt.

**2 ▲** Process until a ball of dough is formed, adding more water, 1 teaspoon at a time, if the dough is too dry, or the remaining flour, 1 tablespoon at a time, if it is too wet.

**3 ▲** Put the dough in an oiled bowl and turn it so the ball of dough is oiled all over. Cover the bowl and let the dough rise in a warm place until doubled in size, about 1 hour.

**4 ▲** Meanwhile, cook the broccoli florets in boiling salted water or steam them until just tender, about 5 minutes. Drain well and set aside.

**5** Preheat the oven to the highest setting. Oil a 12 in (30 cm) round pizza pan and sprinkle with the cornmeal.

**6** When the dough has risen, turn out onto a lightly floured surface. Punch down the dough to deflate it, and knead it briefly.

~ **COOK'S TIP** ~

If more convenient, the pizza dough can be used as soon as it is made, without any rising.

**7 ▲** Roll out the dough to a 12 in (30 cm) round. Lay the dough on the pizza pan and press it down evenly.

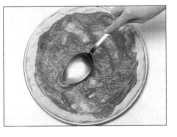

**8 ▲** Spread the tomato sauce evenly onto the pizza base, leaving a rim of dough uncovered around the edge about ½ in (1 cm) wide.

**9 ▲** Arrange the broccoli florets, tomatoes, and olives on the tomato sauce and sprinkle with the cheeses. Drizzle the olive oil over the top.

**10** Bake until the cheese melts and the edge of the pizza base is puffed and browned, 10–15 minutes.

# Pitta-Bread Pizzas

**SERVES 4**

4 × 6 in (15 cm) round pitta breads, split in half horizontally

2 fl oz (65 ml) olive oil

salt and pepper

1 small red pepper, seeded and sliced

1 small yellow pepper, seeded and sliced

8 oz (225 g) small red potatoes, cooked and sliced

1 tbsp chopped fresh rosemary, or 1 tsp dried rosemary

1½ oz (45 g) Parmesan cheese, freshly grated

1 Preheat a 350°F/180°C/Gas 4 oven.

2 ▼ Place the pitta rounds on a baking tray. Brush them on both sides with 2 tablespoons of the oil. Sprinkle with salt. Bake until pale golden and crisp, about 10 minutes.

3 ▲ Heat the remaining oil in a frying pan. Add the peppers and cook until softened, about 5 minutes, stirring frequently.

4 ▲ Add the potatoes and rosemary to the peppers. Heat through, about 3 minutes, stirring well. Season with salt and pepper.

5 Preheat the grill.

6 ▲ Divide the pepper-potato mixture between the pitta rounds. Sprinkle with the Parmesan cheese and transfer to the grill pan.

7 Grill about 3 in (8 cm) from the heat until golden, 3–4 minutes.

# Onion, Olive and Anchovy Pizza

**SERVES 4**

6 tbsp olive oil

1 lb (450 g) onions, thinly sliced

3 garlic cloves, crushed

1 bay leaf

2 tsp dried thyme

salt and pepper

2 cans anchovy fillets, drained and blotted dry on kitchen paper

12 olives, mixed black and green

FOR THE PIZZA DOUGH

4 oz (115 g) wholewheat flour

3 oz (85 g) plain flour

1¼ tsp active dry yeast

⅛ tsp sugar

5 fl oz (150 ml) tepid water

2 tbsp olive oil

½ tsp salt

**1** For the pizza dough, in a food processor combine the flours, yeast and sugar. With the motor running, pour in the tepid water. Turn the motor off. Add the oil and salt. Process until a ball of dough is formed.

**2** Put the dough in an oiled bowl and turn it to coat with oil. Cover and let rise until doubled in size.

**3** ▲ Heat 3 tablespoons of the oil in a frying pan. Add the onions, garlic and herbs. Cook over a low heat until the onions are very soft and the moisture has evaporated, about 45 minutes. Season with salt and pepper.

**4** Preheat the oven to the highest setting. Oil a 13 × 9 in (33 × 23 cm) baking tray.

**5** ▼ Transfer the risen dough onto a lightly floured surface. Punch down the dough and knead it briefly. Roll it out into a rectangle to fit the baking tray. Lay the dough on the tray and press it up the edges of the tray.

**6** Brush the dough with 1 tablespoon olive oil. Discard the bay leaf, and spoon the onion mixture onto the dough. Spread it out evenly, leaving a ½ in (1 cm) border around the edge.

**7** ▲ Arrange the anchovies and olives on top of the onions. Drizzle the remaining 2 tablespoons olive oil over the top.

**8** Bake the pizza until the edges are puffed and browned, 15–20 minutes.

# Spicy Sausage Pizza

**SERVES 2–3**

| |
|---|
| 2 tbsp cornmeal |
| 4 fl oz (125 ml) tomato sauce |
| 8 oz (225 g) pepperoni sausage, cut in thin slices |
| 8 oz (225 g) mozzarella cheese, grated |
| Pizza Dough |

**1** Make the pizza dough as directed in steps 1–3 of Broccoli and Goat Cheese Pizza.

**2** Preheat a 475°F/240°C/gas 9 oven. Oil a 12 in (30 cm) round pizza pan and sprinkle with the cornmeal.

**3** Transfer the risen dough to a lightly floured surface. Punch down the dough to deflate it and knead it briefly.

**4 ▼** Roll out the dough to a 12 in (30 cm) round. Lay the dough on the pizza pan and press it down evenly.

**5 ▲** Spread the tomato sauce evenly on the pizza base, leaving a ½ in (1 cm) rim of dough uncovered around the edge. Arrange the sausage slices on top. Sprinkle with the cheese.

**6** Bake until the cheese melts and the edge of the pizza base is puffed and browned, 10–15 minutes.

---

# Folded Pizza with Peppers and Aubergine

**SERVES 2**

| |
|---|
| 3–4 tbsp olive oil |
| ½ small aubergine, cut in ½ in (1 cm) sticks |
| ½ red pepper, seeded and sliced |
| ½ yellow pepper, seeded and sliced |
| 1 small onion, halved and sliced |
| 1 garlic clove, crushed |
| salt and pepper |
| 4 oz (125 g) mozzarella cheese, chopped |
| Pizza Dough |

**1** Make the pizza dough as directed in steps 1–3 of Broccoli and Goat Cheese Pizza.

**2** Heat 3 tbsp olive oil in a frying pan. Add the aubergine and cook until golden, about 6–8 minutes. Add the pepper strips, onion and garlic, with more oil if necessary. Cook, stirring occasionally, until softened, about 5 minutes longer. Season to taste.

**3** Preheat a 475°F/240°C/gas 9 oven.

**4** Transfer the risen pizza dough to a lightly floured surface. Punch down the dough to deflate it and knead it briefly. Divide the dough in half.

**5** Roll out each piece of dough into a 7 in (18 cm) round. With the back of a knife, make an indentation across the centre of each round to mark it into halves.

**6 ▲** Spoon half of the vegetable mixture onto one side of each dough round. Divide the cheese evenly between them.

**7 ▲** Fold the dough over to enclose the filling. Pinch the edges to seal them securely.

**8** Set the folded pizza on an oiled baking sheet. Bake until puffed and browned, 20–25 minutes. To serve, break or cut each pizza in half.

*Spicy Sausage Pizza (top), Folded Pizza with Peppers and Aubergine*

# Pizza Toasts with Cheesy Topping

**Serves 4**

2 small aubergines, cut across into thin slices (about 8 oz/225 g)

1 tbsp salt

4 fl oz (125 ml) olive oil

1 garlic clove, crushed with the side of a knife

8 slices French bread, ½ in (1 cm) thick

8 oz (225 g) Mozzarella cheese, cut into 8 slices

3 tbsp chopped fresh chives

3 tbsp chopped fresh basil

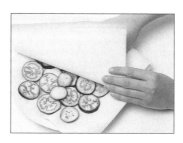

**1 ▲** Put the aubergine slices in a colander and sprinkle with the salt. Let stand at least 30 minutes to drain. Rinse the aubergine slices under cold water, then blot dry with kitchen paper.

**2** Heat half the olive oil in a frying pan. Add the aubergine slices and fry until golden brown, about 5 minutes on each side. Add more oil if necessary when the slices are turned over. Drain on kitchen paper.

**3** Preheat a 325°F/170°C/Gas 3 oven.

**4 ▲** In a small bowl, combine the remaining olive oil and the garlic. Brush both sides of the bread slices with the garlic oil. Place the slices on a baking tray. Bake until golden brown, about 10 minutes.

**5** Preheat the grill.

**6 ▲** Top each slice of garlic bread with a slice of aubergine and a slice of Mozzarella. Arrange on a baking tray.

**7** Grill about 3 in (8 cm) from the heat until the cheese melts, 5–7 minutes. Sprinkle the toasts with the chopped herbs before serving.

# Mini Tomato Pastry 'Pizzas'

**SERVES 6**

| |
|---|
| 4 large or 8 small sheets of frozen filo pastry, thawed |
| 2 fl oz (65 ml) olive oil |
| 1 lb (450 g) tomatoes, peeled, seeded and diced |
| 2 oz (55 g) Parmesan cheese, grated |
| 4 oz (115 g) feta cheese, crumbled |
| 9 black olives, stoned and halved |
| ¼ tsp dried oregano |
| ½ tsp fresh thyme leaves, or ⅛ tsp dried thyme |
| salt and pepper |
| fresh thyme or basil, for garnishing |

**1** Preheat a 350°F/180°C/Gas 4 oven. Grease 2 baking trays.

**2 ▲** Stack the filo sheets. With a sharp knife, cut into 24 × 6 in (15 cm) rounds, using a small plate as a guide.

**3 ▲** Lay 3 filo rounds on each baking tray. Brush the rounds lightly with olive oil. Lay another pastry round on top of each oiled round and brush it with oil. Continue layering the pastry rounds, oiling each one, to make 6 stacks of 4 rounds each.

**4** Bake the filo bases until they are crisp and golden brown, about 5 minutes.

**5 ▲** In a bowl, combine the tomatoes, cheeses, olives and herbs. Mix well. Season with salt and pepper.

**6 ▲** Spoon the tomato mixture on top of the filo pastry bases, leaving the edges bare. Return to the oven to bake until heated through, about 5 minutes.

**7** Serve hot, garnished with fresh herb sprigs.

# Couscous with Vegetables

**SERVES 4**

2 tbsp olive oil

8 button onions, peeled

1 red pepper, seeded and quartered

1 leek, cut across into 1 in (2.5 cm) lengths

¼ tsp saffron strands

½ tsp turmeric

¼ tsp cayenne pepper

1 tsp ground ginger

1 × 3 in (8 cm) cinnamon stick

3 large carrots, cut diagonally into 1 in (2.5 cm) lengths

1 swede, peeled and cubed

2 potatoes, peeled and quartered

1 × 16 oz (450 g) can chopped tomatoes

1¼ pt (750 ml) chicken stock

salt and pepper

2 courgettes, cut across into 1 in (2.5 cm) lengths

4 oz (115 g) whole green beans, trimmed

1 × 15 oz (420 g) can chick peas, drained

2 tbsp chopped fresh coriander

2 tbsp chopped fresh parsley

**FOR THE COUSCOUS**

1 pt (575 ml) water

½ tsp salt

9 oz (250 g) instant couscous

**1** Heat the oil in a large saucepan or cast iron casserole. Add the onions, red pepper and leek. Cook for 2–3 minutes.

~ **COOK'S TIP** ~

This couscous makes a filling vegetarian meal, and the recipe can be doubled or tripled. When multiplying a recipe, increase spices by less and taste.

**2 ▲** Stir in the saffron, turmeric, cayenne, ginger and cinnamon stick.

**3 ▲** Add the carrots, swede, potatoes, tomatoes and chicken stock. Season with salt. Bring to the boil. Reduce the heat to low, cover and simmer until the vegetables are nearly tender, about 25 minutes.

**4 ▲** Meanwhile, for the couscous, put the water and salt in a saucepan and bring to the boil. Stir in the couscous. Remove the pan from the heat, cover and set aside until all the liquid is absorbed, about 10 minutes.

**5 ▲** Stir the courgettes, green beans and chick peas into the vegetable mixture. Simmer 5 minutes longer.

**6 ▲** Stir in the herbs and add pepper to taste.

**7 ▲** Lightly fluff the couscous grains with a fork. Pile the couscous in a mound in the middle of a shallow, round platter. Spoon the vegetables over the couscous and serve.

# Tangy Bulgur Wheat Salad

**SERVES 6**

4 oz (115 g) fine bulgur wheat

8 fl oz (250 ml) water

3 oz (85 g) fresh parsley, finely chopped

4 tbsp chopped fresh mint, or 2 tbsp dried mint

2 spring onions, finely chopped

½ small red onion, finely chopped

1 large tomato, chopped

2 fl oz (65 ml) olive oil

3 fl oz (85 ml) fresh lemon juice

salt and pepper

½ head of cos lettuce, leaves separated

**1** Place the bulgur wheat in a bowl. Pour the water over the wheat. Let stand until the wheat swells and softens, about 30 minutes.

**2 ▲** A handful at a time, squeeze excess water out of the bulgur wheat and put it in a mixing bowl.

**3 ▲** Add the parsley, mint, spring onions, red onion and tomato to the bulgur wheat. Stir in the olive oil and lemon juice. Season to taste.

**4** Line a large serving platter with the lettuce leaves. Pile the bulgur wheat salad in the middle.

# Cheesy Vegetarian Slice

**SERVES 6**

1¼ pt (750 ml) water

¼ tsp salt

4 oz (115 g) instant polenta

1 egg

6 oz (175 g) Cheddar cheese, grated

1 oz (30 g) butter or margarine

⅛ tsp cayenne pepper

**1** Preheat a 350°F/180°C/Gas 4 oven. Grease a 13 × 9 in (33 × 23 cm) baking dish.

**2** Put the water and salt in a medium saucepan and bring to the boil.

~ **COOK'S TIP** ~

Served with salad or a tomato sauce, this makes a delicious snack. Try it instead of rice or potatoes with a main course, too.

**3 ▲** Stir in the polenta. Reduce the heat to low, cover the pan and cook the polenta until thickened, 5–7 minutes, stirring occasionally.

**4 ▲** In a small bowl, beat the egg lightly. Add a large spoonful of the cooked polenta and stir well to mix.

**5** Stir the egg mixture into the remaining cooked polenta. Add two-thirds of the cheese, the butter, and the cayenne. Stir over low heat until the cheese melts.

**6 ▲** Transfer the mixture to the prepared dish. Sprinkle the remaining cheese over the top. Bake until the cheesy polenta is set and golden on top, 35–40 minutes. Let cool 5 minutes before cutting and serving.

*Tangy Bulgur Wheat Salad (top), Cheesy Vegetarian Slice*

# Mixed Rice Ring

**SERVES 8**

2 tbsp vegetable oil

1 large onion, chopped

12 oz (350 g) mixed long-grain and wild rice

2 pt (1.25 litres) chicken stock

2½ oz (75 g) currants

salt

6 spring onions, cut diagonally into ¼ in (5 mm) lengths

parsley sprigs, for garnishing

**1** Oil a 2¾ pt (1.75 litre) ring.

**2 ▼** Heat the oil in a large saucepan. Add the onion and cook until softened, about 5 minutes.

**3 ▲** Add the rice to the pan and stir well to coat the rice with the oil.

**4 ▲** Stir in the chicken stock and bring to the boil.

**5** Reduce the heat to low. Stir the currants into the rice mixture. Add salt to taste. Cover and simmer until the rice is tender and the stock has been absorbed, about 20 minutes.

**6** Drain the rice if necessary and transfer it to a mixing bowl. Stir in the spring onions.

**7 ▲** Pack the rice mixture into the prepared mould. Unmould it onto a warmed serving platter. If you like, put parsley sprigs into the centre of the ring before serving.

# Green and Orange Riso

**SERVES 4**

2 pt (1.25 litres) chicken stock

1½ oz (45 g) butter or margarine

1 small onion, chopped

2 oz (55 g) peeled and coarsely grated
   acorn squash or pumpkin

9 oz (250 g) short-grain rice

1 courgette, quartered lengthwise and
   chopped

5 oz (140 g) frozen peas, thawed

1½ oz (45 g) Parmesan cheese, grated

salt and pepper

**1** In a saucepan, bring the stock to a simmer. Keep it simmering gently.

**2** Melt one-third of the butter or margarine in a heavy saucepan. Add the onion and cook until softened, about 5 minutes.

**3** ▲ Add the grated squash to the onion. Cook 1 minute, stirring.

**4** ▲ Add the rice and stir to coat all the grains well with butter. Cook 1 minute, stirring.

**5** Add a ladleful of the simmering stock to the rice. Cook, stirring frequently, until the stock is absorbed. Continue adding the stock, one ladleful at a time, allowing each addition to be absorbed before adding the next, and stirring frequently.

**6** ▲ After about 5 minutes, stir in the courgette pieces. After about 10 minutes, stir in the peas. The risotto will be cooked in about 20 minutes.

**7** ▲ Remove the pan from the heat. Add the remaining butter or margarine and the Parmesan and stir well. Season with salt and pepper. If you like, serve in hollowed-out cooked acorn squash halves.

# Red Beans and Rice

**SERVES 4**

1 onion, chopped

1 green pepper, seeded and chopped

4 rashers of bacon, chopped

1 garlic clove, chopped

6 oz (170 g) long-grain rice

2–3 tsp chilli powder

2 tsp fresh thyme leaves or ½ tsp dried
thyme

16 fl oz (450 ml) canned chopped
tomatoes

8 fl oz (250 ml) chicken or beef stock

salt and pepper

1 × 15 oz (420 g) can red kidney beans,
drained and rinsed

1 ▼  In a medium saucepan, cook the
onion, green pepper, bacon and garlic
until the vegetables are softened and
the bacon has rendered its fat, about 5
minutes.

2 ▲  Add the rice and stir until all
the grains are coated with bacon fat.
Stir in the chilli powder and cook
1 minute.

3 ▲  Add the thyme, chopped
tomatoes and stock and stir well.
Season with salt and pepper. Bring to
the boil.

4  Reduce the heat to low, cover the
pan and simmer until the rice is nearly
tender, about 15 minutes.

5 ▲  Stir in the kidney beans. Cover
again and simmer until the rice is
tender and all the stock has been
absorbed, about 5 minutes longer.

6  Fluff the rice and beans with a fork,
then transfer to a warmed serving
dish.

# Nut Pilaf

**SERVES 4**

| |
|---|
| 1 oz (30 g) butter or margarine |
| 1 onion, finely chopped |
| 12 oz (350 g) long-grain brown rice |
| ½ tsp finely grated lemon rind |
| 16 fl oz (450 ml) chicken stock |
| 16 fl oz (450 ml) water |
| ¼ tsp salt |
| 4 spring onions, finely chopped |
| 2 tbsp fresh lemon juice |
| 1½ oz (45 g) pecan halves, toasted |

**1 ▲** Melt the butter or margarine in a medium saucepan. Add the onion and cook until softened, about 5 minutes.

**2 ▲** Stir in the rice and cook 1 minute, stirring.

**3 ▲** Add the lemon rind, chicken stock, water and salt and stir well. Bring to the boil. Reduce the heat to low, cover the pan and simmer until the rice is tender and all the liquid is absorbed, 30–35 minutes.

**4 ▼** Remove the pan from the heat and let stand 5 minutes, still covered. Stir in the spring onions, lemon juice and pecan halves. Transfer to a warmed serving dish.

# Fried Rice with Prawns and Asparagus

**SERVES 4**

3 tbsp vegetable oil

12 oz (350 g) asparagus, cut diagonally into 1 in (2.5 cm) lengths

3 oz (85 g) brown or button mushrooms, sliced

12 oz (350 g) cooked long-grain rice

1 tsp finely grated fresh root ginger

8 oz (225 g) cooked peeled prawns, deveined

4 oz (115 g) canned water chestnuts, drained and sliced

3 tbsp soy sauce

pepper

1 ▲ Heat the oil in a wok over high heat. Add the asparagus and mushrooms and stir-fry, 3–4 minutes.

3 ▲ Add the prawns and stir-fry for 1 minute.

2 ▲ Stir in the rice and ginger. Cook, stirring, until heated through, about 3 minutes.

4 ▲ Add the water chestnuts and soy sauce and stir-fry 1 minute longer. Season with pepper and serve.

~ VARIATION ~

Ingredients for fried rice are infinitely variable. Instead of prawns, try scallops or cubes of firm-fleshed fish.

---

# Saffron Rice

**SERVES 6**

4 tbsp butter or margarine

⅛ tsp crumbled saffron strands

1 lb (450 g) long-grain rice

1¾ pt (1 litre) chicken stock

½ tsp salt

~ COOK'S TIP ~

If preferred, bring the saffron rice to the boil in a flameproof casserole, then transfer to a preheated 375°F/190°C/Gas 5 oven.

1 Melt the butter or margarine in a large saucepan. Stir in the saffron.

2 ▲ Add the rice and stir to coat all the grains well with the saffron butter.

3 ▼ Stir in the stock and salt. Bring to the boil. Reduce the heat to low, cover and simmer until the rice is tender and all the stock has been absorbed, about 20 minutes.

4 Fluff the rice grains with a fork before serving.

*Fried Rice with Prawns and Asparagus (top), Saffron Rice*

# SALADS, VEGETABLES, EGGS & CHEESE

~

*Here is a bright selection of tasty vegetable main dishes and accompaniments, colourful salads, and economical and quick egg and cheese dishes for lunches and suppers.*

# Avocado, Grapefruit and Melon Salad

**SERVES 6**

| |
|---|
| 1 pink grapefruit |
| 1 yellow grapefruit |
| 1 cantaloup melon |
| 2 large, ripe but firm avocados |
| 2 tbsp fresh lemon juice |
| 2 tbsp vegetable oil |
| 1 tbsp clear honey |
| 3 tbsp chopped fresh mint |
| salt and pepper |
| fresh mint leaves, for garnishing |

1 ▲ Peel the grapefruit. Cut out the segments, leaving the membranes. Put the segments in a bowl.

2 Cut the melon in half. Remove the seeds and discard them. With a melon baller, scoop out balls from the melon flesh. Add the melon balls to the grapefruit sections. Chill the fruit at least 30 minutes.

3 ▲ Cut the avocados in half and discard the stones. Cut each half in two. Peel off the skin, then cut the flesh into small pieces.

4 ▲ Toss the avocado pieces in the lemon juice. Using a slotted spoon, transfer the avocado to the grapefruit mixture.

5 ▲ For the dressing, whisk the oil into the reserved lemon juice. Stir in the honey, chopped mint and salt and pepper to taste.

6 Pour the dressing over the fruit mixture and toss gently. Garnish with mint leaves and serve immediately.

# Sweet and Savoury Salad

**SERVES 4**

1 medium red onion, thinly sliced into rings

salt and pepper

2 oranges, peeled and cut in segments

1 firm jícama, peeled and cut in matchstick strips, or drained canned water chestnuts

2 heads of radicchio, cored, or 1 head of red leaf lettuce, leaves separated

3 tbsp chopped fresh parsley

3 tbsp chopped fresh basil

1 tbsp white wine vinegar

2 fl oz (65 ml) walnut oil

**1 ▲** Put the onion in a colander and sprinkle with 1 teaspoon salt. Let drain 15 minutes.

**2** In a mixing bowl combine the orange and jícama or water chestnuts.

**3** Spread out the radicchio or lettuce leaves in a large shallow bowl or serving platter.

**4 ▲** Rinse the onion and dry on kitchen paper. Toss it with the jícama or water chestnuts and orange.

**5 ▼** Arrange the jícama or water chestnut, orange and onion mixture on top of the radicchio leaves. Sprinkle with the parsley and basil.

**6 ▲** Combine the vinegar, oil and salt and pepper to taste in a screwtop jar. Shake well to combine. Pour the dressing over the salad and serve immediately.

# Crispy Coleslaw

**SERVES 6**

12 oz (350 g) green or white cabbage, cut in wedges and cored

4 oz (115 g) red cabbage, cored

3 spring onions, finely chopped

2 medium carrots, grated

1 tsp sugar

2 tbsp fresh lemon juice

2 tsp distilled white vinegar

4 fl oz (125 ml) soured cream

4 fl oz (125 ml) mayonnaise

¾ tsp celery seeds

salt and pepper

**1** ▼ Slice the green and red cabbage thinly across the leaves.

**2** Place the cabbage in a mixing bowl and add the spring onions and carrots. Toss to combine.

**3** In a small bowl, combine the sugar, lemon juice, vinegar, soured cream, mayonnaise and celery seeds.

**4** ▲ Pour the mayonnaise dressing over the vegetables. Season with salt and pepper. Stir until well coated. Spoon into a serving bowl.

---

# Tangy Potato Salad

**SERVES 8**

3 lb (1.35 kg) small new potatoes

2 tbsp white wine vinegar

1 tbsp Dijon mustard

3 tbsp vegetable or olive oil

3 oz (85 g) chopped red onion

salt and pepper

4 fl oz (125 ml) mayonnaise

2 tbsp chopped fresh tarragon, or 1½ tsp dried tarragon

1 celery stick, thinly sliced

**1** Cook the unpeeled potatoes in boiling salted water until tender, 15–20 minutes. Drain.

**2** In a small bowl, mix together the vinegar and mustard until the mustard dissolves. Whisk in the oil.

**3** ▲ When the potatoes are cool enough to handle, slice them into a large mixing bowl.

**4** ▲ Add the onion to the potatoes and pour the dressing over them. Season, then toss gently to combine. Let stand at least 30 minutes.

**5** ▲ Mix together the mayonnaise and tarragon. Gently stir into the potatoes, along with the celery. Taste and adjust the seasoning before serving.

> **~ VARIATION ~**
>
> Substitute 3 tablespoons dry white wine for the wine vinegar, if preferred. When available, use small red potatoes to give a nice colour to the salad.

*Crispy Coleslaw (top), Tangy Potato Salad*

# Caesar Salad

**SERVES 4**

2 eggs

1 garlic clove, crushed

½ tsp salt

4 fl oz (125 ml) olive oil

juice of 1 lemon

¼ tsp Worcestershire sauce

1 lb (450 g) cos lettuce, torn into bite-sized pieces

1½ oz (45 g) Parmesan cheese, freshly grated

pepper

8 canned anchovy fillets, drained and blotted dry on kitchen paper (optional)

**FOR THE CROUTONS**

1 garlic clove

¼ tsp salt

2 fl oz (65 ml) olive oil

4–6 slices French bread, cubed

1  Preheat a 350°F/180°C/Gas 4 oven.

2 ▲  For the croûtons, crush the garlic with the salt in a mixing bowl and mix in the oil. Add the bread cubes to the bowl and toss to coat with the garlic oil.

3  Spread the bread cubes on a baking tray. Bake until golden brown, 20–25 minutes.

4  Meanwhile, put the eggs in a small pan of boiling water and simmer gently for 7 minutes. Transfer the eggs to a bowl of cold water and shell them as soon as they are cool enough to handle.

5 ▼  Mash the garlic clove with the salt in the bottom of a salad bowl. Whisk in the olive oil, lemon juice and Worcestershire sauce.

6  Add the lettuce to the salad bowl and toss well to coat with the dressing.

7  Add the Parmesan cheese and season with pepper. Add the croûtons and toss well to combine.

8  Cut the hard-boiled eggs in quarters. Arrange on top of the salad with the anchovies, if using. Serve immediately.

# Green Salad with Blue Cheese Dressing

**SERVES 6**

4 handfuls mixed salad leaves, torn in bite-size pieces

1 small bunch of lamb's lettuce (mâche), rocket or watercress

**FOR THE DRESSING**

4 fl oz (125 ml) plain yoghurt

1½ tsp white wine vinegar

½ tsp sugar

1 tbsp fresh lemon juice

1 garlic clove, crushed

1 oz (30 g) blue cheese, crumbled

1 ▼  For the dressing, combine the yoghurt, wine vinegar, sugar, lemon juice and garlic in a small bowl and mix well. Fold in the cheese. The dressing should be lumpy.

2 ▲  Put the salad leaves in a salad bowl. Add the dressing and toss until all the leaves are coated. Serve immediately.

*Caesar Salad (top), Green Salad with Blue Cheese Dressing*

# Spinach and Bacon Salad

**SERVES 4**

1 hard-boiled egg

3 fl oz (85 ml) white wine vinegar

1 tsp Dijon mustard

2 tbsp vegetable or olive oil

salt and pepper

1 lb (450 g) fresh young spinach leaves

2 oz (55 g) small mushrooms, sliced

3 rashers of bacon

1 medium onion, chopped

2 garlic cloves, crushed

1  Separate the egg yolk and white. Chop the egg white and set aside.

2 ▲ To make the dressing, press the egg yolk through a sieve into a bowl. Whisk in the vinegar, mustard, oil and salt and pepper to taste.

3  Put the spinach in a salad bowl with the mushrooms.

4  In a small frying pan, fry the bacon until crisp. Remove the bacon and drain on kitchen paper.

5 ▼ When cool, crumble the bacon over the spinach.

6  Add the onion and garlic to the bacon fat in the frying pan and cook until softened, about 5 minutes, stirring frequently.

7  Pour the onion and garlic over the spinach, with the bacon fat. Add the dressing and toss well to combine. Sprinkle the egg white on top and serve immediately.

# Warm Red Cabbage Salad with Spicy Sausage

**SERVES 4**

1 lb (450 g) red cabbage, cut in wedges and cored

2 fl oz (65 ml) olive oil

2 shallots or 1 small onion, chopped

2 garlic cloves, chopped

3 tbsp cider vinegar

4 oz (115 g) chorizo or other cooked spicy sausage, cut diagonally in ¼ in (5 mm) slices

salt and pepper

2 tbsp chopped fresh chives

2 tbsp chopped fresh parsley

1  Slice the cabbage wedges very thinly across the leaves.

2 ▲ Heat the oil in a frying pan. Add the shallots and garlic and cook until softened, about 4 minutes. Transfer from the pan to a salad bowl using a slotted spoon.

3  Add the cabbage to the hot oil and cook until wilted, about 10 minutes, stirring occasionally. Add 1 tablespoon of the vinegar and cook 1 minute longer, stirring. Transfer the cabbage and the oil from the pan to the salad bowl.

4 ▼ Add the sausage slices to the pan and fry until well browned. Transfer the sausage to the salad bowl using the slotted spoon.

5  Pour the remaining vinegar over the salad and toss well to combine. Season with salt and pepper. Sprinkle with the chopped herbs and serve.

*Spinach and Bacon Salad (top), Warm Red Cabbage Salad with Spicy Sausage*

# Pasta, Olive and Avocado Salad

**SERVES 6**

8 oz (225 g) pasta spirals, or other small pasta shapes

4 oz (115 g) drained canned sweetcorn, or frozen sweetcorn, thawed

½ red pepper, seeded and diced

8 black olives, stoned and sliced

3 spring onions, finely chopped

2 medium avocados

FOR THE DRESSING

2 sun-dried tomato halves, loose-packed (not preserved in oil)

1½ tbsp balsamic or white wine vinegar

1½ tbsp red wine vinegar

½ garlic clove, crushed

½ tsp salt

5 tbsp olive oil

1 tbsp chopped fresh basil

**1 ▼** For the dressing, drop the sun-dried tomatoes into a pan containing 1 in (2.5 cm) of boiling water and simmer until tender, about 3 minutes. Drain and chop finely.

**2 ▲** Combine the tomatoes, vinegars, garlic and salt in a food processor. With the machine on, add the oil in a stream. Stir in the basil.

**3** Cook the pasta in a large pan of boiling salted water until just tender (check packet instructions for timing). Drain well.

**4 ▲** In a large bowl, combine the pasta, sweetcorn, red pepper, olives and spring onions. Add the dressing and toss well together.

**5 ▲** Just before serving, peel the avocados and cut the flesh into cubes. Mix gently into the pasta salad and serve at room temperature.

# Ham and Bean Salad

**SERVES 8**

6 oz (175 g) dried black-eyed beans

1 onion

1 carrot

8 oz (225 g) smoked ham, diced

3 medium tomatoes, peeled, seeded and diced

salt and pepper

**FOR THE DRESSING**

2 garlic cloves, crushed

3 tbsp olive oil

3 tbsp red wine vinegar

2 tbsp vegetable oil

1 tbsp fresh lemon juice

1 tbsp chopped fresh basil, or 1 tsp dried basil

1 tbsp whole-grain mustard

1 tsp soy sauce

½ tsp dried oregano

½ tsp caster sugar

¼ tsp Worcestershire sauce

½ tsp chilli sauce

**1** Soak the black-eyed beans in water to cover overnight. Drain.

**2** ▲ Put the beans in a large saucepan and add the onion and carrot. Cover with fresh cold water and bring to the boil. Lower the heat and simmer until the beans are tender, about 1 hour. Drain, reserving the onion and carrot. Transfer the beans to a salad bowl.

**3** ▼ Finely chop the onion and carrot. Toss with the beans. Stir in the ham and tomatoes.

**4** For the dressing, combine all the ingredients in a small bowl and whisk to mix.

**5** ▲ Pour the dressing over the beans. Season with salt and pepper. Toss to combine.

# Egg, Bacon and Avocado Salad

**SERVES 4**

1 large head of cos lettuce, sliced into strips across the leaves

8 rashers of bacon, fried until crisp and crumbled

2 large avocados, peeled and diced

6 hard-boiled eggs, chopped

2 beef tomatoes, peeled, seeded and chopped

6 oz (170 g) blue cheese, crumbled

FOR THE DRESSING

1 garlic clove, crushed

1 tsp sugar

½ tbsp fresh lemon juice

1½ tbsp red wine vinegar

4 fl oz (125 ml) groundnut oil

salt and pepper

1 For the dressing, combine all the ingredients in a screwtop jar and shake well.

2 ▲ On a large rectangular or oval platter, spread out the lettuce to make a bed.

3 ▲ Reserve the bacon, and arrange the remaining ingredients in rows, beginning with the avocados. Sprinkle the bacon on top.

4 Pour the dressing over the salad just before serving.

---

# Spicy Sweetcorn Salad

**SERVES 4**

2 tbsp vegetable oil

1 lb (450 g) drained canned sweetcorn, or frozen sweetcorn, thawed

1 green pepper, seeded and diced

1 small fresh red chilli pepper, seeded and finely diced

4 spring onions, cut diagonally into ½ in (1 cm) lengths

3 tbsp chopped fresh parsley

8 oz (225 g) cherry tomatoes, halved

salt and pepper

FOR THE DRESSING

½ tsp sugar

2 tbsp white wine vinegar

½ tsp Dijon mustard

1 tbsp chopped fresh basil, or 1 tsp dried basil

1 tbsp mayonnaise

¼ tsp chilli sauce

1 Heat the oil in a frying pan. Add the sweetcorn, pepper, chilli pepper and spring onions. Cook over a medium heat until softened, about 5 minutes, stirring frequently.

2 ▲ Transfer the vegetables to a salad bowl. Stir in the parsley and tomatoes.

3 ▲ For the dressing, combine all the ingredients in a small bowl and whisk together. Pour the dressing over the sweetcorn mixture. Season with salt and pepper. Toss well to combine, and serve.

*Egg, Bacon and Avocado Salad (top), Spicy Sweetcorn Salad*

# Scalloped Potatoes

**SERVES 6**

2½lb (1.2kg) potatoes, peeled and cut in ⅛in (3mm) slices

salt and pepper

1 large onion, thinly sliced

1oz (30g) plain flour

2oz (55g) butter or margarine, cut in small pieces

6oz (175g) Cheddar cheese, grated

7floz (200ml) milk

16floz (500ml) single cream

**1** Preheat a 350°F/180°C/Gas 4 oven. Butter a 10in (25cm) oval gratin dish.

**2** Layer one-quarter of the potato slices in the prepared dish. Season with salt and pepper.

**3 ▼** Layer one-quarter of the sliced onion over the potatoes. Sprinkle with one-quarter of the flour and dot with one-quarter of the butter or margarine. Sprinkle with one-quarter of the cheese.

**4** Continue layering these ingredients, making 4 layers.

**5 ▲** Heat the milk and single cream in a small saucepan. Pour the mixture evenly over the potatoes.

**6** Cover the gratin dish with foil. Place it in the oven and bake for 1 hour. Remove the foil and bake until the potatoes are tender and the top is golden, 15–20 minutes longer.

# New Potatoes with Savoury Butter

**SERVES 6**

1¼lb (575g) small new potatoes

2oz (55g) butter or margarine

3 shallots or 1 small to medium onion, finely chopped

2 garlic cloves, crushed

salt and pepper

1 tsp chopped fresh tarragon

1 tsp chopped fresh chives

1 tsp chopped fresh parsley

**1** Bring a saucepan of salted water to the boil. Add the potatoes and cook until just tender, 15–20 minutes. Drain well.

**2 ▼** Melt the butter or margarine in a frying pan. Add the shallots or onion and garlic and cook over low heat until softened, about 5 minutes.

**3 ▲** Add the potatoes to the pan and stir well to mix with the savoury butter. Season with salt and pepper. Cook, stirring, until the potatoes are heated through.

**4** Transfer the potatoes to a warmed serving bowl. Sprinkle with the chopped herbs before serving.

*Scalloped Potatoes (top), New Potatoes with Savoury Butter*

# Mashed Potatoes with Garlic

**SERVES 6**

2–3 heads of garlic, according to taste, cloves separated

2 oz (55 g) butter or margarine

2½ lb (1.2 kg) potatoes, peeled and quartered

salt and pepper

4 fl oz (125 ml) whipping cream

3 tbsp chopped fresh chives

**1** Drop the garlic cloves into a pan of boiling water and boil 2 minutes. Drain and peel.

**2 ▲** Melt half the butter or margarine in a small saucepan over a low heat. Add the peeled garlic. Cover and cook until very soft, 20–25 minutes, stirring frequently.

**3** Meanwhile, cook the potatoes in boiling salted water until tender, 15–20 minutes. Drain well and return to the pan. Set over medium heat to evaporate excess moisture, 2–3 minutes.

**4 ▲** Push the potatoes through a potato ricer or mash them with a potato masher. Return them to the saucepan and beat in the remaining butter or margarine, in two batches. Season with salt and pepper.

**5 ▲** Remove the pan of garlic from the heat and mash the garlic and butter together with a fork until smooth. Stir in the cream. Return to the heat and bring just to the boil.

**6** Beat the garlic cream into the potatoes, 1 tablespoon at a time. Reheat the potatoes if necessary.

**7** Fold most of the chives into the potatoes. Transfer the potatoes to a warmed serving bowl and sprinkle the remaining chives on top.

# Candied Sweet Potatoes

**SERVES 8**

3 lb (1.35 kg) sweet potatoes, peeled

1½ oz (45 g) butter or margarine

4 fl oz (125 ml) maple syrup

¾ tsp ground ginger

1 tbsp fresh lemon juice

**1** Preheat a 375°F/190°C/Gas 5 oven. Grease a large shallow baking dish.

**2** ▲ Cut the potatoes in ½ in (1 cm) slices. Cook them in boiling water for 10 minutes. Drain. Let cool.

**3** ▲ Melt the butter or margarine in a small saucepan over a medium heat. Stir in the maple syrup until well combined. Stir in the ginger. Simmer 1 minute, then add the lemon juice.

**4** ▼ Arrange the potato slices in one layer in the prepared baking dish, overlapping them slightly.

**5** ▲ Drizzle the maple syrup mixture evenly over the potatoes. Bake until the potatoes are tender and glazed, 30–35 minutes, spooning the cooking liquid over them once or twice.

# Creamy Sweetcorn with Peppers

**SERVES 4**

1 oz (30 g) butter or margarine

1 small red pepper, seeded and finely diced

1 small green pepper, seeded and finely diced

4 corn cobs, trimmed

4 fl oz (125 ml) whipping cream

salt and pepper

**2 ▼** Cut the kernels off the corn cobs. Scrape the cobs with the back of a knife to extract the milky liquid. Alternatively, use a corn scraper to remove the kernels and liquid.

**3 ▲** Add the sweetcorn with the liquid to the saucepan. Stir in the cream. Bring to the boil and simmer until thickened and the sweetcorn is tender, 3–4 minutes. Season with salt and pepper.

**1 ▲** Melt the butter or margarine in a saucepan. Add the peppers and cook 5 minutes, stirring occasionally.

~ **VARIATION** ~

1 lb (450 g) frozen sweetcorn, thawed, can be substituted if fresh corn cobs are not available.

# Fried Okra

**SERVES 6**

1½ lb (700 g) okra

2 oz (55 g) cornmeal, or polenta

⅛ tsp black pepper

3 fl oz (85 ml) bacon dripping or oil

¾ tsp salt

~ **COOK'S TIP** ~

When removing the stems of the okra, slice through the point where it joins the vegetable. Cutting into the vegetable allows the release of the viscous insides.

**1** Wash the okra well and drain in a colander. Cut off the stems.

**2 ▲** Combine the cornmeal and pepper in a mixing bowl. Add the still damp okra and toss to coat evenly with cornmeal.

**3 ▼** Heat the bacon drippings or oil in a frying pan. Add the okra and fry until tender and golden, 4–5 minutes. Drain on kitchen paper.

**4** Sprinkle the fried okra with the salt just before serving.

*Creamy Sweetcorn with Peppers (top), Fried Okra*

# Brussels Sprouts with Chestnuts

**SERVES 6**

1 lb (450 g) Brussels sprouts, trimmed

4 oz (115 g) butter or margarine

3 celery sticks, cut diagonally in ½ in (1 cm) lengths

1 large onion, thinly sliced

1 × 14 oz (400 g) can whole chestnuts in brine, drained and rinsed

¼ tsp grated nutmeg

salt and pepper

grated rind of 1 lemon

**2 ▲** Melt the butter or margarine in a frying pan over low heat. Add the celery and onion and cook until softened, about 5 minutes.

**1 ▲** Drop the Brussels sprouts into a pan of boiling salted water and cook 3–4 minutes. Drain well.

**3 ▲** Raise the heat to medium and add the chestnuts and Brussels sprouts to the frying pan.

**4** Stir in the nutmeg and salt and pepper to taste. Cook until piping hot, about 2 minutes, stirring frequently.

**5 ▲** Stir in the grated lemon rind. Transfer to a warmed serving dish.

> **~ VARIATION ~**
>
> For a tasty alternative, substitute grated orange rind for the lemon rind, especially when serving with pork or turkey.

---

# Green Peas and Baby Onions

**SERVES 6**

½ oz (15 g) butter or margarine

12 baby onions, peeled

1 small butterhead lettuce, shredded

10 oz (300 g) shelled fresh green peas or frozen peas, thawed

1 tsp sugar

2 tbsp water

salt and pepper

2 sprigs fresh mint

**1** Melt the butter or margarine in a frying pan. Add the onions and cook over medium heat until they just begin to colour, about 10 minutes.

**2 ▼** Add the lettuce, peas, sugar and water. Season with salt and pepper. Bring to a boil. Reduce the heat to low, cover and simmer until the peas are tender, about 15 minutes for fresh peas and 10 minutes for frozen peas, stirring occasionally.

**3 ▲** Strip the mint leaves from the stems. Chop finely with a sharp knife. Stir the mint into the peas. Transfer to a warmed serving dish.

*Brussels Sprouts with Chestnuts (top), Green Peas and Baby Onions*

# Broccoli and Cauliflower Bake

**SERVES 6**

1–1½ lb (450–700 g) broccoli, trimmed

1–1½ lb (450–700 g) cauliflower, trimmed

FOR THE CHEESE SAUCE

3 tbsp butter or margarine

1 oz (30 g) plain flour

12 fl oz (375 ml) milk

3 oz (85 g) Cheddar cheese, grated

⅛ tsp grated nutmeg

salt and pepper

**1** Preheat a 300°F/150°C/Gas 2 oven. Butter a 1¾ pt (1 litre) ovenproof bowl or round mould.

**2** Break the broccoli into florets. Drop into a pan of boiling salted water and cook 5 minutes. Drain and rinse with cold water to stop the cooking. Drain thoroughly, then spread on kitchen paper to dry.

**3** Break the cauliflower into florets. Drop into a pan of boiling salted water and cook 5 minutes. Drain and rinse with cold water. Drain thoroughly, then spread the florets on kitchen paper to dry.

**4 ▲** Place a cluster of cauliflower on the bottom of the prepared bowl, stems pointing inwards. Add a layer of broccoli, heads against the side and stems pointing inwards. Fill the centre with smaller florets.

**5 ▲** Add another layer of cauliflower florets. Finish with a layer of broccoli.

**6** Cover the bowl with buttered foil. Bake until the vegetables are heated through, 10–15 minutes.

**7** Meanwhile, for the sauce, melt the butter or margarine in a saucepan. Add the flour and cook 2 minutes, stirring. Stir in the milk. Bring to the boil, stirring constantly, and simmer until thickened, about 5 minutes. Stir in the cheese. Season with the nutmeg and salt and pepper to taste. Keep the sauce warm over a very low heat.

**8 ▲** Hold a warmed serving plate over the top of the bowl, turn them over together and lift off the bowl. Serve the moulded vegetables with the cheese sauce.

# Green Bean and Red Pepper Stir-Fry

**SERVES 4**

1 lb (450 g) fine green beans, cut diagonally in 1 in (2.5 cm) lengths

2 tbsp olive oil

1 red pepper, seeded and cut in matchstick strips

½ tsp soy sauce

1 tsp fresh lemon juice

**1** Drop the green beans into a pan of boiling salted water and cook 3 minutes. Drain and refresh in cold water. Pat dry with kitchen paper.

**2 ▼** Heat the oil in a frying pan. Add the green beans and red pepper and stir-fry until just tender, about 2 minutes.

**3 ▲** Remove the pan from the heat and stir in the soy sauce and lemon juice. Transfer the vegetables to a warmed serving dish.

*Broccoli and Cauliflower Bake (top), Green Bean and Red Pepper Stir-Fry*

# Baked Onions with Sun-Dried Tomatoes

**SERVES 4**

1 lb (450 g) button onions

2 tsp chopped fresh rosemary, or ¾ tsp dried rosemary

2 garlic cloves, chopped

1 tbsp chopped fresh parsley

salt and pepper

4 fl oz (125 ml) sun-dried tomatoes in oil, drained and chopped

6 tbsp olive oil

1 tbsp white wine vinegar

**1** Preheat a 300°F/150°C/Gas 2 oven. Grease a shallow baking dish.

**2 ▼** Drop the onions into a pan of boiling water and cook 5 minutes. Drain in a colander.

**3 ▲** Spread the onions in the bottom of the prepared baking dish.

**4 ▲** Combine the rosemary, garlic, parsley, salt and pepper and sprinkle over the onions.

**5 ▲** Scatter the tomatoes over the onions. Drizzle the olive oil and vinegar on top.

**6** Cover with a sheet of foil and bake 45 minutes, basting occasionally. Remove the foil and bake until the onions are golden, about 15 minutes longer.

# Special Stewed Tomatoes

**SERVES 6**

| |
|---|
| 2 lb (900 g) very ripe tomatoes, stems removed |
| 1 oz (30 g) butter or margarine |
| 2 celery sticks, diced |
| 1 small green pepper, seeded and diced |
| 2 spring onions, finely chopped |
| salt and pepper |
| 2 tbsp chopped fresh basil |

**1**  Fill a mixing bowl with boiling water and another bowl with iced water. Three or four at a time, drop the tomatoes into the boiling water and leave them 30 seconds.

**2 ▲**  Remove the tomatoes with a slotted spoon and transfer to the iced water. When they are cool enough to handle, remove the tomatoes from the iced water.

**3 ▲**  Peel the tomatoes and cut them into wedges.

**4 ▼**  Heat the butter or margarine in a flameproof casserole or saucepan. Add the celery, green pepper and spring onions and cook until softened, about 5 minutes.

~ **VARIATION** ~

To make stewed tomatoes into a tomato sauce, cook uncovered in a frying pan, stirring occasionally, until thickened to the desired consistency.

**5 ▲**  Stir in the tomatoes. Cover and cook until the tomatoes are soft but not mushy, 10–15 minutes, stirring occasionally. Season with salt and pepper.

**6**  Remove the pan from the heat and stir in the basil.

# Braised Red Cabbage with Apple

**SERVES 6**

2 lb (900 g) red cabbage, quartered and cored

salt and pepper

2 medium red onions, halved and thinly sliced

2 Red Delicious apples, peeled, cored, halved and thinly sliced

1½ tsp caraway seeds

3 tbsp light brown sugar

3 tbsp red wine vinegar

1 oz (30 g) butter or margarine, diced

**1** Preheat a 400°F/200°C/Gas 6 oven.

**2** Slice the cabbage quarters thinly across the leaves.

~ **VARIATION** ~

For a sharper flavour, substitute Granny Smith or other tart varieties of eating apple for the Red Delicious apples in this recipe.

**3 ▲** Make a layer of one-quarter of the cabbage in a large, deep baking dish. Season with salt and pepper.

**4 ▲** Layer one-third of the sliced onions and apples on top of the cabbage. Sprinkle with some of the caraway seeds and 1 tablespoon of the brown sugar.

**5** Continue layering until all the ingredients have been used, ending with a layer of cabbage on top.

**6 ▲** Pour in the vinegar and dot the top with the butter or margarine. Cover and bake 1 hour.

**7** Remove the cover and continue baking until the cabbage is very tender and all the liquid has evaporated, about 30 minutes longer.

# Glazed Carrots with Spring Onion

**SERVES 6**

1 lb (450 g) baby carrots, trimmed and peeled if necessary

1½ oz (45 g) butter or margarine

2 tbsp honey

2 tbsp fresh orange juice

8 oz (225 g) spring onions, cut diagonally into 1 in (2.5 cm) lengths

salt and pepper

**1** Cook the carrots in boiling salted water or steam them until just tender, about 10 minutes. Drain if necessary.

**2 ▼** In a frying pan, melt the butter or margarine with the honey and orange juice, stirring until the mixture is smooth and well combined.

**3 ▲** Add the carrots and spring onions to the pan. Cook over medium heat, stirring occasionally, until the vegetables are heated through and glazed, about 5 minutes. Season with salt and pepper before serving.

*Braised Red Cabbage with Apple (top), Glazed Carrots with Spring Onion*

# Spanish Omelette

**SERVES 4**

4 rashers of bacon

3 tbsp olive oil

1 onion, thinly sliced

½ small red pepper, seeded and sliced

½ small green pepper, seeded and sliced

1 large garlic clove, crushed

12 oz (350 g) small potatoes, cooked and sliced

4 eggs

2 tbsp single cream

salt and pepper

**1** Preheat a 350°F/180°C/Gas 4 oven.

**2** In a heavy 8 in (20 cm) frying pan with an ovenproof handle, fry the bacon until crisp. Drain on kitchen paper.

**3** Pour off the bacon fat from the frying pan. Add 1 tablespoon oil to the pan and cook the onion and peppers until softened, about 5 minutes.

**4** ▲ Remove the frying pan from the heat and stir in the garlic. Crumble in the bacon. Reserve the mixture in a bowl until needed.

**5** ▲ Heat the remaining oil in the frying pan. Lay the potato slices in the bottom of the pan, slightly overlapping. Spoon the bacon, onion, and pepper mixture evenly over the potatoes.

**6** In a small bowl, beat together the eggs, cream and salt and pepper to taste.

**7** ▲ Pour the egg mixture into the frying pan. Cook over low heat until the egg is set, lifting the edge of the omelette with a knife several times to let the uncooked egg seep down.

**8** Transfer the frying pan to the oven to finish cooking the omelette, 5–10 minutes longer. Serve hot or warm, cut into wedges.

# Spinach and Cheese Pie

**SERVES 8**

3 lb (1.35 kg) fresh spinach leaves,
    coarse stems removed

2 tbsp olive oil

1 medium onion, finely chopped

2 tbsp chopped fresh oregano, or 1 tsp
    dried oregano

4 eggs

1 lb (450 g) cottage cheese

6 tbsp freshly grated Parmesan cheese

grated nutmeg

salt and pepper

12 small sheets of frozen filo pastry,
    thawed

2 oz (55 g) butter or margarine,
    melted

**1** Preheat a 375°F/190°C/Gas 5 oven.

**2** ▲ Stack handfuls of spinach leaves, roll them loosely and cut across the leaves into thin ribbons.

**3** Heat the oil in a large saucepan. Add the onion and cook until softened, about 5 minutes.

**4** Add the spinach and oregano and cook over high heat until most of liquid from the spinach evaporates, about 5 minutes, stirring frequently. Remove from the heat and let cool.

**5** Break the eggs into a bowl and beat. Stir in the cottage cheese and Parmesan cheese, and season generously with nutmeg, salt and pepper. Stir in the spinach mixture.

**6** ▲ Brush a 13 × 9 in (33 × 23 cm) baking dish with a little butter or margarine. Arrange half the filo sheets in the bottom of the dish to cover evenly and extend about 1 in (2.5 cm) up the sides. Brush with butter.

**7** ▲ Ladle in the spinach and cheese filling. Cover with the remaining filo pastry, tucking under the edges neatly.

**8** Brush the top with the remaining butter. Score the top with diamond shapes using a sharp knife.

**9** Bake until the pastry is golden brown, about 30 minutes. Cut into squares and serve hot.

# Spinach Moulds with Tomato Dressing

**SERVES 6**

| |
|---|
| 1½ lb (700 g) frozen chopped spinach, thawed |
| 1 oz (30 g) butter or margarine |
| 3 oz (85 g) fresh breadcrumbs |
| salt and pepper |
| 2 eggs |
| 1 egg yolk |
| 12 fl oz (350 ml) milk |
| 3 tbsp freshly grated Parmesan cheese |
| fresh thyme sprigs, for garnishing |
| FOR THE DRESSING |
| 5 tsp fresh lemon juice |
| 1 tsp sugar |
| ½ tsp whole-grain mustard |
| ½ tsp fresh thyme leaves, or ⅛ tsp dried thyme |
| 4 fl oz (125 ml) olive oil |
| 3 tomatoes, peeled, seeded and diced |

**1** Preheat a 350°F/180°C/Gas 4 oven. Butter 6 ramekins. Place them in a shallow baking tin.

**2** ▲ A handful at a time, squeeze the thawed spinach to remove as much water as possible.

**3** Melt the butter or margarine in a saucepan. Stir in the spinach and cook 1 minute over a high heat, stirring.

**4** ▲ Remove the pan from the heat. Stir the breadcrumbs into the spinach. Season with salt and pepper.

**5** In a small bowl, beat the whole eggs with the egg yolk. Scald the milk in a small saucepan. Lightly beat it into the eggs.

**6** ▲ Add the Parmesan cheese to the milk mixture and stir into the spinach mixture.

**7** ▲ Spoon the mixture into the ramekins, dividing it evenly. Cover each ramekin tightly with foil.

**8** ▲ Add hot water to the baking tin to come halfway up the sides of the ramekins. Bake until a knife inserted in a flan comes out clean, about 35 minutes.

**9** ▲ Meanwhile, for the dressing, combine the lemon juice, sugar, mustard and thyme in a bowl. Whisk in the olive oil. Stir in the tomatoes and salt and pepper to taste.

**10** To serve, unmould the flans onto individual plates. Spoon a little dressing over each flan and garnish with a sprig of fresh thyme.

> **~ COOK'S TIP ~**
>
> Fresh breadcrumbs are easy to make using a food processor. Remove and discard the crusts from several slices of bread. Tear the bread into smaller pieces and process.

# Sweetcorn Fritters

**SERVES 4**

5 garlic cloves

3 eggs, beaten

3 oz (85 g) plain flour

salt and pepper

6 oz (175 g) drained canned sweetcorn, or frozen sweetcorn, thawed

8 fl oz (250 ml) soured cream

2 tbsp chopped fresh chives

3 tbsp corn oil

1 Preheat the grill.

2 Thread the garlic cloves onto a skewer. Grill close to the heat, turning, until charred and soft. Let cool.

3 ▼ Peel the garlic cloves. Place them in a bowl and mash with a fork. Add the eggs, flour and salt and pepper to taste and stir until well mixed. Stir in the sweetcorn. Set aside for at least 30 minutes.

4 In a small bowl, combine the soured cream and chives. Cover and refrigerate.

5 ▲ To cook the fritters, heat the oil in a frying pan. Drop in spoonfuls of the batter and fry until lightly browned on both sides, about 2 minutes, turning once. Drain on kitchen paper.

6 Serve the fritters hot with the chive dip.

# Cheese and Mushroom Open Omelette

**SERVES 4**

2 tbsp olive oil

4 oz (115 g) small mushrooms, sliced

3 spring onions, finely chopped

6 eggs

4 oz (115 g) Cheddar cheese, grated

1 tbsp chopped fresh dill, or ¼ tsp dried dill

salt and pepper

1 Heat the oil in a heavy 8 in (20 cm) frying pan, preferably with an ovenproof handle. Add the mushrooms and spring onions and cook over medium heat until wilted, about 3 minutes, stirring occasionally.

2 ▲ Break the eggs into a bowl and beat to mix. Add the cheese, dill and salt and pepper to taste.

3 Preheat the grill.

4 ▼ Spread the vegetables evenly in the frying pan. Pour the egg mixture over them. Cook until the omelette is set at the edge, and the underside is golden, 5–6 minutes.

5 Place the frying pan under the grill, about 3 in (8 cm) from the heat. Grill until the top has set and is lightly browned, 3–4 minutes. Transfer to a warmed platter for serving.

*Sweetcorn Fritters (top), Cheese and Mushroom Open Omelette*

# Baked Cheeses with Red Pepper Sauce

**SERVES 4**

| |
|---|
| 12 oz (350 g) log of goat cheese, cut into 12 equal slices |
| 4 oz (115 g) dry breadcrumbs |
| 1 tbsp chopped fresh parsley |
| 1½ oz (45 g) Parmesan cheese, freshly grated |
| 2 eggs, beaten |
| fresh parsley, for garnishing |
| FOR THE SAUCE |
| 4 tbsp olive oil |
| 4 garlic cloves, chopped |
| 2 red peppers, seeded and chopped |
| 1 tsp fresh thyme leaves |
| 2 tsp tomato purée |
| salt and pepper |

1 Preheat a 450°F/230°C/Gas 8 oven.

2 ▼ For the sauce, heat the olive oil in a saucepan. Add the garlic, red peppers and thyme and cook until the vegetables are soft, about 10 minutes, stirring frequently.

3 Pour the pepper mixture into a food processor or blender and purée. Return the puréed mixture to the saucepan. Stir in the tomato purée and salt and pepper to taste. Set aside.

4 ▲ Place each slice of cheese between two pieces of greaseproof paper. With the flat side of a large knife, flatten the cheese slightly.

5 ▲ In a small bowl, combine the breadcrumbs, parsley and Parmesan cheese. Pour the mixture onto a plate.

6 ▲ Dip the cheese rounds in the beaten egg, then in the breadcrumb mixture, coating well on all sides. Place on an ungreased baking tray.

7 Bake the cheese until golden, about 5 minutes. Meanwhile, gently reheat the sauce.

8 To serve, spoon some sauce on 4 heated plates. Place the baked cheese slices on top and garnish with parsley. Pass the remaining sauce.

# Cheese and Dill Soufflés

**SERVES 6**

| |
|---|
| 2 tbsp grated Parmesan cheese |
| 2 oz (55 g) butter or margarine |
| 1½ oz (45 g) plain flour |
| 10 fl oz (300 ml) milk |
| 4 oz (115 g) mature Cheddar cheese, grated |
| 3 eggs, separated |
| 2 tbsp chopped fresh dill |
| salt and pepper |

**1** Preheat a 400°F/200°C/Gas 6 oven. Butter 6 ramekins, and dust with the Parmesan cheese.

**2 ▲** Melt the butter or margarine in a saucepan. Add the flour and cook 2 minutes, stirring. Stir in the milk. Bring to a boil, stirring constantly, and simmer until thickened, about 5 minutes. Remove from the heat and let cool about 10 minutes.

**3 ▲** Stir the cheese, egg yolks and dill into the sauce. Season with salt and pepper. Transfer to a bowl.

**4** In a clean mixing bowl, beat the egg whites with ⅛ teaspoon salt until stiff peaks form.

**5 ▲** Stir one-quarter of the egg whites into the cheese sauce mixture to lighten it. Fold in the remaining egg whites.

**6 ▲** Divide the mixture evenly between the prepared dishes. Bake until the soufflés are puffed and golden, 15–20 minutes. Serve immediately.

# Asparagus, Sweetcorn and Red Pepper Quiche

**Serves 6**

8 oz (225 g) fresh asparagus, woody stalks removed

1 oz (30 g) butter or margarine

1 small onion, finely chopped

1 red pepper, seeded and finely chopped

4 oz (115 g) drained canned sweetcorn, or frozen sweetcorn, thawed

2 eggs

8 fl oz (250 ml) single cream

2 oz (55 g) Cheddar cheese, grated

salt and pepper

For the pastry

6½ oz (190 g) plain flour

½ tsp salt

4 oz (115 g) lard or vegetable fat

2–3 tbsp iced water

1　Preheat a 400°F/200°C/Gas 6 oven.

2　For the pastry, sift the flour and salt into a mixing bowl. Using a pastry blender or 2 knives, cut in the fat until the mixture resembles coarse breadcrumbs. Sprinkle in the water, 1 tablespoon at a time, tossing lightly with your fingertips or a fork until the dough forms a ball.

3　▲　On a lightly floured surface, roll out the dough. Use it to line a 10 in (25 cm) quiche dish or loose-bottomed tart tin, easing the pastry in and being careful not to stretch it. Trim off excess pastry.

4　▲　Line the pastry case with greaseproof paper and weigh it down with pastry weights or dried beans. Bake 10 minutes. Remove the paper and weights or beans and bake until the pastry is set and beige in colour, about 5 minutes longer. Let cool.

5　Trim the stem ends of 8 of the asparagus spears to make them 4 in (10 cm) in length. Set aside.

6　▲　Finely chop the asparagus trimmings and any remaining spears. Place in the bottom of the case.

7　▲　Melt the butter or margarine in a frying pan. Add the onion and red pepper and cook until softened, about 5 minutes. Stir in the sweetcorn and cook 2 minutes longer.

8　Spoon the sweetcorn mixture over the chopped asparagus.

9　▲　In a small bowl, beat the eggs with the cream. Stir in the cheese and salt and pepper to taste. Pour into the pastry case.

10　▲　Arrange the reserved asparagus spears like the spokes of a wheel on top of the filling.

11　Bake until the filling is set, 25–30 minutes.

~ **VARIATION** ~

To make individual tarts, roll out the pastry and use to line a 12-cup bun tray. For the filling, cut off and reserve the asparagus tips and chop the tender part of the stalks. Mix the asparagus and the cooked vegetables into the egg mixture with the cheese. Spoon the filling into the pastry cases and bake as directed, decreasing baking time by about 8–10 minutes.

# Bread and Cheese Bake

**SERVES 4**

| |
|---|
| 3 tbsp butter or margarine |
| 1 pt (625 ml) milk |
| 3 eggs, beaten |
| 1½ oz (45 g) Parmesan cheese, freshly grated |
| ⅛ tsp cayenne pepper |
| salt and pepper |
| 5 large, thick slices of crusty white bread |
| 8 oz (225 g) Cheddar cheese, grated |

1  Grease an oval baking dish with the butter or margarine.

2 ▼  In a bowl combine the milk, eggs, 3 tablespoons of the Parmesan cheese, the cayenne and salt and pepper to taste.

3 ▲  Cut the bread slices in half. Arrange 5 of them in the bottom of the prepared dish, overlapping the slices if necessary.

4 ▲  Sprinkle the bread with two-thirds of the Cheddar cheese. Top with the remaining bread.

5  Pour the egg mixture evenly over the bread. Press the bread down gently so that it will absorb the egg mixture. Sprinkle the top evenly with the remaining Parmesan and Cheddar cheeses. Let stand until the bread has absorbed most of the egg mixture, at least 30 minutes.

6  Preheat a 425°F/220°C/Gas 7 oven.

7  Set the baking dish in a roasting tin. Add enough boiling water to the tin to come halfway up the sides of the baking dish.

8  Place in the oven and bake 30 minutes, or until the pudding is lightly set and browned. If the pudding browns too quickly before setting, cover loosely with foil. Serve hot.

# Italian Savoury Tarts

**MAKES 12–18**

2 eggs

3 tbsp whipping cream

3 tbsp crumbled feta cheese

salt and pepper

8 oz (225 g) tomatoes, peeled, seeded and chopped

12 fresh basil leaves, cut in thin ribbons

FOR THE PASTRY

6½ oz (190 g) plain flour

½ tsp salt

4 oz (115 g) lard or vegetable fat

2–3 tbsp iced water

**1** Preheat a 400°F/200°C/Gas 6 oven.

**2** For the pastry, sift the flour and salt into a mixing bowl. Using a pastry blender or 2 knives, cut in the fat until the mixture resembles coarse breadcrumbs. Sprinkle in the water, 1 tablespoon at a time, tossing lightly with your fingertips or a fork until the pastry forms a ball.

**3** ▲ On a lightly floured surface, roll out the pastry thinly. With a fluted 2½ in (6 cm) pastry cutter, cut out 18 rounds. Use the rounds to line 18 cups in a small bun tray. Cut out larger rounds, if necessary, and make fewer tarts.

**4** In a bowl, combine the eggs and cream and beat together. Stir in the cheese and salt and pepper to taste.

**5** ▼ In a small saucepan, warm the tomatoes with the basil. Drain the tomatoes, then stir them into the egg mixture.

**6** ▲ Divide the tomato mixture evenly between the pastry cases. Bake 10 minutes. Reduce the heat to 350°F/180°C/Gas 4 and bake until the filling has set and the pastry is golden brown, about 10 minutes longer. Let cool on a wire rack before serving.

# BREADS, CAKES, PIES & BISCUITS

~

*Both old favourites and lots of new ideas are here, for quick
breads and buns, simple cakes and gateaux, fruit pies,
nut pies, biscuits and delicious teatime treats.*

# Savoury Sweetcorn Bread

**MAKES 9**

2 eggs, lightly beaten

8 fl oz (250 ml) buttermilk

4 oz (115 g) plain flour

4 oz (115 g) cornmeal, or polenta

2 tsp baking powder

½ tsp salt

1 tbsp caster sugar

4 oz (115 g) Cheddar cheese, grated

8 oz (225 g) sweetcorn, fresh or frozen and thawed

1 Preheat a 400°F/200°C/Gas 6 oven. Grease a 9 in (23 cm) square baking tin.

2 Combine the eggs and buttermilk in a small bowl and whisk until well mixed. Set aside.

3 ▼ In another bowl, stir together the flour, cornmeal, baking powder, salt and sugar. Add the egg mixture and stir with a wooden spoon to combine. Stir in the cheese and sweetcorn.

4 ▲ Pour the mixture into the prepared tin. Bake until a skewer inserted in the centre comes out clean, about 25 minutes.

5 Unmould the bread onto a wire rack and let cool. Cut into 3 in (8 cm) squares for serving.

~ VARIATION ~

For a spicy bread, stir 2 tablespoons chopped fresh chilli peppers into the mixture with the cheese and sweetcorn.

---

# American-Style Corn Sticks

**MAKES 6**

1 egg

4 fl oz (125 ml) milk

1 tbsp vegetable oil

4 oz (115 g) cornmeal, or polenta

2 oz (55 g) plain flour

2 tsp baking powder

3 tbsp caster sugar

1 Preheat a 375°F/190°C/Gas 5 oven. Grease a cast iron corn-stick mould.

2 Beat the egg in a small bowl. Stir in the milk and oil. Set aside.

3 ▼ In a mixing bowl, stir together the cornmeal or polenta, flour, baking powder and sugar. Pour in the egg mixture and stir with a wooden spoon to combine.

4 ▲ Spoon the mixture into the prepared mould. Bake until a skewer inserted in the centre of a corn stick comes out clean, about 25 minutes. Let cool in the mould on a wire rack for 10 minutes before unmoulding.

~ COOK'S TIP ~

You can also cook the corn sticks in éclair tins or an ordinary bun tray, reducing the cooking time by about 10 minutes.

*Savoury Sweetcorn Bread (top), American-Style Corn Sticks*

# Courgette Loaf

**MAKES 2 LOAVES**

8 oz (225 g) flour

2 tsp bicarbonate of soda

1 tsp baking powder

1 tsp salt

1 tsp ground cinnamon

1 tsp grated nutmeg

3 eggs

10 oz (300 g) sugar

12 fl oz (315 ml) corn oil

1 tsp vanilla essence

about 8 oz (225 g) courgettes, grated

**1** Preheat a 350°F/180°C/gas 4 oven. Grease 2 5½ × 4½ in (13 × 11 cm) tins or 1 9 × 5 in (23 × 13 cm) tin.

**2** ▼ Sift the flour, bicarbonate of soda, baking powder and salt in a mixing bowl. Add the cinnamon and nutmeg, and stir to blend.

**3** ▲ With an electric mixer, beat the eggs and sugar together until thick and pale. With a wooden spoon, stir in the oil, vanilla and courgettes.

**4** ▲ Add the flour mixture and stir until just combined. Do not overmix the batter.

**5** ▲ Pour the batter into the prepared tin. Bake in the middle of the oven until a skewer inserted in the centre comes out clean, about 1 hour for 2 smaller tins or 1¼ hours for a larger tin.

**6** Let cool in the tins on a wire rack for 15 minutes, then unmould onto the wire rack to cool completely.

# Sweet Potato and Raisin Bread

**MAKES 1**

| |
|---|
| 10 oz (300 g) plain flour |
| 2 tsp baking powder |
| ½ tsp salt |
| 1 tsp ground cinnamon |
| ½ tsp grated nutmeg |
| 1 lb (450 g) mashed cooked sweet potatoes |
| 3½ oz (100 g) light brown sugar |
| 4 oz (115 g) butter or margarine, melted and cooled |
| 3 eggs, beaten |
| 3 oz (85 g) raisins |

**1 ▼** Preheat a 350°F/180°C/Gas 4 oven. Grease a 9 × 5 in (23 × 13 cm) loaf tin.

**2** Sift the flour, baking powder, salt, cinnamon and nutmeg into a small bowl. Set aside.

**3 ▼** With an electric mixer, beat the mashed sweet potatoes with the brown sugar, butter or margarine and eggs until well mixed.

**4 ▼** Add the flour mixture and the raisins. Stir with a wooden spoon until the flour is just mixed in.

**5 ▲** Transfer the batter to the prepared tin. Bake until a skewer inserted in the centre comes out clean, 1–1¼ hours.

**6** Let cool in the tin on a wire rack for 15 minutes, then unmould the bread from the tin onto the wire rack and let cool completely.

# Banana and Nut Buns

**Makes 8**

5 oz (140 g) plain flour

1½ tsp baking powder

2 oz (55 g) butter or margarine, at room temperature

6 oz (170 g) caster sugar

1 egg

1 tsp vanilla essence

about 3 medium bananas, mashed

2 oz (55 g) chopped pecans

3 fl oz (85 ml) milk

~ **VARIATION** ~

Use an equal quantity of walnuts instead of the pecans.

1 Preheat a 375°F/190°C/Gas 5 oven. Grease a bun tray.

2 Sift the flour and baking powder into a small bowl. Set aside.

3 ▲ With an electric mixer, cream the butter or margarine and sugar together. Add the egg and vanilla and beat until fluffy. Mix in the banana.

4 ▼ Add the pecans. With the mixer on low speed, beat in the flour mixture alternately with the milk.

5 Spoon the mixture into the prepared bun cups, filling them two-thirds full. Bake until golden brown and a skewer inserted into the centre of a bun comes out clean, 20–25 minutes.

6 Let cool in the tray on a wire rack for 10 minutes. To loosen, run a knife gently around each bun and unmould onto the wire rack. Let cool 10 minutes longer before serving.

# Fruit and Cinnamon Buns

**Makes 8**

4 oz (115 g) plain flour

1 tbsp baking powder

⅛ tsp salt

2½ oz (65 g) light brown sugar

1 egg

6 fl oz (175 ml) milk

3 tbsp vegetable oil

2 tsp ground cinnamon

5 oz (140 g) fresh or thawed frozen blueberries, or blackcurrants

1 Preheat a 375°F/190°C/Gas 5 oven. Grease a bun tray.

2 With an electric mixer, beat the first 8 ingredients together until smooth.

3 ▲ Fold in the blueberries or blackcurrants.

4 ▲ Spoon the mixture into the bun cups, filling them two-thirds full. Bake until a skewer inserted in the centre of a bun comes out clean, about 25 minutes.

5 Let cool in the bun tray on a wire rack for 10 minutes, then unmould the buns onto the wire rack and allow to cool completely.

*Banana and Nut Buns (top), Fruit and Cinnamon Buns*

# Buttermilk Scones

**MAKES 10**

8 oz (225 g) plain flour

1 tsp baking powder

½ tsp bicarbonate of soda

1 tsp salt

2 oz (55 g) butter or margarine, chilled

6 fl oz (175 ml) buttermilk

1  Preheat a 425°F/220°C/Gas 7 oven.

2 ▼  Sift the flour, baking powder, bicarbonate of soda and salt into a mixing bowl. Cut in the butter or margarine with a fork until the mixture resembles coarse breadcrumbs.

~ COOK'S TIP ~

If time is short, drop heaped tablespoonfuls of the biscuit mixture onto the baking tray without kneading or cutting it out.

3 ▲  Add the buttermilk and mix until well combined to a soft dough.

4 ▲  Turn the dough onto a lightly floured board and knead 30 seconds.

5 ▲  Roll out the dough to ½ in (1 cm) thickness. Use a floured 2½ in (6 cm) pastry cutter to cut out rounds.

6  Transfer the rounds to a baking tray and bake until golden brown, 10–12 minutes. Serve hot.

# Savoury Parmesan Puddings

**MAKES 6**

| |
|---|
| 8 tbsp freshly grated Parmesan cheese |
| 4 oz (115 g) plain flour |
| ¼ tsp salt |
| 2 eggs |
| 8 fl oz (250 ml) milk |
| 1 tbsp butter or margarine, melted |

**1 ▼** Preheat a 450°F/230°C/Gas 8 oven. Grease 6 individual baking tins. Sprinkle each pan with 1 tablespoon of the grated Parmesan. Alternatively, you can use ramekins, in which case, heat them on a baking tray in the oven, then grease and sprinkle with Parmesan just before filling.

**2** Sift the flour and salt into a small bowl. Set aside.

**3 ▲** In a mixing bowl, beat together the eggs, milk and butter or margarine. Add the flour mixture and stir until smoothly blended.

**4 ▼** Divide the batter evenly among the containers, filling each one about half full. Bake for 15 minutes, then sprinkle the tops of the puddings with the remaining grated Parmesan cheese. Reduce the heat to 350°F/180°C/Gas 4 and continue baking until the puddings are firm and golden brown, 20–25 minutes.

**5 ▲** Remove the puddings from the oven. To unmould, run a thin knife around the inside of each tin to loosen them. Gently ease out, then transfer to a wire rack to cool.

# Traditional Chocolate Cake

**SERVES 10**

4 oz (115 g) plain chocolate

9 fl oz (275 ml) milk

7 oz (200 g) light brown sugar

1 egg yolk

9 oz (260 g) plain flour

1 tsp bicarbonate of soda

½ tsp salt

5 oz (140 g) butter or margarine, at room
    temperature

9 oz (260 g) caster sugar

3 eggs

1 tsp vanilla essence

FOR THE ICING

8 oz (225 g) plain chocolate

¼ tsp salt

6 fl oz (175 ml) soured cream

**1**  Preheat a 350°F/180°C/Gas 4 oven.
Line 2 × 8–9 in (20–23 cm) round
cake tins with greaseproof paper.

**2** ▲  In a heatproof bowl set over a
pan of simmering water, or in a double
boiler, combine the chocolate, one-
third of the milk, the brown sugar and
egg yolk. Cook, stirring, until smooth
and thickened. Let cool.

**3** ▲  Sift the flour, bicarbonate of
soda and salt into a bowl. Set aside.

**4** ▲  With an electric mixer, cream
the butter or margarine with the caster
sugar until light and fluffy. Beat in the
whole eggs, one at a time. Mix in the
vanilla.

**5**  On low speed, beat the flour
mixture into the butter mixture
alternately with the remaining milk,
beginning and ending with flour.

**6** ▲  Pour in the chocolate mixture
and mix until just combined.

**7**  Divide the cake mixture evenly
between the cake tins. Bake until a
skewer inserted in the centre comes
out clean, 35–40 minutes.

**8**  Let·cool in the tins on wire racks
for 10 minutes, then unmould the
cakes from the tins onto the wire racks
and let cool completely.

**9** ▲  For the icing, melt the
chocolate in a heatproof bowl set over
a pan of hot, not boiling, water, or in
the top of a double boiler. Remove the
bowl from the heat and stir in the salt
and soured cream. Let cool slightly.

**10** ▲  Set 1 cake layer on a serving
plate and spread with one-third of the
icing. Place the second cake layer on
top. Spread the remaining icing all
over the top and sides of the cake,
swirling it to make a decorative finish.

# Coconut Cake

**SERVES 10**

| 6 oz (175 g) icing sugar |
| 4 oz (115 g) plain flour |
| 12 fl oz (375 ml) egg whites (about 12) |
| 1½ tsp cream of tartar |
| 8 oz (225 g) caster sugar |
| ¼ tsp salt |
| 2 tsp almond essence |
| 3½ oz (100 g) desiccated coconut |

FOR THE ICING

| 2 egg whites |
| 4 oz (115 g) caster sugar |
| ¼ tsp salt |
| 2 tbsp cold water |
| 2 tsp almond essence |
| 7 oz (200 g) desiccated coconut, toasted |

**1 ▲** Preheat a 350°F/180°C/Gas 4 oven. Sift the icing sugar and flour into a bowl. Set aside.

**2** With an electric mixer, beat the egg whites with the cream of tartar on medium speed until very thick. Turn the mixer to high speed and beat in the caster sugar, 2 tablespoons at a time, reserving 2 tablespoons.

**3 ▲** Continue beating until stiff and glossy. Swiftly beat in the reserved 2 tablespoons of sugar, with the salt and almond essence.

**4 ▲** One heaped teaspoon at a time, sprinkle the flour mixture over the meringue, quickly folding until just combined. Fold in the desiccated coconut in 2 batches.

**5 ▲** Transfer the cake mixture to an ungreased 10 in (25 cm) non-stick tube tin, and cut gently through the mixture with a metal spatula. Bake until the top of the cake springs back when touched lightly, 30–35 minutes.

**6 ▲** As soon as the cake is done, turn the tin upside down and suspend its funnel over the neck of a funnel or bottle. Let cool, about 1 hour.

**7 ▲** For the icing, combine the egg whites, sugar, salt and water in a heatproof bowl. Beat with an electric mixer until blended. Set the bowl over a pan of boiling water and continue beating on medium speed until the icing is stiff, about 3 minutes. Remove the pan from the heat and stir in the almond essence.

**8 ▲** Unmould the cake onto a serving plate. Spread the icing gently over the top and sides of the cake. Sprinkle with the toasted coconut.

# Carrot Cake

**SERVES 10**

| |
|---|
| 1 lb (450 g) caster sugar |
| 8 fl oz (250 ml) vegetable oil |
| 4 eggs |
| about 8 oz (225 g) carrots, finely grated |
| 8 oz (225 g) plain flour |
| 1½ tsp bicarbonate of soda |
| 1½ tsp baking powder |
| 1 tsp ground allspice |
| 1 tsp ground cinnamon |
| FOR THE ICING |
| 8 oz (225 g) icing sugar |
| 8 oz (225 g) cream cheese, at room temperature |
| 2 oz (55 g) butter or margarine, at room temperature |
| 2 tsp vanilla essence |
| 6 oz (175 g) chopped walnuts or pecans |

**1** Preheat a 375°F/190°C/Gas 5 oven.

**2** Butter and flour 2 × 9 in (23 cm) round cake tins.

**3** ▲ In a mixing bowl, combine the caster sugar, vegetable oil, eggs, and carrots. Beat for 2 minutes.

**4** Sift the dry ingredients into another bowl. Add in 4 equal batches to the carrot mixture, mixing well after each addition.

**5** ▲ Divide the cake mixture evenly between the prepared cake tins. Bake until a skewer inserted in the centre of the cake comes out clean, 35–45 minutes.

**6** Let cool in the tins on wire racks for 10 minutes, then unmould the cakes from the tins onto the wire racks and let cool completely.

**7** For the icing, combine everything but the nuts in a bowl and beat until smooth.

**8** ▲ To assemble, set 1 cake layer on a serving plate and spread with one-third of the icing. Place the second cake layer on top. Spread the remaining icing all over the top and sides of the cake, swirling it to make a decorative finish. Sprinkle the nuts around the top edge.

# Apple and Pear Frying-Pan Cake

**SERVES 6**

1 apple, peeled, cored and thinly sliced

1 pear, peeled, cored and thinly sliced

2 oz (55 g) chopped walnuts

1 tsp ground cinnamon

1 tsp grated nutmeg

3 eggs

3 oz (85 g) plain flour

1 oz (30 g) light brown sugar

6 fl oz (175 ml) milk

1 tsp vanilla essence

2 oz (55 g) butter or margarine

icing sugar, for sprinkling

**1 ▲** Preheat a 375°F/190°C/Gas 5 oven. In a mixing bowl, toss together the apple and pear slices, walnuts, cinnamon and nutmeg. Set aside.

**2 ▲** With an electric mixer, beat together the eggs, flour, brown sugar, milk and vanilla.

**3 ▼** Melt the butter or margarine in a 9–10 in (23–25 cm) ovenproof frying pan (preferably cast iron) over medium heat. Add the apple mixture. Cook until lightly caramelized, about 5 minutes, stirring occasionally.

**4 ▲** Pour the mixture over the fruit and nuts. Transfer the frying pan to the oven and bake until the cake is puffy and pulling away from the sides of the pan, about 30 minutes.

**5** Sprinkle the cake lightly with icing sugar and serve hot.

# Ginger Cake with Spiced Whipped Cream

**SERVES 9**

6 oz (170 g) plain flour

2 tsp baking powder

½ tsp salt

2 tsp ground ginger

2 tsp ground cinnamon

1 tsp ground cloves

¼ tsp grated nutmeg

2 eggs

8 oz (225 g) caster sugar

8 fl oz (250 ml) whipping cream

1 tsp vanilla essence

icing sugar, for sprinkling

FOR THE SPICED WHIPPED CREAM

6 fl oz (175 ml) whipping cream

1 tsp icing sugar

¼ tsp ground cinnamon

¼ tsp ground ginger

⅛ tsp grated nutmeg

1  Preheat a 350°F/180°C/Gas 4 oven. Grease a 9 in (23 cm) square baking tin.

2  Sift the flour, baking powder, salt and spices into a bowl. Set aside.

3 ▲ With an electric mixer, beat the eggs on high speed until very thick, about 5 minutes. Gradually beat in the caster sugar.

4 ▲ With the mixer on low speed, beat in the flour mixture alternately with the cream, beginning and ending with the flour. Stir in the vanilla.

5 ▲ Pour the cake mixture into the tin and bake until the top springs back when touched lightly, 35–40 minutes. Let cool in the tin on a wire rack for 10 minutes.

6 ▲ Meanwhile, to make the spiced whipped cream, combine the ingredients in a bowl and whip until the cream will hold soft peaks.

7  Sprinkle icing sugar over the hot cake, cut in 9 squares, and serve with spiced whipped cream.

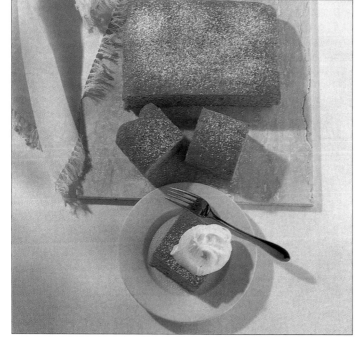

# Madeira Cake

**SERVES 12**

8 oz (225 g) plain flour

1 tsp baking powder

8 oz (225 g) butter or margarine, at room temperature

8 oz (225 g) caster sugar

grated rind of 1 lemon

1 tsp vanilla essence

4 eggs

**1** Preheat a 325°F/170°C/Gas 3 oven. Grease a 9 × 5 in (23 × 13 cm) loaf tin.

**2** Sift the flour and baking powder into a small bowl. Set aside.

**3** ▲ With an electric mixer, cream the butter or margarine, adding the sugar 2 tablespoons at a time, until light and fluffy. Stir in the lemon rind and vanilla.

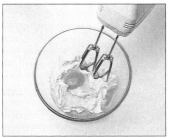

**4** ▲ Add the eggs one at a time, beating for 1 minute after each addition.

**5** ▼ Add the flour mixture and stir until just combined.

**6** ▲ Pour the cake mixture into the tin and tap lightly. Bake until a metal skewer inserted in the centre comes out clean, about 1¼ hours.

**7** Let cool in the tin on a wire rack for 10 minutes, then unmould the cake from the tin onto the wire rack and let cool completely.

# Apple Cake

**SERVES 10**

1½ lb (700 g) apples, peeled, cored and quartered

1 lb 2 oz (500 g) caster sugar

1 tbsp water

12 oz (350 g) plain flour

1¾ tsp bicarbonate of soda

1 tsp ground cinnamon

1 tsp ground cloves

6 oz (170 g) raisins

5 oz (140 g) chopped walnuts

8 oz (225 g) butter or margarine, at room temperature

1 tsp vanilla essence

FOR THE ICING

4 oz (115 g) icing sugar

¼ tsp vanilla essence

2–3 tbsp milk

**1 ▲** Combine the apples, 2 oz (55 g) of the sugar and the water in a medium saucepan and bring to a boil. Simmer 25 minutes, stirring occasionally with a wooden spoon to break up any lumps. Let cool.

~ **COOK'S TIP** ~

Be sure to grease the cake tin generously and allow this cake to become completely cold before unmoulding it.

**2 ▲** Preheat a 325°F/170°C/Gas 3 oven. Butter and flour a 3–3½ pt (1.75–2 litre) tube tin.

**3** Sift the flour, bicarbonate of soda and spices into a mixing bowl. Remove 2 tablespoons of the mixture to a bowl and toss with the raisins and all but 1 oz (30 g) of the walnuts.

**4 ▲** With an electric mixer, cream the butter or margarine and remaining sugar together until light and fluffy. Fold in the apple mixture gently with a wooden spoon.

**5 ▲** Fold the flour mixture into the apple mixture. Stir in the vanilla and the raisin and walnut mixture.

**6** Pour the cake mixture into the prepared tin. Bake until a skewer inserted in the centre comes out clean, about 1½ hours.

**7** Let cool in the tin on a wire rack for 20 minutes, then unmould the cake from the tin onto the wire rack and let cool completely.

**8 ▲** For the icing, put the sugar in a bowl and stir in the vanilla and 1 tablespoon of the milk. Add the remaining milk, teaspoon by teaspoon, until the icing is smooth and has a thick pouring consistency.

**9 ▲** Transfer the cooled cake to a serving plate and drizzle the icing on top. Sprinkle with the remaining nuts. Let the cake stand for 2 hours before slicing, so the icing can set.

# Pumpkin Pie

**SERVES 8**

| |
|---|
| about 9 oz (250 g) puréed pumpkin |
| 16 fl oz (450 ml) single cream |
| 4½ oz (135 g) light brown sugar |
| ¼ tsp salt |
| 1 tsp ground cinnamon |
| ½ tsp ground ginger |
| ¼ tsp ground cloves |
| ⅛ tsp grated nutmeg |
| 2 eggs |
| FOR THE PASTRY |
| 5½ oz (165 g) plain flour |
| ½ tsp salt |
| 4 oz (115 g) lard or vegetable fat |
| 2–3 tbsp iced water |
| 1½ oz (45 g) pecans, chopped |

1  Preheat a 425°F/220°C/Gas 7 oven.

2 ▲  For the pastry, sift the flour and salt into a mixing bowl. Using a pastry blender, cut in the fat until the mixture resembles coarse breadcrumbs. Sprinkle in the water, 1 tablespoon at a time, tossing lightly with a fork until the mixture forms a ball.

3 ▲  On a lightly floured surface, roll out the pastry to ¼ in (5 mm) thickness. Use it to line a 9 in (23 cm) pie tin. Ease the pastry in without stretching it. Trim off the excess.

4 ▲  If you like, use the pastry trimmings to make a decorative rope edge. Cut in strips and twist together in pairs. Dampen the rim of the pastry case and press on the rope edge. Or, with your thumbs, make a fluted edge. Sprinkle the chopped pecans over the bottom of the case.

5  With a whisk or an electric mixer on medium speed, beat together the puréed pumpkin, cream, brown sugar, salt, spices and eggs.

6  Pour the pumpkin mixture into the pastry case. Bake 10 minutes, then reduce the heat to 350°F/180°C/Gas 4 and continue baking until the filling is set, about 45 minutes. Let the pie cool in the tin, set on a wire rack.

# Maple Syrup and Pecan Pie

**SERVES 8**

| |
|---|
| 3 eggs, beaten |
| 3½ oz (100 g) dark brown sugar |
| 5 fl oz (150 ml) golden syrup |
| 3 fl oz (85 ml) maple syrup |
| ½ tsp vanilla essence |
| ⅛ tsp salt |
| 4 oz (115 g) pecan halves |
| FOR THE PASTRY |
| 5½ oz (165 g) plain flour |
| ½ tsp salt |
| 1 tsp ground cinnamon |
| 4 oz (115 g) lard or vegetable fat |
| 2–3 tbsp iced water |

**1** Preheat a 425°F/220°C/Gas 7 oven.

**2** For the pastry, sift the flour, salt and cinnamon into a mixing bowl. Using a pastry blender, cut in the fat until the mixture resembles coarse breadcrumbs. Sprinkle in the water, 1 tablespoon at a time, tossing lightly with your fingertips or a fork until the mixture forms a ball.

**3** On a lightly floured surface, roll out the pastry to a circle 15 in (38 cm) in diameter. Use it to line a 9 in (23 cm) pie tin, easing in the pastry and being careful not to stretch it.

**4 ▲** With your thumbs, make a fluted edge. Using a fork, prick the bottom and sides of the pastry case all over. Bake until lightly browned, 10–15 minutes. Let cool in the tin.

**5 ▼** Reduce the oven temperature to 350°F/180°C/Gas 4. In a bowl, stir together the eggs, sugar, syrups, vanilla and salt until well mixed.

**6 ▲** Sprinkle the pecans evenly over the bottom of the baked pastry case. Pour in the egg mixture. Bake until the filling is set and the pastry is golden brown, about 40 minutes. Let cool in the tin, set on a wire rack.

# Traditional Apple Pie

**SERVES 8**

about 2 lb (900 g) tart eating apples,
  such as Granny Smith, peeled, cored
  and sliced

1 tbsp fresh lemon juice

1 tsp vanilla essence

4 oz (115 g) caster sugar

½ tsp ground cinnamon

1½ oz (45 g) butter or margarine

1 egg yolk

2 tsp whipping cream

FOR THE PASTRY

8 oz (225 g) plain flour

1 tsp salt

6 oz (170 g) lard or vegetable fat

4–5 tbsp iced water

1 tbsp quick-cooking tapioca

**1**  Preheat a 450°F/230°C/Gas 8 oven.

**2**  For the pastry, sift the flour and salt into a bowl. Using a pastry blender, cut in the fat until the mixture resembles coarse breadcrumbs.

**3 ▲**  Sprinkle in the water, 1 tablespoon at a time, tossing lightly with your fingertips or with a fork until the pastry forms a ball.

**4 ▲**  Divide the pastry in half and shape each half into a ball. On a lightly floured surface, roll out one of the balls to a circle about 12 in (30 cm) in diameter.

**5 ▲**  Use it to line a 9 in (23 cm) pie tin, easing the dough in and being careful not to stretch it. Trim off the excess pastry and use the trimmings for decorating. Sprinkle the tapioca over the bottom of the pie shell.

**6 ▲**  Roll out the remaining pastry to ⅛ in (3 mm) thickness. With a sharp knife, cut out 8 large leaf-shapes. Cut the trimmings into small leaf shapes. Score the leaves with the back of the knife to mark veins.

**7 ▲**  In a bowl, toss the apples with the lemon juice, vanilla, sugar and cinnamon. Fill the pastry case with the apple mixture and dot with the butter or margarine.

**8 ▲**  Arrange the large pastry leaves in a decorative pattern on top. Decorate the edge with small leaves.

**9 ▲**  Mix together the egg yolk and cream and brush over the leaves to glaze them.

**10**  Bake 10 minutes, then reduce the heat to 350°F/180°C/Gas 4 and continue baking until the pastry is golden brown, 35–45 minutes. Let the pie cool in the tin, set on a wire rack.

# Rich Chocolate Pie

**SERVES 8**

| |
|---|
| 3 oz (85 g) plain chocolate |
| 2 oz (55 g) butter or margarine |
| 3 tbsp golden syrup |
| 3 eggs, beaten |
| 5 oz (140 g) caster sugar |
| 1 tsp vanilla essence |
| 4 oz (115 g) milk chocolate |
| 16 fl oz (500 ml) whipping cream |
| FOR THE PASTRY |
| 5½ oz (165 g) plain flour |
| ½ tsp salt |
| 4 oz (115 g) lard or vegetable fat |
| 2–3 tbsp iced water |

**1** Preheat a 425°F/220°C/Gas 7 oven.

**2** For the pastry, sift the flour and salt into a mixing bowl. Using a pastry blender, cut in the fat until the mixture resembles coarse breadcrumbs. Sprinkle in the water, 1 tablespoon at a time. Toss lightly with a fork until the pastry forms a ball.

**3** On a lightly floured surface, roll out the pastry. Use to line an 8 or 9 in (20 or 23 cm) pie tin, easing in the pastry and being careful not to stretch it. Make a fluted edge.

**4** Using a fork, prick the bottom and sides of the pastry case all over. Bake until lightly browned, 10–15 minutes. Let cool, in the tin, on a wire rack.

**5** ▲ In a heatproof bowl set over a pan of simmering water, or in a double boiler, melt the plain chocolate, the butter or margarine and golden syrup. Remove the bowl from the heat and stir in the eggs, sugar and vanilla.

**6** Reduce the oven temperature to 350°F/180°C/Gas 4. Pour the chocolate mixture into the case. Bake until the filling is set, 35–40 minutes. Let cool in the tin, set on a rack.

**7** ▲ For the decoration, use the heat of your hands to soften the chocolate bar slightly. Draw the blade of a swivel-headed vegetable peeler along the side of the chocolate bar to shave off short, wide curls. Chill the chocolate curls until needed.

**8** Before serving, lightly whip the cream until soft peaks form. Using a rubber spatula, spread the cream over the surface of the chocolate filling. Decorate with the chocolate curls.

# Creamy Banana Pie

**Serves 6**

7 oz (200 g) ginger biscuits, finely
crushed

2½ oz (70 g) butter or margarine, melted

½ tsp grated nutmeg or ground
cinnamon

6 oz (175 g) ripe bananas, mashed

12 oz (350 g) cream cheese, at room
temperature

2 fl oz (65 ml) thick plain yogurt or
soured cream

3 tbsp dark rum or 1 tsp vanilla essence

**For the topping**

8 fl oz (250 ml) whipping cream

3–4 bananas

**1** Preheat a 375°F/190°C/Gas 5 oven.

**2 ▲** In a mixing bowl, combine the
crushed biscuits, butter or margarine
and spice. Mix thoroughly with a
wooden spoon.

**3 ▲** Press the biscuit mixture into a
9 in (23 cm) pie dish, building up
thick sides with a neat edge. Bake 5
minutes. Let cool, in the dish.

**4 ▼** With an electric mixer, beat the
mashed bananas with the cream
cheese. Fold in the yogurt or soured
cream and rum or vanilla. Spread the
filling in the biscuit base. Refrigerate
at least 4 hours or overnight.

**5 ▲** For the topping, whip the cream
until soft peaks form. Spread on the
pie filling. Slice the bananas and
arrange on top in a decorative pattern.

# Lime Meringue Pie

**SERVES 8**

| |
|---|
| 3 egg yolks |
| 12 fl oz (350 ml) sweetened condensed milk |
| finely grated rind and juice of 4 limes |
| 7 egg whites |
| ⅛ tsp salt |
| squeeze of fresh lemon juice |
| 4 oz (115 g) sugar |
| ½ tsp vanilla essence |
| FOR THE PASTRY |
| 5½ oz (165 g) plain flour |
| ½ tsp salt |
| 4 oz (115 g) lard or vegetable fat |
| 2–3 tbsp iced water |

**1** Preheat a 425°F/220°C/Gas 7 oven.

**2** ▲ For the pastry, sift the flour and salt into a mixing bowl. Using a pastry blender or 2 knives, cut in the fat until the mixture resembles coarse breadcrumbs. Sprinkle in the water, 1 tablespoon at a time, tossing lightly with a fork until the mixture forms a ball.

> ## ~ COOK'S TIP ~
>
> When beating egg whites with an electric mixer, start slowly, and increase speed after they become frothy. Turn the bowl constantly.

**3** ▲ On a lightly floured surface, roll out the pastry. Use it to line a 9 in (23 cm) pie tin, easing in the pastry. Make a fluted edge.

**4** Using a fork, prick the bottom and sides of the pastry case all over. Bake until lightly browned, 10–15 minutes. Let cool, in the tin, on a wire rack. Reduce oven temperature to 350°F/ 180°C/Gas 4.

**5** ▲ With an electric mixer on high speed, beat the yolks and condensed milk. Stir in the lime rind and juice.

**6** ▲ In another clean bowl, beat 3 of the egg whites until stiff. Fold into the lime mixture.

**7** ▲ Spread the lime filling in the pastry case. Bake 10 minutes.

**8** ▲ Meanwhile, beat the remaining egg whites with the salt and lemon juice until soft peaks form. Beat in the sugar, 1 tablespoon at a time, until stiff peaks form. Add the vanilla.

**9** ▲ Remove the pie from the oven. Using a metal spatula, spread the meringue over the lime filling, making a swirled design and covering the surface completely.

**10** Bake until the meringue is lightly browned and the pastry is golden brown, about 12 minutes longer. Let cool, in the tin, on a wire rack.

# Cherry Pie

### SERVES 8

| |
|---|
| 2 lb (900 g) fresh Morello cherries, stoned, or 2 × 1 lb (450 g) cans or jars, drained and stoned |
| 2½ oz (70 g) caster sugar |
| 1 oz (30 g) plain flour |
| 1½ tbsp fresh lemon juice |
| ¼ tsp almond essence |
| 1 oz (30 g) butter or margarine |
| FOR THE PASTRY |
| 8 oz (225 g) plain flour |
| 1 tsp salt |
| 6 oz (175 g) lard or vegetable fat |
| 4–5 tbsp iced water |

**1** For the pastry, sift the flour and salt into a mixing bowl. Using a pastry blender, cut in the fat until the mixture resembles coarse breadcrumbs.

**2** ▲ Sprinkle in the water, 1 tablespoon at a time, tossing lightly with your fingertips or a fork until the pastry forms a ball.

**3** Divide the pastry in half and shape each half into a ball. On a lightly floured surface, roll out one of the balls to a circle about 12 in (30 cm) in diameter.

**4** ▲ Use it to line a 9 in (23 cm) pie tin, easing the pastry in and being careful not to stretch it. With scissors, trim off excess pastry, leaving a ½ in (1 cm) overhang around the pie rim.

**5** ▲ Roll out the remaining pastry to ⅛ in (3 mm) thickness. Cut out 11 strips ½ in (1 cm) wide.

**6** ▲ In a mixing bowl, combine the cherries, sugar, flour, lemon juice and almond essence. Spoon the mixture into the pastry case and dot with the butter or margarine.

**7** ▲ To make the lattice, place 5 of the pastry strips evenly across the filling. Fold every other strip back. Lay the first strip across in the opposite direction. Continue in this pattern, folding back every other strip each time you add a cross strip.

**8** ▲ Trim the ends of the lattice strips even with the case overhang. Press together so that the edge rests on the pie-tin rim. With your thumbs, flute the edge. Refrigerate 15 minutes.

**9** Preheat a 425°F/220°C/Gas 7 oven.

**10** Bake the pie 30 minutes, covering the edge of the pastry case with foil, if necessary, to prevent over-browning. Let cool, in the tin, on a wire rack.

# Ginger Biscuits

**MAKES 60**

| |
|---|
| 10 oz (300 g) plain flour |
| 1 tsp bicarbonate of soda |
| 1½ tsp ground ginger |
| ¼ tsp ground cinnamon |
| ¼ tsp ground cloves |
| 4 oz (115 g) butter or margarine, at room temperature |
| 12 oz (350 g) caster sugar |
| 1 egg, beaten |
| 4 tbsp treacle |
| 1 tsp fresh lemon juice |

**1** Preheat a 325°F/170°C/Gas 3 oven. Grease 3–4 baking trays.

**2** Sift the flour, bicarbonate of soda and spices into a small bowl. Set aside.

**3** With an electric mixer, cream the butter or margarine and two-thirds of the sugar together.

**4** ▲ Stir in the egg, treacle and lemon juice. Add the flour mixture and mix in thoroughly with a wooden spoon to make a soft dough.

**5** ▲ Shape the dough into ¾ in (2 cm) balls. Roll the balls in the remaining sugar and place about 2 in (5 cm) apart on the baking trays.

**6** Bake until the biscuits are just firm to the touch, about 12 minutes. With a slotted spatula, transfer the biscuits to a wire rack and let cool.

# Chocolate-Chip Oat Biscuits

**MAKES 60**

| |
|---|
| 4 oz (115 g) plain flour |
| ½ tsp bicarbonate of soda |
| ¼ tsp baking powder |
| ¼ tsp salt |
| 4 oz (115 g) butter or margarine, at room temperature |
| 4 oz (115 g) caster sugar |
| 3½ oz (100 g) light brown sugar |
| 1 egg |
| ½ tsp vanilla essence |
| 3 oz (85 g) rolled oats |
| 6 oz (170 g) plain chocolate chips |

**1** Preheat a 350°F/180°C/Gas 4 oven. Grease 3–4 baking trays.

**2** Sift the flour, bicarbonate of soda, baking powder and salt into a mixing bowl. Set aside.

**3** With an electric mixer, cream the butter or margarine and sugars together. Add the egg and vanilla and beat until light and fluffy.

**4** ▲ Add the flour mixture and beat on low speed until thoroughly blended. Stir in the rolled oats and chocolate chips, mixing well with a wooden spoon. The dough should be crumbly.

**5** ▲ Drop heaped teaspoonfuls onto the prepared baking trays, spacing the dough about 1 in (2.5 cm) apart. Bake until just firm around the edge but still soft to the touch in the centre, about 15 minutes. With a slotted spatula, transfer the biscuits to a wire rack and let cool.

*Ginger Biscuits (top), Chocolate-Chip Oat Biscuits*

# Traditional Sugar Biscuits

**MAKES 36**

12 oz (350 g) plain flour

1 tsp bicarbonate of soda

2 tsp baking powder

¼ tsp grated nutmeg

4 oz (115 g) butter or margarine, at room temperature

8 oz (225 g) caster sugar

½ tsp vanilla essence

1 egg

4 fl oz (125 ml) milk

coloured or demerara sugar, for sprinkling

**1**  Sift the flour, bicarbonate of soda, baking powder and nutmeg into a small bowl. Set aside.

**2** ▲ With an electric mixer, cream the butter or margarine, caster sugar and vanilla together until the mixture is light and fluffy. Add the egg and beat to mix well.

**3** ▲ Add the flour mixture alternately with the milk, stirring with a wooden spoon to make a soft dough. Wrap the dough in cling film and refrigerate at least 30 minutes, or overnight.

**4** ▲ Preheat a 350°F/180°C/Gas 4 oven. Roll out the dough on a lightly floured surface to ⅛ in (3 mm) thickness. Cut into rounds or other shapes with biscuit cutters.

**5** ▲ Transfer the biscuits to ungreased baking trays. Sprinkle each one with coloured or demerara sugar.

**6**  Bake until golden brown, 10–12 minutes. With a slotted spatula, transfer the biscuits to a wire rack and let cool.

# Chocolate Chip Nut Biscuits

**MAKES 36**

4 oz (115 g) plain flour

1 tsp baking powder

¼ tsp salt

3 oz (85 g) butter or margarine, at room temperature

4 oz (115 g) caster sugar

1¾ oz (50 g) light brown sugar

1 egg

1 tsp vanilla essence

4½ oz (130 g) chocolate chips

2 oz (55 g) hazelnuts, chopped

**1** ▲ Preheat a 350°F/180°C/Gas 4 oven. Grease 2–3 baking trays.

**2** Sift the flour, baking powder and salt into a small bowl. Set aside.

**3** ▲ With an electric mixer, cream the butter or margarine and sugars together. Beat in the egg and vanilla.

**4** Add the flour mixture and beat well with the mixer on low speed.

**5** ▼ Stir in the chocolate chips and half of the hazelnuts using a wooden spoon.

**6** Drop teaspoonfuls of the mixture onto the prepared baking trays, to form ¾ in (2 cm) mounds. Space the biscuits 1–2 in (2–5 cm) apart.

**7** ▲ Flatten each biscuit lightly with a wet fork. Sprinkle the remaining hazelnuts on top of the biscuits and press lightly into the surface.

**8** Bake until golden brown, about 10–12 minutes. With a slotted spatula, transfer the biscuits to a wire rack and let cool.

# Spicy Pepper Biscuits

**MAKES 48**

| |
|---|
| 7 oz (200 g) plain flour |
| 2 oz (55 g) cornflour |
| 2 tsp baking powder |
| ½ tsp ground cardamom |
| ½ tsp ground cinnamon |
| ½ tsp grated nutmeg |
| ½ tsp ground ginger |
| ½ tsp ground allspice |
| ½ tsp salt |
| ½ tsp freshly ground black pepper |
| 8 oz (225 g) butter or margarine, at room temperature |
| 3½ oz (100 g) light brown sugar |
| ½ tsp vanilla essence |
| 1 tsp finely grated lemon rind |
| 2 fl oz (65 ml) whipping cream |
| 3 oz (85 g) finely ground almonds |
| 2 tbsp icing sugar |

1 Preheat a 350°F/180°C/Gas 4 oven.

2 Sift the flour, cornflour, baking powder, spices, salt and pepper into a bowl. Set aside.

3 With an electric mixer, cream the butter or margarine and brown sugar together until light and fluffy. Beat in the vanilla and lemon rind.

4 ▲ With the mixer on low speed, add the flour mixture alternately with the cream, beginning and ending with flour. Stir in the ground almonds.

5 ▲ Shape the dough into ¾ in (2 cm) balls. Place them on ungreased baking trays about 1 in (2.5 cm) apart. Bake until the biscuits are golden brown underneath, 15–20 minutes.

6 Let the biscuits cool on the baking trays about 1 minute before transferring them to a wire rack to cool completely. Before serving, sprinkle them lightly with icing sugar.

---

# Chocolate and Coconut Slices

**MAKES 24**

| |
|---|
| 6 oz (175 g) digestive biscuits, crushed |
| 2 oz (55 g) caster sugar |
| ⅛ tsp salt |
| 4 oz (115 g) butter or margarine, melted |
| 3 oz (85 g) desiccated coconut |
| 9 oz (260 g) plain chocolate chips |
| 8 fl oz (250 ml) sweetened condensed milk |
| 4 oz (115 g) chopped walnuts |

1 Preheat a 350°F/180°C/Gas 4 oven.

2 ▼ In a bowl, combine the crushed biscuits, sugar, salt and butter or margarine. Press the mixture evenly over the bottom of an ungreased 13 × 9 in (33 × 23 cm) baking dish.

3 ▲ Sprinkle the coconut over the biscuit base, then scatter over the chocolate chips. Pour the condensed milk evenly over the chocolate. Sprinkle the walnuts on top.

4 Bake 30 minutes. Unmould onto a wire rack and let cool, preferably overnight. When cooled, cut into slices.

*Spicy Pepper Biscuits (top), Chocolate and Coconut Slices*

# Lemon Squares

**MAKES 12**

8 oz (225 g) plain flour

2 oz (55 g) icing sugar

¼ tsp salt

6 oz (170 g) cold butter or margarine

1 tsp cold water

FOR THE LEMON LAYER

4 eggs

1 lb (450 g) caster sugar

1 oz (30 g) plain flour

½ tsp baking powder

1 tsp grated lemon rind

2 fl oz (65 ml) fresh lemon juice

icing sugar, for sprinkling

1  Preheat a 350°F/180°C/Gas 4 oven.

2 ▼  Sift the flour, icing sugar and salt into a mixing bowl. Using your fingertips or a pastry blender, rub or cut in the butter or margarine until the mixture resembles coarse breadcrumbs. Add the water and toss lightly with a fork until the mixture forms a ball.

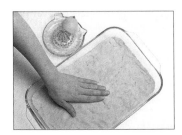

3 ▲  Press the mixture evenly into an ungreased 13 × 9 in (33 × 23 cm) baking dish. Bake until light golden brown, 15–20 minutes. Remove from oven and let cool slightly.

4  Meanwhile, with an electric mixer, beat together the eggs, caster sugar, flour, baking powder and lemon rind and juice.

5 ▲  Pour the lemon mixture over the baked base. Return to the oven and bake 25 minutes. Let cool, in the baking dish, on a wire rack.

6 ▲  Before serving, sprinkle the top with icing sugar. Cut into squares with a sharp knife.

# Hazelnut Squares

MAKES 9

2 oz (55 g) plain chocolate

2½ oz (70 g) butter or margarine

8 oz (225 g) caster sugar

2 oz (55 g) plain flour

½ tsp baking powder

2 eggs, beaten

½ tsp vanilla essence

4 oz (115 g) skinned hazelnuts, roughly
   chopped

1 Preheat a 350°F/180°C/Gas 4 oven.
Grease an 8 in (20 cm) square baking
tin.

2 ▲ In a heatproof bowl set over a
pan of barely simmering water, or in a
double boiler, melt the chocolate and
butter or margarine. Remove the bowl
from the heat.

3 ▲ Add the sugar, flour, baking
powder, eggs, vanilla and half the
hazelnuts to the melted mixture and
stir well with a wooden spoon.

4 ▼ Pour the mixture into the
prepared tin. Bake 10 minutes, then
sprinkle the reserved hazelnuts over
the top. Return to the oven and
continue baking until firm to the
touch, about 25 minutes.

5 ▲ Let cool in the tin, set on a wire
rack, for 10 minutes, then unmould
onto the rack and let cool completely.
Cut into squares for serving.

# HOT & COLD DESSERTS

~

There's always a little space left at the end of a meal for
dessert, particularly if it's rich and creamy, fruity and spiced,
crisp and nutty, icy cold, or, best of all, chocolatey.
You'll find a sweet idea here for every occasion.

# Hot Spiced Bananas

**SERVES 6**

6 ripe bananas

7 oz (200 g) light brown sugar

8 fl oz (250 ml) unsweetened pineapple juice

4 fl oz (125 ml) dark rum

2 cinnamon sticks

12 whole cloves

**1 ▼** Preheat a 350°F/180°C/Gas 4 oven. Grease a 9 in (23 cm) baking dish.

**2 ▲** Peel the bananas and cut them into 1 in (2.5 cm) pieces on the diagonal. Arrange the banana pieces evenly over the bottom of the prepared baking dish.

**3 ▲** In a saucepan, combine the sugar and pineapple juice. Cook over a medium heat until the sugar has dissolved, stirring occasionally.

**4** Add the rum, cinnamon sticks and cloves. Bring to the boil, then remove the pan from the heat.

**5 ▲** Pour the pineapple and spice mixture over the bananas. Bake until the bananas are very tender and hot, 25–30 minutes. Serve hot.

# Apple and Walnut Crisp

**SERVES 6**

| |
|---|
| about 2 lb (900 g) tart eating apples, such as Granny Smith, peeled, cored and sliced |
| grated rind of ½ lemon |
| 1 tbsp fresh lemon juice |
| 3½ oz (100 g) light brown sugar |
| 3 oz (85 g) plain flour |
| ¼ tsp salt |
| ¼ tsp grated nutmeg |
| ½ tsp ground cardamom |
| ½ tsp ground cinnamon |
| 4 oz (115 g) butter or margarine, diced |
| 2 oz (55 g) chopped walnuts |

**1** Preheat a 350°F/180°C/Gas 4 oven. Grease a 9–10 in (23–25 cm) oval gratin dish or shallow baking dish.

**2 ▲** Toss the apples with the lemon rind and juice. Arrange them evenly in the bottom of the prepared dish.

**3** In a mixing bowl, combine the brown sugar, flour, salt, nutmeg, cardamom and cinnamon. With 2 knives, or a pastry blender, cut in the butter or margarine until the mixture resembles coarse breadcrumbs. Mix in the walnuts.

**4 ▼** With a spoon, sprinkle the walnut and spice mixture evenly over the apples. Cover with foil and bake for 30 minutes.

**5 ▲** Remove the foil and continue baking until the apples are tender and the topping is crisp, about 30 minutes longer. Serve warm.

# Baked Apples with Caramel Sauce

**Serves 6**

| |
|---|
| 3 Granny Smith apples, cored but not peeled |
| 3 Red Delicious apples, cored but not peeled |
| 5 oz (140 g) light brown sugar |
| 6 fl oz (175 ml) water |
| ½ tsp grated nutmeg |
| ¼ tsp freshly ground black pepper |
| 1½ oz (45 g) walnut pieces |
| 1½ oz (45 g) sultanas |
| 2 oz (55 g) butter or margarine, diced |
| **For the caramel sauce** |
| ½ oz (15 g) butter or margarine |
| 4 fl oz (125 ml) whipping cream |

**1** Preheat a 375°F/190°C/Gas 5 oven. Grease a baking tin just large enough to hold the apples.

**2** ▲ With a small knife, cut at an angle to enlarge the core opening at the stem-end of each apple to about 1 in (2.5 cm) in diameter. (The opening should resemble a funnel in shape.)

~ **VARIATION** ~

Use a mixture of firm red and gold pears instead of the apples, preparing them the same way. Cook for 10 minutes longer.

**3** ▲ Arrange the apples in the prepared tin, stem-end up.

**4** ▲ In a small saucepan, combine the brown sugar, water, nutmeg and pepper. Bring the mixture to the boil, stirring. Boil for 6 minutes.

**5** ▲ Mix together the walnuts and sultanas. Spoon some of the walnut-sultana mixture into the opening in each apple.

**6** ▲ Top each apple with some of the diced butter or margarine.

**7** ▲ Spoon the brown sugar sauce over and around the apples. Bake, basting occasionally with the sauce, until the apples are just tender, about 50 minutes. Transfer the apples to a serving dish, reserving the brown sugar sauce in the baking tin. Keep the apples warm.

**8** ▲ For the caramel sauce, mix the butter or margarine, cream and reserved brown sugar sauce in a saucepan. Bring to the boil, stirring occasionally, and simmer until thickened, about 2 minutes. Let the sauce cool slightly before serving.

# Upside-Down Pear Pudding

**Serves 8**

2 oz (55 g) plain flour

1 tsp baking powder

¼ tsp salt

7 oz (200 g) plain chocolate

4 oz (115 g) butter or margarine

2 eggs

4 oz (115 g) caster sugar

½ tsp vanilla essence

1 tbsp strong black coffee

1½ oz (45 g) plain chocolate chips

3 oz (85 g) walnuts, chopped

1½ lb (700 g) ripe pears, or 2 × 14 oz
   (400 g) cans pear quarters, drained

**1** Preheat a 375°F/190°C/Gas 5 oven. Grease a 9 in (23 cm) round non-stick baking dish.

**2** Sift the flour, baking powder and salt into a small bowl. Set aside.

**3** In a heatproof bowl set over a pan of simmering water, or in a double boiler, melt the chocolate and butter or margarine. Remove the bowl from the heat and let cool slightly.

**4** ▲ Beat the eggs, sugar, vanilla and coffee into the melted chocolate mixture. Stir in the flour mixture, chocolate chips and walnuts.

**5** ▲ If using fresh pears, peel, quarter and core them. Arrange the pear quarters in the prepared baking dish, with the rounded ends against the side of the dish. Pour the pudding mixture evenly over the pears.

**6** Bake 1 hour, covering with foil after 30 minutes. Let cool 15 minutes, then hold an upturned plate tightly over the top of the baking dish, invert and unmould. Serve hot.

---

# Baked Pears with Ginger

**Serves 6**

6 large firm pears, peeled, cored and
   sliced lengthwise

3 fl oz (85 ml) honey

2 oz (55 g) light brown sugar

1 tbsp finely grated fresh root
   ginger

4 fl oz (125 ml) whipping cream

~ **VARIATION** ~

Substitute firm (even under-ripe) peaches for the pears. To peel, dip the peaches in boiling water for about a minute, then slip off the skins. Cook as for pears.

**1** ▼ Preheat a 400°F/200°C/Gas 6 oven. Butter a 10 in (25 cm) oval gratin dish or shallow baking dish. Fan the pear slices in a spiral design in the bottom of the baking dish.

**2** ▲ In a small bowl, mix together the honey, brown sugar, grated root ginger and cream. Pour this mixture over the pears.

**3** Bake until the pears are tender and the top is lightly golden, about 30 minutes. Serve hot.

*Upside-Down Pear Pudding (top), Baked Pears with Ginger*

# Summer Berry Pudding

**SERVES 8**

8 oz (225 g) plain flour

2 tsp baking powder

½ tsp salt

4 oz (115 g) butter or margarine, at room temperature

5 oz (140 g) caster sugar

1 egg

½ tsp vanilla essence

6 fl oz (175 ml) milk

10 oz (300 g) blueberries, or blackcurrants

whipped cream, for serving

FOR THE TOPPING

3½ oz (100 g) light brown sugar

2 oz (55 g) plain flour

½ tsp salt

½ tsp ground allspice

2 oz (55 g) butter or margarine

2 tsp milk

1 tsp vanilla essence

1 Preheat a 375°F/190°C/Gas 5 oven. Grease a 9 in (23 cm) round gratin dish or shallow baking dish.

2 Sift the flour, baking powder and salt into a small bowl. Set aside.

3 ▲ With an electric mixer, or using a wooden spoon, cream together the butter or margarine and caster sugar. Beat in the egg and vanilla. Add the flour mixture alternately with the milk, beginning and ending with the flour.

4 ▲ Pour the mixture into the prepared dish. Sprinkle the fruit evenly over the mixture.

5 ▲ For the topping, combine the brown sugar, flour, salt and allspice in a bowl. With a pastry blender, cut in the butter until the mixture resembles coarse breadcrumbs.

6 ▲ Mix together the milk and vanilla. Drizzle over the flour mixture and toss lightly with a fork to mix.

7 Sprinkle the topping over the fruit. Bake until a skewer inserted in the centre comes out clean, about 45 minutes. Serve warm, with whipped cream, if wished.

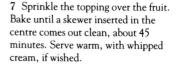

# Peach Cobbler

**SERVES 6**

about 3 lb (1.35 kg) peaches, peeled and sliced

3 tbsp caster sugar

2 tbsp peach brandy

1 tbsp fresh lemon juice

1 tbsp cornflour

FOR THE TOPPING

4 oz (115 g) plain flour

1½ tsp baking powder

¼ tsp salt

1½ oz (45 g) finely ground almonds

2 oz (55 g) caster sugar

2 oz (55 g) butter or margarine

3 fl oz (85 ml) milk

¼ tsp almond essence

1  Preheat a 425°F/220°C/Gas 7 oven.

2  In a bowl, toss the peaches with the sugar, peach brandy, lemon juice, and cornflour.

3  Spoon the peach mixture into a 3½ pt (2 litre) baking dish.

4 ▲ For the topping, sift the flour, baking powder and salt into a mixing bowl. Stir in the ground almonds and all but 1 tablespoon of the sugar. With 2 knives, or a pastry blender, cut in the butter or margarine until the mixture resembles coarse breadcrumbs.

5 ▼  Add the milk and almond essence and stir until the topping mixture is just combined.

6 ▲  Drop the topping in spoonfuls onto the peaches. Sprinkle with the remaining tablespoon of sugar.

7  Bake until the cobbler topping is browned, 30–35 minutes. Serve hot, with ice cream, if wished.

# Spiced Milk Pudding

**SERVES 6**

1¾pt (1 litre) milk

1½oz (45g) semolina

½tsp salt

¼tsp ground ginger

¾tsp ground cinnamon

2oz (55g) butter or margarine

8floz (250ml) treacle

2 eggs, beaten

1 Heat three-quarters of the milk in a saucepan.

2 In a heatproof bowl set over a pan of boiling water, or in a double boiler, combine the semolina, salt, ginger, cinnamon and remaining milk.

3 ▼ Pour in the heated milk, stirring to combine. Cook, stirring constantly, until smooth.

4 Reduce the heat so the water is just simmering, and cook 25 minutes, stirring frequently.

5 Preheat a 350°F/180°C/Gas 4 oven. Grease a deep 1¾pt (1 litre) earthenware baking dish.

6 ▲ Remove the bowl from the heat. Stir in the butter or margarine and treacle until the mixture is smooth. Stir in the eggs.

7 Pour the mixture into the prepared baking dish. Bake 1 hour. Serve warm.

---

# Lemon Sponge Pudding

**SERVES 6**

4oz (115g) plain flour

1 tsp baking powder

¼ + ⅛tsp salt

4oz (115g) butter or margarine, at room temperature

10oz (300g) caster sugar

finely grated rind and juice of 4 large lemons

4 eggs, separated

10floz (300ml) milk

1 Preheat a 350°F/180°C/Gas 4 oven. Butter a 10in (25cm) baking dish.

2 Sift the flour, baking powder and ¼ teaspoon salt into a small bowl. Set aside.

3 ▼ With an electric mixer, beat together the butter or margarine, sugar and lemon rind. Beat in the egg yolks, one at a time. Mix in the flour mixture alternately with the milk and lemon juice (reserving a squeeze of juice), beginning and ending with the flour.

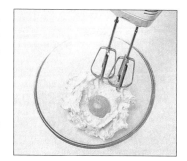

4 ▲ In a clean bowl, beat the egg whites with the ⅛ teaspoon salt and squeeze of lemon juice until stiff peaks form. Fold into the lemon mixture.

5 Pour into the prepared baking dish. Bake until golden brown, 40–45 minutes. Serve hot.

*Spiced Milk Pudding (top), Lemon Sponge Pudding*

# Bread Pudding with Whiskey Sauce

**Serves 8**

about 6 oz (170 g) stale French bread, in ¾ in (2 cm) cubes

16 fl oz (450 ml) milk

2 eggs

8 oz (225 g) caster sugar

1 tbsp vanilla essence

½ tsp ground cinnamon

¼ tsp grated nutmeg

2 oz (55 g) butter or margarine, melted and cooled slightly

3 oz (85 g) raisins

For the sauce

2 egg yolks

4 oz (115 g) butter or margarine

8 oz (225 g) sugar

3 fl oz (85 ml) bourbon or Irish whiskey

**3 ▲** With an electric mixer on high speed, beat the eggs with the sugar until pale and thick. Stir in the vanilla, cinnamon, nutmeg, butter or margarine and raisins.

**4 ▲** Add the soaked bread cube mixture and stir well to mix. Let stand 10 minutes.

**6 ▲** Meanwhile, make the sauce. With an electric mixer, beat the egg yolks until thick and pale.

**7 ▲** Melt the butter or margarine and sugar in a saucepan. Pour the butter and sugar mixture over the egg yolks, beating constantly, until well thickened. Stir in the whiskey.

**8** Serve the warm pudding from its baking dish. Pass the hot whiskey sauce separately.

**1 ▲** Preheat a 350°F/180°C/Gas 4 oven. Grease an 8 in (20 cm) baking dish.

**2 ▲** Put the bread cubes in a bowl with the milk and squeeze the bread with your hands until well saturated.

**5 ▲** Transfer the mixture to the prepared baking dish. Bake until firm and a knife inserted in the middle comes out clean, 45–50 minutes. Let it cool slightly in the dish, set on a wire rack.

~ COOK'S TIP ~

It is important to allow enough time for the egg mixture to soak the bread thoroughly; otherwise the bread cubes will float on top, leaving a layer of custard on the bottom when the dish is cooked.

# Rich Chocolate Pudding

**SERVES 6**

| |
|---|
| 3 oz (85 g) plain flour |
| 2 tsp baking powder |
| ⅛ tsp salt |
| 2 oz (55 g) butter or margarine, at room temperature |
| 1 oz (30 g) plain chocolate |
| 4 oz (115 g) caster sugar |
| 3 fl oz (85 ml) milk |
| ¼ tsp vanilla essence |
| whipped cream, for serving |
| FOR THE TOPPING |
| 2 tbsp instant coffee |
| 10 fl oz (315 ml) hot water |
| 3½ oz (100 g) dark brown sugar |
| 2½ oz (70 g) caster sugar |
| 2 tbsp unsweetened cocoa powder |

**1** Preheat a 350°F/180°C/Gas 4 oven. Grease a 9 in (23 cm) square non-stick baking tin.

**2** Sift the flour, baking powder and salt into a small bowl. Set aside.

**3** In a heatproof bowl set over a pan of simmering water, or in a double boiler, melt the butter or margarine, chocolate and caster sugar, stirring occasionally. Remove the bowl from the heat.

**4 ▲** Add the flour mixture and stir well. Stir in the milk and vanilla.

**5 ▲** Pour the mixture into the prepared baking tin.

**6** For the topping, dissolve the coffee in the water. Let cool.

**7 ▲** Mix together the sugars and cocoa powder and sprinkle over the pudding mixture.

**8 ▲** Pour the coffee evenly over the surface. Bake 40 minutes. Serve immediately with whipped cream.

# Individual Chocolate Soufflés

**SERVES 6**

2½ oz (70 g) caster sugar

2 oz (55 g) plus 1 tbsp unsweetened cocoa powder

3 fl oz (85 ml) cold water

6 egg whites

icing sugar, for dusting

**1** Preheat a 375°F/190°C/Gas 5 oven. Lightly butter 6 individual soufflé dishes or ramekins. Mix together 1 tablespoon of the sugar and 1 tablespoon of cocoa powder. Sprinkle this mixture over the bottom and sides of the dishes and shake out any excess.

**2 ▲** In a saucepan, combine the remaining cocoa powder and the cold water. Bring to the boil over medium heat, whisking constantly. Pour into a mixing bowl.

**3 ▲** With an electric mixer, beat the egg whites until soft peaks form. Add the remaining sugar and continue beating until the peaks are stiff.

**4 ▼** Add one-quarter of the egg whites to the chocolate mixture and stir well to combine. Add the remaining egg whites and fold gently but thoroughly, until no streaks of white are visible.

**5 ▲** Divide the chocolate mixture between the prepared dishes, filling them to the top. Smooth the surface with a metal spatula. Run your thumb around the rim of each dish so the mixture will not stick when rising.

**6** Bake until well risen and set, 14–16 minutes. Dust with icing sugar and serve immediately.

# Fruit Kebabs with Mango and Yoghurt Sauce

**SERVES 4**

½ pineapple, peeled, cored and cubed

2 kiwi fruit, peeled and cubed

5 oz (140 g) strawberries, hulled and cut
in half lengthwise, if large

½ mango, peeled, stoned and cubed

FOR THE SAUCE

4 fl oz (125 ml) fresh mango purée, from
1–1½ peeled and stoned mangoes

4 fl oz (125 ml) thick plain yoghurt

1 tsp sugar

⅛ tsp vanilla essence

1 tbsp finely shredded fresh mint leaves

1  To make the sauce, beat together
the mango purée, yoghurt, sugar and
vanilla with an electric mixer.

2 ▼  Stir in the mint. Cover the
sauce and refrigerate until
required.

3 ▲  Thread the fruit onto 12 × 6 in
(15 cm) wooden skewers, alternating
the pineapple, kiwi fruit, strawberries
and mango cubes.

4  Arrange the kebabs on a large
serving platter with the mango and
yoghurt sauce in the centre.

# Tropical Fruits in Cinnamon Syrup

**SERVES 6**

1 lb (450 g) caster sugar

1 cinnamon stick

1 large or 2 medium papayas (about
1½ lb/700 g), peeled, seeded and cut
lengthwise into thin pieces

1 large or 2 medium mangoes (about
1½ lb/700 g), peeled, stoned and cut
lengthwise into thin pieces

1 large or 2 small starfruit (about 8 oz/
225 g), thinly sliced

1  Sprinkle one-third of the sugar over
the bottom of a large saucepan. Add
the cinnamon stick and half the
papaya, mango and starfruit pieces.

~ **COOK'S TIP** ~

Starfruit is sometimes called
carambola.

2 ▼  Sprinkle half of the remaining
sugar over the fruit pieces in the pan.
Add the remaining fruit and sprinkle
with the remaining sugar.

3  Cover the pan and cook the fruit
over medium-low heat until the sugar
dissolves completely, 35–45 minutes.
Shake the pan occasionally, but do
not stir or the fruit will collapse.

4 ▲  Uncover the pan and simmer
until the fruit begins to appear
translucent, about 10 minutes.
Remove the pan from the heat and let
stand to cool. Remove the cinnamon
stick.

5  Transfer the fruit and syrup to a
bowl, cover and refrigerate overnight.

*Fruit Kebabs with Mango and Yoghurt Sauce (top), Tropical Fruits in Cinnamon Syrup*

# Rice Pudding with Soft Fruit Sauce

**Serves 6**

12 oz (350 g) short-grain rice

11 fl oz (335 ml) milk

⅛ tsp salt

3½ oz (100 g) light brown sugar

1 tsp vanilla essence

2 eggs, beaten

grated rind of 1 lemon

1 tsp fresh lemon juice

1 oz (30 g) butter or margarine

For the sauce

5 oz (140 g) strawberries, hulled and quartered

4 oz (115 g) raspberries

4 oz (115 g) caster sugar

grated rind of 1 lemon

**1** Preheat a 325°F/170°C/Gas 3 oven. Grease a deep 3½ pt (2 litre) baking dish.

**2** ▼ Bring a saucepan of water to the boil. Add the rice and boil 5 minutes. Drain. Transfer the rice to the prepared baking dish.

**3** In a bowl, combine the milk, salt, brown sugar, vanilla, eggs and lemon rind and juice. Pour this mixture over the rice and stir well.

**4** ▲ Dot the surface of the rice mixture with the butter or margarine. Bake until the rice is cooked and creamy, about 50 minutes.

**5** ▲ Meanwhile, for the sauce, combine the fruit and sugar in a small saucepan. Stir over low heat until the sugar dissolves completely and the fruit is becoming pulpy. Transfer to a bowl and stir in the lemon rind. Refrigerate until required.

**6** ▲ Remove the rice pudding from the oven. Let cool completely, and serve with the berry sauce.

# Surprise Fruit Baskets

**SERVES 6**

| |
|---|
| 4 large or 8 small sheets of frozen filo pastry, thawed |
| 2½ oz (70 g) butter or margarine, melted |
| 8 fl oz (250 ml) whipping cream |
| 3 tbsp strawberry jam |
| 1 tbsp Cointreau or other orange flavoured liqueur |
| 4 oz (115 g) seedless black grapes, halved |
| 4 oz (115 g) seedless white grapes, halved |
| 5 oz (140 g) fresh pineapple, cubed, or drained canned pineapple chunks |
| 4 oz (115 g) raspberries |
| 2 tbsp icing sugar |
| 6 sprigs of fresh mint, for garnishing |

**1** Preheat a 350°F/180°C/Gas 4 oven. Grease 6 cups of a bun tray.

**2** ▲ Stack the filo sheets and cut with a sharp knife or scissors into 24 × 4½ in (11 cm) squares.

**3** ▲ Lay 4 squares of pastry in each of the 6 greased cups. Press the pastry firmly into the cups, rotating slightly to make star-shaped baskets.

**4** ▼ Brush the pastry baskets lightly with butter or margarine. Bake until the pastry is crisp and golden, 5–7 minutes. Let cool on a wire rack.

**5** In a bowl, lightly whip the cream until soft peaks form. Gently fold the strawberry jam and Cointreau into the cream.

**6** ▲ Just before serving, spoon a little of the cream mixture into each pastry basket. Top with the fruit. Sprinkle with icing sugar and decorate each basket with a small sprig of mint.

# Strawberry Shortcake

**SERVES 6**

1 lb (450 g) strawberries, hulled and halved or quartered, depending on size

3 tbsp icing sugar

8 fl oz (250 ml) whipping cream

mint leaves, for garnishing

**FOR THE SHORTCAKE**

8 oz (225 g) plain flour

3 oz (85 g) caster sugar

1 tbsp baking powder

½ tsp salt

8 fl oz (250 ml) whipping cream

1  Preheat a 400°F/200°C/Gas 6 oven. Lightly grease a baking tray.

2 ▲  For the shortcake, sift the flour into a mixing bowl. Add 2 oz (55 g) of the caster sugar, the baking powder and salt. Stir well.

3 ▲  Gradually add the cream, tossing lightly with a fork until the mixture forms clumps.

4 ▲  Gather the clumps together, but do not knead the dough. Shape the dough into a 6 in (15 cm) log. Cut into 6 slices and place them on the prepared baking tray.

5 ▲  Sprinkle with the remaining 1 oz (30 g) caster sugar. Bake until light golden brown, about 15 minutes. Let cool on a wire rack.

6 ▲  Meanwhile, combine one-quarter of the strawberries with the icing sugar. Mash with a fork. Stir in the remaining strawberries. Let stand 1 hour at room temperature.

7 ▲  In a bowl, whip the cream until soft peaks form.

8 ▲  To serve, slice each shortcake in half horizontally using a serrated knife. Put the bottom halves on individual dessert plates. Top each half with some of the whipped cream. Divide the strawberries among the 6 shortcakes. Replace the tops and garnish with mint. Serve with the remaining whipped cream.

~ COOK'S TIP ~

For best results when whipping cream, refrigerate the bowl and beaters until thoroughly chilled. If using an electric mixer, increase speed gradually, and turn the bowl while beating to incorporate as much air as possible.

# Italian Trifles

**SERVES 4**

8 oz (225 g) mascarpone cheese

1½ tbsp caster sugar

2 eggs, at room temperature, separated

⅛ tsp salt

squeeze of fresh lemon juice

4 fl oz (125 ml) very strong cold black coffee

2 tbsp coffee liqueur

4 oz (115 g) biscuits, macaroons or Madeira cake, coarsely crumbled

2 tbsp cocoa powder, sifted

~ **COOK'S TIP** ~

Buying very fresh eggs from a reputable producer is especially important when using them raw.

1 With an electric mixer, beat the cheese, sugar and egg yolks together until blended and creamy.

2 ▲ In a clean mixing bowl, beat the egg whites with the salt and lemon juice until stiff peaks form. Fold into the cheese mixture.

3 In a small bowl, combine the coffee and liqueur.

4 ▲ Divide half the crushed biscuits among 4 stemmed glasses. Drizzle over 1–1½ tablespoons of the liqueur mixture. Top the moistened biscuits with half the mascarpone mixture. Layer the remaining biscuits, coffee mixture and mascarpone mixture in the same way.

5 Cover and refrigerate the desserts for 1–2 hours. Sprinkle with the sifted cocoa powder before serving.

# White Chocolate Mousse

**SERVES 8**

9 oz (250 g) white chocolate

3 fl oz (85 ml) milk

12 fl oz (350 ml) whipping cream

1 tsp vanilla essence

3 egg whites, at room temperature

⅛ tsp salt

squeeze of fresh lemon juice

chocolate covered coffee beans, for decoration (optional)

1 In a heatproof bowl set over a pan of barely simmering water, or in a double boiler, melt the chocolate.

2 Scald the milk in a small saucepan. Remove the bowl of chocolate from the heat and whisk in the warm milk until smooth. Let cool.

3 In a mixing bowl, whip the cream with the vanilla until soft peaks form. Refrigerate until needed.

4 ▲ Using an electric mixer and a clean bowl, beat the egg whites with the salt and lemon juice until stiff peaks form (do not overbeat or the mousse will be grainy). Fold into the chocolate mixture.

5 ▲ Gently fold the chocolate and egg white mixture into the vanilla flavoured whipped cream.

6 Transfer to a pretty serving bowl or individual stemmed glasses. Cover and refrigerate at least 1 hour. Sprinkle with chocolate covered coffee beans before serving, if wished.

*Italian Trifles (top), White Chocolate Mousse*

# Chocolate Cheesecake

## SERVES 12

1 lb (450 g) plain chocolate, broken into pieces

4 oz (115 g) caster sugar

2 tsp vanilla essence

4 eggs

1½ lb (700 g) cream cheese, at room temperature

2–3 tbsp icing sugar, for decoration

### FOR THE BASE

4 oz (115 g) digestive biscuits, crushed

2½ oz (70 g) butter or margarine, melted

2 tbsp grated plain chocolate

1 oz (30 g) caster sugar

**1 ▲** Preheat a 325°F/170°C/Gas 3 oven. Grease a 9–10 in (23–25 cm) springform tin and line the bottom with greased greaseproof paper.

---

~ **VARIATION** ~

For an all-chocolate cheesecake, substitute an equal quantity of finely crushed chocolate wafers for the digestive biscuits when preparing the base. For a special topping, pipe whipped cream around the top of the cheesecake and sprinkle with icing sugar.

---

**2 ▲** For the base, mix together the crushed biscuits, melted butter or margarine, grated chocolate and sugar. Pat evenly over the bottom and up the sides of the prepared tin. (The base will be thin.)

**3 ▲** In a heatproof bowl set over a pan of barely simmering water, or in a double boiler, melt the chocolate with the caster sugar. Remove the bowl from the heat and stir in the vanilla. Let cool briefly.

**4 ▲** In another bowl, beat together the eggs and cream cheese until smooth and well combined. Gently stir in the cooled chocolate mixture until completely blended.

**5 ▲** Pour the chocolate filling into the biscuit base. Bake until the filling is set, 45 minutes.

**6 ▲** Let cool, in the tin, on a wire rack. Refrigerate at least 12 hours.

**7 ▲** Remove the side of the tin and transfer the cheesecake to a serving plate. To decorate, lay a paper doily on the surface of the cake and sift the icing sugar evenly over the doily. With two hands, carefully lift off the doily.

# Coffee Ice Cream Sandwiches

**MAKES 8**

4 oz (115 g) butter or margarine, at room temperature

2 oz (55 g) caster sugar

4 oz (115 g) plain flour

2 tbsp instant coffee

icing sugar, for sprinkling

16 fl oz (450 ml) coffee ice cream

2 tbsp cocoa powder, for sprinkling

1  Lightly grease 2–3 baking trays.

2  With an electric mixer or wooden spoon, beat the butter or margarine until soft. Beat in the caster sugar.

3 ▲ Add the flour and coffee and mix by hand to form an evenly blended dough. Wrap in a plastic bag and refrigerate at least 1 hour.

4  Lightly sprinkle the work surface with icing sugar. Knead the dough on the sugared surface for a few minutes to soften it slightly.

5 ▼ Using a rolling pin dusted with icing sugar, roll out the dough to ⅛ in (3 mm) thickness. With a 2½ in (6 cm) fluted pastry cutter, cut out 16 rounds. Transfer the rounds to the prepared baking trays. Refrigerate for at least 30 minutes.

6  Preheat a 300°F/150°C/Gas 2 oven. Bake the biscuits until they are lightly golden, about 30 minutes. Let them cool and firm up before removing them from the trays to a wire rack to cool completely.

7  Remove the ice cream from the freezer and let soften 10 minutes at room temperature.

8 ▲ With a metal spatula, spread the ice cream evenly on the flat side of eight of the biscuits, leaving the edges clear. Top with the remaining biscuits, flat-side down.

9  Arrange the ice cream sandwiches on a baking tray. Cover and freeze at least 1 hour, longer if a firmer sandwich is desired. Sift the cocoa powder over the tops before serving.

# Chocolate Mint Ice Cream Pie

**SERVES 8**

3 oz (85 g) plain chocolate chips

1½ oz (45 g) butter or margarine

2 oz (55 g) crisped rice cereal

1¾ pt (1 litre) mint-chocolate-chip ice cream

3 oz (85 g) plain chocolate

**1** Line a 9 in (23 cm) pie tin with foil. Place a round of greaseproof paper over the foil in the bottom of the tin.

**2** In a heatproof bowl set over a pan of barely simmering water, or in a double boiler, melt the chocolate chips and butter or margarine.

**3 ▲** Remove the bowl from the heat and gently stir in the cereal, a little at a time. Let cool 5 minutes.

**4 ▲** Press the chocolate-cereal mixture evenly over the bottom and up the sides of the prepared tin, forming a ½ in (1 cm) rim. Refrigerate until completely hard.

**5** Carefully remove the cereal base from the tin and peel off the foil and greaseproof paper. Return the base to the pie tin.

**6** Remove the ice cream from the freezer and let soften 10 minutes.

**7 ▼** Spread the ice cream evenly in the crust. Freeze until firm, about 1 hour.

**8** For the decoration, use the heat of your hands to soften the chocolate slightly. Draw the blade of a swivel-headed vegetable peeler along the smooth surface of the chocolate to shave off short, wide curls.

Refrigerate the chocolate curls until needed.

**9 ▲** Scatter the chocolate curls over the ice cream just before serving.

# Hazelnut Sundaes with Hot Fudge Sauce

**SERVES 8**

1 recipe Hazelnut Squares

16 fl oz (500 ml) vanilla ice cream

16 fl oz (500 ml) chocolate ripple ice cream

2 oz (55 g) walnuts, chopped

FOR THE HOT FUDGE SAUCE

1½ oz (45 g) butter or margarine

2½ oz (70 g) caster sugar

2 oz (55 g) dark brown sugar

2 oz (55 g) unsweetened cocoa powder

3 fl oz (85 ml) whipping cream

⅛ tsp salt

1 ▼ For the sauce, combine all the ingredients in a saucepan. Cook gently, stirring, until smooth.

2 Put a hazelnut square in each of the 8 glass serving dishes.

3 ▼ Top each serving dish with a scoop of each ice cream. Spoon the hot fudge sauce on top. Sprinkle with chopped walnuts and serve immediately.

# Chocolate Biscuit Ice Cream

**MAKES 2½ PT (1.5 LITRES)**

16 fl oz (500 ml) whipping cream

3 egg yolks

12 fl oz (375 ml) condensed milk

4 tsp vanilla essence

about 12 chocolate sandwich biscuits, coarsely crushed

2 In a mixing bowl, whip the cream until soft peaks form. Set aside.

3 ▼ In another bowl, beat the egg yolks until thick and pale. Stir in the condensed milk and vanilla. Fold in the crushed biscuits and the whipped cream.

5 ▲ To serve, remove the ice cream from the pan and peel off the foil. Cut into thin slices with a sharp knife.

1 ▲ Line a 9 × 5 in (23 × 13 cm) loaf tin with foil, leaving enough overhang to cover the top.

4 Pour into the prepared loaf tin. Cover with the foil overhang and freeze until firm, about 6 hours.

~ COOK'S TIP ~

Buying very fresh eggs from a reputable producer is especially important when using them raw.

*Hazelnut Sundaes with Hot Fudge Sauce (top), Chocolate Biscuit Ice Cream*

# INDEX